Financing The Raj

The City of London and Colonial India, 1858–1940

Financing The Raj

The City of London and Colonial India, 1858–1940

David Sunderland

THE BOYDELL PRESS

First published 2013
The Boydell Press, Woodbridge

ISBN 978 1 84383 795 4

The Boydell Press is an imprint of Boydell & Brewer Ltd
PO Box 9, Woodbridge, Suffolk IP12 3DF, UK
and of Boydell & Brewer Inc.
668 Mount Hope Ave, Rochester, NY 14620-2731, USA
website: www.boydellandbrewer.com

A catalogue record for this book is available
from the British Library

The publisher has no responsibility for the continued existence or accuracy of URLs for external
or third-party internet websites referred to in this book, and does not guarantee that any content
on such websites is, or will remain, accurate or appropriate

Papers used by Boydell & Brewer Ltd are natural, recyclable products
made from wood grown in sustainable forests

Typeset by
Frances Hackeson Freelance Publishing Services, Brinscall, Lancs
Printed and bound in Great Britain by
TJ International Ltd, Padstow, Cornwall

Contents

Figures and Tables

Figures

Tables

Preface

In January 2006 I took my place in the Asian and African Reading Room at the British Library and began to read the evidence presented to the *Royal Commission on Indian Finance and Currency*. To say the least, I was utterly appalled at the portrait of the India Office that emerged from those pages. Not only was it grossly incompetent, but it acted purely in the interests of its financial advisors and the City of London, and to the detriment of India. At the end of the first day of my new project, I vowed to expose the ineptitude and dishonesty of this truly depraved organisation.

Six years later I have produced a book which, if not exactly eulogising the Office, at least demonstrates that it was an efficient institution, staffed and advised by committed and highly knowledgeable individuals, who wished to and generally succeeded in protecting India from City exploitation. This 360-degree change in my views arose from a study of India Office files, the material lodged in the Bank of England, Crown Agents and other archives, and contemporary accounts of how the financial centre of the World actually operated. The research was aided by numerous individuals and institutions. I would thus like to thank the staff of the British Library Asian and African Reading Room, who helped me solve the many mysteries of the India Office archive; the librarians at the John Rylands Library, the British Library of Political & Economic Science, the Guildhall Library and the Marshall Library; and the archivists and staff at the National Archives, Kew, the Bank of England, the National Westminster Bank and the Crown Agents. The book was also much improved by the suggestions of the Boydell & Brewer anonymous reviewer, and, as ever, I would like to acknowledge Peter Sowden, the Boydell & Brewer History Editor, for his interest in my work and his great efficiency, and Professor Avner Offer, my former doctorial supervisor at Oxford University, whose advice on the craft and purpose of scholarship I have never forgotten.

Finally, research is a lonely business, and I would like to thank Dr Geoffrey Tweedale, Mary Tweedale, Professor David Jeremy, Dr Young Chan Kim and Dr Tesfa Mehari for their friendship, and the many students I have taught over the past six years, who have both appalled and very occasionally delighted me.

Abbreviations

B of E	Bank of England
BE	Bank of England Archive, London
BL	British Library, London
CAAL	Crown Agents' Archive, Liverpool
CAs	Crown Agents
CAS	Crown Agents' Archive, Sutton
CO	Colonial Office
d	pennies
DA	Documents on Acceptance
DP	Documents on Payment
G of I	Government of India
GSR	Gold Standard Reserve
H of C	House of Commons
HMG	His/Her Majesty's Government
IO	India Office
NA	National Archives, Kew
NDC	National Debt Commissioners
PCR	Paper Currency Reserve
PP	Parliamentary Paper
rs	rupees
s	shillings
S of S	Secretary of State for India
SF	Sinking Fund

Introduction

Lionel Abrahams saw India's London financial operations as a large waterway system comprising 'rivers running into a lake at one side and so many rivers running out of the lake at the other side'. The goal of India Office (IO) officials like himself was to connect 'incoming rivers with ... outgoing rivers', a task he acknowledged was 'sometimes difficult'.[1] To truly understand the IO's financial operations one must extend this analogy. India's waterways did not exist in isolation. They formed part of a much larger system, the City of London, which in turn was connected to and fed a vast ocean of international finance and trade. Moreover, as in nature, the IO's collection of rivers, lakes and streams comprised a highly complex ecosystem, a community of diverse self-interested institutions and individuals, which through mutual dependency ultimately operated in a manner that was both harmonious and sustainable, and ensured that each organisation and actor achieved at least some of their goals. Previous commentators on Indian finance have overlooked this ecosystem. To them, India was an interloper in a primeval jungle, where it was ruthlessly savaged by its denizens, which fed on its entrails for decades. This book disagrees. It rather argues that Indian finance was an integral component of the City environment, contributing to and benefitting from the natural balance this habitat attained. To demonstrate that this was the case, it seeks to investigate how the Indian financial ecosystem operated (disentangling the complex relationships and interactions between individuals and institutions), how it achieved balance and how it adapted when the natural order was damaged.

To begin this exploration, it is first necessary to briefly examine the City's ecosystem and to delineate in very broad strokes the place India occupied in this habitat through a description of those involved in Indian finance. The financial might of Britain was based on its adoption of a gold standard, the commitment by a country that its basic unit of currency will be equal in value to and exchangeable for a

---

1   Parliamentary Paper (PP) 1920 [Cmd.528] *Committee Appointed to Enquire into Indian Exchange and Currency, Volumes 1 and 2*, q. 5603.

specified amount of gold. Instituted in 1717 and enshrined in the 1844 Bank Charter Act, which inaugurated the issue by the Bank of England of notes that were exchangeable for gold sovereigns, this monetary regime rapidly spread across the World, and, by the late 1870s, the US, Scandinavia, Germany, France and several other European countries had acquired gold-based currencies.[2] The rate of exchange between these areas was thus effectively fixed, and traders and investors were spared the risk that the relative exchange value of their domestic currency would move against them, increasing the price of their goods or reducing the value of their investment returns. Trade between nations thus grew considerably, the temptation by governments to adopt inflationary policies was curbed, and capital began to flow from the developed to the developing World.[3]

The trade generated was increasingly financed by bills of exchange, used to recompense sellers of goods, which stated that payment would be made at the end of a given period (known as the maturity of the bill), usually three to six months hence. The popularity of these bills grew rapidly in the later nineteenth century for a number of reasons. Payment in the form of gold involved relatively high transportation costs and the possibility of loss through theft or accident, and, as international trade took off, the demand for bullion outpaced supply. Bills also allowed sellers of produce to obtain payment almost immediately rather than on the delivery of their goods. Bills were sold (discounted) to discount houses and bill brokers, and the proceeds used to finance the purchase or production of the goods traded. Bills thus effectively allowed commerce to be financed by credit, and, not surprisingly, this development further boosted the growth of international trade.[4]

Other explanations for the greater use of bills include the arrival of the telegraph, which allowed suppliers to receive drafts within minutes rather than after a lengthy sea voyage, and the development of the London discount market, where sterling bills could be bought and sold. By the end of the nineteenth century, this market financed 60 per cent of World trade, only a small proportion of which passed through the UK or involved British buyers and sellers.[5] The reasons for its dominance are not hard to find. Britain was the World's leading trading nation, possessed an international

2   L. H. Officer, 'Gold Standard', at http://eh.net/encyclopedia/article/officer.gold.standard (accessed January 2011).

3   Inflationary policies would force an expansion of the responsible government's gold reserves.

4   R. Vasudevan, 'International Trade, Finance and Uneven Development', *Export-Import Bank of India Occasional Paper*, 133 (2009), p. 29; P. H. Lindert, *Key Currencies and Gold, 1900–13*, Princeton 1967, p. 26.

5   D. Kynaston, *The City of London, Volume 2: Golden Years, 1890-1914*, London 1995, p. 8; D. Williams, 'The Evolution of the Sterling System', in C. R. Whittlesey and J. S. G. Wilson (eds), *Essays in Money and Banking in Honour of R. S. Sayers*, Oxford 1968, p. 268. In 1913/14, two-thirds of the bills discounted on the market had no involvement with British trade (M. Ball and D. Sunderland, *An Economic History of London, 1800-1914*, London 2001, p. 344).

banking network and the funds necessary to lubricate such a market, and, as discussed below, was the centre of a triangular settlements network.[6]

The growth of the market was also related to the evolution of bills from a medium of exchange, representing an actual mercantile transaction, to a financial instrument purchased for interest rate or American exchange rate speculation. When rates were lower in London than elsewhere, foreign speculators would draw a sixty or ninety day bill, the price of which was based on UK interest rates, on a London associate. The bill would then be discounted and the proceeds invested in their own country at the higher rate of interest, the profit constituting the difference between the two rates.[7] Likewise, in the spring of each year when the dollar was weak, US financiers would borrow on the bills and repay the amount due in the harvest season when foreign demand for dollars to purchase crops caused the dollar to appreciate.[8] Such operations in 1913 accounted for 60 per cent of London's outstanding bank acceptances and greatly increased the amount of money flowing into and out of the City.[9]

The second financial sector to benefit from the gold standard and the low level of exchange risk was UK overseas investment. From 1865 to 1914, foreign governments and companies trading overseas floated £4.2 billion of securities on the London capital and stock markets, 40 per cent of which went to the Empire (66 per cent in the 1920s), around 35 per cent to North America and much of the remainder to Latin America.[10] The impact of this outpouring of funds on the City was significant. The issue of the loans generated business for issuing houses, brokers, underwriters and jobbers, and the use of the proceeds to finance railways and other infrastructure stimulated international trade, the issue of exchange bills and the expansion of the London discount market. More importantly, the outflow induced foreign borrowers to accumulate in Britain large caches of sterling in order to meet their loan interest

---

6   In 1914, for example, British banks controlled one-third of Brazilian deposits and a quarter of Argentinean and Chilean deposits (R. Vasudevan, 'The Borrower of Last Resort: International Adjustment and Liquidity in Historical Perspective', *Journal of Economic Issues*, 42 (4) (2008), p. 1067).

7   F. Silver, *Modern Banking: Commercial and Credit Paper*, New York 1920; A. I. Bloomfield, *Short-term Capital Movements under the Pre-1914 Gold Standard*, Princeton 1963, p. 38. When the amount to be paid became due, the necessary funds would be transferred back to the London associate, who would pay off the bill.

8   E. W. Tallman and J. R Moen, 'Lessons from the Panic of 1907', *Economic Review*, May/June 1990, p. 3.

9   Vasudevan, 'The Borrower', p. 1064.

10 R. C. Michie, *The City of London*, London 1992, p. 109; M. Simon, 'The Pattern of New British Portfolio Foreign Investment, 1865–1914', in A. R. Hall (ed.), *The Export of Capital from Britain, 1870–1919*, London 1968 , p. 24; A. Fishlow, 'Lessons from the Past: Capital Markets during the Nineteenth Century and the Interwar Period', *International Organization*, 39 (3) (1985), p. 394; P. J. Cain and A. G. Hopkins, *British Imperialism, 1688–2000*, Harlow 2002, p. 439. Overseas investments accounted for 40 per cent of British savings and 10 per cent of UK GDP (R. Triffin, 'The Evolution of the International Monetary System: Historical Reappraisal and Future Perspectives', *Princeton Studies in International Finance*, 12 (1964)).

payments, much of which was temporarily placed in short-term investments or deposited in London banks.[11]

The outflow was the result of a combination of pull and push factors. Foreign countries required money for economic development and offered relatively high returns, even taking into account the greater risk of default, and there was relatively little domestic demand for funds, as British manufacturers tended to draw capital from retained profits, savings, friends and relatives.[12] Such investment, however, was only possible because of the Empire. Britain possessed a trade deficit with Europe, the US and Latin America, imports from these countries being greater than the exports to them. British industry largely manufactured basic goods that were increasingly produced by domestic manufacturers in these regions, and it had difficulty competing with the US and Germany in the production of the more technically advanced 'new' products. In North America, British industry also faced high tariff barriers. [13] With no Empire, the imports from these areas would have been financed with domestic funds and the income generated from previous overseas investment. In the event, this was unnecessary, as the UK possessed trade surpluses with the Empire, which, in turn, had trade surpluses with Europe and the US. Although there was little demand for Britain's manufacturing output in the developed World, this was not the case in the colonies and particularly in India, where industries producing such goods had yet to develop.[14] Likewise, Europe and the US had an insatiable hunger for the raw materials produced by these colonies. A triangular settlement system thus developed, whereby the money the Empire obtained from selling commodities to Europe/the US was used to purchase British imports, and the UK employed the money acquired from these sales to pay for the goods it imported from Europe/the US.[15]

Britain's surplus funds and the income from previous overseas investment could thus be lent overseas, advancing World trade and avoiding the international monetary illiquidity that would have occurred had the interest paid on loans not been returned to borrower countries in the form of further advances. Moreover, the system further promoted the development of the London discount market. The bulk of the trade between the Empire and Britain was centralised in London, and, as the colonial banking system was largely UK owned, Imperial trade with Europe/the US was also largely financed by sterling bills settled in London. European and US

11   Vasudevan, 'The Borrower', p. 1070; S. Sen, *Colonies and the Empire: India, 1890–1914*, London 1992, p. 72.
12   M. Edelstein, 'Realised Rates of Return of UK Home and Overseas Portfolio Investment in the Age of High Imperialism', *Explorations in Economic History*, 13 (3) (1976), pp. 302–6.
13   M. de Cecco, *The International Gold Standard: Money and Empire*, London 1984, pp. 34, 37; P. Rag, 'Indian Nationalism, 1885–1905: An Overview', *Social Scientist*, 23 (263–5) (April/June 1995), p. 72.
14   India, in 1910/11, absorbed 39 per cent of all British exports of finished cotton goods, and, in 1913, sourced 80 per cent of its total imports from the UK (de Cecco, *The International Gold Standard*, pp. 31, 33).
15   S. B. Saul, *Studies in British Overseas Trade, 1870–1914*, Liverpool 1960, pp. 57–63.

merchants thus accumulated large sums of money in the capital and used these funds to finance their trade with non-Empire countries through the purchase/discounting of yet more sterling bills. Bilateral clearing was thus gradually transformed into multilateral clearing.[16] To maintain this system, however, Britain had to ensure that the Empire remained undeveloped and thus continued to import large amounts of basic British goods, and, as the UK's trade deficits with the rest of the World worsened, that the Empire met the ever-increasing demand for its exports from the US and Europe. The system also inevitably led to a trade-off between finance and industry. Although the City benefitted, the underdevelopment of the Empire caused manufacturing to be yoked to markets that grew relatively slowly, and the guaranteed Imperial demand for basic goods discouraged much-needed industrial restructuring.[17]

Appearing at first glance robust, the international financial system possessed two potentially fatal flaws. The most damaging weakness was that the Bank of England, the issuer of Britain's currency notes, possessed very little gold, even though sterling was the international currency, and massive sums of foreign money were held in London. During the period the gold standard was in operation, its gold reserves rarely exceeded £40m, equal to 2–3 per cent of the UK's money supply and 5 per cent of its imports.[18] A commercial organisation, the Bank wished to keep as few of its funds as possible in non-interest-earning specie, and, in any case, the Bank Act of 1844 had precluded the extent to which it could use its reserves to defend sterling.[19] The other source of gold, the joint stock banks, was simply not utilised, the banks being under no obligation to lodge their reserves with the Bank.[20] The possible consequences of this lack of gold did not bear thinking about. A run on sterling, the demand that UK currency notes be exchanged for gold, caused by either a domestic or foreign economic crisis, would not only force an abandonment of the standard, but would trigger a World financial crash and depression, since London was the lynchpin of international finance and trade, and the pound was regarded as a currency of unquestioned convertibility. A second related but more minor flaw was the annual outflow of short-term capital from London to the US. Because of the uneven development of the American banking system, the funds sent each year by the Eastern banks westward to finance the grain harvest only returned after the crops had been sold and the farmers had purchased goods produced in the East. In

---

16   Williams, 'The Evolution of the Sterling System', pp. 285–6; Vasudevan, 'The Borrower', p. 1067.

17   de Cecco, *The International Gold Standard*, pp. 37, 71.

18   R. S. Sayers, *The Bank of England 1891-1944, Volume 1*, Cambridge 1975, pp. 9–10; A. I. Bloomfield, *Monetary Policy under the International Gold Standard*, New York 1959, p. 21. In comparison, France possessed reserves of £120m, equal to 40–50 per cent of imports (*ibid.*).

19   J. Dutton, 'The Bank of England and the Rules of the Game', in M. D. Bordo and A. J. Schwartz (eds), *A Retrospective on the Classical Gold Standard, 1821–1931*, London 1984, pp. 178–9; Vasudevan, 'The Borrower', p. 1058.

20   Vasudevan, 'International Trade', p. 26.

the interim, the shortage of money in the Eastern states of America prompted a rise in New York interest rates, which drew money from London, much of it in the form of finance bills.[21]

The Bank overcame its lack of gold and US seasonal instability partly through 'gold devices' (which were particularly popular in the 1880s), but largely via the manipulation of the bank rate. Gold devices involved the alteration of the terms of exchange by which the Bank purchased gold and redeemed notes for gold sovereigns. To make it more advantageous for customers to import gold and lodge it at the Bank, interest-free loans were provided or the purchase price raised; conversely, to increase the cost of removing and exporting gold, the sale of bars was banned, the selling price raised or notes redeemed in underweight domestic coin.[22] Bank rate was adopted from the 1890s. If it appeared that there was to be a loss of gold overseas and a possible run on sterling, the Bank would raise bank rate (the rate at which it lent money), which would cause all other rates to rise and maximise inflows and minimise outflows of gold. The high rates would attract to London 'hot money', liquid foreign balances seeking temporary investment, and stimulate arbitrage operations – the borrowing of money at low interest rates in one country and its investment at higher rates in another country. At the same time, foreign loan issues in the capital market would be delayed, the proceeds of previous flotations would be temporarily retained in the UK, there would be less overseas speculative investment (much of which was again financed with debt), the demand for finance bills would plummet, and less money would leave the UK via the discount market. Discount houses and bill brokers obtained the funds used to purchase bills of exchange from the joint stock banks. A rise in interest rates thus reduced the availability and increased the cost of these loans, which meant that the discount houses/brokers bought fewer bills or paid lower prices for them, far more were held to maturity and the movement abroad of the bill proceeds was thus delayed for up to six months.[23]

Bank rate, however, had a number of drawbacks. A sudden rise in UK interest rates damaged the profitability of City institutions, including the Bank of England, and could cause economic calamity in countries on the periphery of the gold standard area. Gold would flow from these countries to London, reducing their gold reserves and forcing them to suspend note convertibility and depreciate their currencies. To prevent such an outcome, governments could raise their own interest rates, but

---

21   Bloomfield, *Monetary Policy*; G. Balachandran, *John Bullion's Empire: Britain's Gold Problem and India between the Wars*, Richmond 1996, p. 31. Had the US Treasury and banks been prepared to provide a countervail to the withdrawal of short-term funds in the form of long-term investments in London, there would have been far less instability (*ibid.*).

22   Dutton, 'The Bank of England', pp. 177–8, 462; Vasudevan, 'International Trade', p. 25.

23   Vasudevan, 'International Trade', pp. 30–1; Vasudevan, 'The Borrower', pp. 1058, 1064–5; M. D. Bordo, 'The Gold Standard: The Traditional Approach', in Bordo and Schwartz (eds), *A Retrospective*, p. 50. The loans were less available as the banks could obtain higher rates by lending their funds elsewhere, in particular to the government via the purchase of Treasury bills.

this would damage trade and lead to deflation.[24] Over the period, there was also a weakening of the effectiveness of bank rate. The explosion in joint stock banking from the 1850s had reduced the Bank of England's share of money market business, and a rise in bank rate often failed to immediately elicit a rise in other rates.[25] The Bank was thus forced to combine changes in bank rate with other activities, known as open market operations. To ensure that a rate increase would have an impact on other interest rates it sought to force financial institutions to have recourse to its higher interest rate loans by limiting other possible sources of funds.[26] During periods when the gold standard was under threat, it also strengthened its control of the amount of bills of exchange purchased and the prices offered for them. From the start of the First World War, it increased its sales of Treasury bills, short-term government investments that offered a relatively high interest rate. These were rapidly taken up by the joint stock banks, which thus lent less funds to discount houses/brokers, who bought fewer bills at a lower price, and the sale proceeds increased Bank gold stocks.[27] Likewise, from 1830 to 1858 and again from 1890, it bought bills of exchange from discount houses/bill brokers in need of funds, but only at a relatively low price, forcing the houses/brokers to pay an equally low price for traders' bills.[28]

Aware that the effectiveness of bank rate was suspect and that its application could damage British financial interests and the economies of periphery countries, the Bank looked to foreign central banks and governments to make the sacrifices necessary to prevent the collapse of the system when major crises occurred. During the 1890 Barings crisis, for example, inconvertibility was prevented by the inflow of gold from the Bank of France and gold coin from Russia. In the 1907 sterling crisis, the Bank of France heavily discounted British bills of exchange, the proceeds of which flowed to the UK, and the German Reichsbank supplied gold drawn from the

24 G. M. Gallarotti, *The Anatomy of an International Monetary Regime: The Classical Gold Standard 1880–1914*, Oxford 1999; Lindert, *Key Currencies*, pp. 47–50. In the 1890s, Argentina, Brazil and Chile were all forced to suspend convertibility (Bloomfield, *Monetary Policy*).

25 H. James, *International Monetary Cooperation since Bretton Woods*, Oxford 1996, p. 37. Although the capital of the joint stock banking sector rose from £35m to £50m from 1881 to 1891, only 2 per cent of their deposits were held by the Bank of England (de Cecco, *The International Gold Standard*, p. 95).

26 Dutton, 'The Bank of England', p. 177. Prior to 1890, this policy was rarely used (*ibid.*).

27 James, *International Monetary Cooperation*, p. 195; W. F. Jopling, *Foreign Exchange and Foreign Bills in Theory and Practice*, London 1925, p. 210.

28 The Bank first bought bills of exchange from discount houses and brokers in 1830. The bankruptcy and near bankruptcy of two discount houses and a realisation of the riskiness of the practice then caused it to be abandoned until 1890 when the Bank began to buy bills with a currency of just fifteen days. From 1897, the Bank began to buy three month bills and, from 1900, four month and exceptionally six month bills (Ball and Sunderland, *An Economic History*, pp. 341–2; Vasudevan, 'The Borrower', p. 1060).

Russian State Bank.[29] The reserves of special depositors in London, including the governments of India and Japan, were also occasionally called upon. [30]

India Office

The role of the Indian government in the City's ecosystem was managed by various officials, the Under Secretary of State, the Assistant Under Secretary of State and a Finance Council (grouped together in this book as the India Office). They in turn employed service providers, in the form of the Bank of England, brokers and underwriters, and performed their duties with the help of various City institutions. The Assistant Under Secretaries of State supervised the Finance, Accountant General's, Public Works, and Stores Departments, and advised and often eventually became Under Secretaries of State.[31] Although they had no financial training, they devoted their careers to finance and thus possessed vast experience and expertise. Three were also Jews, which led to much distrust and outright hostility, but at the same time benefitted India.[32] Although anti-Semitism was rife in the City, many of the most prominent financiers were Jewish, some of whom, like two of the Assistant Under Secretaries, were members of various Jewish political and charitable groups.[33] The shared ethnicity and social connections inevitably led to the development of strong bonds of trust, and, no doubt, explains the preponderance of Jewish firms with which the IO did business.[34]

The Finance Council, a subcommittee of the India Council, normally met once per week, and more regularly in times of crisis, in order to formulate policy and monitor the work of the Under Secretary and Assistant Under Secretary of State and officials.[35] Oddly, critics of the Council claimed that it was controlled both by

---

29   R. S. Sayers, *Bank of England Operations 1890-1914*, Connecticut 1970, pp. 102, 110–13; B. Eichengreen, *Globalizing Capital: A History of the International Monetary System*, Princeton 1996, pp. 34–5.

30   Lindert, *Key Currencies*, p. 32.

31   S. A. Husain, 'The Organisation and Administration of the India Office, 1910-1924', University of London, PhD thesis, 1978, p. 47. Three of the five Assistant Under Secretaries of State from 1859 to 1919 became Under Secretaries. From 1914, there were two Assistant Under Secretaries of State (*ibid.*).

32   Sir Lionel Abrahams, Sir Cecil Kisch and Sir Arthur Hirtzel.

33   Kynaston, *The City ... Vol. 2*, p. 225. Abrahams was President of the Jewish Historical Society and a member of the 1917 committee to convene a conference of Anglo-Jewry on the Balfour Declaration, on which also sat the financiers Lord Rothschild and Sir Stuart Samuel (D. S. Zakheim, 'The British Reaction to Zionism, 1895 to the 1990s', *Round Table*, 88 (350) (1999), p. 326; *Canadian Jewish Chronicle*, 5 Feb. 1915, p. 4). Kisch was active in Zangwills, the Jewish territorial organisation (*ibid.*, 29 Sept. 1943, p. 32).

34   For example, nine of the stockbrokers who obtained IO loans were Jewish (British Library, London (BL), L/F/5/144).

35   PP 1896 [C.8258], *Indian Expenditure Commission, Volume 1*, q. 2405–6, 2416; C. N. Vakil, *Financial Developments in Modern India, 1860-1924*, London 1924, p. 53.

'high priests of …Whitehall', whose lack of financial knowledge and unwillingness to innovate 'had cost India dear by throwing away millions of her finance', and by a 'Lombard Street clique' of financial virtuosos, who 'dispensed financial patronage on a colossal scale' and subordinated the interests of India to those of the London money market.[36] Of the two accusations, the former has very little foundation, as this book will testify. As for the second claim, the Council certainly always contained at least one City member and these often had some involvement in the financial areas in which the IO operated (Table 1). It seems unlikely, however, that they took up their positions in order to 'feather their own nests'. More likely motivations were patriotism or a wish to burnish their reputations for trustworthiness or professional/social status; to increase their chances of gaining a public honour; or, in some cases, to put into effect their belief in Christian economic rationality – that moral progress and the spread of the gospel could only be achieved through effective financial management.[37] Their presence also greatly benefitted India. All had great financial knowledge and thus prevented financiers using their expertise to exploit IO officials.[38] Sir Felix Schuster, for example was 'one of the highest authorities in Europe on business and banking', and Bertram Currie was considered the City's 'most eminent financial authority'.[39] Moreover, they were fabulously wealthy and unlikely to use their positions for financial gain, had immaculate reputations on which the IO could free ride, and, wishing to maintain these reputations, made sure the IO operated in a competent and honest manner.[40] Many had political influence and all had links of family, background and schooling with major City figures, and belonged to a myriad of City networks.[41] They thus possessed ascribed trust, had access to information on the trustworthiness of others and could use their various relationships to obtain favours for India.[42]

---

36 S. V. Doraiswami, *Indian Finance, Currency and Banking*, Madras 1915, pp. 64, 132; *ibid.*, appendix, pp. lxxv–lxxvi; PP 1921 [153] *Return of Indian Financial Statement and Budget*, p. 124; PP 1920 [Cmd.529] *Report of the Committee Appointed to Enquire into Indian Exchange and Currency, Volume 3*, p. 86.

37 Doraiswami, *Indian Finance*, appendix, p. lxxiii; Cain and Hopkins, *British Imperialism, 1688–2000*, p. 547.

38 The impact of the 'knowledge gap' is discussed in E. Green, 'The Influence of the City over British Economic Policy, c.1880–1960', in Y. Cassis (ed.), *Finance and Financiers in European History, 1880–1960*, Cambridge 1992, pp. 193–218, and S. Sweeney, 'Indian Railroading: Floating Railway Companies in the Late Nineteenth Century', *Economic History Review*, 62 (S1) (2009), p. 78.

39 *Toronto World*, 23 July 1913, p. 1; Y. Cassis, *City Bankers, 1890–1914*, Cambridge 1994, p. 25, n. 32.

40 Owing to public interest in India, inappropriate actions would receive maximum media attention and have the potential to destroy the reputations of Council members.

41 Schuster, for example, had stood as a Liberal in the 1906 election, was close to the Party and was a friend of Charles Ritchie, a former Governor at the Union Bank and, from 1902, Chancellor of the Exchequer (*Financial Times*, 15 May 1936, p. 6; *Oxford Dictionary of National Biography*, Oxford 2004, vol. 49).

42 The theory of ascribed trust suggests trust arises where two people have similar characteristics and that individuals will not act against the interests of partners with a similar background

Table 1. Council member City connections

Council member (membership period)	City connections	Connections with IO work
Bertram Currie (1880–95)	Partner of the bank Glyn Mills Currie & Co. Close friend of the banker Edward Baring and associate of Nathaniel Rothschild.	Glyn Mills Currie & Co. received loans from IO balances.
James Lyle MacKay (Lord Inchcape) (1897–1911)	Chairman of P & O Steamship Navigation Co. Director of National Provincial Bank, Royal Bank of Scotland, Atlas Assurance Co.	P & O Banking Corp. (founded 1920) was an Indian exchange bank.
Francis Charles Le Marchant (1896–1906)	Director of National Provincial Bank. Senior Partner of merchant bank H. S. Lefevre & Co.	National Provincial Bank purchased council bills.
Sir Felix Schuster (1906–16)	Director, Deputy Governor and Governor of Union Bank/Union of London & Smiths Bank. Director of Imperial Bank and London & Liverpool Bank of Commerce. Deputy Chairman/Chairman of Committee of London Clearing Banks (1904–5, 1925). President of Council of the Institute of Bankers (1907–9). Chairman of Central Association of Bankers (1913–15). President of British Bankers Association.	Father was director of General Credit & Finance, later to become Union Discount, a major discount house. Union of London & Smiths Bank was a major purchaser of India export bills, and received loans from IO balances.
Frederick Cranford Goodenough (1918–30)	Assistant Secretary of Union Bank. Director and Chairman of Barclay & Co. Director of Alliance Assurance Co.	Partner of Nivisons, IO broker. Barclays purchased council bills and received loans from IO balances.

Sources. Currie: Y. Cassis, *City Bankers, 1890–1914*, Cambridge 1994, p. 25, n. 32; N. Ferguson, *The House of Rothschild*, New York 1998, p. 344; BL, L/AG/14/14. Inchcape: G. Jones, *British Multinational Banking, 1830–1990*, Oxford 1993, p. 158; *Financial Times*, 24 May 1932, p. 7; Jones, *British Multinational Banking*, p. 158. Le Marchant: BL, L/F/5/144, memo, deposits with Banks for Mr Baker's speech, 6 Feb. 1913; *Financial Times*, 11 Dec. 1930, p. 6; BL, L/AG/24/36. Schuster: D. Gutwein, 'Jewish Financiers and Industry 1890-1914: Germany and England', *Jewish History*, 8 (1–2) (1994), p. 181; *Financial Times*, 15 May 1936, p. 6; *Oxford Dictionary of National Biography*, Oxford 2004, vol. 49; G. Cleaver and P. Cleaver, *The Union Discount: A Centenary Album*, London 1985, p. 19; R. S. Sayers, *Gilletts in the London Money Market*, Oxford 1968, p. 47; BL, L/AG/14/14. Goodenough: *Oxford Dictionary*, vol. 22; *Directory of Directors*, 1921; BL, L/AG/29/1/153, 138/1, Nivisons, 1 April 1924; BL, L/AG/24/36.

---

to themselves, as in doing so they would suffer a psychological loss (D. Sunderland, *Social Capital, Trust and the Industrial Revolution, 1780–1880*, London 2007, pp. 6–7). The reciprocal exchange of favours (gifts) will also have helped to strengthen trust relationships/friendships (*ibid.*, p. 8).

As trust was essential to its operations, only a small number of large high status City financial institutions were used by the IO. Many worked with the IO for decades and provided services in more than one financial area. Over time, their executives formed close working relationships and friendships with IO officials. Highly successful, such firms had no financial need to act against the interests of India, and their managers were well aware that any short-term gains from such actions would be offset by long-term losses. Self-interested behaviour would end their friendships with IO staff, damage their own and their firm's hard-won reputation for trustworthiness and lose them a great deal of future business.[43]

Approach and structure of the book

As John Maynard Keynes acknowledged when discussing Indian finance, 'it is impossible to say everything at once and an author must sacrifice from time to time the complexity and interdependence of fact in the interest of the clearness of his exposition'.[44] This book thus discusses the various activities of the IO in turn, and the interconnections between the various tasks undertaken are referred to within the chapters and briefly summarised in the conclusion. It is divided into four sections. The first part explores the issue and sale/purchase on the London market of Indian government debt. The first three chapters examine the most important component of this debt – Indian government sterling loans. Chapter 1 attempts to discover the reasons these securities were issued, why they were raised in London rather than in India and the identities of those who purchased them. The following chapter then considers how the IO maximised demand – by the use of a powerful broker and issuing house, the careful timing, widespread advertisement and underwriting of issues and the inclusion in prospectuses of attractive terms. The most important term, the yield earned by buyers, is the main subject matter of the third chapter, which also looks at the assets issued, and traces the fall in the popularity of these securities among the investing public and their eventual repatriation to India. The section concludes with a chapter on the sale and purchase in London of government stock issued in India and denominated in rupees, and the IO's other activities in the capital market – its involvement in the flotation of the debentures of government-owned guaranteed railway companies and the sale of sterling bills, short-term loans that had to be repaid within months.[45]

The second part comprises a single chapter, which discusses the purchase of silver for the minting of rupee coins and the 'scandal' of 1912, when the award of a

---

43 Long relationships will also have allowed the IO to monitor their service providers for dishonesty and to discover their capabilities.

44 J. M. Keynes, *Indian Currency and Finance*, London 1913, pp. 181–2.

45 The guaranteed railway companies were so-called because the Indian government guaranteed the dividends and the repayment of their capital. The history of the railways is summarised in Chapter 7.

major contract for the supply of this metal to the family firm of the Under Secretary of State for India, Edwin Samuel Montagu, led to accusations of cronyism and fraud. The following section investigates perhaps the most complex topic of this book, the management of the Indian/UK exchange rate and the transfer from India to London of the money needed to meet the Indian government's UK commitments. To understand how these tasks were achieved one must first appreciate how the exchange banks financed Indian trade. Chapter 6 thus examines each side of the trading relationship. Exporters of Indian goods to the UK sold bills/drafts of exchange, known as export bills, to Indian exchange banks for rupees, using the proceeds to finance their future purchases of Indian produce. The exchange banks then transferred the bills to London, where they were held until they were paid in sterling by the purchasers of the goods or immediately sold (discounted) on the discount market. Exporters of British manufactures to India, meanwhile, sold for sterling in London import bills of exchange to the banks, which conveyed them to India, where they were held until they were paid in rupees by the buyer of the materials. The banks used the sterling gained in London from the encashment of export drafts to buy import bills and the rupees obtained in India from the payment of import bills to buy export bills. Unfortunately, exports from India to the UK exceeded trade in the opposite direction and the banks could not transfer all the funds required in India for the purchase of export bills via import drafts. Money was thus also moved from London to India in the form of specie, rupee Indian government stock, bills of exchange issued by Indian railway companies and council bills of exchange, which were sold by the IO to the banks in London for sterling and cashed in India by the Indian government for rupees.

Chapters 7 and 8 throw the focus onto council bills, which were used by the Indian government to move funds to the UK, where they met India's various financial commitments in the country. After describing these commitments, known as the home charges, and critically examining the claims that they were excessive, Chapter 7 describes the three main types of council bill and the auction issuing process, identifies the purchasers and investigates the trade and non-trade factors that influenced the demand for and the supply of the bills. Chapter 8 then examines the prices charged for the drafts, which effectively determined the Indian/British exchange rate, as it dictated the prices paid by the exchange banks for export and import bills. The fall in silver prices from the early 1870s reduced the value of the silver rupees exchange banks obtained in India in exchange for council bills and prompted them to offer lower prices for the bills, thus forcing the IO to issue more drafts in order to obtain the sterling required to meet the home charges. To staunch this loss, it was first decided in 1893 that India should have a gold currency, and, in 1898, that the silver rupee should be retained, but its value should be fixed to gold at an exchange rate of 1s 4d, the so-called gold exchange standard.

In the event, the IO sold council bills within a narrow price range. The upper limit was set at 1s 4 ⅛d, as above this price it was cheaper for the exchange banks to send money to India in the form of gold, which would reduce council bill proceeds, making it more difficult to meet the home charges; lead to a contraction in London gold stocks, which could elicit a rise of interest rates that would damage both the City and India; and force the IO to ship the gold back to the UK. When the price breached 1s 4 ⅛d, the IO sold drafts far in excess of the amounts needed to meet India's UK commitments (thus removing the need for banks to turn to gold), and purchased any Australian or Egyptian gold that the banks were shipping to India, redirecting it to England. Both policies also possessed secondary benefits. The sale of bills in excess of UK commitments helped the exchange banks meet the great increase in export bills that accompanied the expansion of India's trade and allowed the reserve in which the proceeds of the bills were placed, known as the home balances, to be built up and more of its surplus funds to be lent to City institutions, again to the advantage of India. The purchase and redirection of Australian and Egyptian gold, meanwhile, reduced the amount of specie arriving in the subcontinent and again built up London's gold stocks.

The lower limit of the price range was 1s 3$^{29}/_{32}$d, the price at which it was financially beneficial for the exchange banks to move gold from India to Britain in order to buy council bills, the profit from the purchase of the bills (the 1s 4d obtained in India minus the lower price paid) being large enough to offset the cost of buying and shipping the gold to London. When the price dropped below this level, the IO halted the resultant dangerous outflow of specie from India and prevented further falls and even greater losses on the sale of bills by offering fewer bills and selling reverse council bills, which were sold by the Indian government in India for rupees and cashed in sterling in London by the IO.

Ironically, whilst the setting of the 1s 4d exchange rate was prompted by the fall in silver prices, that of 2s, established in 1920, was the result of a rise in the price of the metal. The remainder of Chapter 8 investigates the introduction and the eventual abandonment of this rate and its replacement by the more realistic 1s 6d. It is followed (Chapter 9) by a description of how the IO responded when the Indian government lacked the rupee funds to cash council bills on their arrival in India and the myriad ways in which the IO met the home charges when council bills were not an effective mode of remittance. Money was despatched in the form of advances, export bills, specie and via earmarking, an early form of multilateral netting.[46] Within Britain, commitments were discharged by issuing loans on the London capital market; obtaining advances from City institutions, the Treasury, the Bank of England and the Indian railway companies; tapping the Gold Standard Reserve, one of the investment funds managed by the IO; and from debts owed by HMG to the Indian government that were paid in London. After 1923, the Indian government also began to purchase sterling within India.

In the fourth and final part of the book, attention is turned to the IO's investment role. India had three reserves located in London, the aforementioned Gold Standard Reserve (GSR), the UK branch of the Paper Currency Reserve (PCR) and the home balances. The GSR was established in 1899 and underpinned the exchange, providing

---

46   C. W. L. Hill, *International Business: Competing in the Global Marketplace*, London 2010, pp. 685–7.

a pool of money to cash reverse council bills when the price of ordinary council bills dipped below the gold export point. The PCR provided financial backing for currency notes, ensuring that holders could at any time exchange them for coin. Both were largely invested in UK government securities, thus helping to finance public expenditure, and their operation and portfolios are explored in Chapter 10 – along with a brief description of the Indian Silver Reserve, established in India in 1904 to allow the rapid coinage of silver rupees if demand suddenly and unexpectedly surged.

The third reserve, the home balances, is discussed in the final chapter. Holding the proceeds of council bills awaiting expenditure, the size of this Fund was inflated by the 1904 decision to sell drafts in excess of UK commitments when prices exceeded 1s 4 ⅛d. Part of its contents were kept in the IO's current account at the Bank of England, thus augmenting the Bank's gold stocks, but until the First World War the vast proportion was lent to City institutions, much to the advantage of India. Not only did the advances increase market liquidity, again acting against the imposition of high interest rates, but the money borrowed was used to purchase Indian government loans, sterling bills, export bills and council bills, and recipients had to provide collateral in the form of Indian government stock to obtain the loans, which further strengthened demand for these securities. Unfortunately, the Bank of England, for largely self-interested reasons, restricted this lending, forcing the IO from 1914 to invest the majority of the funds in UK government securities.

In summary, this book seeks to demonstrate that the IO was a constituent part of the City's ecosystem, contributing to and benefitting from its operation through the formation of close symbiotic and trust relationships, the exchange of gifts in the form of favours, the recycling of resources, and, perhaps most significantly, its help in supporting the operation of the gold standard. The IO lent significant sums to the City, helping to maintain liquidity; retained a current account at the Bank of England, thus supplementing the Bank's gold stocks; and complied with the Bank's various diktats on the timing of loan flotations. It acted in this way because its assistance was reciprocated by the Bank of England and Treasury, and its officials were well aware that low interest rates increased broker demand for Indian government and railway company loans (which could thus offer a lower yield), and, most importantly, boosted Indian trade. The low rates increased the amount of funds in the discount market and allowed the exchange banks to discount export bills and to obtain a better price for the drafts. They thus had more funds available to purchase council bills and could offer higher prices in India for export bills, enabling merchants to pay slightly higher prices for their Indian produce. A low rate and the availability of funds, similarly, enabled UK importers of Indian goods to cheaply finance their purchases and discouraged exchange banks investing the proceeds of discounted export bills in London or moving funds from India to London to gain from the difference between London/Indian rates, actions that again damaged export bill purchases.[47] The crucial role the IO played in the operation of the gold

---

47   PP 1914 [Cd.7069], q. 2745–6.

standard and the City as a whole is discussed in the Conclusion, which seeks to delineate and explain the various interactions and relationships through the prism of principal agent theory and the concepts of trust, the gift economy and enlightened self-interest.

1

The Issue of Government Loans:
Purpose, Location of Issue and Purchasers

The amount of Indian government debt on the London markets rose from £1.49m in 1800/1 to £272m in 1938/9 (Figure 1). It comprised the government loans discussed in this and the following two chapters, and the sterling bills and the securities of the guaranteed railway companies, which are considered in Chapter 4. In addition, a large proportion of the rupee stock issued in India was also held by British investors, purchases that are again explored in Chapter 4. From 1857/8 to 1935/6, when the last government loan was issued, the IO sold £407.71m of debentures/stock for which it obtained approximately £392.1m (the loans were generally sold at a discount) (Figure 2).[1] The debt represented around half of total British investments in India (1910 and 1939); between 6.56 per cent (1857) and 43 per cent (1934) of India's total public debt; in 1861 and 1899, respectively 13.6 per cent and 15 per cent of its National Domestic Product; and a minute percentage of the total government bonds floated on the London market (just 2.77 per cent and 3.58 per cent in 1875 and 1905 respectively).[2]

---

1   BL, L/AG/14/10/1. Amounts exclude the debentures/stock created for conversions, i.e. exchanged for existing debentures/stock.

2   R. W. Goldsmith, *The Financial Development of India, 1860-1977*, London 1983, p. 18; A. Maddison, *Class Structure and Economic Growth: India and Pakistan since the Moghuls*, London 1971, chap. 3; R. N. Poduval, *Finance of the Government of India since 1935*, Delhi 1951, p. 93; A. Mukherjee, *Imperialism, Nationalism and the Making of the Capitalist Class, 1920–47*, London 2002, p. 26; M. Desai, 'Drains, Hoards and Foreigners: Does the Nineteenth Century Indian Economy have any Lessons for the Twenty First Century India?', in K. Uma (ed.) *Indian Economy*, New Delhi 2004, pp. 17–32; P. Mauro, N. Sussman, and Y. Yafeh, *Emerging Markets and Financial Globalization: Sovereign Bond Spreads in 1870–1913 and Today*, Oxford 2007, p. 13, table 2.1. From 1893/4 to 1919/20, sterling government loans averaged 63 per cent of total Indian government debt (PP 1906 [Cd.2754] *East India (Statistical Abstract). 1894–95 to 1903–04*, no. 76; PP 1914–16 [Cd.7799] *East India (Statistical Abstract), 1903–04 to 1912–13*, no. 76; PP 1922 [Cmd.1778] *East India (Statistical Abstract). 1910–11 to 1919–20*, no. 76).

Figure 1. Total sterling debt and repayment, 1800/1–1941/2

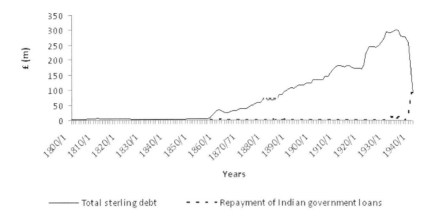

Sources. BL, L/AG/14/10/1; PP 1859 [201] *East India (Loans)*; BL, L/F/5/60; BL, L/F/5/79; PP 1930–31 [Cmd.3670] *Explanatory Memorandum, of the Accounts and Estimates for 1930-31*, p. 12; PP 1929-30 [Cmd. 3386] *Explanatory Memorandum, of the Accounts and Estimates for 1929-30*, pp. 11, 13.

Notes. Total sterling debt = Indian government loans, guaranteed railway company debentures and sterling bills. It does not include liability for the British government 5 per cent war loan 1929–47 taken over by India. The repayment of Indian government debt does not include conversions.

Figure 2. Sterling loan issues, 1857/8–1935/6

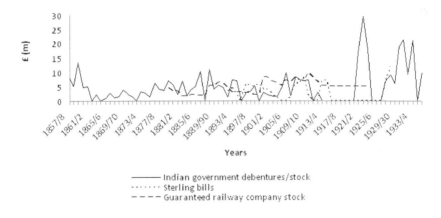

Sources. BL, L/AG/14/10/1; PP 1859 [201]; BL, L/F/5/60; BL, L/F/5/79; PP 1930–31 [Cmd.3670], p. 12; PP 1929-30 [Cmd.3386], pp. 11, 13.

Notes. Indian government debentures/stock = receipts and not totals issued. Amounts exclude the debentures/stock created for conversions. Guaranteed railway company debentures comprise the debentures of the East Indian Railway, Eastern Bengal Railway, Oudh and Rohilkhand Railway, South Indian Railway, Great Indian Peninsula Railway, and the Bombay, Baroda & Central India Railway.

The debentures/stock were either publicly issued by the Bank of England and the IO's brokers (79.3 per cent from 1857/8 to 1935/6) or created and sold privately/exchanged for guaranteed railway company debentures, and either had a stated date of repayment or no repayment date, though the latter loans could be repaid or exchanged for new securities after the passage of twenty to thirty years. They were sold at a price fixed by the IO or one determined by those who tendered for allotments, which was above or below the 'par' price (100) at which they would eventually be repaid, and offered a given annual rate of interest (a percentage of an issue's par value), usually related to the ruling market rate. After they had been sold, they were quoted on the Stock Market, which enabled investors to sell and buy stock/debentures, with the resultant changes in supply and demand causing the quoted price to rise or fall. The initial purchasers of the publicly issued loans were stockbrokers, who, in the fullness of time, offloaded their allocations at a profit onto general investors; financial institutions, which retained their purchases as reserves; and those members of the public who 'stagged' popular issues, that is, bought securities in the hope that the price would rise soon after issue, when they would be immediately resold.[3]

When issuing debentures/stock, the goal of the IO was to maximise the amount of money raised. This could be achieved in three ways – by maximising the amount it was allowed to issue, by ensuring that all the securities floated were purchased and by paying as low a yield as possible, i.e. seeing that the debentures/stock were sold at a relatively high price and paid a relatively low rate of interest. Unfortunately, the latter two objectives were at variance with each other. Low yields would discourage investors making purchases; debentures/stock would remain unsold; brokers, unable to offload their purchases onto the public, would have fewer funds to purchase other issues; and the market price of all Indian government sterling loans would fall, triggering a drop in UK government security prices.[4] Confidence in Indian government loans, i.e. the 'credit' of the country, would thus be damaged and investors would be reluctant to buy new debentures/stock, reducing the amount that could be issued, and would demand higher yields, minimising loan returns. When floating securities, the IO thus concentrated on the maximisation of demand.

Purposes of issue

Issues had a number of purposes – the finance of railways (approximately £58.38m from 1879/80 to 1935/6), the payment of the home charges (at least £25m) and the repayment or conversion of old debentures/stock and sterling bills (approximately

---

3   To prevent stagging, some brokers refused to allow clients to withdraw applications, and requests for stock in excess of £1,000 had to be in multiples of £1,000 (National Archives, Kew (NA), CAOG 9/107; *The Economist*, 16 Oct. 1943; Crown Agents' Archive, Liverpool (CAAL), WN 13, a055803, Scrimgeours to Crown Agents (CAs), 4 Dec. 1962).
4   E.g. *Financial Times*, 3 Nov. 1922, p. 1.

£60m). There were also a variety of miscellaneous reasons. Early flotations partly financed the various wars waged by the East India Company within and outside India, the 1932 issue was to raise funds for the launch of the Reserve Bank of India and to finance the transfer of funds from the home balances to the GSR, and, in 1893, £96,000 of stock was created to pay off the trustees of the estate of the Maharajah Duleep Singh.[5] Railway loans were floated to finance construction, to purchase the guaranteed railway companies, and, after acquisition, to provide these firms with advances. Generally the companies raised capital through the flotation of their own loans, but when the yield was expected to be relatively high, the IO issued government debentures/stock and advanced the firms the proceeds.[6]

Borrowing primarily for construction occurred from 1869/70 to 1873/4.[7] Finance was then raised in India except for the £7.7m issued in 1885 and 1886. The U-turn was prompted by the 1884 Select Committee on railways, which recommended that if UK interest rates were considerably below those in India then borrowing should occur in London. In 1885/6, a trade depression and a collapse in the exchange caused such a situation to arise, and the money was duly raised in the UK.[8] Flotations for the purchase of the share capital and debentures of guaranteed railway companies began from 1879.[9] The Indian government's original contracts with the firms were ridiculously generous, and ran for fifty to ninety-nine years, but provided the right to purchase the companies after twenty-five to thirty years, though in the case of two railways the IO relinquished this prerogative in return for contract modifications.[10] Such was the criticism of the original and renegotiated contracts that on the activation of these early purchase clauses/completion of the contracts, India bought out eight companies (six of which were allowed to continue to operate their lines), but in doing so was further 'fleeced'. Under the contract terms, remuneration was determined by the average market value of shares in the three years preceding a buyout, and, to maximise their remuneration, directors during this period artificially minimised expenditures, causing receipts and share prices to soar.[11]

The companies' share capital and debentures were either purchased (the funds for the purchase being raised by the issue of sterling government loans) or exchanged

5   B. Dhar, *The Sterling Balances of India*, Calcutta 1956, p. 10; BL, L/F/7/803, IO to Schuster, 10 March 1932; BL, L/AG/9/8/5, vol. 5, p. 889, IO to Bank of England (B of E), 14 Dec. 1893; BL, L/F/7/806, Secretary of State for India (S of S) to Government of India (G of I), 9 Nov. 1932.

6   PP 1896 [C.8258], q. 7438–9. E.g. BL, L/F/5/64, memo, 1889; PP 1902 [187] *Indian Financial Statement for 1902–03*, p. 63.

7   Poduval, *Finance*, p. 94.

8   PP 1896 [C.8258], q. 7444, 7452.

9   The IO also purchased two guaranteed irrigation companies (*ibid.*, q. 8783).

10   The contracts are discussed in Chapter 7. The modified contracts (for the Great Indian Peninsula and the Bombay, Baroda & Central India railways) permitted the equal division of profits over interest (A. Prasad, *Indian Railways: A Study in Public Utility Administration*, London 1960, p. 55).

11   S. C. Ghose, Lectures on Indian Railway Economics, Part One, Calcutta 1922, p. 22; Investors Review, 5 (Jan./June 1900), p. 582.

for sterling debentures/stock or for annuities, financial instruments that paid holders an annual sum for a given number of years.[12] Over the period, £81.8m of annuities were issued for five railway companies, the size of the debt falling as the annual payments were made to reach £33.76m in 1939/40.[13] The advantage of such instruments was that they helped to maintain India's credit in the London markets, as they avoided the issue of sterling loans, and, until 1924/5, they were 'off balance sheet' (not recorded as debt in Government accounts). Drawbacks were that they were costly to administer, the size of the annual dividends could not be reduced over time in line with market interest rates, as was the case with debentures/stock, and trust funds were unwilling to invest in them. The IO thus had to exchange some of the annuities issued for sterling debentures/stock or stock issued in the name of the companies.[14]

The payment of the home charges partly occurred as an adjunct to the issue process. All loan proceeds were placed in the home balances until needed and were thus used to pay the charges or lent out to the City, the amount of money available depending on the purpose of the issue and the extent to which purchasers paid for their debentures/stock immediately or in instalments.[15] Securities were also specifically floated to meet the home charges – when the Indian government faced difficulties remitting, owing to famine, low exports or (as in 1930–31) the flight of capital abroad, or when the IO suspended the sale of council bills, either because there was insufficient demand or it wished to 'gerrymander' the exchange.[16] Inevitably, these issues were criticised; borrowing to 'bolster the exchange' was 'contrary to every sound principle of finance'. Although the loans in the short term reduced

12   E.g. PP 1889 [123] *Financial Statement of Government of India, 1889–90*, p. 36; PP 1890 [140] *Financial Statement of Government of India, 1890–91*, p. 44; BL, L/AG/14/11/1, memo, 13 March 1886; BL, L/F/5/59, note, no date. £31.01m of stock was issued/exchanged to purchase the India Midland Railway (bought in 1910/11 at a cost of £5.9m) , the Madras Railway (1907/8, £2.14m), the Oudh and Rohilkhand Railway (1893/4, £0.729m), South Indian Railway (1893/4, £0.52m) and the Great Indian Peninsula Railway (1900/1, £5.92m) (PP 1906 [Cd.2754], no. 72; PP 1914–16 [Cd.7799], no. 72).

13   Dhar, *The Sterling Balances*, p. 42; PP 1942–43 [Cmd. 6441] *East India (Statistical Abstract), 1930–31 to 1939–40*. Annuities were issued for the East Indian Railway, the Eastern Bengal Railway, the Scinde Punjab and Delhi Railway, the Great Indian Peninsula Railway and the Madras Railway (PP 1930–31 [Cmd.3882], no. 102).

14   PP 1900 [225] *Financial Statement of Government of India, 1900–01*, p. 57; D. L. Dubey, *The Indian Public Debt*, London 1930, p. 27; *Investors Review*, 15 (Jan./June 1905), p. 756; Doraiswami, *Indian Finance*, p. 131; PP 1896 [C.8258], q. 11905.

15   *The Statist*, 26 May 1888, p. 582.

16   *Ibid.*, 21 Jan. 1928, p. 90; BL, L/F/7/783, Cook to Kisch, 5 May 1921. E.g. PP 1878–79 [312] *Select Committee on Expediency of Constructing in India Public Works*, q. 526; Balachandran, *John Bullion's Empire*, p. 171; V. G. Kale, *India's National Finance since 1921*, Delhi 1932, p. 90; PP 1871 [363] *Select Committee on Finance and Financial Administration of India*, q. 9436; B. R. Tomlinson, 'Monetary Policy and Economic Development', in K. N. Chaudhuri and C. J. Dewey (eds), *Economy and Society*, Oxford 1979, p. 200; *Investors Review*, 3 (Jan./June 1899), p. 406.

remittances, in the long run the greater interest payments enhanced the movement of funds to Britain, and loans issued to overcome trade imbalances, by being spent on goods produced in the UK and exported to India, often only worsened those imbalances.[17]

Location of issue

The location of borrowing was the subject of much controversy. Those in favour of rupee issues argued that they would benefit both India and the UK. As the Indian government was free to borrow in India without Parliamentary authority, more funds could be raised, and such borrowing would power economic growth. Indian capitalists would have an interest in the development of their country, large money markets would develop, interest payments would be reinvested, and the taxation paid on dividends would increase government revenues.[18] More significantly, the elimination of sterling interest payments would dissipate some of the anger generated by the home charges, and the fall in remittances/council bill sales would result in less loss by exchange and a lower and more stable exchange rate.[19] Meanwhile, in the UK, rupee loans would cure 'india-gestation', the overissue of sterling loans that damped down gilt prices, and finally free the City 'from the mercy of India' – the fear that political disturbances or even another mutiny could lead to a default that would wreak havoc on the financial markets.[20] It was also argued, more improbably, that the disappearance of Indian loans would improve liquidity, lowering interest rates and making it easier for British businesses to raise funds, and that a portion of the dividends earned by Indian investors would be spent on UK-produced goods.[21]

Opponents of Indian issues regarded such arguments, at best, as facile, and, at worst, as plain ridiculous. Until the turn of the century, there was paltry domestic demand for rupee stock. There was little capital to invest, particularly during times

---

17 *The Statist*, 9 Sept. 1899, p. 398; H. Fawcett, *Indian Finance*, London 1880, p. 97; *Investors Review*, 10 (June/Dec. 1902), p. 567.

18 *The Statist*, 19 June 1880, p. 354; *ibid.*, 25 Feb. 1893, p. 212; PP 1900 [Cd.130] *Indian Expenditure Commission, Volume 3*, q. 18594; Dhar, *The Sterling Balances*, p. 16; PP 1882 [181] *Financial Statement of Government of India, 1882–83*, p. 260.

19 BL, L/F/7/787, Kisch to Goodenough, 22 Nov. 1928; PP 1878–79 [312], q. 27; PP 1920 [Cmd. 528], q. 5855.

20 *Financial Times*, 13 Nov. 1933, p. 1; A. Banerji, *Finances in the Early Raj: Investments and the External Sector*, London 1995, p. 47; PP 1873 [354] *Select Committee on Finance and Financial Administration of India, Third Report*, q. 6852.

21 Dubey, *The Indian Public Debt*, pp. 22–3, 81–3; PP 1878 [333] *Report from the Select Committee on East India (Public Works)*, p. 352; PP 1873 [354], q. 6808.

of famine, and this was hoarded, lent or invested in land or trade.[22] The reasons for such behaviour were legion. Many Indians had no wish to financially prop up British rule, feared that 'the Empire might go smash', and could obtain higher returns from alternate investments. They were also put off by the nature of rupee loans and the undeveloped nature of Indian money markets.[23] The securities were sold in relatively large batches, there was always the possibility that they would be converted into lower interest yielding stock, and the payment of interest, the transference of ownership and the sale of holdings could be difficult.[24] The gilt-edged market, even in the 1920s, was narrow, market demand was often low or non-existent and market prices were subject to wide fluctuations.[25]

It was thus highly improbable that Indians would buy any rupee stock issued, and, even if they did, a higher yield would have to be offered and the predicted fall in remittances/council bill sales and the exchange would be far less than envisaged.[26] Sterling loans were often used to meet the home balances and some of the proceeds of rupee debt would still have to be remitted to England to pay for railway materials, the vast majority of which were bought in the UK.[27] There was also the possibility that Indian investment in rupee stock would starve the rest of the economy of funds and lead to permanently high interest rates that would be especially damaging to trade.[28] A more likely scenario was that the rupee stock would be bought by British investors, though some doubted that even they would 'take-up the slack', given the difficulties of investing in India. If such purchases did indeed occur, many of the benefits put forward by the proponents of Indian flotations would disappear, particularly the fall in remittances/exchange, as council bills would be purchased to transfer to India payments for the stock and private drafts to move the dividends back to Britain.[29]

Although there were exceptions, borrowing in London was generally frowned upon until the mid 1880s. The positive attitude of the 1884 Select Committee on

22   PP 1873 [354], q. 6868, 6869; PP 1899 [254] *Financial Statement of Government of India, 1899–1900*, p. 68; *The Statist*, 19 Nov. 1892, p. 579; S. Bhattacharayya, *Financial Foundations of the British Raj*, Simla 1971, p. 134; PP 1872 [327], *Select Committee on Finance and Financial Administration of India*, q. 3467.

23   PP 1872 [327], q. 3464. In the 1870s, the returns from trade, landed property and loans to farmers were respectively 9 per cent, 12–15 per cent, and 20–25 per cent (PP 1873 [354], q. 6880, 6882).

24   PP 1878 [333], q. 1868; *The Statist*, 7 July 1894, p. 16; PP 1914 [Cd.7069] *Royal Commission on Indian Finance and Currency, Volume 1*, q. 6362–3.

25   *India Finance*, 17 March 1928, p. 85.

26   C. A. K. Banerji, *Aspects of Indo-British Economic Relations, 1858–1898*, Oxford 1982, p. 101; D. Rothermund, *An Economic History of India from Pre-Colonial times to 1991*, London 1993, p. 51; A. Bagchi, *Private Investment in India, 1900–1939*, Cambridge 1972, p. 38.

27   *The Statist*, 30 April 1881, p. 475; PP 1914 [Cd. 7069], q. 1337.

28   *The Statist*, 19 Nov. 1892, p. 579; PP 1898 [C.9037] *Committee to Inquire into Indian Currency: Evidence*, q. 1043; PP 1878–79 [312], q. 732.

29   *The Statist*, 30 April 1881, p. 475; *ibid.*, 19 June 1880, p. 354; *ibid.*, 13 Sept. 1879, p. 50.

railways towards sterling debt and the stability of the exchange from 1893 then caused the number of loans to rise.[30] From the start of the First World War, the IO also considered the use of the New York market. During the war, its use would not only have overcome the closure of the London market to government loans, but also would have released the £14m City institutions invested in Indian sterling bills for investment in UK Treasury bills, prevented the problems that arose from the expansion of the rupee debt, and, through the movement of loan proceeds to the UK, benefitted the British exchange rate.[31] Post-war advantages were that borrowing in America did not require Parliamentary sanction and would give relief to the London market and to Indian credit, and would allow the IO to issue long-term loans rather than the short-term debentures floated in the UK.[32] In the event, the market was never used. A 1917 request for an American issue was blocked by the Treasury, which predicted that the American government would reject any plan that increased the outflow of gold from the country.[33] In 1922 and 1930, it was the IO itself that decided not to act. It was believed that American issue would be expensive, higher yields would have to be offered, and there was a possibility that brokers would simply offload their purchases onto the London market. Also, although there appeared to be sufficient demand in 1922, in 1930 a fall in the market and media reports of Indian political unrest made it unlikely that sufficient investors would make subscriptions for the loan.[34]

Purchasers

The purchasers of debentures/stock can be divided into two classes – issue and post-issue buyers. The monetary value and the number of applications for loans at flotation appear impressive. Issues on average were oversubscribed by more than three times, and, from 1921 to 1933, the mean number of applications was 6,204.[35]

30   Vakil, *Financial Developments*, p. 295.

31   NA, T 120/1, Treasury to IO, 16 Aug. 1916; K. T. Shah, *Sixty Years of Indian Finance*, London 1927, p. 399.

32   BL, L/F/7/773, note, 28 July 1922; *ibid.*, Kisch to Laithwaite, 31 July 1922.

33   NA, T120/1, Treasury to IO, 20 Sept. 1917.

34   BL, L/F/7/773, Kisch to Duke, 19 Aug. 1922; BL, L/F/7/794, S of S to Viceroy, 4 Feb. 1930. In 1922, the investment bank J. P. Morgan was convinced that the market could handle $50m of Indian stock (BL, L/F/7/773, J. P. Morgan to Morgan Grenfell & Co., 18 Aug. 1922; *ibid.*, Lamont to Blackett, 20 Jan. 1923).

35   The oversubscription mean is based on the 29 loans for which subscription details are available (PP 1904 [193] *Indian Financial Statement for 1904–05*, p. 72; *The Statist*, 10 May 1902, p. 952; *ibid.*, 20 July 1901, p. 119; *ibid.*, 16 July 1898, p. 100; *ibid.*, 9 July 1898, p. 63; *ibid.*, 24 May 1884, p. 586; *ibid.*, 26 May 1906, p. 998; *ibid.*, 8 April 1905, p. 647; *ibid.*, 30 April 1904, p. 857; BL, L/F/5/59, B of E, 30 July 1874; *Journal of the Statistical Society*, 24 (1861), pp. 128–9; BL, L/F/7/784, B of E to IO, 18 May 1923; *ibid.*, Kisch to Finance Dept., 24 May 1923; BL, L/F/7/783, B of E to IO, 25 April 1921; BL, L/F/5/79; PP 1908 [170] *Indian Financial Statement for 1908–09*, p. 67; BL, L/F/7/809, B of E to IO, 11 May 1933; BL, L/F/7/803, B of E, 28 April 1932;

The reality was less remarkable. A large number of subscriptions were from stags and were for small sums, and most City institutions made numerous applications for excessive amounts in order to ensure that they obtained the stock/debentures that they actually required.[36] Both practices were disliked by the IO. Oversubscription fuelled criticism of its yields and stagging increased flotation costs, and, via the post-flotation sale of allotments, caused the price of the issued debentures/stock to fall to a discount, making it more difficult to offload onto the public.[37] Officials, however, did nothing to halt either practice. Oversubscription strengthened India's credit and increased the post-issue demand for debentures/stock, and, when City demand for a loan was sluggish, stagging could provide a useful stopgap.[38]

The loans were largely bought by British financial institutions and brokers. City institutions used them to obtain short-term funds. All Indian debentures/stock, as discussed in Chapter 11, could be given as collateral for advances from the home balances, and, as a last resort, from the Bank of England; while short-term bonds and the stock of loans within a few years of being repaid, known as 'floaters' or 'shorts', could be used to obtain funds from the discount market (Appendix 1).[39] The main purchasers were insurance companies and merchant and exchange banks, and, in the case of floaters, discount houses and retail banks. Discount houses used the short-term bonds as collateral for the short-term bank loans that financed their activities, and retail banks bought them to cover their deposits-at-call, deposits that clients could insist be repaid immediately.[40]

Demand for debentures/stock peaked in the first decade of the twentieth century and for shorts in the 1930s, when trading bills became scarce and the vast amount of short-term securities issued by the UK government during the First World War began to dry up.[41] On purchase, both were placed in the buying institution's reserves, which, to minimise risk, contained cash and a range of other short-term securities, and were regarded more highly than other reserve investments owing to their safety, price stability and relatively high return.[42] Floaters, if not discounted, would be held until the end

---

BL, L/F/7/801, note, 23 May 1931; BL, L/F/5/62; BL, L/F/7/796, B of E to IO, 17 Oct. 1930; BL, L/F/7/795, B of E to IO, 22 May 1930; BL, L/F/7/787, B of E to IO, 7 Jan. 1929; BL, L/F/7/786, B of E to IO, 18 Jan. 1902; Dhar, *The Sterling Balances*, p. 36; BL, L/F/7/810, B of E to IO, 10 Nov. 1933).The largest oversubscriptions were for the October 1930 and 1935 loans, which were seven times oversubscribed (BL, L/F/7/796, B of E to IO, 17 Oct. 1930; Dhar, *The Sterling Balances*, p. 36). The applications mean is for the thirteen loans for which data is available (NA, CO 323/945, c12397, loans issued in London since the war).

36   BL, L/F/7/773, Cook to Kisch, 6 July 1922; *The Statist*, 3 Aug. 1895, p. 148.
37   BL, L/F/7/809, Baxter, 10 May 1933; *Financial Times*, 2 Nov. 1931, p. 1.
38   BL, L/F/7/796, Kisch to Denning, 21 Oct. 1930.
39   BL, L/F/7/797, Kisch to Schuster, June 1930.
40   B. Supple, *The Royal Exchange Assurance*, London 1970, p. 346; PP 1889 [123], p. 92; *Financial Times*, 11 Jan. 1881, p. 1; BL, L/AG/9/8/6, p. 339; BL, L/F/7/797, Goodenough, 23 June 1930; Sayers, *Gilletts*, pp. 49–50, 104.
41   *Financial Times*, 11 Feb. 1930, p. 6.
42   BL, L/F/7/816, note, 27 June 1935; *The Statist*, 27 April 1912, p. 181.

of their lives; while evidence from the Union Bank suggests that ordinary debentures/ stock could be retained for as long as nine years.[43]

Institutions wishing to tap the discount market either discounted their purchases or used them as collateral for loans. Discounting involved selling the floater to a discounting house at a discount to the par (100) repayment value. The discounting house would then either resell the short or hold it until the end of its life when it received the par repayment value from the IO. To increase demand, the Stock Exchange in 1930 was persuaded to quote the market price of Indian bonds rather than the accrued price (market price plus the ensuing dividend payment), as some claimed that the latter made them difficult to value and thus discouraged their purchase.[44] If used as collateral, the short would be bundled with other securities (since lenders generally required collateral comprising a variety of different securities to minimise risk) and given to the lender, who would provide a short-term loan in return. Generally, the interest payable on the loan would be less (in 1931 a third less) than the dividend paid by the IO, and the purchaser would thus reap a profit on the transaction.[45]

Brokers bought Indian debentures/stock for their clients and for after-issue resale, though a small proportion would be retained for use as collateral for advances from the IO/discount market or for discounting. The main purchasers were the prominent City firms, who, in the early days, were part of the IO's underwriting syndicate, and, through their access to IO advances/the discount market, possessed the capacity to raise the funds necessary to acquire a large proportion of an issue, and, if a loan failed, had the resources and could be trusted not to dump their allotments onto the market and precipitate a price fall. Applications from provincial brokers were discouraged. Most were small and made on behalf of private clients, many of whom were stags, and, if a loan failed, most provincial brokers would simply dump the stock, lacking the resources to do otherwise. Prospectuses were thus 'sparingly distributed' and despatched on the day prior to a flotation, which, as most issues closed a few hours after opening, ensured that applications arrived too late to be considered for allotments.[46]

Indian purchase was negligible. Both private individuals and institutions lacked the necessary funds, particularly if a London flotation closely followed one in India, and investment was discouraged by the payment of interest and repayment of capital in England. Dividends and repayments were thus liable to British income tax and had to be remitted to India, which created much inconvenience and could result in exchange

---

43 C. A. E. Goodhart, *The Business of Banking, 1891–1914*, London 1972, p. 493.
44 BL, L/F/7/797, Kisch to Rickett, 16 Oct. 1930; *ibid., Financial Times*, 15 Oct. 1930; *ibid.*, Schuster to Niemeyer, 3 June 1930; *ibid.*, B of E to Kisch, 15 Oct. 1930. Some officials disputed the claim (*ibid.*, Goodenough, 23 June 1930; *ibid.*, Kisch to Schuster, June 1930).
45 *The Statist*, 23 May 1931, p. 827.
46 *Financial Times*, 13 Feb. 1930, p. 5; *ibid.*, 12 May 1933, p. 1; BL, L/F/7/815, Freeuard & Co. to IO, 14 Feb. 1930.

loss.[47] Indian applications also tended to arrive well after issues had closed and applicants thus received no allotment.[48] As with applications from provincial brokers, there was a reluctance to solve the problem. Some officials believed Indian demand to be relatively unimportant to the success of an issue, that the purchase of sterling debentures/stock would have a negative impact on sales of rupee loans, and that the transfer of purchase funds to England negated one of the main purposes of sterling issues – the minimisation of Indian government remittances to the UK and the associated fall in the exchange.[49] Others disagreed, arguing that the flow of purchase funds to England was offset by the transfer of dividends in the opposite direction and that Indian demand helped to raise prices.[50]

Over time, as the British appetite for the loans waned, it was the latter view that gained the upper hand, and the IO began to encourage Indian applications. In 1929, for example, the IO agreed to accept any applications received during the day of issue.[51] The change of heart was also related to a rise in demand. Of the eleven loans issued from 1923 to 1933 for which data is available, 8.54 per cent were bought by Indians, and, in the case of the 1931 issue, this figure soared to 50 per cent.[52] Reasons for the upturn included the increased wealth of Indian capitalists and institutions; the need for Indian businesses to hold some of their reserves in sterling; in the mid 1920s, the relatively low price of sterling securities, as compared to their rupee equivalent, and an expectation of a recovery; and, from the early 1930s, nationalistic fervour.[53]

After issue, the brokers offloaded their stock onto the public, and, over time, the securities were bought and sold on the market. The main after-issue purchasers were trusts and various City institutions, the relatively large amounts bought by institutions pushing the average holding of Indian stock in 1905 up to a sizeable £2,020.[54] Financial trusts were attracted to Indian loans by the low default risk, the stability of their market prices, their long lives and simply because they were one of a relatively limited number of securities in which trustees were allowed to invest by the 1872 and

---

47   BL, L/F/7/783, S of S to Viceroy, 30 April 1921; BL, L/F/7/809, Finance Dept. to IO, 11 May 1933; PP 1872 [327], q. 1565; PP 1878–79 [312], q. 119.

48   E.g. BL, L/F/7/755, Kisch to Cook, 2 June 1921.

49   BL, L/F/7/801, note, 23 May 1931.

50   BL, L/F/7/785, IO to G of I, 8 July 1926; *ibid.*, Kisch, 8 June 1926.

51   BL, L/F/7/787, S of S to Viceroy, 3 Jan. 1929.

52   BL, L/F/7/810, Imperial Bank, 10 Nov. 1933; BL, L/F/7/809, Imperial Bank to IO, 11 May 1933; BL, L/F/7/803, Imperial Bank to IO, 28 April 1932; BL, L/F/7/801, Imperial Bank to IO, 22 May 1931; *ibid.*, note, 23 May 1931; BL, L/F/7/799, Imperial Bank to IO, 10 Feb. 1931; BL, L/F/7/796, Imperial Bank to IO, 20 Oct. 1930; BL, L/F/7/795, Imperial Bank to IO, 26 May 1930; *ibid.*, Baxter to Finance Dept., 23 May 1930; BL, L/F/7/793, note, no date; BL, L/F/7/787, B of E to IO, 7 Jan. 1929; BL, L/F/7/786, Imperial Bank to IO,18 Jan. 1928; BL, L/F/7/784, Imperial Bank to IO, 19 May 1923. The figures are from the Imperial Bank of India, through which most applications were made.

53   BL, L/F/7/785, Jukes to S of S, 10 May 1926; *ibid.*, Kisch, 8 June 1926; *Financial Times*, 18 Jan. 1928, p. 6.

54   BL, L/F/7/173, fol. 1394, memo, no date; BL, L/F/7/164, B of E Chief Accountant, 22 Nov. 1905.

1893 Trustee Acts.[55] By the 1890s, the scarcity of such securities had greatly increased trustee demand for Indian debentures/stock, but this dissipated after the passage of the 1900 Colonial Stocks Act, which anointed Crown colony loans with trustee status, and the 1929 Colonial Development Act's extension of the status to the issues of protectorates and mandated territories.[56]

Institutional purchasers included finance companies, which, as discussed, purchased stock close to its repayment date, and, if necessary, short-term bonds; the Bank of England for its reserves; from 1935, the Reserve Bank of India; the Crown Agents; and the IO itself.[57] The Reserve Bank of India bought for its reserves short-term bonds close to their repayment date, the bonds providing a higher return and the same level of liquidity as UK Treasury bills.[58] The Crown Agents acquired Indian debentures/stock (by 1939, £6.479m worth) for the colonial investment funds that they managed, the contents of which were restricted to those securities listed in the Trustee Acts.[59] The IO, meanwhile, purchased loans for its discount sterling loan Sinking Funds (1920: £7.503m) and for five discount Sinking Funds that were established for guaranteed railway companies (1920: £6.01m), for various charity funds, the GSR, and, from 1934/5 to 1938/9, for the Commissioners of four family pension funds (1938/9: £9.5m).[60] By 1912, it held 22 per cent of the sterling securities issued, which helped to keep market prices high.[61]

Conclusion

The issue of government loans was one of many ways in which the IO sought to attain its two primary goals – the maximisation of Indian exports and the payment of India's UK commitments. Securities were floated in order to finance the construction of the infrastructure that was essential to the development of trade, to raise funds needed to meet the country's commitments in Britain when the issue

---

55 PP 1889 [123], p. 92; PP 1872 [327], q. 7637; A. E. Davies, *The Money and the Stock and Share Markets*, London 1909, p. 65. From 1873 to 1886, the annual market price of Indian government 4 per cent stock varied by an average of just 4.3 per cent (PP 1887 [C.5099] *Gold and Silver Commission*, p. 342).

56 *The Statist*, 26 May 1894, p. 671; Anon, *The Investor's Handy Book of Active Stocks and Shares*, London 1910, p. 2; D. Sunderland, *Managing British Colonial and Post-Colonial Development: The Crown Agents 1920–1980*, London 2007, p. 14.

57 Bank of England Archive (BE), ADM 19/7, 28 Feb. 1882; BL, L/F/7/799, Viceroy to IO, 23 March 1936.

58 BL, L/F/7/816, note, 27 June 1935; BL, L/F/7/820, note, 25 May 1937.

59 NA, CO 323/1202/11, Gowers to Colonial Office (CO), 24 Oct. 1932; NA, CO 323/1623/19, CAs to CO, 26 Oct. 1939.

60 BL, L/AG/14/11/3; BL, L/F/7/825, note, 24 July 1942; PP 1934–35 [17] *Government of India: A Bill to make Further Provision for the Government of India*, pp. 140, 146; Dhar, *The Sterling Balances*, p. 14.

61 PP 1914 [Cd.7070] *Royal Commission on Indian Finance and Currency: Appendices, Volume 1*, statement no. 1, p. 317.

of council bills was not possible and to permit the purchase of the guaranteed railway companies, the extravagant interest payments of which had increased the home charges. More importantly, issues fuelled the IO's re-lending cycle, providing some of its funds and a means of access. Loan proceeds were placed in the home balances until needed, from whence they were advanced to City institutions, and Indian government securities were accepted as guarantees for home balance/discount market loans, could be sold in the latter market or presented by discount houses as warranties for advances from joint stock banks. The funds raised were then recycled—used by the brokers and banks to buy more Indian government securities, by the exchange banks to purchase further council/import bills, and by the discount houses to discount Indian export drafts.

The importance of sterling issues to this recycling of resources precluded the raising of all loans in India, though until the inter-war period this was always a non-starter. As will be discussed later, a large proportion of the securities were bought by British investors, whose purchases aided the finance of trade. There was also a lack of capital and enthusiasm for rupee stock in India, and the Indian government was well aware that any loan proceeds used to meet the home charges would have to be remitted to England, damaging the exchange, and that the withdrawal of funds from the Indian capital market would have raised interest rates, again to the detriment of traders.

2

The Issue of Government Loans: Demand

The demand for Indian debentures/stock was high for reasons unconnected to the machinations of the IO. In the early part of the period, there was little competition for investors' funds from foreign governments or domestic industry, and there was a patriotic element to the purchase of Indian securities.[1] Much of the railway equipment bought with the proceeds of issues was sourced in the UK and the completed infrastructure, built by British engineers, ultimately increased UK exports and reduced the cost of imports.[2] More importantly, investors believed Indian loans to be secure and that the Indian government would default neither on the payment of dividends nor on the repayment of capital.[3] Until the inter-war period, they thus had a good appetite for the securities, which allowed the IO to offer relatively low yields. Their confidence was also based on the state of the country's finances, its membership of the British Empire, and a mistaken (though essentially accurate) belief that the loans were guaranteed by the UK government. Indian finances were regarded as extremely sound – government debt was exceeded by the value of public sector assets, the revenue of which exceeded interest charges over time – and this situation was expected to continue as long as the country remained part of an Empire on which the sun would never set.[4] The might of the British army and navy ensured that there would be little internal political discontent (a precursor of default) or external aggression; the country's adoption of a semi-gold standard from 1898 and the efforts of the IO to maintain a stable exchange promoted trade; and the

1   A. R. Hall, *The London Capital Market and Australia, 1870–1914*, Canberra 1963, p. 15. The large number of issues may also have been influential; investors were attracted to seasoned borrowers (M. Tomz, *Reputation and International Cooperation*, Oxford 2007, p. 67).

2   PP 1914 [Cd.7069], q. 9938; Dubey, *The Indian Public Debt*, p. 57; *Journal of the Royal Society of Arts*, 79 (4028) (31 Jan. 1930).

3   W. H. S. Aubrey, *Stock Exchange Investments*, London 1896, p. 178; PP 1889 [123], p. 92.

4   Anon, *The Investor's Handy Book*, p. 2; Dubey, *The Indian Public Debt*, p. 56; PP 1872 [327], q. 7642. In the 1870s, some argued that the Indian 'surplus' was the result of creative accounting (PP 1871 [363], q. 9822–36).

country was administered by able, honest and white administrators operating under the British legal system.[5] Worshipping the Gladstoneian trinity of balanced budgets, sound money and free trade, these upright bureaucrats would do their utmost to prevent the country reaching a position where it was unable to pay its debts, and, if this eventuality ever came to pass, would extract the deficit from the Indian people, if necessary, by force.[6] They, in turn, were supervised by the IO, managed by some of the finest financial minds in City, which in its turn was monitored by Parliament.[7]

Investors also believed that the payment of dividends and loan repayment were guaranteed by the UK government, a misconception that the IO did little to overturn.[8] The reasons for this conviction are not hard to find. The loans could only be raised with the authority of Parliament and the Secretary of State; like UK government securities, they were recorded in the books of the Bank of England, which managed all transfers and made all interest payments; and they were excluded from the provisions of the 1877 Colonial Inscribed Stock Act that required colonial borrowers to state clearly on prospectuses that the securities floated carried no Imperial guarantee.[9] Many investors were also convinced that the guarantee given to Indian railway companies extended to government loans and were confused by the Stock Exchange listing. Because the loans were raised with the authority of Parliament, they were placed in the 'British funds' market section, which additionally contained UK government consols and exchequer bills, rather than the more appropriate

5   N. Ferguson and M. Schularick, 'The Empire Effect: The Determinants of Country Risk in the First Era of Globalisation, 1880–1913', *Journal of Economic History*, 66 (2) (2006), pp. 287, 289; Dubey, *The Indian Public Debt*, p. 58; PP 1873 [354], q. 1430; M. D. Bordo and H. Rockoff, 'The Gold Standard as a "Good Housekeeping Seal of Approval"', *Journal of Economic History*, 56 (1996), pp. 389–428; M. Obstfeld and A. M. Taylor, 'Sovereign Risk, Credibility and the Gold Standard 1870–1913 versus 1925–31', *Economic Journal*, 113 (487) (2003), pp. 1–35; K. J. Mitchener and M. D. Weidenmei, 'Country Risk, Currency Risk and the Gold Standard', at http://www.frbatlanta.org/news/CONFEREN/06workshop/mitchener.pdf (accessed August 2010), p. 33.

6   Ferguson and Schularick, 'The Empire Effect', pp. 284, 287; PP 1896 [C.8258], q. 7507. Mitchener and Weidenmei also believe India's partial membership of the gold standard was significant, though this view is not shared by others (M. Flandreau and F. Zumer, *The Making of Global Finance*, Paris 2004; N. Ferguson and M. Schularick, 'The "thin film of gold": Monetary Rules and Policy Credibility in Developing Countries', NBER Working Paper, no. 13918 (2008)).

7   PP 1932–33 [112] *Report of the Joint Committee (Indian Constitutional Reform)*, par. 11320; PP 1871 [363], q. 9468.

8   PP 1871 [363], q. 9466; *The Statist*, 13 March 1886, p. 283; M. Edelstein, 'Imperialism: Cost and Benefit', in R. Floud and D. McCloskey, *The Economic History of Britain, Volume 2*, Cambridge 1984, p. 206. Some of those who did not share this view strongly suspected that any default would be met from the Indian government's home balances, GSR or PCR (Dubey, *The Indian Public Debt*, p. 57).

9   NA, T 160/472, Indian Government securities, note, no date, early 1930s; BL, L/F/7/792, IO to Thompson, 20 Oct. 1933; PP 1871 [363], q. 9458; BL, L/F/5/64, memo, 8 Nov. 1880, p. 2; NA, CAOG 9/94, CAs to CO, 31 March 1908.

'Dominion, provincial and colonial government securities' sector.[10] An attempt by the Treasury in 1934 to alter this anomaly was, not surprisingly, strongly and successfully opposed by the IO.[11]

Aware of the impact an actual guarantee would have on demand, the IO and others actively campaigned for government protection. Among the arguments put forward were that a guarantee would allow higher prices and lower interest rates to be set, allowing more money to be raised and reducing the size of the home charges; facilitate loan conversion; strengthen Parliamentary control of Indian finances; and safeguard the interests of British investors.[12] All were summarily rejected. It was pointed out that colonial loans similarly lacked a guarantee, lower yields would further discourage Indian purchase of sterling loans, and that the announcement of government safeguards and the consequent increase in the UK's national debt would lead to a collapse in the price of consols and could even trigger a sell-off. Moreover, a guarantee was unnecessary.[13] Most investors already believed that there was government protection, and, in the event of a collapse in Indian finances, the UK government would have little option but to safeguard investor interests.[14] It had a moral obligation to do so and would be under such intense pressure that to do otherwise would be political suicide.[15] Default would also damage the legitimacy of the Empire and have devastating financial consequences – investors would withdraw their funds from private sector initiatives in India; Indian and Imperial credit would be destroyed, forcing colonial administrations to turn to the Imperial Exchequer for financial support; and the fall in investor wealth and incomes would reduce demand for home and foreign loans and damage consumer demand.[16] No guarantee was thus ever provided, though in the early 1930s, when independence reared its 'ugly head' and non-payment would have had serious implications for sterling, which was becoming increasingly vulnerable, the government issued a number of statements that essentially stated that default would never be countenanced.[17]

10   PP 1878 [C.2157] *London Stock Exchange Commission: Report*, q. 493; NA, T 160/649, note, 17 Feb. 1934; *ibid.*, Coats to Chancellor, 5 Feb. 1934; Edelstein, 'Imperialism', p. 206.

11   NA, T 160/649, Coats to Chancellor, 5 Feb. 1934; *ibid.*, note, 4 Feb. 1934 . The Stock Exchange was also reluctant to alter the listing (*ibid.*, note, 17 Feb. 1934).

12   PP 1871 [363], p. 516, par. 36; PP 1873 [354], q. 5645, 5650, 6812; K. M. Purkayastha, *The ABC of Indian Finance*, Calcutta 1924, p. 160.

13   *The Statist*, 8 March 1924, p. 350; PP 1873 [354], q. 6849, 6858, 6862–3, 6872, 6895.

14   One commentator stated that the latter claim was 'the the greatest illusion that was ever passed off on a credulous and ignorant nation' (R. H. Elliot, *Our Indian Difficulties*, London, 1874, p. 43).

15   PP 1871 [363], p. 516, par. 36; PP 1873 [354], q. 5646, 5648.

16   PP 1873 [354], q. 3477, 5646, 5648; NA, CAOG 9/101, memo, 18 July 1935; NA, CAOG 9/324, notes, p. 21.

17   Cain and Hopkins, *British Imperialism, 1688–2000*, p. 556. Reassurances were made in Parliament (NA, T 160/649, Parliamentary question of 26 June 1931); at the 1931 Round Table Conference (BL, L/F/7/792, Official statements relating to Indian credit and financial stability, no date); at the Joint Committee on Constitutional Reform (NA, T 160/649, Coats to

Despite this inherent demand for Indian debentures/stock, the IO could neither assume that its issues would be fully subscribed nor exploit the public's appetite by reducing yields. As its calls on the London market increased and became more urgent, the public's hunger for its securities became sated and then began to wane. It was thus imperative that it maximise demand and avoid credit-destroying loan failures, goals achieved through the choice of an appropriate issuing house and broker; the careful timing, advertisement and support/underwriting of issues; and the setting of attractive terms.

Choice of broker/issuing house

Issuers of government debentures/stock employed a broker (who recruited underwriters and provided advice as to the loan terms that the market would accept and the timing of flotations) and an issuing house (which organised flotations and managed the securities sold). The IO's brokers were Nivisons and Mullens Marshall & Co, whose Senior Partner acted as government broker and no doubt used his close links with the Bank of England to ensure that India's issues avoided clashes with other flotations.[18] Nivisons, broker to New Zealand, the Australian States and South Africa, had an excellent reputation, on which India free rode; was a member of the Committee of the Stock Exchange, the decisions of which it could influence in the IO's favour; and, since it was almost part of the fabric of the City, could provide accurate and timely market advice.[19] It had close links with and, in some cases, acted for many of the trusts that purchased India's issues. Through its brokerage of dominion loans, which appealed to a similar market, it also ensured that Indian and dominion flotations were evenly spread over the year and possessed a coterie of reliable underwriters.[20]

The IO was less enamoured by its issuing house, the Bank of England. The Bank's involvement in flotations did add value. It increased public confidence and the Bank provided useful advice on market conditions, though Randolph Churchill during his brief tenure at the IO suspected its market knowledge to be grossly exaggerated and

---

Chancellor, 5 Feb. 1934); in an IO letter to the British Chamber of Commerce (BL, L/F/7/792, IO to Treasury, 10 Feb. 1933); and in the 1935 Government of India Bill (NA, T 160/649, Hilton Young to Foy, 11 April 1935).

18   D. Wainwright, *Government Broker: The Story of an Office and of Mullens & Co.*, London 1990, pp. ix, 55; BL, L/AG/9/8/6, pp. 869–70, memo, 16 July 1913.

19   Wainwright, *Government Broker*, p. 55. See also R. S. Gilbert, 'London Financial Intermediaries and Australian Overseas Borrowing, 1900–29', *Australian Economic History Review*, 10 (1) (1971), pp. 39–47.

20   H. Colebatch, 'Australian Credit as Viewed from London', *Economic Record* (Nov. 1927), p. 225; Senate of the United States, Speech by Hon. William M. Stewart, 1 May 1888, at http://www.yamaguchy.com/library/uregina/stewart.html (accessed July 2012); Gilbert, 'London Financial Intermediaries', p. 42.

recommended its replacement by Rothschilds.[21] The Bank's relatively high management fee, alternatively, was much criticised by IO officials. Oddly, its repayment, conversion and issue fees were reasonable. The 'unnecessarily generous' conversion and redemption charges were £500 per million with a minimum fee of £2,500 from 1887 to 1930, and, thereafter, £750 per million on amounts up to £2.5m and £500 per million on amounts above this sum.[22] In comparison, the Crown Agents charged £5,000 per million (1880–1912) and £1,000 per million (1912–14) for redemptions, and £5,000 per million (1880–87), £2,500 per million (1887–1912) and £1,000 per million (1912–14) for conversions; similarly, the Bank required its dominion government clients to pay £1,000 per million (1880–1908) and £600 per million (1908–14) for conversion, and £1,000 per million for redemptions.[23] The issue fee was equally competitive at £500 per million of debentures/stock floated in tender issues, raised in 1904 to £625 per million in line with UK government issue fees; and £1,000 per million, increased to £1,250 per million in 1904, for fixed price flotations, which attracted more public applications and therefore involved more administrative work.[24] Mechanisation then allowed these charges in 1930 to be reduced to £250 per million for tender issues, and £1,000 per million up to £2.5m and thereafter £750 per million for fixed price flotations.[25] In contrast, the Crown Agents, who lacked the economies of scale of the Bank, variously charged £2,500 per million (1863–86 and 1893–1914) and £5,000 per million (1886–93), and the Bank's dominion government clients paid £5,000 per million from 1880 to 1908 and £2,500 per million from 1908 to 1914.[26] The IO's only disagreement with the Bank as regards these fees occurred in 1910 when it was asked henceforth to pay £1,250 per million, as opposed to £625 per million, for the tender issue of bonds. Despite protests, the Bank refused to alter its decision, arguing that the higher fee was due to increased bond printing costs and that the same commission was paid by the UK government.[27]

There was far less satisfaction with the Bank's charges for the management of loans, which comprised the payment of dividends and the recording of transfers of ownership. Action, however, was constrained by the fact that all loan statutes required the use of the Bank and a fear that it would exercise its influence in the City

21 Kynaston, *The City of London … Vol. 1*, p. 374.

22 BL, L/F/7/173, fol. 5607, note, 24 Jan. 1935; *ibid.*, fol. 1393, note, 20 Feb. 1931; BE, AC 30/121, IO to B of E, 26 April 1887.

23 NA, CO 323/364/5665, CAs to CO, 2 April 1886; NA, CO 323/393/11909, CAs to CO, 13 July 1903; NA, CAOG 9/40, Antrobus to CO, 23 March 1912; BE, AC 14/14, memo, 12 Aug. 1908; *ibid.*, memo, 20 April 1914.

24 PP 1896 [C.8258], q. 11880; BE, AC 30/121, memo, 9 Nov. 1904; *ibid.*, IO to B of E, 15 Dec. 1904; *ibid.*, B of E to IO, 23 July 1900.

25 BL, L/F/7/173, fol. 1393, revised B of E terms, no date.

26 NA, CO 323/364/5665, CAs to CO, 2 April 1886; NA, CO 323/393/11909, CAs to CO, 13 July 1903; NA, CAOG 9/40, Antrobus to CO, 23 March 1912; BE, AC 14/14, memo, 12 Aug. 1908.

27 BL, L/F/7/163, no. 22, file 4, fol. 720, note, 1910; *ibid.*, no. 22, file 4, fol. 720, B of E to IO, 17 Nov. 1910.

to destroy Indian issues if future empowering Acts dispensed with its employment.[28] On obtaining the management role in 1859, the Bank charged a fee of £340 per million of stock/debentures managed, the same amount paid by the British government for the management of the first £600m of UK public debt. The IO believed this was fair, but in 1887 demanded a reduction. The main reasons were that two years earlier the Bank had introduced a management fee of £400 per million for loans that paid quarterly rather than biannual dividends; HMG's charge had been reduced to £300m in 1861, and it was not required to pay a higher commission for quarterly dividend payment; the size of the Indian sterling debt had risen from £5m to £90m, permitting management economies of scale; and it had been discovered that the Bank was earning a significant sum lending out unclaimed dividends.[29] In response, the Bank pointed out that quarterly payments doubled its labour outlays, and that the cost of the issue of council bills and the management of the home balances was no longer covered by the interest the Bank earned on the IO's current account, as the money kept in the account had fallen. It nonetheless agreed to reduce its charges for half-yearly dividend stock to £300 per million and that for quarterly dividend stock to £360 per million. Although suspicious of the Bank's claims, the IO accepted the compromise and agreed that the terms would be renegotiated when the quarterly dividend debt reached £100m, which occurred in 1896 when the charge on quarterly dividend debt over £100m was reduced to £100 per million.[30]

The IO returned to the fray in 1904. Eight years earlier, the UK Treasury's quarterly dividend charges had been reduced to £325 per million on debt up to £500m and £100 per million thereafter. The IO thus requested that its fees on the first £100m of such debt be similarly cut.[31] The Bank's reaction was to demand an even higher fee, an investigation of their work having revealed that the cost of managing India quarterly dividend stock was far higher than formerly believed, as the average holding was smaller (and therefore the number of interest payments were higher than for UK government debt) and there were relatively more transfers of ownership.[32] Unable to disprove the data presented, the IO agreed to pay £360 per million when the debt was below £125m, and, when it exceeded this figure, £300 per million on the first £125m and £60 per million thereafter.[33] Emboldened by its success, the Bank in 1910, on the flotation of debentures, demanded £100 per million for their management, even though

28   BL, L/F/7/177, fol. 1326, note, E. L. Ball, 26 Jan. 1938; BL, L/F/7/173, fol. 1393, IO to Sir R. Mant, 17 Sept. 1930.
29   BL, L/F/5/64, IO to B of E, 20 July 1887; BL, L/AG/9/8/5, vol. 6, pp. 683–7.
30   BL, L/F/5/64, B of E to IO, 19 Aug. 1887; *ibid.*, B of E to IO, 24 Jan. 1888; *ibid.*, Currie, 8 Dec. 1887; *ibid.*, IO to B of E, 8 Feb. 1888; BE, G 8/48, p. 66, note, 11 March 1896.
31   BL, L/AG/9/8/5, vol. 6, pp. 683–7.
32   *Ibid.*, vol. 6, pp. 705–8, memo, no date. There was an average of 495 accounts per million pounds of India stock and an average of 245 transfers per annum. The same figures for UK government stock were 237 accounts and 190 transfers (BL, L/F/7/164, fol. 8093, note, no date, 1905).
33   BL, L/AG/9/8/5, vol. 6, p. 709.

it had previously received no remuneration for this work since it involved neither the recording of changes of ownership nor the payment of dividends. The IO wrote a strongly worded letter of protest and Schuster and Inchcape met the Bank's Governor, but to no avail, the Bank arguing that a similar charge was paid by the UK Treasury.[34]

By the time the 1905 agreement expired, the battles between the IO and the Bank over the purchase of silver and the lending of the home balances, described in Chapters 5 and 11, had come to an end with the resounding victory of the Bank. IO officials thus made no protest when the Bank delayed renegotiations for nine years owing to 'pressures of work' and mildly accepted its 1924 demand for a new charge of £330 per million for deed stocks, which it claimed were relatively costly to manage.[35] It was only in the 1930s that it made a stand, prompted by its financial difficulties, the desertion of other Bank clients to the joint stock banks, and the criticisms of the government auditor, who believed it 'ridiculous' that the Bank had never provided a breakdown of its costs and that no comparison had been made of India's charges with those of other institutions and the Bank's other clients.[36]

The case built by the IO concentrated on the Bank's costs. Although it refused to provide details, the IO argued that these must have declined given the increased size of its debt and the accompanying economies of scale, the expansion of its debenture debt, and the Bank's adoption of labour-saving devices.[37] It also pointed out that its fees were three times those of the Crown Agents, even though the Agents managed a smaller amount of debt and thus lacked the Bank's scale economies, and slightly higher than those of the UK government, whose debt was presumably managed in conjunction with its own loans.[38] The case was presented to the Bank in 1930, 1932 and 1934, and, in 1932 and 1934, the IO attempted but failed to organise 'concerted action' with the UK Treasury.[39] The Bank, however, refused to give way, and, in 1938, increased the quarterly dividend charge to £325 per million on the first £750m of

34 BL, L/F/7/163, no. 22, file 4, IO to B of E, 2 Nov. 1910; *ibid.*, no. 22, file 4, fol. 720, note, 1910; *ibid.*, no. 22, file 4, fol. 720, note, 1910; *ibid.*, no. 22, file 4, fol. 720, B of E to IO, 17 Nov. 1910.

35 BL, L/F/7/164, fol. 1372, note, 9 Jan. 1919; BL, L/F/7/172, IO to B of E, 3 April 1923; BL, L/F/7/173, fol. 700, note, no date; *ibid.*, fol. 1393, revised B of E terms, no date.

36 BL, L/F/7/177, Auditor, 18 Sept. 1937; *ibid.*, fol. 1326, note, E. L. Ball, 26 Jan. 1938. Among others, New South Wales and Middlesex County Council transferred their business (BL, L/F/7/173, fol. 1394, Turner, 24 Jan. 1930).

37 BL, L/F/7/177, IO to B of E, 8 Nov. 1937; BL, L/F/7/173, fol. 1393, note, Cecil Kisch, 31 Oct. 1930; *ibid*, fol. 1394, memo, no date; *ibid.*, G of I to IO, 20 April 1903; *ibid.*, Baxter to Treasury, 6 Feb.1934.

38 BL, L/F/7/173, fol. 1394, Turner, 24 Jan. 1930; *ibid.*, Kisch to G of I, 12 March 1931; BL, L/F/7/177, note, 14 Oct. 1937. The Crown Agents charged £100 per million for loans prior to 1928 and £200 per million on later loans (BL, L/F/7/173, note, 25 Jan. 1932). There was some disagreement over whether UK government and Indian debt were managed jointly (BL, L/F/7/177, fol. 1326, Ball, 26 Jan. 1938).

39 BL, L/F/7/173, fol. 1393, note, Cecil Kisch, 31 Oct. 1930; *ibid.*, IO to G of I, 6 July 1932; *ibid.*, Baxter to Treasury, 6 Feb. 1934; *ibid.*, G of I to IO, 20 April 1932; *ibid.*, Treasury to IO, 13 Feb. 1934.

debt and £150 per million on the balance on the grounds that the average holding of Indian stock had fallen, increasing the number of interest payments.[40]

Timing and advertisement of issues

Timing was crucial to the success of flotations. Dates of issue, along with the terms, were determined via correspondence between the IO, its brokers and the Bank of England, and confirmed and occasionally changed at a formal meeting between the Under Secretary of State, the Governor, one or two directors of the Bank of England and the two brokers immediately before the announcement of a flotation.[41] Until 1921, the government of India played little part in these discussions. Government officials had no financial experience or City contacts, and it was feared that their involvement could lead to the setting of issue dates/terms unacceptable to the market, and, as regards the pre-announcement meeting, to the IO 'missing the tide', an upturn in market demand.[42] There was also a danger that they would leak the date of an issue, causing the market price of existing Indian loans to fall and allowing the market manipulation described below to occur. Not surprisingly, the Indian government objected to its exclusion from the raising of its own debt, and, in 1921, after the calamity of that year's issue, the IO agreed to henceforth consult it 'as far as practicable before taking the final decision'.[43] In reality, little changed until the 1927 arrival of George Schuster as finance member of the Viceroy's Council. Mistakenly regarding himself as a financial expert, and 'difficult to handle', Schuster constantly interfered in the issue process, often to the fury of Bank of England and IO officials, and usually to the detriment of India. [44]

In order to allow advantage to be taken of market upturns and to avoid down-turns, the IO issued loans well before the proceeds were required.[45] Although the strategy was costly in interest payments, in general the additional dividends paid were offset by the higher prices secured, by the interest charged on lending out the loan proceeds until needed to City institutions, and the other benefits that accrued from these advances. Ideal times for flotations were periods of low interest rates and cheap and freely available money; after the repayment of Indian or other loans, when the recipients were searching for substitute investments; immediately before the payment of Indian loan dividends, when the market price of debentures/stock

---

40   BL, L/F/7/173, fol. 1393, note, Cecil Kisch, 31 Oct. 1930; *ibid.*, IO to G of I, 6 July 1932; BL, L/F/7/177, fol. 1326, Ball, 26 Jan. 1938.

41   PP 1909 [Cd.4474] *Committee of Enquiry into the Organisation of the Crown Agents' Office*, q. 703.

42   PP 1914 [Cd.7069], q. 11656; BL, L/F/7/806, note, 9 Jan. 1933.

43   BL, L/F/7/783, S of S to Iveroy, no date.

44   BE, G 1/323, Kisch to Norman, 15 May 1930. See, for example, *ibid.*, Norman to Kisch, 25 Sept. 1929; *ibid.*, Norman to Baxter, 15 Oct. 1929; *ibid.*, Harvey to Norman, 20 Jan. 1931.

45   BL, L/F/5/144, Schuster's statement with reference to silver purchases and IO balances (Schuster's statement), 7 Feb. 1913.

was high and holders, anticipating the arrival of dividends, were more likely to add to their portfolios; and prior to the distribution of the dividends of UK government securities, which mostly occurred in January and February.[46] Periods avoided by the IO included immediately after the flotation of other trustee securities, and following the flotation of very large loans, especially if they failed, which would increase the time required for brokers/underwriters to offload their allotments and downgrade the public's perception of a 'fair price'.[47] The IO also avoided periods of political disturbance in India, the summer months when much of the City closed down, and before or after the flotation of rupee loans.[48] As a large proportion of rupee stock was purchased by British investors, issues prior to or at the same time as a rupee loan flotation would reduce demand for that loan and issues afterwards would minimise demand for the sterling debentures/stock.

Unfortunately, the IO's ability to avoid market downturns was constrained by Bank of England control of the timing of issues, designed to prevent issuers entering the market simultaneously, as they were wont to do during upturns. Such market stampedes inevitably led to the failure of loans, which damaged the reputation of the City and its ability to attract foreign issuers, diminished liquidity, could lead to a dangerous outflow of gold and reduced the number of issues that could occur by 'clogging' the market with unsold stock. As demand for flotations increased, the Bank's control strengthened, though the IO benefitted from the post-war decision to give preference to Empire over foreign issues and to loans for funds that would be spent in the UK or the Empire and would thus aid British trade.[49] In late 1931, it was also granted special treatment when the Treasury embargo on issues was extended to 'provide a fair field' for a loan that it had previously agreed to postpone.[50] Nonetheless, the Bank's interference did occasionally act against the interests of India – the 1922 loan, for example, failed as the slot for its issue granted by the Bank happened to coincide with a market downturn, and the IO believed a higher price could have been obtained for the May 1933 issue if the Bank had not insisted that it be postponed until after the publication of the White Paper on Indian constitutional change.[51]

46   BL, L/F/7/773, Kisch to Cook, 25 July 1922; PP 1914 [Cd.7069], q. 4594.

47   PP 1914 [Cd.7069], q. 10853–4; *Investors Review*, 8 (June/Dec. 1901), p. 70.

48   *The Statist*, 3 April 1897, p. 508; NA, CAOG 9/118, CAs to Nigeria, 1 Feb. 1927; NA, T 160/474, Indian loans, 1932 and 1933, S of S to G of I, 13 Jan. 1933.

49   J. Atkin, 'Official Regulation of British Overseas Investment, 1914–31', *Economic History Review*, 23 (2) (1970), p. 325.

50   NA, T 175/70, Chancellor, Jan. 1933; K. Tsokhas, 'Coldly Received: Australia and the London Capital Market in the 1930s', *Australian Journal of International Affairs*, 46 (1) (1992), pp. 61–80. The embargo was designed to leave the market free for the conversion of UK government debt and to avoid an increase in interest rates undermining the government's cheap money policy. In the event, the loan was further delayed by a decline in the market (*ibid.*, p. 65).

51   BL, L/F/7/773, Cook to Kisch, 6 July 1922; BL, L/F/7/806, Hare, 17 Feb. 1933.

Once the timing of an issue had been decided upon, the IO set about advertising the flotation, which they achieved through newspaper advertisements and meetings with editors.[52] As the majority of loans were purchased by the City, and few of the readers of some of the newspapers in which advertisements appeared were regular purchasers of securities, the advertisements had little impact on demand at issue. Their true purpose was to alert readers of the appearance of debentures/stock that they could later buy through their brokers (which increased the likelihood that the City would be able to offload its purchases quickly and at a high price) and to ensure 'good write-ups' of the issues and Indian affairs in general.[53] Indian advertisement was a good source of revenue for newspapers, and there was a strong belief that advertisements in such outlets as the *Daily Chronicle* and *Daily News*, which the IO accepted were 'almost valueless', encouraged the proprietors to include positive news stories on the outcome of flotations and Indian politics.[54] To further encourage post-issue take-up and affirmative reporting, Under Secretaries of State and Bank of England officials prior to flotations held private meetings with journalists and representatives of the leading newspapers, during which they were sometimes 'economical with the truth'.[55] In 1933, for example, 'the greatest possible prominence' was given to the strengthening of the position of the Reserve Bank of India as the 'real object' of the issue, when in reality the flotation was to replenish the home balances.[56] Occasionally, immediately before or after flotations, the IO also planted positive news stories about India or made announcements designed to rally support. In 1930, Kisch in an 'entirely private' letter to the editors of the major papers enclosed correspondence from the Secretary of State to a private investor, who was assured that the UK government would never allow India to default on its debts.[57] The leak paid off 'very handsomely', as the following morning all the newspapers carried articles on the letter, and the market price of Indian securities rose by 2 to 4 per cent.[58] Likewise, in 1932, an announcement that £10m was to be transferred from the home balances to the GSR was delayed until the day the prospectus for the loan of that year appeared. As the proceeds of the issue were to be used to increase

---

52   A 1922 proposal that the IO place advertisements in the press extolling the general virtues of the Indian economy was rejected (BL, L/F/7/773, Cook to Kisch, 6 July 1922; *ibid.*, Kisch to Cook, 25 July 1922).

53   BL, L/F/7/791, B of E, 16 Dec. 1929. From 1900, underwriters generally required that a certain sum be spent on publicity (Crown Agents' Archive, Sutton (CAS), CA M 5, Memorandum on the procedures followed in connection with the issue of Crown colony loans, 1919, p. 21).

54   BL, L/F/7/791, note, 20 Jan. 1929; *ibid.*, B of E, 16 Dec. 1929.

55   BL, L/F/7/796, note, 22 Oct. 1930; BL, L/F/7/787, Kisch, 7 Jan. 1929.

56   BL, L/F/7/809, note, 9 May 1933; *ibid.*, Baxter, 8 May 1933; *ibid.*, note, 15 May 1933.

57   E.g. BL, L/F/7/792, IO to Editor, *Daily News*, 27 Jan. 1930; *ibid.*, Kisch to Leith, *Financial Times*, 27 Jan. 1930.

58   *Ibid.*, Kisch to S of S, 28 Jan. 1930.

GSR funds, it was believed that the announcement would 'have a reassuring affect on investors' and give 'a fill up' to the flotation.[59]

Unfortunately, some newspapers proved resistant to the IO's financial lures and embellishments. Much to the IO's fury, the *Daily Mail* from 1929 to 1931 and the *Morning Post* from 1933 to 1934 published negative articles on Indian finance. The *Daily Mail*, for example, in a 1929 editorial strongly advised potential buyers of sterling bills to think again, describing purchase as 'an act of weakness and short-sightedness', and it later dismissed the IO's 1930 leaked letter as 'a childish assurance'. The IO was convinced that such 'unscrupulous propaganda' was politically motivated, designed to strengthen the position of opponents of greater Indian independence by reducing Indian loan and sterling bill subscriptions and market prices. As to how it should respond, it was divided. Some officials believed no action should be taken, regarding the *Daily Mail* as a 'silly newspaper' that had little impact on the decisions of investors.[60] Others, including Kisch, believed that the articles were having an 'adverse' affect on subscriptions and market prices and that it was imperative that 'something was done'.[61] Strategies discussed included no longer placing advertisements in the papers; using 'private channels', such as the Governor of the Bank of England, to talk to the proprietors, without mentioning 'that the suggestion emanated' from themselves; and sending letters to other newspapers refuting the criticisms. As correspondence from the IO could 'do more harm than good', it was proposed that Sir Basil Blackett, a former member of the Finance Committee and currently a member of the Union of Britain and India, be conscripted to put his name to a letter that described the newspapers' tactics as 'disgraceful'.[62] In the event, no action was taken, and, after the emergence of the new constitution, both papers eventually moved on to other campaigns.

Underwriting

Informal underwriting first appeared in the 1860s and involved the recruitment by Nivisons of a group or syndicate of brokers and City institutions, which agreed to tender for a given portion of a loan at the minimum price, or, in the case of

59   BL, L/F/7/806, S of S to G of I, 9 Nov. 1932; *ibid.*, Kisch to Governor, B of E, 9 Nov. 1932; *ibid.*, B of E to Kisch, 10 Nov. 1932.
60   BL, L/F/7/791, *Daily Mail*, 17 Dec. 1929; BL, L/F/7/792, *Daily Mail*, 29 Jan. 1930. See also BL, L/F/7/799, Kisch, 9 Feb. 1931; BL, L/F/7/801, note, 23 May 1931; BL, L/F/7/792, *Morning Post*, 9 Oct. 1933; *ibid.*, *Morning Post*, 23 Feb. 1934; *ibid.*, *Morning Post*, 23 May 1934; *ibid.*, note, 25 May 1934; *ibid.*, *Morning Post*, 12 Sept. 1934; *ibid.*, IO to Thompson, 20 Oct. 1933; *ibid.*, note, 19 Jan. 1930; *ibid.*, note, 2 March 1934.
61   E.g. *ibid.*, Kisch, 31 Jan. 1930; *ibid.*, Kisch to S of S, 29 Jan. 1930; BL, L/F/7/799, Kisch, 9 Feb. 1931; BL, L/F/7/801, note, 23 May 1931; BL, L/F/7/792, IO to Thompson, 20 Oct. 1933.
62   BL, L/F/7/791, note, 17 Dec. 1930; BL, L/F/7/792, Kisch to S of S, 29 Jan. 1930; *ibid.*, Kisch, 31 Jan. 1930; *ibid.*, IO to Thompson, 20 Oct. 1933.

fixed price issues, to purchase an agreed amount of the debenture/stock at a price discount.[63] After the flotation, the syndicate then sold the debentures/stock it had purchased for a profit, having, in the case of tender loans, rigged the minimum price upwards. Syndicates' applications for debentures/stock encouraged others and particularly the public (which was unaware of the practice) to subscribe, and, if take-up was poor, the IO at least received a proportion of the money required. Moreover, the failure of a loan remained secret. India's credit in the market and among the investing public was thus secure, and there was no post-issue collapse in prices and demand, allowing syndicate brokers to rapidly offload their allotments at a reasonable price.

Formal underwriting began in 1907 and involved the IO entering into legal contracts with brokers, who agreed to buy at a given price and in return for a commission those portions of loans that had not been purchased at issue. Many at the IO opposed the introduction of the practice, arguing that it increased flotation expenses, damaged confidence in the commercial viability of Indian loans and discouraged applications, as investors were aware that a loan failure would result in the post-issue sale of debentures/stock by underwriters at a discount. Officials, however, had little option but to accept formal underwriting, facing pressure to do so from both brokers and the Bank of England. Brokers, who had lost money in the early 1890s as a result of informal underwriting, wished to gain guaranteed remuneration for their support activities and either refused to purchase securities that were not underwritten or would only buy them at a deep discount.[64] The Bank of England, meanwhile, strongly urged issuers to adopt the practice, which it believed would minimise the failure of loans and thus improve the reputation of the capital market and its use by foreign governments, and would increase loan turnaround, owing to fewer issue delays caused by brokers having to offload unsold debentures/stock.[65] There was also a growing realisation among IO officials that underwriting possessed a number of benefits. Although loan failures no longer remained secret, the very fact that underwriters were willing to support an issue gave the public confidence to invest, and underwriting ensured that India would receive all the funds required even if the take-up of loans proved inadequate, as seemed increasingly likely given the massive expansion of issues.[66] The Office could thus set a fair rather than an excessively low price for its securities and avoid

---

63   PP 1875 [367] *Report from the Select Committee on Loans to Foreign States*, q. 137, 139, 347, 352, 357, xlvi, xlvii; Hall, *The London Capital Market*, pp. 77, 79. The 1872 syndicate included Gilletts, the discounting house that specialised in Indian bills of exchange (Sayers, *Gilletts*, p. 50).

64   Hall, *The London Capital Market*, p. 102; PP 1914 [Cd.7069], q. 11703–4, 11709, 11712; NA, CAOG 9/29, Blake to Hong Kong, 23 Feb. 1906; B. Attard, 'Marketing Colonial Debt in London: Financial Intermediaries and Australasia, 1855–1914', *Association of Business Historians Conference*, Jan. 2004, p. 12.

65   *ibid.*, p. 19.

66   PP 1914 [Cd.7069], q. 11705, 11710.

the 'embarrassment' of being unable to meet its commitments and the extra cost and inconvenience of 'raising the wind by other means'.[67]

Underwriting was organised by Nivisons, which managed a large group of underwriters who were expected to support all the company's loans, both good and bad, with a refusal to do so leading to ejection from the group, and, as their lack of loyalty became common knowledge, from other underwriting circles.[68] The underwriters were large and prestigious banks, insurance and broking companies, discount houses and, from the late 1920s, the Crown Agents.[69] All possessed large amounts of surplus capital (in the case of the Crown Agents, colonial investment funds) or could easily raise funds in the discount market, and could be relied upon not to dump debentures/stock onto the market, and, if necessary, in some cases to hold it as a permanent investment. It was also unlikely that they would engage in sub-underwriting, that is, passing a portion of the support taken on to another firm in order to reduce their risk exposure. The practice was frowned upon by issuers, as, in the past, sub-underwriters had refused or lacked the funds to take up unsold stock or had immediately sold it on the market at a deep discount.[70]

Nivisons' arrangements broke down only once, in 1921, when the firm announced that it was unable to organise underwriting for that year's loan owing to its large £7.5m size and the high interest rates then ruling. It was thus decided that the Bank of England would underwrite the issue, and, to guarantee success and avoid any damage to India's credit, would make applications for the whole amount. Unfortunately, the experiment proved disastrous. The Bank charged a fee of 2 per cent, as against the usual 1⅛ per cent. To maximise public applications, it demanded that the loan should carry a massive 7 per cent interest rate, and perhaps leaked its own applications for stock to the City.[71] The result was that the loan was five times oversubscribed, attracting £36.5m worth of subscriptions. Moreover, a day after the issue was announced the Bank cut base rate, making the 7 per cent interest rate appear even more outlandish. Although IO officials, in answer to the many critics of the loan, claimed that they had 'anticipated' the rate reduction and that a high dividend was crucial to the success of the flotation and the re-establishment of

---

67   BL, L/F/7/786, Kisch to Burden, 20 March 1928.

68   CAS, Notes on the issue of loans by the Crown Agents, 1926, p. 11; Gilbert, 'London Financial Intermediaries', p. 42; BL, L/F/7/795, B of E to Kisch, 30 July 1930.

69   *The Statist*, 27 April 1912, p. 181; NA, CAOG 9/104, Abbott, 16 Oct. 1933; Sayers, *Gilletts*, p. 50. From 1928 to 1933, the Crown Agents underwrote ten Indian loans (NA, CAOG 9/104, memo, 16 Oct. 1933, statement A).

70   *The Statist*, 27 April 1912, p. 181; NA, CAOG 9/101, note, 15 Oct. 1923.

71   BL, L/F/7/783, note, no date; *ibid.*, memo, 16 April 1920; *ibid.*, Howard to B of E, 24 March 1921; *ibid.*, B of E to IO, 13 May 1921; *ibid.*, *Financial News*, 22 April 1921. The Indian government believed the rate to be 'ruinous' (*ibid.*, Viceroy to S of S, 27 April 1921).

India's credit (the loan was the first since 1912), privately they fumed at the Bank's duplicity.[72]

After its introduction, the only criticism of underwriting was its cost. For arranging underwriting, Nivisons obtained a commission (known as an overriding fee) of ⅛ per cent, half of which it passed to Mullens Marshall & Co.[73] The sum was half that charged by the company for the flotation of Australian loans and by the Crown Agents' broker, but was nonetheless resented.[74] It was rightly claimed that in return for its fee the company performed very little work, simply calling upon and later phoning its group of underwriters, and that its role as the IO's broker granted it valuable benefits that constituted remuneration. The prestige of being India's broker and its underwriting patronage attracted business, it could use inside information on the likely demand for loans to make lucrative applications on its own account and employ the lure of participation in Indian underwriting to entice underwriters to support more risky flotations.[75] The remuneration of the underwriters – 1 per cent, the market average – was similarly claimed to be excessive.[76] Like Nivisons, they obtained inside information that they could use for their own benefit, and the underwriting of Indian loans carried relatively little risk. Only six issues failed, leaving underwriters with a total of just £47.345m of unsold debentures/stock, and, even if underwriters were forced to take an unsold balance, the demand from trusts meant that it would eventually be offloaded and usually at a slight profit.[77]

The IO, however, like the other London issuers, had no power to alter the fees. It was well aware that no other London broker would be prepared to offer lower overriding or underwriting commissions and that a 1922 attempt by the Crown Agents to transfer their underwriting business to the British Stockbrokers Trust Ltd, an alliance of provincial stockbrokers that offered lower rates, had been abandoned when they were informed that all London broker applications for their loans would cease if the transfer went ahead.[78] The only alternative, Indian government underwriting of loans, was simply not feasible. It would have been strongly opposed by the

72   *Ibid.*, B of E to IO, 25 April 1921; *ibid.*, Viceroy to S of S, 10 May 1921; *ibid.*, S of S to Viceroy, 30 April 1921; *ibid.*, Kisch to S of S, 5 July 1921.

73   BL, L/F/5/144, House of Commons (H of C), 6 Nov. 1912, Baker; *ibid.*, H of C, 10 Jan. 1913, Gwynne; *ibid.*, H of C, 8 Jan. 1913.

74   NA, CAOG 9/40, CAs to CO, 26 Jan. 1928.

75   NA, CAOG 9/102, Bickersteth to Gowers, 17 June 1935; *ibid.*, memo, 20 Feb. 1934; *ibid.*, Bickersteth to Thornton, 21 July 1932. Australian issuers also allowed the firm's own applications to take precedence over those from the public (Gilbert, 'London Financial Intermediaries', p. 42).

76   PP 1914 [Cd.7069], q. 11703.

77   BL, L/F/5/62; NA, CO 323/945, c12397, loans issued in London since the war; *Financial Times*, 25 April 1912, p. 6; *ibid.*, 14 Jan. 1910, p. 4; Gilbert, 'London Financial Intermediaries', p. 44.

78   D. Sunderland, *Managing the British Empire: The Crown Agents for the Colonies 1833–1914*, London 2004, pp. 26–7; Gilbert, 'London Financial Intermediaries', p. 43.

City, the Indian government lacked the necessary funds, and, in 1923, the Finance Committee judged that it involved an unacceptable level of risk.[79]

Method of issue, purpose and size

The IO's determination to ensure that India obtained and paid a low yield for its funds did not end with the timing and advertisement of issues, and the organisation of support/underwriting. Demand could be further maximised and yield minimised through its determination of the terms of loans, the information that appeared in prospectuses. Terms included the method of issue, the power to borrow, the loan's purpose, size and yield and the form of asset issued. In the inter-war period, it was suggested that prospectuses should also include positive details of India's finances and a statement that loan proceeds would be spent in the UK.[80] In the event, both proposals were rejected. Although transparency regarding Indian finances would help to sell debentures/stock in good years, during periods of deficit it would restrict demand, and waving the flag of British purchase would run counter to the policy of sourcing as many supplies as possible from India and 'raise a great outcry', reminding Indians of their supposed exploitation.[81]

Initially loans were sold in 'open offers'. The East India Company and the IO would create a given amount of stock/debentures and these would then be gradually sold to brokers and City institutions privately as need or demand arose over the following few months to a year.[82] The practice ensured that money was raised only when needed and that unemployed loan proceeds did not sit in the home balances earning relatively little interest, and it increased the likelihood that a 'fair' price would be obtained. The small amounts sold at any one time prevented a fall in the market price, and, if the prices proffered were too low, sales were simply suspended.[83]

Tenders were introduced from the early 1860s, largely because it was believed that they encouraged the public to participate in issues, increasing demand and prices.[84] They also introduced competition to the issuing process, again raising prices, absolved the IO and the Bank of England from responsibility/criticism for the price attained, and reduced the extravagant expenditure supposedly engendered

---

79   BL, L/F/7/784, note, 8 Aug. 1923.
80   BL, L/F/7/805, Kisch, 14 Nov. 1928; BL, L/F/7/807, note, 8 May 1931.
81   BL, L/F/7/805, Kisch, 3 Dec. 1928; BL, L/F/7/810, note, 2 Nov. 1933; BL, L/F/7/807, note, 8 May 1931. Statements indicating British purchase did appear in the prospectus of the 1921 loan, which was expected to fail, and, under Treasury and Parliamentary pressure, in the prospectuses of the 1931 and 1933 issues (*ibid.*, note, 8 May 1931; *ibid.*, H of C, 22 May 1931; BL, L/F/7/810, note, 2 Nov. 1933).
82   PP 1871 [363], q. 9444, 9446, 9452.
83   BL, L/F/5/169, p. 43, Secombe, 2 Aug.1869; PP 1871 [363], q. 9446, 9449.
84   BL, L/F/5/64, Perry, 20 May 1879, p. 3.

by open offers.[85] At first, the minimum price at which the IO was prepared to sell was concealed, in the belief that investors lacking a guide would increase the prices bid. Later, when it was realised that the reverse often occurred and that concealed prices discouraged applications, the minimum price was listed in the prospectus.[86] In the event, tenders failed to significantly increase demand – investors were discouraged from making applications by the complexity of the process, the need to make a rapid decision to buy, and their lack of knowledge of likely bid prices, which could cause them to obtain no allotments or the full amount applied for at an excessive price.[87] In the 1890s, therefore, tenders were replaced with fixed price sales in which subscribers made applications to buy stock at a fixed price and were allotted stock pro rata to total subscriptions.[88]

Despite the arrival of tenders and fixed prices, private sales did not disappear completely. Stock continued to be privately sold to brokers, though these deals became increasingly rare and the sales were largely made to just two brokers, Hopkins & Giles and Wedd Jefferson, who were trusted to pay a fair price. After the failure of the 1901 loan, £0.7m of the unsold stock was offloaded to these brokers at the issue price plus the immediate payment of the first dividend for £0.4m of the stock. Private sales were also made in 1888, when the proceeds of the loan for the purchase of the Oudh and Rohilkhand Railway fell short by £0.2m of the sum required to buy the line; in 1889, when £4m of stock was sold for railway purposes; in 1891, to meet the home charges; and in 1896, to raise the £2m required to repay a terminable loan.[89]

In order to issue securities on the market, India had to apply to Parliament for one of two borrowing powers – 'special' powers when a loan was for railway purposes and 'ordinary' powers when it was for general expenditure. After securities to the value of the borrowing authority had been issued, the power disappeared, but was revived when the loan was repaid.[90] On many occasions, the IO wished to issue securities, but lacked the necessary borrowing authority and was reluctant to apply to Parliament for additional rights, either because it believed that they would not be granted or feared that their award would damage India's credit in the market by indicating additional borrowing.[91] It thus carefully 'managed' its powers to ensure that it could always borrow funds without fresh Parliamentary sanction.

85   PP 1878–79 [312], q. 665, 815.
86   *Investors Review*, 12 (July/Dec. 1898), p. 155; PP 1896 [C.8258], q. 11875–6.
87   Hall, *The London Capital Market*, p. 102.
88   Gilbert, 'London Financial Intermediaries', p. 42.
89   BL, L/AG/9/8/5, vol. 5, p. 423, note, 26 Oct. 1888; *ibid.*, vol. 5, p. 685, Scott to IO, 27 Nov. 1891; *ibid.*, vol. 6, p. 273, memo, no date; *ibid.*, vol. 6, pp. 265–7; *ibid.*, vol. 6, p. 275; *ibid.*, vol. 5, p. 427, memo, 30 Nov. 1888; *ibid.*, vol. 5, pp. 531–2, memo, 15 April 1889; *ibid.*, vol. 5, pp. 679–81, memo, 6 Nov. 1891; *ibid.*, vol. 5, p. 841.
90   Vakil, *Financial Developments*, p. 306; BL, L/F/7/757, note, 1921; BL, L/AG/4/12/1, fol. 12198, note, 4 Nov. 1921.
91   E.g. BL, L/F/7/772, note, 27 Nov. 1922; BL, L/AG/4/12/1, note, 18 Sept. 1931.

When deciding which loans to repay, officials generally took account of the borrowing authority that would be revived, repaying loans with powers that they needed to issue fresh loans. Likewise, the stated purpose of loans was determined according to their existing sanctions and the powers they believed would be required in the future. In late 1920s, for example, they possessed more 'special' than 'ordinary' powers, but wished to conserve the latter in case a financial emergency forced the issue of an 'ordinary' loan. They thus stated that the £6m sterling bills issued in December 1929 for general expenditure were for railway purposes and claimed that the 1931 and 1932 loans, the prospectus purposes of which were listed as 'railway and general purposes', were used to finance railway capital expenditure when, in fact, the majority of the proceeds was used to supplement the home balances.[92]

Not everyone at the IO was comfortable with these actions. Some opposed the 1931 manipulation, claiming that it was dishonest and could lead to difficulties if Parliament later questioned the division of the loan's proceeds. Others argued that the allocations only 'strained the facts' in that the railway expenditure had actually occurred, albeit some years previously and financed from other funds. It was also maintained that most investors cared little about the use made of their money, that it was not 'conceivable that anyone will believe that we are really borrowing ... for railway purposes', and that the subterfuge was unlikely to be discovered.[93] The latter claim proved over-optimistic. Soon after the loan, *The Statist*, having noticed a discrepancy between the size of the loan and the value of railway material exports to India, accused the IO of 'misrepresenting' its investors and attempting to hide its support of the rupee.[94] The story, however, attracted little attention and officials again manipulated their powers in the 1932 issue.

The amount to be borrowed in England and India was decided upon during the budget negotiations between the Indian government and the Secretary of State that occurred at the start of each financial year. Critics claimed that the practice led to unnecessary borrowing, as after the borrowing targets had been agreed there was no further discussion on the subject, and, when budget estimates proved to be overly pessimistic, the IO continued to issue loans and bills, often at high prices. In reality, the IO received monthly revenue statements and altered its borrowing plans accordingly, though it accepted that in 1911 it renewed debt that could possibly have been paid off.[95] The actual size of loans was determined by the IO in conjunction with the Bank of England and its brokers, who estimated how much Indian debentures/stock the market could absorb. The loans were considerably bigger than those floated by the

---

92   BL, L/AG/4/12/1, 5581/32, Baxter, note, no date; *ibid.*, 12798/29, Accountant General, 27 Feb. 1930; BL, L/F/7/782, Baxter, 20 Sept. 1932. See also BL, L/AG/4/12/1, Kisch to Cook, 12 April 1923.

93   BL, L/F/7/782, Baxter, 20 Feb. 1931; *ibid.*, Turner, 22 Oct. 1930; *ibid.*, Turner, 5 Sept. 1930.

94   *The Statist*, 23 May 1931, p. 826.

95   PP 1914 [Cd.7069], q. 4386–7, 4478, 4390–3, 9506–8.

Crown colonies and Australia, though smaller than those of foreign governments.[96] Large issues had to be sold relatively cheaply and their announcement led to a relatively steep fall in market prices.[97] Alternatively, they created more attention, increasing subscription, and avoided India having to regularly enter the market, which could create a perception of overissue.[98]

Conclusion

The demand for Indian debentures/stock was high for a variety of inherent reasons, the most important of which were that India was part of the Imperial project, with all the benefits that entailed, and investors truly believed that the payment of dividends and loan repayment were guaranteed by the UK government, a misconception the IO did little to overturn. Aware that this inherent demand could evaporate overnight and that a loan failure would destroy its credit in the market, the IO also sought to maximise demand through its choice of issuing house/broker, the careful timing, advertisement and underwriting of flotations and the sale of large amounts of debentures/stock via minimum, and later fixed price, tenders.

The Bank of England and Nivisons were inspired choices as respectively issuing house and broker. Nivisons had strong links to the large trustee market, and both it and the Bank possessed valuable market knowledge and influence, as well as excellent reputations that ensured they would perform their tasks honestly and competently, and on which the IO could free ride. The only downside was the self-interested behaviour of the Bank of England, which sought to maximise its loan management commission, and, in the process, damaged relations with the IO. The scheduling of loans was also impressive. Issues were carefully timed to ensure that maximum advantage was taken of market upturns and that the home balances possessed sufficient funds and could make the loans to the City that were so beneficial to India. True, the IO's freedom of choice as regards issuing dates was constrained by the Bank of England. However, this was an eminently reasonable strategy that benefitted all issuers, including India, and, on at least one occasion, the Bank relaxed its rules in the subcontinent's favour. As regards the marketing of loans and prospectus descriptions of their purpose, the IO adopted rather disreputable strategies that had more in common with the private than the public sector to achieve results. When marketing issues, officials were occasionally economical with the truth, planted 'good news' stories in the press and used their advertising budget to procure positive

---

96   The average size of publicly issued Indian government loans from 1858 to 1935 was £5.74m (BL, L/F/5/59; BL, L/AG/14/10/1). Their mean size from 1883 to 1912 was £3.68m, as compared with £1.91m for responsible government colonies, £0.76m for Crown colonies and £4.66m for foreign governments (Sunderland, *Managing the British Empire*, p. 154).

97   E.g. *The Statist*, 5 Jan. 1929, p. 4; BL, L/F/7/799, note, 26 Jan. 1931.

98   NA, CAOG 9/94, CAs to CO, 31 March 1908. India also needed more money than the Crown colonies/Australia.

reporting. To ensure that they always possessed sufficient Parliamentary borrowing powers, they deliberately falsified the proposed expenditure of a number of loans, safe in the knowledge that their dishonesty would not be discovered. As will be seen later in this book, such behaviour was replicated in other areas.

3

The Issue of Government Loans: Yields, Assets and Repatriation

One of the main lures used by the IO to attract timid investors to Indian government loans was yield, the annual dividend paid, which was determined by each issue's interest rate, the price paid for the debentures/stock at issue and various other factors. From 1880 to the First World War, the annual yields of Indian loans, as calculated by the formula interest rate/price x 100, were lower than those of the securities floated by the Crown Agents for the Crown colonies and by the Australian dominions, and far smaller than foreign government issues. The Indian government thus paid relatively less for the money that it borrowed than its counterparts, though, as will be seen, the saving was not as great as first appears.[1] After the First World War, however, yields were higher than those offered by the Crown Agents, and, in some years, greater than Australian loans, though still far below those provided to subscribers of foreign securities (Figure 3).[2]

To further investigate the mysteries of yield, this chapter will examine the prices demanded by the IO for its debentures/stock and the interest rates and 'extras' paid to subscribers. It will then examine the type of assets issued before tracing the fall in the popularity of Indian government loans and their eventual repatriation.

Prices

On issue, each debenture/stock was sold for a minimum/fixed price that was above or below the 'par' price (£100) at which it would eventually be repaid. The IO generally chose below-par prices, as trustees were averse to purchasing stock at

---

1 A discussion of basic yields can be found in Ferguson and Schularick, 'The Empire Effect'.
2 From 1920 to 1935, the mean yields at issue of foreign government loans was 6.3 per cent, of Crown colony loans 4.55 per cent, of Australian loans 4.9 per cent, and of Indian loans 5.1 per cent (NA, CAOG 9/33–CAOG 9/35; *Stock Exchange Official Intelligence*, London 1921–32, 1939; BL, L/AG/14/10/1).

Figure 3. Average annual yields of government publicly issued loans, 1880–1935

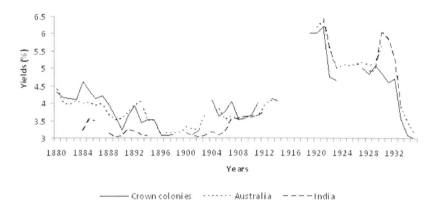

Sources. CAS, Prospectuses; Guildhall Library, London, Prospectuses; NA, CAOG 9/33–CAOG 9/35; *Stock Exchange Official Intelligence*, London 1921–32, 1939; BL, L/AG/14/10/1.

Notes. Yield = interest rate/price x 100. Australian issues = S. Australia, W. Australia, New South Wales, Tasmania, Victoria and Queensland.

a considerable premium and they were prohibited by law from buying above-par securities if they managed trusts with less than fifteen years to run.[3] The minimum/fixed prices set were dependent on a variety of factors, including the level of UK interest rates, many brokers borrowing the money with which they bought loans; the price of recently issued Indian and colonial stock; and the market price of Indian securities.[4] The IO always ensured that issue prices were higher than the price of existing Indian government debentures/stock (by a relatively high average of 2.68 per cent from 1885 to 1912), since this allowed the brokers who purchased loans to make a profit, known as a 'turn', when they resold the debentures/stock to the public.[5] Issue prices were therefore partly determined by market prices (which, in turn, were dependent on the general state of the Stock Market, and, in particular, the price of other trustee securities, which had a tendency to fluctuate in unison) and on the state of the Indian economy, especially the amount of rupee debt in existence.[6] Market prices also tended to fall on the issue of new loans, as the flotation increased the supply of securities on the market and occasionally offered better

---

3 NA, CAOG 9/324, note, p. 14.
4 BL, L/F/7/783, Viceroy to S of S, 10 May 1921.
5 *Investors Review*, 8 (June/Dec. 1901), p. 43; *Daily List*, 1885–1912. The average quoted is the difference between issue prices and market prices one week before issue. The colonial premium was 3.162 per cent (*ibid.*).
6 *Financial Times*, 24 Jan. 1914, p. 1. E.g. Kale, *India's National Finance*, pp. 61, 63.

terms; when another trustee or Indian guaranteed railway loan was floated; or, in the case of individual stocks priced at above 100, as the date at which they would be repaid (at 100) approached.[7]

Unlike the Crown Agents, the IO did not rig the market before or after issues, though it allowed its syndicates/underwriters to do so. Rigging involved an issuing house buying before a flotation on the market large amounts of stock similar to that being issued, and, after an issue, the stock of the floated loan, thus forcing the price to rise. A price increase prior to flotation allowed a high minimum/fixed price to be set, and a rise after flotation encouraged public purchase by giving the impression that there was a great demand for the new debentures/stock and further rises were likely. From 1885 to 1912, on average the market price of Indian securities fell by 0.0119 per cent in the month before issue, as compared to a Crown colony rise of 0.82 per cent, and, in the month after flotation, rose by just 0.7 per cent, as opposed to a 1.7 per cent rise for colonial loans.[8] The sheer amount of Indian debentures/ stock on the market meant that purchases prior to issue, unless extremely large, would have little impact on prices, and the IO, unlike the Crown Agents, lacked the investment funds to make acquisitions. The IO, however, on at least four occasions, did seek to reverse the slight fall in market prices that occurred immediately after a loan was announced, a reaction to the future increase in the supply of debentures/ stock, which some thought had a minor impact on demand. Purchases for the discount Sinking Funds, described below, were made immediately after the price fall, allowing the debentures/stock to be bought cheaply and the fall to be reversed.[9] Aware of these market interventions, the Indian government in 1930 requested that a far more major operation be launched to reverse the price collapse caused by the financial crisis that had badly damaged Indian prices. After much consideration, the IO refused. Given the severity of the fall, very large purchases would be required to correct it and the necessary funds were unavailable; the home balances were low, only one Sinking Fund had money to purchase stock and the issue of a loan or bills would be impossible, given market conditions.[10]

The IO syndicates/underwriters rigged markets after issues, in order to increase the demand for and the price at which they could sell their allotments, and also

---

7 H. Lowenfeld, *All About Investment*, London 1909, p. 20; *Financial Times*, 24 Jan. 1914, p. 1; PP 1887 [C.5099], q. 1772.

8 *Daily List* 1885–1912. The Crown Agents were enthusiastic pre- and post-issue riggers (Sunderland, *Managing the British Empire*, p. 165). Both the Bank of England and the London and Westminster Bank also occasionally indulged in post-issue price manipulation (*ibid.*, p. 167).

9 BL, L/AG/14/11/4, note, 6 Sept. 1921. There are records of support purchases in 1900, 1901, 1905 and 1921 (BL, L/AG/14/11/1, memo, 27 June 1901; *ibid.*, memo, 21 March 1905; *ibid.*, memo, 21 June 1921).

10 BL, L/F/7/792, Viceroy to IO, 4 Jan. 1930; *ibid.*, Kisch to Schuster, 3 Dec. 1929; *ibid.*, Kisch, 1 Jan. 1930; *ibid.*, S of S to Finance Dept., 4 Jan. 1930.

during the flotation process.[11] On the announcement of an issue, syndicate members/ underwriters would apply for stock at the minimum price. This apparent enthusiastic support for the loan would boost after-issue purchase and encourage the public and brokers to make more applications at a higher price prior to the application deadline in the belief that there were after-issue profits to be made and that allotments would be poor. The final price of the loan was thus advanced and the chance of failure reduced, and, even if subscriptions were inadequate, the underwriters' applications disguised the extent of the debacle and minimised the severity of the price fall, thus making it easier to offload unsold stock.[12] The syndicates/underwriters also actively participated in the 'grey' market in which brokers and the public bought and sold the as yet to be issued scrip via buy or sell time bargains for delivery after the issue. Purchases removed the risk that buyers would obtain no or only a small allotment if a loan was oversubscribed, and, if the grey market price was lower than the after-issue market price, allowed them to sell purchases at a profit.[13] The IO syndicates/underwriters bought large amounts of new stock on the grey market at a relatively high price, causing the grey market price to rise, which prompted yet more high price applications from brokers and the public by suggesting that after-issue demand would be high.[14]

Their dealings in the grey market also allowed them to make big profits. After agreeing to buy large amounts of debentures/stock at high prices, thus causing the grey market price to rise, they then began to make agreements to sell debentures/ stock at the bidded-up price, meeting these bargains after the issue was over with the scrip they had already purchased at the lower grey market prices then ruling, and, in the case of syndicates, with the stock they bought from the IO at a discounted price. Sometimes, however, no sale agreements were entered into. There were occasional conspiracies to 'defeat' a loan. Brokers who had not been allowed to join a syndicate/underwriting group, who had a personal vendetta against members or the issuer/issuing house, or who wished to force the issuer to float future loans at a very low price would themselves sell debentures/stock in the grey market and thus force the price down. On such occasions, the syndicate/underwriters would continue to make purchase bargains in the hope of reversing the price fall.[15] Likewise, there was a danger that brokers who had agreed to sell stock at an advanced price would continue to make sale bargains in the hope that the falling grey market price that the sales precipitated would reduce subscription, result in a low post-issue market price

11   BL, L/F/7/786, Kisch to Burden, 20 March 1928.
12   NA, CAOG 9/103, memo, 31 March 1936; *ibid.*, memo, June 1936; NA, CAOG 9/101, memo, 23 Nov. 1927.
13   PP 1878 [C.2157], q. 5312.
14   PP 1875 [367], q. 137, 139, 347; *Investors Review*, 5 (July/Dec. 1895), p. 180; *Banker's Magazine*, 875 (1909), pp. 875, 902–3; Lowenfeld, *All About Investment*, pp. 177–9. The practice was known as the 'premium dodge'.
15   PP 1875 [367], pp. xlvi–xlvii; *ibid.*, q. 5179; PP 1878 [C.2157], q. 3158, 3166; *Investors Review*, 8 (June/Dec. 1901), p. 70.

and permit them to buy the stock required to meet their sale bargains at a price lower than the purchase price. When it appeared that such a process was about to occur, the syndicate/underwriters again began to make purchase bargains.[16]

Inevitably, the prices paid for the IO's loans were the subject of much criticism from the Indian government and others, who claimed that they were set too low and that this reduced the amount of money raised and increased the cost of repayment (at £100).[17] It was also argued that low prices reduced demand by giving an impression of poor quality; had a negative, though temporary, impact on the market price of both sterling and rupee stock; and forced the Indian government to adopt a similar policy when floating its rupee loans.[18] Some of the prices were indeed too low, the result of officials misreading the market (which, when it occurred, they privately admitted), and, in the case of the 1921 loan, as already discussed, the perfidy of the Bank of England. Generally, however, the IO was correct to set relatively modest prices, particularly after the fall in demand for Indian securities from the early 1900s. Steeper prices would have increased the likelihood of failure and damaged India's credit in the market, which, given its insatiable hunger for sterling loans, had to be defended at any cost.

Low prices were also demanded by the IO's underwriters, brokers and the Bank of England.[19] High prices could result in underwriters and brokers being left with large amounts of unsold securities; if there was a post-issue collapse in price, could lead to broker losses; and, by reducing demand, forced brokers to hold onto their purchases, and pay interest on the discount market loans with which they were bought, for long periods before the debentures/stock were sold on to the public.[20] Moreover, there was a danger that underwriters and brokers would 'cut their losses' and sell their allotments at any price. Such action would force those who retained their acquisitions to hold them even longer and lead to a steep collapse in market prices that would destroy Indian credit.[21] There would also be wider market implications, which could also impact India. Large underwriter and broker holdings of unsold Indian debentures/stock would reduce liquidity and demand for HMG and other issues, and the dumping of Indian securities would cause all market prices to fall and make it difficult for new issuers to obtain reasonable prices for their loans.[22]

16 PP 1878 [C.2157], q. 3059.
17 E.g. *Journal of the Statistical Society*, 24 (1861), pp. 128–9; *The Statist*, 9 July 1898, p. 63; Dhar, *The Sterling Balances*, p. 36; *Financial Times*, 22 March 1911, p. 6.
18 *The Statist*, 9 July 1898, p. 63; PP 1902 [187], p. 17; BL, L/F/7/783, Viceroy to S of S, 27 April 1921.
19 G. Chand, *The Financial System of India*, London 1926, p. 315; BL, L/F/7/799, note, 26 Jan. 1931.
20 *The Statist*, 9 July 1898, p. 6. Broker losses were particularly large when interest rates were high (*Investors Review*, 12 (July/Dec. 1898), p. 7).
21 *Investors Review*, 12 (July/Dec. 1898), p. 7.
22 NA, CAOG 9/300, CAs to Wilson, 8 Dec. 1927.

Interest rate and 'extras'

After price, the next most important loan term was the interest rate or dividend. The rate set depended on the interest charges of other issuing houses and the Bank of England base rate, which reflected the amount of money in the market, though there were rumours in 1897 and 1904 that the Bank had brought forward interest rate cuts in order to increase the demand for Indian loans.[23] When base rates were low, dividends and 'extras' tended to be relatively meagre (and vice versa), as brokers could easily obtain funds at a low cost, and, if a loan failed, they were less likely to dump their unsold allotments onto the market to cut their debt charges. Where possible, the IO sought to float loans with the same interest rate and dividend/repayment dates as previous issues. Thus, though interest rates varied over the period from 2.5 per cent to 6 per cent, there was £94.4m of 3.5 per cent stock issued, £78.9m of 3 per cent stock, and £11.9m of 2.5 per cent stock.[24] The flotation of loans with identical interest rates/terms encouraged holders of previous flotations to purchase more stock, as the security was familiar and their new and old holdings could be sold together, reducing selling fees, and, for the Bank of England, the payment of vast amounts of dividends on the same dates reduced administration costs.[25] More importantly, the resultant large blocks of stock overcame the tendency of trustee purchasers to rarely sell their holdings and ensured a relatively liquid market, which again encouraged subscription.[26] Holders were assured that there would always be someone willing to buy their holdings, an advantage that particularly appealed to City institutions that held stock as short-term investments.[27]

The rates offered were far higher than first appears, as subscribers obtained a variety of 'extras' in the form of early payment discounts, unearned interest, the payment of stamp duty and redemption yields, all of which effectively increased the rate paid. Those who decided to pay for their purchases in one lump sum received a discount on the amount paid. The size of the discount varied according to whether the IO required the funds immediately to meet the home charges, and, from 1883 to 1912, averaged 2.38 per cent, as against the Crown colonies' 2.44 per cent and the responsible government colonies' 2.33 per cent.[28] Generally, brokers opted for full

23   *Financial Times*, 22 April 1904, p. 1; PP 1921 [Cmd.1512] *Report of the Committee Appointed by the Secretary of State for India to Enquire into the Administration and Working of Indian Railways*, p. 29. The *Financial Times* believed the unexpected 1897 cut in the base rate on the day the 2.5 per cent loan was announced was 'rather remarkable' and had saved the issue from certain failure (*Financial Times*, 15 May 1897, p. 4).
24   BL, L/F/5/61, no. 70.
25   CO 137/552/2931, CAs to CO, 12 Feb. 1892.
26   BE, C40/289, Reserve Bank of India to B of E, 29 April 1937; H. Lowenfeld, *The Investment of Trust Funds in the Safest and Most Productive Manner*, London 1908, p. 15; BL, L/F/5/64, memo, March 1885.
27   PP 1889 [123], p. 92.
28   Sunderland, *Managing the British Empire*, p. 170.

payment when the discount was high and they intended to hold the stock for only a short period, and when interest rates were low and they could easily and cheaply borrow the sum required for the payment.

Unearned interest was bestowed as part of the first six month dividend payment and consisted of accrued and free interest. Accrued interest was a fictional back-dated remittance. If a loan was floated on 1 June and the first six month interest payment was made on 31 August (three months later), only three months of the dividend paid would actually have been earned, and the remainder, accrued interest, unearned. Free interest, meanwhile, was given to those who opted to pay for securities in instalments spread over a number of months. Although during the first six months of ownership they had not fully paid for their purchases, they nevertheless obtained the full rate of interest when the first six month dividend payment was made.[29] The amount of free interest earned was dependent on the size and period between payment instalments, which, in turn, depended on when the money was required and the likely demand for the debentures/stock. If a loan was likely to fail, more free interest would be provided in order to attract investors and to discourage brokers from dumping unsold stock onto the market.[30] Over the period 1883–1912, the accrued/free interest offered by the IO averaged 0.577 per cent – midway between the amount given by the Crown Agents (0.494 per cent) and responsible government colonies (0.964 per cent).[31]

The rate of return from stock was further increased by the IO payment from 1885 of stamp duty (a tax usually paid by investors whenever they wanted to sell their stock) and the early repayment of loans.[32] Most Indian issues allowed the Secretary of State to repay the sum borrowed at par (100) at any time after a given date. A loan's rate of return was thus greater the earlier it was repaid. So, for example, if debentures/stock that were sold at £91 could be repaid at £100 at any date after 1920, a repayment in 1921 would give the holder a slightly higher return overall than if the loan was repaid in 1931, as he or she would have the use of the repayment premium (the difference between the purchase price and the repayment price: £100 minus £91= £9) for a longer period.[33] To make this additional yield more prominent, after the First World War the IO gave its loans early and final repayment dates, and, to further increase the additional amount earned on early repayment, occasionally offered to redeem a loan at the earliest date at a price above par – 102 in the case of

29 *The Statist*, 10 May 1902, p. 952. E.g. *ibid.*, 17 Dec. 1921, p. 1090; *Financial Times*, 1 April 1905, p. 4; BL, L/F/7/784, IO to Finance Dept., 10 May 1923.
30 E.g. BL, L/F/5/64, memo, 'Conversion of 4pc stock', no date; BE, G 1/323, note, 23 Dec. 1930
31 Sunderland, *Managing the British Empire*, p. 169.
32 In 1885, the Treasury allowed the IO immediately after an issue to make a composition payment, a lump sum that covered all future stamp duty payments (NA, T 20/6, p. 544, Treasury to IO, 17 Feb. 1887).
33 The additional income earned comprised the interest the repayment premium could earn if invested at the current base rate from the early repayment date to the last possible date of repayment.

the 1921 loan.[34] The additional yield, known as the redemption yield, was generally small, averaging just 0.029 per cent for the eleven issues that were redeemed early, had a final redemption date and for which data is available; however, it could be much higher – 0.833 per cent as regards the 1928 loan.[35]

Type of asset issued

Indian loans were 'first charges' on the revenues of India (that is, they would be repaid before other debts if the government was unable to pay its obligations) and took the form of debentures, stock or a combination of the two.[36] Debentures were bearer securities, the ownership of which was not recorded, and could therefore be sold without reference to the issuing house or payment of stamp duty.[37] Although popular with the City, they were disliked by the public, as they were liable to theft or misappropriation, and, to obtain dividends, coupons attached to the certificate had to be sent to the issuing house.[38] The IO therefore, like other issuers, in the mid 1880s began to sell stock, the ownership of which was recorded at the Bank of England, allowing interest payments to be sent to the holder's home address. Unfortunately, the Bank had to be notified personally of any changes of ownership by the sellers of stock or their legal representatives, which was inconvenient, increased costs and dampened demand. The solution, transfer by deed, was repeatedly blocked by the Bank (concerned at the impact the increase in its workload and the greater likelihood of fraud would have on its costs), but was finally introduced in 1920.[39] Other benefits of stock were that from 1885 and the IO's agreement with the Treasury, purchasers no longer had to pay stamp duty on sales, and, unlike debentures, which could only be sold in given amounts (£500, £1,000), it could be disposed

---

34 *Financial Times*, 21 April 1921, p. 4.

35 Redemption yield data from *The Statist*, 17 Dec. 1921, p. 1090; *ibid.*, 21 Jan. 1928, p. 90; *ibid.*, 5 Jan. 1929, p. 34; *ibid.*, 24 May 1930, p. 1010; *ibid.*, 11 Nov. 1933, p. 791; *ibid.*, 13 July 1935, p. 66; *ibid.*, 13 May 1933, p. 743; BL, L/F/5/62. A drawback of this strategy was that if the IO did not redeem at the first opportunity, many investors would sell their stock, causing the price to fall. In the case of the 1930 loan, therefore, the final redemption price was higher than the early redemption price (*The Statist*, 15 Feb. 1930).

36 BL, L/F/5/64, Perry, 20 May 1879, p. 3. A 1929 proposal that the charge should be placed on railway revenues was rejected by the IO, as it would involve costly legal changes and no additional security would be provided (BL, L/F/7/782, Kisch to legal advisor, 23 Sept. 1929; *ibid.*, legal advisor, 25 Sept.1929).

37 Anon, *Guidebook for Investors in Government of India Securities*, Calcutta 1921, p. 16.

38 NA, T 172/238, Chamberlain, 6 July 1915; NA, CAOG 9/324, notes, p. 3.

39 BL, L/F/7/763, minute, 13 Oct. 1909; *ibid.*, note, no date; *ibid.*, IO to B of E, 26 Feb. 1920. Attempts to introduce deed stocks were made in 1909, 1911, 1914 and 1916. In 1914/16, the Bank claimed that it lacked sufficient staff to undertake the additional work (*ibid.*, B of E to IO, 19 Dec. 1911; *ibid.*, note, 1914; *ibid.*, B of E to IO, 21 Sept. 1916).

of in parcels of any value.[40] The sale of a combination of debentures and stock began in 1921 in an attempt to increase demand by appealing to both City and public investors. Buyers were either given a choice of stock or debentures, or loans were issued as debentures that could be converted into stock without the payment of a fee.[41]

The loans floated were either irredeemable, that is, had no date of repayment, or were terminable, the prospectuses of which explicitly stated when the capital would be repaid. The majority of issues, £200m in 1939, were irredeemable, though the IO usually gave itself the power to repay at a date of its own choosing on one to twelve months' notice and after the passage of twenty to thirty years.[42] The loans removed the need to repay debentures/stock when it was inconvenient to do so and their relatively long life made them more popular with trusts, which disliked having to reinvest capital.[43] More importantly, when market interest rates fell, the IO was able to use its powers of repayment to launch conversion operations. These involved the Office giving holders of high interest loans the choice of repayment or having their holdings replaced with new debentures/stock bearing the new lower market rate, and, when further rate falls were expected, with relatively short lives. Most investors chose to convert, as there were few high rate alternative investments available, the reinvestment of funds would be costly and inconvenient, and the conversion would lengthen the life of their investments. To encourage this choice, the IO also occasionally offered generous conversion rates, and, in 1874 and 1884, the option of conversion into stock or respectively annuities and debentures.[44] Those who rejected the offer were repaid with funds raised from the public sale of additional amounts of the new debentures/stock.[45]

From 1857/8 to 1930/1, £83.07m of debentures/stock were converted to lower rate securities in twelve operations, the practice coming to a halt in 1933 when the UK Treasury unofficially halted conversions in an attempt to conserve market funds and thus maintain low interest rates and a high demand for UK government securities.[46] Apart from reducing Indian government interest payments/home charges, the process had other benefits. Loans were usually converted into 3.5 per cent, 3 per cent or 2.5 per cent stock, thus further increasing the size and liquidity of these securities, and

40 CAS, CA M 5, Memorandum, p. 11; NA, CAOG 9/76, CAs to Gold Coast, 11 Dec. 1907.
41 In the case of the 1922 stock/debenture loan, both the debentures and stock were convertible (*The Statist*, 17 June 1922, p. 1065).
42 Dhar, *The Sterling Balances*, p. 9.
43 *Financial Times*, 10 Feb. 1930, p. 1. For example, repayment was inconvenient when market interest rates were high and the issue of fresh loans to raise the money for repayment would have been costly (Dubey, *The Indian Public Debt*, p. 68).
44 BL, L/F/5/59, note, 22 Dec. 1879; *ibid.*, note, 5 April 1884; *ibid.*, note, 9 Feb. 1889; *ibid.*, note, 27 Jan. 1891; *ibid.*, note, 3 Jan. 1874; *ibid.*, note, 5 April 1884; Sunderland, *Managing the British Empire*, pp. 191–2.
45 E.g. PP 1889 [123], p. 36.
46 BL, L/AG/14/10/1; NA, CAOG 9/300, Treasury to CO, 10 July 1933; *ibid.*, *The Economist*, 3 Sept. 1932. See also S. Howson, 'Sterling's Managed Float: The Operations of the Exchange Equalisation Account, 1932–39', *Princeton Studies in International Finance*, 46 (1980).

the conversion of short-term bonds reduced the amount of bonds on the market, and, as discussed below, their impact on the public's demand for Indian issues.[47] As a failed conversion could damage credit, the IO ensured that all were successful, and the only operation that attracted criticism was that of 1887 when some accused the Office of timidity, arguing that either the 4 per cent securities should have been converted to 3 per cent rather than 3.5 per cent stock, or the 3.5 per cent stock offered should have carried an earlier repayment date, thus allowing a further conversion if interest rates fell further.[48]

Terminable securities with a stated date of repayment, of which £120.69m were issued from 1857/8 to 1933/4, first made their appearance in 1866 and took the form of short-term bonds that had a life of a few months to ten years. Until the First World War, they were issued during the redemption of old loans; investors who rejected repayment would receive bonds paying the same or a lower interest rate and with a given lifespan.[49] After the war, their use was related to the high market interest rates then ruling. The IO expected rates to fall, and, when this occurred, planned to repay the loans with the proceeds of fresh lower rate issues, and the short-term nature of the securities meant that their generous terms had a less negative impact on market prices than would have been the case had they had longer lives.[50] The loans were also part of the IO's determination to maximise demand. The uncertain economic environment caused the public to prefer investments with a fixed and early repayment date, and, as already discussed, the bonds appealed to City institutions, especially insurance companies.[51] Their issue, however, was not without opposition. George Schuster mistakenly questioned the belief that there was a demand for such loans in the City, and Kisch warned that the securities were 'fraught with grave disadvantage'.[52] There was a fear that interest rates rather than falling would rise, that their issue would give the investing public a taste for short-term investments, and that the need to renew or repay vast sums of money in the not-too-distant future would destroy India's credit rating both in London and in India.[53]

The loans were repaid with funds provided by the Indian government, and, where this was not feasible, through the issue of fresh stock or sterling bills or the tapping of the home balances, even though the former damaged Indian credit and the latter could reduce confidence in the adequacy of the balances and have a negative impact on the exchange.[54] To minimise the amount needed, a number of loans permitted

47 *The Statist*, 23 April 1887, p. 443; BL, L/F/7/773, Kisch to Cook, 15 June 1922.
48 BL, L/F/7/795, Viceroy to S of S, 22 April 1930; *The Statist*, 4 June 1887, p. 596.
49 E.g. BL, L/F/5/59, note, 24 Feb. 1866; *ibid.*, note, 6 March 1878; *ibid.*, note, 5 April 1884.
50 BL, L/F/7/755, Kisch to Cook, 2 June 1921; BE, G 1/411, note, 27 Nov. 1929.
51 *Financial Times*, 9 Nov. 1933, p. 1; BL, L/F/7/810, Viceroy to S of S, 2 Nov. 1933.
52 BE, G 1/411, note, 27 Nov. 1929; BL, L/F/7/755, Kisch to Cook, 2 June 1921.
53 BL, L/F/7/773, Kisch to Cook, 15 June 1922; *ibid.*, Cook to Kisch, 6 July 1922.
54 *Financial Times*, 11 Jan. 1932, p. 4; BL, L/AG/14/11/2, capital transactions of 1910–11, p. 3, 19 May 1910; BL, L/AG/9/8/5, vol. 5, p. 841; BL, L/F/7/773, Kisch to Cook, 15 June 1922; BL, L/F/7/795, Cecil Kisch, 22 April 1930.

repayment by annual instalment, the bonds to be paid being chosen by draws.[55] When repayment was not possible, issues (£9.9m from 1857/8 to 1930/1) were converted into same interest securities, and, when market rates were high, into higher dividend stock, which increased Indian government interest payments.[56]

Many believed that the solution to the IO's terminal loan repayment difficulties and the mystery of how the irredeemable loans would eventually be repaid lay in the establishment of repayment investment Funds. Known as Sinking Funds, these were set up by issuers immediately after flotations and received annual payments from the issuer, which were invested in securities, the dividends of which were retained by the Fund. At the end of the loan's life, the investments were sold and the proceeds used to repay the issue.[57] Critics of the IO pointed out that the loans of the Crown Agents and British and Indian local authorities all had such Funds and that the Office's dismissal of them simply passed the problem of the repayment of irredeemable loans on to future generations of administrators and increased yields.[58] The Funds would attract subscribers by minimising the risk of non-repayment and thus allow more parsimonious terms to be offered, and would avoid the need to repay old debentures/stock via the issue of new loans, which damaged India's credit.[59] The IO dismissed these claims: none of the dominions possessed Sinking Funds; future generations, having access to railway profits, would have little difficulty repaying the loans; and there was no evidence that such Funds increased subscription.[60] Moreover, they would increase the home charges and tie up capital that could be used more effectively elsewhere, in particular in the finance of railway construction, which would reduce borrowing and generate returns that could be used for ad hoc repayment.[61]

Despite the Office's rejection of universal Sinking Funds, however, two quasi-Funds were established, and, from the 1880s, Funds were created to repay the losses that accrued when debentures/stock were sold at a discount. The quasi-Funds were the £2m reserve established in 1834 for the repayment of East India Company stocks and the 1878 Famine Insurance Fund, into which the Indian government was to annually pay £1.5m.[62] Theoretically, if harvests were good, half of this amount was

---

55   Dubey, *The Indian Public Debt*, p. 65; PP 1911 [155] *Return of Indian Financial Statement and Budget for 1911–12*, p. 261.
56   E.g. BL, L/F/5/59, note, 10 July 1863; *ibid.*, note, 5 March 1878; BL, L/AG/9/8/5, note, 24 Feb. 1866.
57   Vakil, *Financial Developments*, p. 289.
58   *The Statist*, 4 March 1922, p. 326; PP 1896 [C.8258], q. 11919; Sunderland, *Managing the British Empire*, p. 159. Indian State loans to municipalities also had Sinking Funds (PP 1898 [168] *Financial Statement of Government of India, 1898–99*, p. 161).
59   PP 1898 [168], p. 161.
60   PP 1878 [333], q. 618; PP 1896 [C.8258], q. 11926.
61   Vakil, *Financial Developments*, p. 290.
62   PP 1872 [327], q. 1347; PP 1881 [205] *Financial Statement of Government of India, 1881–82*, par. 68. When the East India Company stocks were repaid in 1874, the £7.5m Fund was insufficient

to be used for the construction of railways for the transportation of food into areas of famine and half for the purchase of sterling stock, which would improve the country's credit and allow fresh borrowing during periods of starvation without increasing aggregate debt.[63] In the event, a lack of funds caused annual payments to be suspended until 1881 and the money remitted to London was often used to pay the home charges, thus diminishing the need for fresh borrowing during market downturns.[64]

The discount Sinking Funds were established in the mid 1880s. Prior to this date, when debentures/stock were sold at a discount, i.e. below par (£100), and India thus obtained less money than it would have to repay, the loss was taken from government revenue.[65] Such a policy was acceptable when most loans were sold at prices above par and with low interest rates, but constituted a heavy charge when it was decided to issue low interest/low price loans in an attempt to raise demand.[66] To avoid the anticipated losses, in 1885 it was decided that the Indian government every three months would pay a sum into a Sinking Fund that, when cashed on the redemption of the loan, would cover the additional payment to be made.[67] Three Funds were set up for the 1885, 1886 and 1888 loans, but thereafter only four further reserves were established.[68] On the arrival of stable interest rates, the IO abandoned its low interest/low price policy, and, in 1889, it was decided that discount losses would be charged against revenue unless they were so great that they would inconvenience the Indian government.[69]

Fund regulations decreed that the sums paid into the Sinking Funds had to be invested in the Indian debentures/stock that provided the highest return, and, apart from the First World War when temporary investments were made in UK government war loans and exchequer bonds, this edict was followed.[70] The investments reduced Indian sterling interest payments/home charges and the amount of debentures/stock to be redeemed and helped to maintain market prices.[71] As the stock was cancelled on purchase, they also released borrowing powers and freed India from the payment of Bank of England management and repayment charges and the composition of stamp

---

to pay the £12m debt and the £4.579m shortfall was covered by the issue of more sterling stock (Vakil, *Financial Developments*, p. 278).

63 PP 1878–79 [312], q. 463, 580, 582; PP 1881 [205], par. 62.

64 V. Anstey, *The Economic Development of India*, London 1952, p. 384; PP 1881 [205], par. 88.

65 BL, L/AG/14/11/1, memo, 15 Nov. 1898. Premiums, likewise, were transferred to revenue (*ibid.*).

66 *Ibid.*, fol. 247, no. 401, note, 7 Nov. 1889.

67 BL, L/AG/14/11/2, note, 18 May 1910.

68 BL, L/AG/14/11/4, 94107, Durrant to Scott, 28 Dec. 1920. The other Funds were created for the 1898, 1909, 1910 and 1911 loans (*ibid.*).

69 PP 1899 [254], pp. 14, 39, 65.

70 BL, L/AG/14/11/2, capital transactions of 1910–11, p. 3, 19 May 1910; BL, L/AG/14/11/4, note, 4 July 1921.

71 BL, L/AG/14/11/1, memo, 18 Feb. 1886; BL, L/F/7/792, Kisch to Schuster, 3 Dec. 1929.

duty fee.[72] Generally, the investments were bought on the market, though in 1921, 3.5 per cent stock was acquired from the Mysore Debenture Sinking Fund, resulting in a small saving in broker commission, and, as discussed above, when an Indian loan was about to be floated, purchases were delayed until after the issue announcement in order to ensure the payment of the lowest possible price.[73]

Decline in demand

The demand for Indian debentures/stock began to shrink from the early 1900s, the decline accelerating after the First World War.[74] The fall was not confined to Indian securities. Other trustee debentures/stock also fell on hard times, many facing far greater struggles to attract investors than Indian issues, which the IO dubbed the 'Cinderellas of the trustee ... market'.[75] The reasons for the slump were many and varied. Like other trustee securities, Indian issues were affected by greater competition and limited market funds. As the ripples of industrialisation spread across the World, foreign states increasingly turned to London for the money needed to finance economic growth, and, after the First World War, were joined by domestic borrowers – municipal authorities; the UK government, seeking to convert the 5 per cent 1929–47 war loan and to finance spending; and companies requiring capital for the rationalisation of industry. Such loans put increasing strain on the pool of funds available for investment, and this pressure intensified during the inter-war period when the depressed condition of the staple industries, the rise in taxation (particularly on higher incomes) and inflation led to a fall in real savings.[76]

India, though, cannot escape blame for the collapse. The fall was also related to the reduction of home balance advances to the City (which caused some institutions to struggle to finance purchases), the country's borrowing policy, and the economic and political situation. The massive increase in the amount of debentures/stock issued in Britain and India and the large size of individual loans caused the supply of securities to vastly exceed demand.[77] Critics claimed that the 'high priests ... of Whitehall' often misread the mood of the market and set prices too high, a criticism

---

72 BL, L/AG/4/12/1, memo, 5 April 1937; BL, L/F/7/799, note, 16 March 1936; *ibid.*, note, 17 June 1935. The dividends earned from the Indian government securities bought were paid into the Sinking Funds from government revenues and were therefore also free of UK income tax (BL, L/F/7/816, note, no date).

73 BL, L/AG/14/11/4, note, 6 Sept. 1921.

74 PP 1914 [Cd.7069], q. 122.

75 *Ibid.*, q. 3371; *The Statist*, 8 March 1924, p. 350.

76 Dubey, *The Indian Public Debt*, pp. 32, 45, 46, 49, 51–3, 55. In 1904–13, domestic issues absorbed 22 per cent of the capital raised; in 1919–28, this figure had reached 74.5 per cent (*ibid.*, p. 47).

77 PP 1914 [Cd.7069], q. 123; Bagchi, *Private Investment*, p. 44; BL, L/F/7/787, *The Times*, 8 Jan. 1929; BE, G 1/323, Norman to Kisch, 5 May 1931.

accepted by Kisch as regards the 1922 loan.[78] More usually, to maximise subscription, the IO offered overly generous terms, which along with the recruitment of under-writers, the failure of a number of issues, the unproductive nature of many loans and the belief that India's hunger for debt would continue for many years, weakened credit.[79] Confidence was further affected by worries about the Indian economy and politics. The collapse of the post-war boom, the instability of the exchange, the fall in exports in the early 1930s, the regular budget deficits, the nationalisation of the large railway companies and the failure of a succession of foreign lenders to meet their debts caused many to fear default, particularly after the struggle to service and repay Indian loans during the 1931 financial crisis.[80] These concerns were intensified by the political situation. During the early 1920s, India became embroiled in the Afghan War and various frontier fracas, and, internally, there was increasing politi-cal disorder and the rise of the non-cooperative movement.[81] After a short period of relative calm, political discontent then re-emerged. 'Native fanatics' launched a civil disobedience campaign, boycotted British goods and declared that on achieving power they would both renege on India's foreign debt and devalue the rupee.[82] The attempt to calm the situation, the new constitution, caused many to believe that the UK government was 'chucking India over-board' and that the new Federation would pursue a course of financial imprudence that would end in national bankruptcy.[83]

The impact of such developments on investors, particularly the 'rather … timid' trusts, was catastrophic.[84] After reading 'alarmist reports' of India's supposed eco-nomic and political collapse in the press, they boycotted new issues and dumped their holdings on the market, causing prices to be heavily marked down.[85] The IO's response was to reduce prices further, increase interest rates and issue short-term bonds. Although it succeeded in raising the funds required, by 1931 officials accepted that the market was 'perilously close to saturation point', and, abiding by the Indian

78 Doraiswami, *Indian Finance*, p. 132; *The Statist*, 20 July 1901; BL, L/F/7/773, Kisch to Cook, 15 June 1922.
79 PP 1914 [Cd.7069], q. 2436, 3368, 11703; BL, L/F/7/792, Kisch, 3 Jan. 1929.
80 BE, G 1/323, Norman to Kisch, 5 May 1903; Bagchi, *Private Investment*, p. 44–5; British-Indian, *Finance and Commerce in Federal India*, Oxford 1932, p. 33; PP 1923 [128] *Return of Indian Financial Statement and Budget*, p. 7; D. Kumar, 'The Fiscal System', in D. Kumar (ed.), *The Cambridge Economic History of India, Volume 2, 1757–1970*, Cambridge 1983, p. 941; N. Charlesworth, 'The Problem of Government Finance in British India: Taxation, Borrowing and the Allocation of Resources in the Inter-War Period', *Modern Asian Studies*, 19 (3) (1985), p. 533.
81 Dubey, *The Indian Public Debt*, p. 63.
82 *Financial Times*, 10 Feb. 1930, p. 1; Anstey, *The Economic Development*, p. 54; Cain and Hopkins, *British Imperialism, 1688–2000*, p. 555.
83 BL, L/F/7/792, note, 2 Jan. 1929; PP 1932–33 [Cmd.4238] *Proceedings during the Third Session, 17th November to 24th December, 1932 (Round Table Conference (1930–31))*, p. 39; NA, T160/472, Indian government securities, Saunders to S of S, 6 April 1933.
84 *The Statist*, 1 Feb. 1930, p. 164.
85 *Ibid.*; BL, L/F/7/792, Kisch, 1 Jan. 1930; BL, L/F/7/809, Baxter, 10 May 1903.

government's policy of minimising debt, four years later the era of sterling borrowing came to an abrupt end.[86]

Repatriation

Over the period 1857/8 to 1941/2, £321.95m of loans were repaid (Figure 1).[87] The possibility of repatriating to India the whole of the sterling debt was first proposed in the early 1880s as a method of reducing interest payments/home charges and improving India's London credit.[88] To achieve these aims, the Indian government suggested that either rupee loans be issued in India and the proceeds used to buy sterling debt or that London securities be converted into rupee stock.[89] The IO, to say the least, was less than enthusiastic. As India's level of debt would remain unchanged, there would be no improvement in overall credit, and both plans would be difficult to implement and be prohibitively expensive.[90] Indians lacked the funds to purchase the large rupee loans necessary to buy up sterling debt, and English investors would be reluctant to support a loan designed to relieve them of their portfolios. The issues would thus have to be offered at a low price or carry a high interest rate. The announcement of government purchase of sterling debentures/stock, meanwhile, would prompt speculators to buy up the securities and cause the price to soar. As for conversion, given the exigencies of the exchange rate, holders of debentures/stock would only convert if they made a significant profit on the transaction and conversion could only occur on or after 1888.[91]

Both plans were resurrected in the 1920s. In 1920, the Indian government again proposed the purchase of sterling debt financed by rupee issues. The high exchange rate would reduce the cost to India of buying the debentures/stock, and Indian investors now possessed both the funds and, because of the lack of alternate investment opportunities, the will to acquire the necessary rupee stock.[92] Moreover, their purchase of rupee securities would release large quantities of hoarded silver, relieving the pressures on the silver market, and, by taking money out of the economy, reduce inflation.[93] The IO remained unconvinced, pointing out that the sterling debt

---

86 BL, L/F/7/801, note, 2 June 1931; D. Rothermund, 'The Great Depression and British Financial Policy in India, 1929–1934', *Indian Economic and Social History Review*, 18 (1) (1981), pp. 1–17.

87 BL, L/AG/14/10/1.

88 *The Statist*, 2 April 1881, p. 362. There was a fear that India's poor credit standing would make it difficult to raise funds on good terms in times of emergency (*ibid.*).

89 BL, L/F/5/64, memo, 7 Aug. 1880, p. 3.

90 PP 1878–79 [312], q. 548.

91 BL, L/F/5/64, memo, 7 Aug. 1880, p. 4; *ibid.*, memo, 8 Nov. 1880, p. 2; *ibid.*, memo, 7 Aug. 1880, p. 3; Dhar, *The Sterling Balances*, p. 16.

92 PP 1920 [Cmd.528], q. 5855; PP 1920 [Cmd.529], p. 124.

93 Silver was hoarded in the form of coins, as there were few banking facilities; the implements and paraphernalia of temples and rajah courts; and as jewellery and ornaments. By Hindu

was much enlarged and that the exchange was unlikely to stay at its present high level.[94] Six years later, the government returned with two further schemes – the conversion of 3.5 per cent stock into its rupee equivalent and the purchase of the 5.5 per cent short-term loan of 1921. Both operations would 'gratify public opinion', and the recent appreciation of the exchange would reduce the cost of the purchase of debt.[95] The IO rejected the conversion plan. The operation would unsettle the Indian market, and, given the political instability of the country, the only participants would be speculators, who would accept the generous exchange terms and then immediately sell their rupee allotments, remitting the money back to London. Alternatively, it believed that the purchase of the 5.5 per cent loan was achievable, though it argued that it should be financed by the Sinking Fund of the 1945/55 rupee loan. The Fund was permitted to purchase and cancel 1945/55 stock only if the price fell below the issue price, and, because this was not the case, it was currently being invested in Municipal and Port rupee debentures, which was less than satisfactory.[96] In the event, the scheme was financed by both the Sinking Fund and from government revenue and purchases continued until 1932/3.[97]

Repatriation of the whole debt began in 1937 when the Secretary of State authorised the Reserve Bank of India to use its large holdings of sterling to purchase debentures/stock. The securities were to be bought in small amounts (to prevent the purchases becoming known and speculation raising the price) and then transferred to the IO for cancellation.[98] Although there was little stock for sale on the market, the Bank in 1937/8 managed to acquire £2.99m of securities for £3.04m, the operation being financed from government revenues for the terminable loans bought, and for the 3/3.5 per cent irredeemable stock (£0.84m) from the issue of rupee securities carrying the same interest rates, which were eventually sold at a price higher than the purchase price of the sterling stock.[99] The following year no repatriation occurred, though the IO cancelled the £9.5m debentures/stock held in the family pension funds.[100]

custom, the latter were the only forms of property that a woman could own and wives thus received large gifts of both when they married and from their husbands during their marriages (D. H. Leavens, *Silver Money*, Bloomington 1939, pp. 66–7).

94 PP 1920 [Cmd.528], q. 4228; PP 1920 [Cmd.529], p. 124.

95 BL, L/F/7/785, Jukes to S of S, 10 May 1926; *ibid.*, Viceroy to IO, 4 May 1926; *ibid.*, Jukes to S of S, 10 May 1926; Shah, *Sixty Years*, p. 408.

96 BL, L/F/7/785, IO to G of I, 8 July 1926; *ibid.*, Kisch, 8 June 1926; *ibid.*, G of I to IO, 7 Oct. 1926. When the market price of the 1945/55 loan fell below the issue price, the Municipal/Port debentures bought would have to be sold leading to a collapse in their price (*ibid.*).

97 *Ibid.*, G of I to IO, 7 Oct. 1926; P. K. Wattal, *The ABC of Indian Government Finance*, Delhi 1945, p. 58; BL, L/F/7/799, note, 15 March 1936.

98 BL, L/F/7/820, S of S to G of I, 22 April 1937; *ibid.*, note, 25 May 1937; *ibid.*, Viceroy to S of S, 25 Oct. 1937. The rupee stock was held by the Indian government and sold as opportunities occurred (BL, L/F/7/785, Taylor to Kelly, 5 July 1937).

99 BL, L/F/7/785, Taylor to Kelly, 5 July 1937; Dhar, *The Sterling Balances*, pp. 13–14.

100 Poduval, *Finance*, p. 24; Dhar, *The Sterling Balances*, p. 14.

The outbreak of the Second World War allowed the repatriation scheme to be greatly expanded, to the extent that by 1946 only £10m of sterling securities remained in existence, representing just 3 per cent of India's total debt.[101] The rise in exports and fall in imports led to a favourable balance of trade and increased the wealth of the country and the ability of its investing classes to purchase rupee stocks.[102] At the same time, the sterling reserves of the Reserve Bank of India rose, allowing it to purchase more sterling securities. As in the First World War, the UK government bought large amounts of raw materials and foodstuffs in India and paid for these purchases in sterling in London. The Bank's reserves of sterling thus increased, supplemented by the British government's contribution towards India's war effort, also paid in the UK, and the proceeds of government sales of silver in London.[103] The IO had the choice of investing these funds in UK government issues that provided a return of around 1 per cent or redeeming sterling debt on which India paid interest at 3 per cent and over. Believing that investment in government securities 'would be sheer exploitation', it opted for repatriation.[104] Surprisingly, given its insistence that India help finance the 1914–18 conflict, the UK government agreed. There were a number of reasons – refusal would have grave political implications that could weaken India's support of the allied cause, the use of sterling surpluses for repatriation would halt the country's investments in gold, and, although India's purchases of UK government securities would cease, the demand from the British investors who benefitted from the repatriation would rise.[105]

Wartime repatriation took four forms. In 1940/1, the holders of six terminable loans were given the option of converting their holdings into rupee stock, and the Reserve Bank continued to purchase securities in the market. Both schemes foundered. The exigencies of the exchange discouraged conversion and rumours that the Reserve Bank was buying debentures/stock caused speculators to enter the market and prices to rise.[106] In February and December 1941, therefore, the government announced the compulsory purchase of respectively its terminable debt and 2.⁵/₃ per cent stock. Holders of the securities were required to surrender their holdings at pre-determined prices and those that held the terminable loans and resided in India were given the option of conversion.[107] Although some denounced the purchases as a breach of contract and an 'indefensible' act of economic opportunism, most City institutions supported the policy.[108] Aware that some form of compulsion

---

101 *Ibid.*, p. 46; Goldsmith, *The Financial Development*, p. 115.

102 Dhar, *The Sterling Balances*, p. 14.

103 Poduval, *Finance*, pp. 97–8.

104 BL, L/F/7/823, note, 20 Feb. 1941.

105 BL, L/F/7/813, Report for Cabinet, Feb. 1941.

106 *The Economist*, 2 March 1940, p. 386; Dhar, *The Sterling Balances*, pp. 15–16. Just £2.2m was converted. The government's denials that prices had risen are unconvincing (*ibid.*, pp. 16, 18–21).

107 Dhar, *The Sterling Balances*, pp. 24, 39; Poduval, *Finance*, p. 101.

108 BL, L/F/7/823, note, 20 Feb. 1941; BL, L/F/7/813, *Truth*, 7 March 1941.

was inevitable, speculators had piled into the market and had driven up the market price, on which the purchase price was based, to new highs.[109] It was also widely believed that repatriation by reducing India's purchase of UK government securities would cause the rates of these securities to become more favourable.[110] Finally, the government announced in December 1941 the repayment the following year of its 3.5 per cent stock, which was redeemable at twelve months' notice, and, in 1942, all guaranteed railway annuities were effectively sold to the British government for £30.054m.[111]

To pay for its purchases of stock, the government rejected the market issue of rupee stock. It was believed that there would be insufficient demand for the securities, the issue of which would cause prices to plummet, increase interest rates and damage the government's flotation of a defence loan. The purchase of the terminable loans was thus financed by the creation and sale of 4.5 per cent rupee stock to the Reserve Bank and government reserves, which it was intended would gradually be offloaded onto the public. In the event, market sales proved difficult and the presence of the securities in the reserves became to be regarded as unsafe. They were therefore either cancelled or converted into 3 per cent stock, which had a more liquid market and an earlier repayment date, and was much in demand from banks and insurance companies. As regards the other repatriations, finance was obtained from a range of sources. The cost of the acquisition of the 2.5/3 per cent stock and 3.5 per cent undated stock was met through the creation and sale to the Reserve Bank of respectively Treasury bills and 3.5 per cent rupee stock, and the purchase losses of the terminable loans (the difference between the purchase price and the face value of the securities bought) by the creation and sale of Treasury bills, Ways and Means advances from the Bank, and the government's cash resources. The sum required to offload the annuities, meanwhile, came from the creation of Treasury bills, Ways and Means, and, on the repayment of the Treasury bills, the issue of 3 per cent rupee stock.[112]

Conclusion

Two important weapons in India's subscription arsenal were yield – annual dividend taking into account price – and loan form. Although the IO did not stoop to rigging its own prices, it was quite happy to turn a blind eye to the activities of its syndicates/underwriters in the pre-issue and grey markets, aware that the public/media were ignorant of their behaviour and that it increased the price of and the demand for Indian securities. Similarly, loan dividends were far more generous than their

---

109   Dhar, *The Sterling Balances*, p. 41.
110   *The Economist*, 15 Feb. 1941, p. 219.
111   Dhar, *The Sterling Balances*, pp. 39, 42.
112   *Ibid.*, pp. 27–30, 43; Poduval, *Finance*, p. 100. The 3 per cent converted stock was used in the discount market.

critics ever imagined, incorporating early payment discounts, unearned interest, stamp duty payments and redemption yields, all of which attracted investors. There were also persistent rumours that prior to flotations the IO occasionally obtained help from the Bank of England, which supposedly brought forward interest rate cuts.

Subscription was further maximised by the form of issues. Loans were first charges on Indian revenues; comprised debentures, stock or a combination of the two; and were largely irredeemable, repayment being at some future date decided by the IO. During periods of low interest rates, debentures/stock could therefore be converted into lower dividend securities, relieving somewhat the burden of the home charges and increasing the size, liquidity and the market/issue price of the three primary securities in existence. Terminable loans became popular only after the First World War when it was thought that the high interest rates then ruling would fall in the near future. Rejecting Sinking Funds, which would further raise the home charges, the IO repaid these issues with Indian government/home balance funds or fresh issues of stock/sterling bills. Sinking Funds, however, were not completely dismissed. Two ad hoc and several discount Funds were established, the investment of their proceeds in Indian government stock increasing demand and again lessening the growth of the home charges.

Unfortunately, the IO ultimately failed in its mission to maximise sales. From the early 1900s, demand for Indian sterling securities fell and then plummeted – a result of over-issue, a general slump in trustee debentures/stock, the disappearance of home balance loans to the City, worries about the Indian economy and the deteriorating political situation. Fighting a rearguard action, the IO offered even more generous terms and issued short-term bonds, but all to no avail; the subcontinent quit the London capital market in 1935. Ironically, as the taste for Indian stock waned in London, it was strengthening in India. The Indian government thus began to buy up sterling debt, financing these purchases with rupee issues, and, at the start of the Second World War, took advantage of the favourable balance of trade to launch a series of buy-back operations, which eliminated sterling debt and the interest component of the home charges once and for all.

4

Other London Debt

The Government of India's presence in the London capital market was not limited to the issue of loans. The IO had some involvement in the flotation of the securities of the purchased guaranteed railway companies, and sold sterling bills, short-term investments with lives of between three to twelve months.[1] There was also at any one time a considerable holding in Britain of Indian rupee stock, and, in 1917/18, the Indian government floated a large rupee war loan, the proceeds of which were used to take over a proportion of the 5 per cent British war loan 1929–47.

The issue of guaranteed railway company debentures

The IO could raise the money required by the purchased guaranteed railway companies through the issue of government loans or the flotation of railway company debentures. Unless the yield for a railway flotation was expected to be high, it preferred to adopt the latter option, and, from 1879/80 to 1923/4, when the companies were nationalised, £217.2m of railway debentures were floated on the London market (Figure 2). The use of railway debentures allowed more money to be raised, as no Parliamentary sanction was needed; the interest payments were not included in the home charges; and, as the loans were not counted as Indian government liabilities and investors did not connect them to the government, they had no impact on Indian credit.[2] Moreover, the issues could often command a higher price than government

---

1 The IO had no responsibility for the flotation of the share capital of the new guaranteed railway companies that appeared from the 1880s. Sweeney has questioned the necessity of some of the new lines/companies and revealed how non-finance IO officials and their advisors were aggressively lobbied by company promoters and the City firms that hoped to issue the share capital (Sweeney, 'Indian Railroading', pp. 57–79. See also S. Sweeney, *Financing India's Imperial Railways, 1875–1914*, London 2011).

2 PP 1872 [327], q. 2861; PP 1878–79 [312], q. 61; PP 1896 [C.8258], q. 12192; Sweeney, 'Indian Railroading', p. 57.

securities. The loans were relatively small, were never converted, financed assets that directly benefitted British trade and produced a reasonable return of over 5 per cent.[3] Government purchase of guaranteed railway company share capital had also created a shortage of Indian railway bonds.[4]

The loans were floated when conditions were most propitious, company needs in the meantime being met through advances from the home balances, and took the form of terminable debentures, and, in the first decade of the century when demand fell, short-term bonds, which at the end of their lives were either renewed or replaced by a long-term issue.[5] Those firms that were purchased with annuities had discount Sinking Funds. These were established when a number of the holders of a company's debt requested that their annuities be exchanged for debentures/stock and were used to pay off this security at the end of its life.[6] From 1879, five such Sinking Funds were established, which received annual sums from government revenues that were invested in Indian government sterling loans.[7] Although the issues were floated and managed by the Bank of England, all the companies had different brokers who organised their underwriting and often purchased large amounts of the stock themselves, which they sold at a profit.[8] Inevitably, the Bank of England fees were considered excessive. After criticism, the issue charge fell from 5 per cent of the amount issued to £2,000 per million, and, in 1906, £1,500 per million.[9] Claiming that there had been an increase in the number of accounts, transfers of ownership and transfers by deed, the Bank in 1905 increased its management fee to 1 shilling per £1,000 of interest paid on the 3/3.5 per cent debentures then in existence, and, in 1915, charged the same amount for the management of 4.5 per cent debentures, thus boosting its earnings.[10]

The bonds were bought by brokers, who then sold the stock on to the public and institutions, the average holding of which was £1,550 in 1905.[11] Institutional purchasers included the Crown Agents, insurance companies, banks, discount houses and

3   Banerji, *Finances*, p. 49; PP 1921 [Cmd.1512], pp. 27, 29.
4   Sweeney, 'Indian Railroading', p. 58.
5   PP 1914 [Cd.7069], q. 10; BL, L/F/7/162, fol. 7389, note, no date; *ibid.* note, no date, c.1906; PP 1909 [Cd.4474], q. 716. The IO charged interest on the advances (PP 1914 [Cd.7069], q. 10). The money raised from the loan of one railway company could, if not immediately required, be advanced to another company (Ghose, *Lectures … Part One*, p. 1).
6   PP 1896 [C.8258], q. 11905; Y. S. Pandit, *India's Balance of Indebtness, 1893–1913*, London 1937, p. 91.
7   BL, L/AG/14/11/311.
8   PP 1909 [Cd.4474], q. 715; BL, L/F/7/164, B of E Chief Accountant, 22 Nov. 1905. See also Sweeney, 'Indian Railroading'.
9   BL, L/F/7/162, fol. 14394, IO to Heath, 22 Nov. 1920; *ibid.*, fol. 7389, note, no date.
10 BL, L/F/7/164, B of E Chief Accountant, 22 Nov. 1905; BL, L/F/7/168, note, 13 Oct. 1915; *ibid.*, IO to B of E, 28 Oct. 1915.
11 BL, L/F/7/164, B of E Chief Accountant, 22 Nov. 1905.

the IO, which, in 1912, held 19 per cent of the bonds issued.[12] The sums raised were placed in the home balances and passed on to the companies only when needed. They thus helped to meet the home charges. Proposals in 1921 and 1930 that company loans should be floated specifically to provide funds for the balances were rejected.[13] Although company loans generally received a better reception in the markets than government debentures/stock and failure would have no impact on Indian credit, Nivisons and the Bank of England remained unconvinced that the market would accept loans of the required size and believed that an excessively high yield would have to be offered.[14] As with the Indian government loans, the securities were eventually repatriated to India via the purchase in January 1943 of the £31.3m of debentures still in existence, the operation being funded from government balances and the issue to the Reserve Bank of ad hoc Treasury bills and coin.[15]

Sterling bills

Sterling bills were short-term investments with lives of three months (21 per cent of issues), nine months (2 per cent) or twelve months (77 per cent) that were sold on the London market.[16] From 1893 to 1929, when they ceased to be used, there were fifty-seven issues for £98m, for which there were £323.6m applications (Figure 2).[17] They were sold variously to meet the home charges when the Indian government found it difficult to remit, or the IO wished to maintain the exchange through the suspension of council bill sales; to provide funds when a sudden decline in market conditions forced the flotation of a sterling loan to be delayed; and, in 1908, to fund the encashment of reverse council bills.[18] As with sterling loans, when it was in their

---

12   NA, CO 323/453/32835, CA to CO, 8 Oct. 1900; Supple, *The Royal Exchange Assurance*, p. 344; Goodhart, *The Business*, pp. 473, 480, 483, 486, 505–7; Sayers, *Gilletts*, p. 50; PP 1914 [Cd.7070], Statement no. 1, p. 317.

13   BL, L/F/7/783, Kisch, 2 June 1920; BL, L/F/7/793, S of S to Viceroy, 14 Jan. 1930.

14   BL, L/F/7/783, Kisch, 2 June 1920; *ibid.*, memo, 16 April 1920; *ibid.*, Norman to Howard, 7 July 1920.

15   Dhar, *The Sterling Balances*, pp. 44–5. Repatriation in the early 1930s was rejected as it was thought the government funds required could be better spent on the construction/extension of lines (*Journal of the Royal Society of Arts*, 79 (4028) (31 Jan. 1930).

16   A 1916 proposal that they be sold in the US was rejected owing to the relatively high American interest rates and repayment difficulties (BL, L/F/7/460, G of I to IO, 26 Aug. 1916).

17   BL, L/F/5/60; BL, L/F/5/79; PP 1930–31 [Cmd.3670] *Explanatory Memorandum, of the Accounts and Estimates for 1930–31*, p. 12; PP 1929–30 [Cmd.3386] *Explanatory Memorandum, of the Accounts and Estimates for 1929–30*, pp. 11, 13.

18   PP 1914 [Cd.7069], q. 4596; PP 1909 [Cd.4474], q. 733; *The Statist*, 7 Dec. 1907, p. 1053. Issues were made to maintain the exchange in 1893, 1921, 1927 and 1928 (PP 1894 [92] *Financial Statement of Government of India, 1894–95*, **p. 12;** G. Balachandran, 'The Sterling Crisis and the Managed Float Regime in India, 1921–1924', *Indian Economic Social History Review*, 27 (1990), p. 15; *The Statist*, 1 Sept. 1928, p. 315).

interest, the IO occasionally economised on the truth when announcing the purposes of sales. To hide its support of the exchange in 1928, for example, it was stated that bills were being sold to finance railway construction.[19]

The bills were sold by tender organised by the Bank of England for an average yield (price divided by interest rate) of 3.31 per cent, 0.37 per cent below the mean ruling base rate, though just under a quarter of the issues paid more than this rate (Figure 4).[20] The yield was largely determined by market interest rates, which dictated the interest rate and demand/price, though the amount paid could be manipulated through the timing of issues and the currencies of the bills. Initially, the IO preferred six month bills, which were generally sold in March/April when market rates were usually low and there was significant demand. There were few more lucrative investment opportunities available and the bills would be repaid in October, when market rates were historically high, enabling purchasers to re-lend the money repaid at the higher rate or to use it themselves as an alternative to borrowing.[21] Over time, as finances became more stretched and bills were increasingly renewed, twelve month bills came into favour. These, again, were sold in the spring, allowing their issue to benefit from low interest rates, but generally paid a higher yield – owing to the longer currency and the possibility of repayment during the low interest rate period.[22]

Figure 4. Sterling bills. Yield versus bank rate, 1893–1915

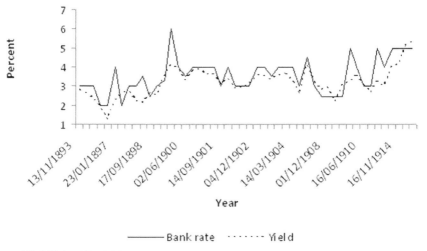

Sources. BL, L/F/5/60; BL, L/F/5/79.

19 *The Statist*, 1 Sept. 1928, p. 315.
20 BL, L/F/5/60; BL, L/F/5/79; PP 1930–31 [Cmd.3670], p. 12; PP 1929–30 [Cmd.3386], pp. 11, 13. For the issue and management of the bills, the Bank was paid a fee of £200 per million (BL, L/AG/9/8/6, p. 499, memo, 15 Dec. 1909; BL, L/F/7/173, fol. 1393, revised B of E terms, no date).
21 BL, L/F/5/64, memo, 'Improvements of Indian credit in England', no date; PP 1909 [Cd.4474], q. 777; *The Statist*, 9 March 1901, p. 452.
22 PP 1909 [Cd.4474], q. 777; *The Statist*, 2 June 1900, p. 849.

Spring issues were only abandoned if funds were needed urgently, market rates temporarily fell, or sales were restricted by the Bank of England/Treasury as part of their management of the capital market/gold stocks.[23] Such interventions multiplied in the First World War when there was a wish to restrict the market to the flotation of UK government stock. In 1915, the Treasury opposed a renewal of bills, but finally relented on the understanding that there would be no further Indian demands on the market in that financial year and that India would curtail its capital expenditure programme and try to borrow more domestically or make greater use of its London reserves. When the IO sought to renew more bills the following year, the Treasury declared that it would only permit the operation if the Office agreed to renew £3m of exchequer bonds held in the GSR, and that India should obtain the money needed from the £3m repaid if this was not possible. Unable to use the GSR due to its depleted state and wishing to avoid the renewal of the low interest exchequer bonds, the IO offered to reinvest the £3m in other government securities – a compromise accepted by the Treasury, though privately they hoped that the funds would be obtained elsewhere.[24]

The bills were bought by a small number of purchasers who acquired large proportions of issues. The £1.5m of bills sold in December 1911, for instance, were purchased by just sixteen investors, two of whom bought 40 per cent of the amount offered.[25] Apart from the Japanese government, which acquired the whole of the May 1898 issue with the proceeds of a recent London loan, all the purchasers were City institutions – UK and foreign banks, the two main discount houses and the leading brokers – most of which also received loans from the IO balances.[26] If the yield was higher than that offered by other short-term investments, the bills would be immediately discounted (sold) at a profit.[27] Otherwise, they were placed in short-term reserves until maturity or used as collateral for loans from the money market, or if cash was needed urgently, sold on. A large purchaser of discounted bills was none other than the IO, which used its GSR/home balance funds to buy bills just before they matured when the price was still less than the repayment price.[28] It thus made a small profit for the GSR/home balances, reduced the administrative cost of

23   *The Statist*, 15 Jan. 1898, p. 103; PP 1914 [Cd.7069], q. 5033–4.
24   NA, T 1/11898, 2637, Treasury to IO, 31 Jan. 1916.; *ibid.*, 21285, Treasury to IO, 6 Sept. 1915; *ibid.*, 4436, note, 11 Feb. 1915; *ibid.*, 4821, Treasury to IO, 25 Feb. 1915; *ibid.*, 24339, Treasury to IO, 7 Dec. 1915; *ibid.*, 2637, Abrahams to Ramsay, 4 Feb. 1916; *ibid.*, 2637, note, 12 Feb. 1916. In the event, the bills were retired (*The Statist*, 30 Sept. 1916, p. 575).
25   BE, C47/333. See also BE, C47/334.
26   *The Statist*, 27 May 1899, p. 810. The foreign banks were Dresdner Bank, National Bank of Egypt, Banca Commerciale Italiana and Banque Belge Pour L'Étranger (BE, C47/333; BE, C47/334). Those purchasers obtaining loans from the home balances included Union Discount, National Discount, Alexanders, Baker Duncombe, Blydensteins and the London City and Midland Bank (BE, C47/334).
27   *The Statist*, 2 June 1900, p. 849; *ibid.*, 28 May 1898, p. 883.
28   E.g. BE, AC 30/471, IO to B of E, 7 Dec. 1927; *ibid.*, IO to B of E, 31 Jan. 1928.

redemption, and increased the demand for the bills and India's credit. In the case of the home balances, however, such purchases only occurred when the saving on repayment was greater than the return obtained from lending out balances.[29]

It goes almost without saying that the issue of the bills was disparaged in India. Among the criticisms made were the IO's failure to include the Indian government in its decisions to sell/renew bills, the supposedly excessive yields and unnecessary renewals.[30] The City and the Bank of England, meanwhile, grumbled that sales/renewals took money out of the market, contributing to higher interest rates, and that they reduced the demand for UK Treasury bills and thus damaged government revenues.[31] In response, the IO pointed out that yields were comparable to those of British government short-term securities and that it had a 'duty' to 'err on the side of caution', as excessively low returns would reduce demand for an issue, forcing it to re-enter the market, by which time interest rates may have risen.[32] If the renewal rate was lower than that obtained from lending the funds to City institutions, it also made good economic sense to renew bills.[33]

European purchase of rupee debt

The amount of rupee debt held by Europeans fell over time (Figure 5). In the early 1830s, between 71 and 75 per cent of rupee loans, known colloquially as 'paper', were held by Europeans.[34] By late 1847, this proportion had fallen to 64 per cent, and it appears to have roughly remained at the 60–80 per cent level until the late 1890s when holdings gradually declined to 50.3 per cent in 1912/13 and approximately 40 per cent in 1927.[35] In money terms, the investments were worth an average of £50.33m in 1868/70, £56m in 1878 and £48.5m in 1896.[36] The stock was held in both

29 BL, L/AG/9/8/5, vol. 5, p. 949, memo, 17 July 1894.
30 PP 1914 [Cd.7069], q. 8164. E.g. *The Statist*, 16 Sept. 1899, p. 429; *ibid.*, 13 Sept. 1902, p. 442; PP 1914 [Cd.7069], q. 3359.
31 *The Statist*, 9 Dec. 1899, p. 884; NA, T 233/1425, memo, 21 April 1958.
32 PP 1914 [Cd.7069], q. 11048.
33 *The Statist*, 25 April 1896, p. 568.
34 PP 1831-32 [734-5] *Select Committee on the Affairs of the East India Company*, p. 45; Banerji, *Aspects*, p. 102.
35 Banerji, *Aspects*, p. 103; PP 1914-16 [Cd.7799], no. 76; Shah, *Sixty Years*, p. 406. See also Goldsmith, *The Financial Development*, pp. 11-12, table 1.5; Vakil, *Financial Developments*, p. 301; PP 1871 [363], appendix 14, p. 746; PP 1878-79 [312], appendix 8, p. 82; PP 1887 [C.5099], q. 1835. Indian holders of the rupee debt included the presidency banks, which held 2 per cent in 1870, 3 per cent in 1890, and 4 per cent in 1913; Indian merchants; the Native States; the public; and the Indian government, whose currency reserve held 11 per cent of 3/3.5 per cent paper in 1896, and, in 1913 and 1934, respectively 6 per cent and 5 per cent of total rupee debt (Goldsmith, *The Financial Development*, pp. 41, 116; PP 1873 [354], q. 6895; PP 1896 [C.8258], q. 7511-3; PP 1897 [193] *Financial Statement of Government of India, 1897-98*, p. 12).
36 PP 1871 [363], appendix 14, p. 746; PP 1878-79 [312], q. 679; PP 1896 [C.8258], q. 7474.

India and the UK. From 1859, the paper lodged in England could be enfaced for the payment of interest. The stock, known as 'enfaced paper', was registered at the Bank of England, which paid dividends in the form of drafts on India that could either be sold on the market or cashed.[37] The practice enabled the IO to determine the likely amount of remittances to India via the use of paper and greatly increased demand for the securities. Registration at the Bank of England allowed them to be quoted and bought/sold on the London Stock Exchange, thus increasing their marketability, and freed holders from the inconvenience of arranging the transfer of dividends from India themselves, either through the purchase/sale of export bills, or, for a brief period from 1866, via the Bank of Bengal.[38] From the enfaced statistics, it would appear that, in 1877, 61 per cent of the European holdings were in London, and, from 1893/4 to 1911/12, an average of 26 per cent, though this may be an under-estimate, as many speculators, intending to keep the stock for only a short period, failed to enface their investments.[39]

Figure 5. Rupee debt inscribed in London, 1867–1940

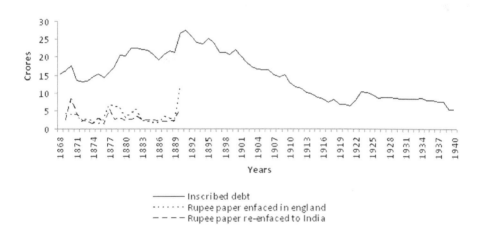

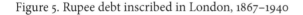

Sources. C. N. Vakil, *Financial Developments in Modern India, 1860–1924*, London 1924, p. 576, table 20; BL, L/F/7/746; BL, L/F/7/768; BL, L/F/7/742; BL, L/F/7/780; *The Statist*, 26 Nov. 1892, p. 607.

Notes. Annual enfacement figures only available from 1869 to 1890.

37   BL, L/AG/9/8/5, vol. 5, p. 643, IO to Inland Revenue, 29 Nov. 1890; BL, L/F/5/139, memo 1043, Hamilton, 1 Dec. 1876; *The Statist*, 13 March 1886, p. 283.
38   *The Statist*, 13 Dec. 1902, p. 1062; BL, L/F/5/59, note, 25 March 1859; BL, L/F/5/139, memo 1043, Hamilton, 1 Dec. 1876. The Bank of Bengal was permitted to transfer the dividends of paper lodged with them to London for payment by the Bank of England or Coutts & Co. (BL, L/F/5/139, IO to G of I, 15 Dec. 1866).
39   PP 1878–79 [312], appendix 8, p. 82; PP 1906 [Cd.2754], no. 76; PP 1914–16 [Cd.7799], no. 76.

These trends in holdings, however, can be somewhat deceptive. Some of the debt stated as belonging to Indians was actually owned by Europeans, and, from 1868 to 1870, an average of 1.29 per cent of enfaced paper presumed to belong to Europeans was actually held by Indians.[40] There were also noteworthy differences in European holdings between loans, and the proportion of the debt owned by Europeans varied quite significantly from month to month and year to year as opportunities for speculation waxed and waned (Figure 5).[41] From 1869/70 to 1940, an annual average of rs2.01.61.758 paper was enfaced in London, but an annual average of rs2.04.10.904 was retransferred to India, and, in 1876/7, the amount of enfaced paper in London ranged from £14.12m (April) to £12.65m (December).[42] Moreover, from 1921 the size of the rupee enfaced debt was greatly enhanced by the transfer of paper from India to England by the Imperial Bank of India – 5.6 crores worth in 1935.[43] The Imperial Bank claimed that the paper was needed as collateral for loans from the Bank of England and other financial institutions that were then advanced to the IO and the Indian government, and that it moved paper rather than cash, which could have been used to purchase UK securities to act as collateral, because of the exchange risks involved in money transfers. The IO was unconvinced. The exchange risks involved in the purchase/use of UK stock/debentures were minimal, other securities had in the past been used to obtain loans, and there was no reason why the paper transferred to the UK had to be enfaced.[44] The true explanation, as discussed below, and as the Imperial Bank eventually admitted, was fraud.

The demand for rupee stock in London was determined by a variety of factors. By far the most significant were the level of interest rates, the value of the rupee and the price of new issues. Low London/Indian interest rates relative to the paper's dividends made the stock more appealing to investors both at and after issue, and there is some evidence that Indian bank rates were deliberately reduced prior to flotations.[45] Exchange rates were significant because dividends were paid and stock repaid in rupees, and a drop in the currency's value reduced both annual returns and the sum obtained at the end of a loan's life.[46] The fall in the exchange to 1893 thus

---

40 PP 1871 [363], appendix 14, p. 746.

41 Whereas UK investors bought 71 per cent of the 5 per cent debentures issued in 1867, they purchased just 36 per cent of the debentures floated the following year (PP 1868–69 [258] *East India (Registered Debt)*).

42 PP 1906 [Cd.2754], nos 76, 82; PP 1914–16 [Cd.7799], no. 80; PP 1922 [Cmd.1778], no. 80; PP 1930–31 [Cmd.3882] *East India (Statistical Abstract) 1919–20 to 1928–29*, no. 104; PP 1938–39 [Cmd.6079] *East India (Statistical Abstract) 1927–28 to 1936–37*, no. 151; PP 1942–43 [Cmd. 6441], no. 141; *The Statist*, 26 Nov. 1892, p. 607; PP 1878–79 [165] *Financial Statement of the Government of India, 1879–80*, appendix b, table 1, p. 83.

43 BL, L/F/7/813, Imperial Bank to Controller of Currency, 20 Feb. 1935; *ibid.*, note, 22 Feb. 1935. A crore was the equivalent of 10m rupees.

44 *Ibid.*, Imperial Bank to Controller of Currency, 20 Feb. 1935; *ibid.*, Kelly, 20 Feb. 1935; *ibid.*, Ball, 28 March 1935.

45 PP 1897 [193], **p. 11**. E.g. *The Statist*, 30 May 1896, p. 76; *ibid.*, 10 July 1897, p. 46.

46 PP 1896 [C.8258], q. 7466; PP 1887 [C.5099], q. 1722.

dampened demand for paper at and after issue, led to sales and initiated a decline in market prices, though many banks and merchant houses escaped the dividend loss by only holding the stock in India, and the total loss was to some extent offset by the high yields offered by the Indian government.[47] In 1893, for example, the return on rupee debt was 3.75 per cent as compared to the 3 per cent offered by sterling stock. Ironically, the 1893 closure of the mints designed to stabilise the exchange led to further sales, investors fearing that the new policy would fail and that the exchange would lurch downwards.[48] Once the new regime was established and proven, however, acquisitions rose, though the possibility of exchange fluctuations still acted as a deterrent.[49] Reluctance to purchase was overcome through the provision of a risk premium on all new issues, and, during flotation periods, high council bill sales to ensure that the exchange remained placid and to facilitate the transfer to India of money for the purchase of stock.[50] In 1902, it was also proposed that rupee paper interest rates be guaranteed at the then fixed exchange rate of 1s 4d.[51] Although many at the IO supported the initiative, fear of political criticism in India resulted in its eventual rejection – the higher interest payments would increase the home charges, and, in periods of slack trade, council bills would be sold for less than the guaranteed rate.[52] The high and rising exchange from 1917 to 1920 then caused demand for stock to again rise, though the higher cost of remitting funds to India to pay for new issues reduced UK subscriptions, and some investors with stock held in India sold their holdings and transferred the proceeds to England, where they were invested in sterling securities.[53]

At issue, the key demand factor was price. When deciding upon the minimum/fixed price, the Indian government took account of the length of the loan, the exchange rate and the existence of a recent London flotation, which would limit British and, in the inter-war period, Indian demand, especially if the stock sold was relatively cheap.[54] The market price of existing paper was also influential, and, in

47 PP 1887 [C.5099], q. 1653, 1771, 1834, 1836, 1892; BL, L/F/5/64, Westland, 12 Jan. 1882, p. 4; *ibid.*, memo, 8 Nov. 1880, p. 2.

48 *The Statist*, 24 June 1893, p. 688; *ibid.*, 5 May 1894, p. 641. Initially, the belief that mint closures would lead to exchange stabilisation increased demand (*ibid.*, 29 July 1893, p. 114). Exchange banks took advantage of the sales/fall in prices by buying up large quantities of the paper and using it as an alternative to council bills for the remittance of funds to India (*ibid.*, 22 July 1893, p. 86).

49 *Ibid.*, 16 Aug. 1902, p. 307.

50 *Ibid.*, 10 July 1897, p. 46. The issue of council bills also kept Indian interests rates low and encouraged Indian purchase (*ibid.*, 21 July 1906, p. 87).

51 *Ibid.*, 2 Aug. 1902, p. 213; PP 1905 [167] *Indian Financial Statement for 1905–06*, p. 20. The proposal caused speculative demand for paper to soar (*The Statist*, 3 Aug. 1902, p. 326).

52 *Ibid.*, 11 Oct. 1902, p. 637; *ibid.*, 2 Aug. 1902, p. 213.

53 PP 1920 [103] *Return of Indian Financial Statement and Budget for 1920–21*, p. 72.

54 PP 1871 [363], q. 9460–1; PP 1899 [C. 9222, 9390] *Committee to Inquire into Indian Currency*, q. 10699–700; BL, L/F/7/795, Finance Dept. to IO, 11 April 1930; BL, L/F/7/806, Viceroy to IO, 3 April 1933.

turn, was dependent on the bank rate, London market prices, the amount of rupee stock floated in previous years, and government and exchange bank rigging of prices prior to issues.[55] While the government was seeking to raise prices by encouraging purchases, the exchange banks were often simultaneously dampening them via sales.[56] After issue, demand was determined by market prices, the possibility of speculation, the state of Indian finances and politics, the likelihood of conversion to a lower interest rate stock, and the closeness of the repayment date, with repayment at par and the usefulness of stock with a short life in the discount market acting as a lure to both ordinary and institutional investors.[57]

Purchasers

Unlike sterling issues, relatively little paper was bought by the public or trusts, which regarded the security with suspicion.[58] Problems included difficulties in purchasing stock at issue; transferring ownership and selling holdings in what was a very narrow market; fluctuating returns due to exchange rate movements; and the manner in which listed prices were calculated (per rs 1,000), which made them appear relatively low.[59] The vast majority of holdings were purchased by the exchange banks and, to a far lesser extent, by other financial institutions.[60] The banks bought the stock both at issue for themselves, clients and to later sell on to Indian and English investors, and after issue on the Indian and London markets.[61] A claim that in the early tender flotations they agreed amongst themselves to submit low bids appears unlikely.[62] A relatively large number of applications were received, an annual average of 1,097 from 1874/5 to 1883/4, and Europeans appear to have tendered far higher prices than native applicants.[63] In India, the paper purchased for their own use was employed as collateral for loans from the presidency banks, used as a temporary investment in the slack season for funds not returned to England, or placed in their reserves. In the case of the Chartered Mercantile Bank, it was also held in India by

55 PP 1893–94 [207] *Financial Statement of Government of India, 1893–94*, p. 17; PP 1898 [168], p. 14.
56 PP 1893–94 [207], p. 17; PP 1898 [168], p. 14.
57 *Investors Review*, 10 (July/Dec. 1897), p. 88; NA, T 172/238, Chamberlain, 6 July 15; *The Statist*, 10 May 1902, p. 953.
58 PP 1905 [167], p. 20; BL, L/F/7/164, B of E Chief Accountant, 22 Nov. 1905.
59 PP 1887 [C.5099], q. 1890; PP 1896 [C.8258], q. 7472; BL, L/F/5/64, memo, 8 Nov. 1880, p. 2; PP 1905 [167], p. 20.
60 A. Crump, *The English Manual of Banking*, London 1879, chap. 17, part 1; PP 1878–79 [312], q. 694; *The Statist*, 10 May 1902, p. 953.
61 *Ibid.*, 15 April 1882, p. 424; *ibid.*, 13 Sept. 1879, p. 50.
62 PP 1878–79 [312], q. 669.
63 BL, L/F/5/64, loans in India, no date. From 1874/5 to 1883/4, 82 per cent of Indian applications were rejected as compared to 68 per cent of European tenders (*ibid.*). Prior to the war, tenders came from just twenty to thirty firms (PP 1920 [Cmd.528], q. 2566).

the Bank's Honk Kong and Shanghai branches, the holdings reaping a relatively high return and being used as security for loans and sold to cover remittances from China. Paper purchased in London was again lodged in reserves; used as collateral for short-term loans, which ideally were obtained at an interest rate less than the rate paid on the paper; and, along with interest warrants and discharge notes, used as an alternative to council bills for the remittance of funds to India when the price of the bills was relatively high.[64] On arrival, the stock would be sold and the proceeds used to buy export bills (if London paper prices were relatively high, the stock would be bought in India, sent to London and then moved back to India).[65] Remittance via interest warrants involved the banks sending out their own drafts or warrants bought in the London market or from clients at the current exchange rate. Although this method of transfer could only be used during periods of dividend payment, considerable sums were sent; in March 1887, of the 20 lakhs of warrants in existence 12 to 15 lakhs were sold in the London market. Similarly, during conversions, if the banks decided to opt for repayment rather than conversion, they would despatch to India their own discharge notes plus purchased notes.[66]

The exchange banks along with some of the institutional buyers also purchased paper in both India and London for themselves and for clients for speculative purposes. Speculators gambled either that paper prices would rise in India/London or that there would be significant differences in London/Indian prices. Speculation on the rise of prices occurred before, during and after flotations. Banks and fellow speculators usually purchased stock prior to the announcement of annual issues, when the market price generally fell in the expectation of an increase in the supply of paper, particularly if they believed that no or a very small rupee loan would eventually be floated. In their prediction of the possibility/size of the issue, the banks took into account the annual budget, the most recent expenditure/revenue data, council bill sales, the state of the Indian government's Treasury balances, future agricultural output and information leaked by government officials.[67]

During flotations, if it was expected that there would be a post-issue rise in price, the banks and other speculators would buy the stock in the market and in the grey market and would make heavy applications for the new loan. Alternatively, if a post-issue fall in price was anticipated, they would sell paper in the grey market for delivery after the flotation at the ruling relatively high price and then meet their sale contracts after the flotation by buying stock at the lower post-issue price, these

64 S. Muirhead, *Crisis Banking in the East*, Aldershot 1996, pp. 114, 208; *The Statist*, 21 Oct. 1882, p. 458. The Chartered Mercantile Bank in 1879 held 86 per cent of its total reserves in rupee paper (*ibid.*, 21 Oct. 1882, p. 458).

65 Muirhead, *Crisis Banking*, p. 217; *The Statist*, 22 July 1893, p. 86; *ibid.*, 4 Sept. 1897, p. 361. The purchase of large amounts of the stock in London naturally caused the UK price to rise (*ibid.*, 4 Sept. 1897, p. 361).

66 *Ibid.*, 12 Jan. 1895, p. 35; *ibid.*, 23 March 1889, p. 330; *ibid.*, 24 Sept. 1887, p. 336; *ibid.*, 19 March 1887, p. 300; *ibid.*, 15 Dec. 1894, p. 724; *ibid.*, 1 Sept. 1894, p. 262.

67 *Ibid.*, 28 June 1902, p. 1272; PP 1890 [140], p. 108.

purchases often causing a small post-issue 'dead cat' bounce in prices. If anything, such speculation was far greater than that associated with London issues of sterling Indian government stock, as the period between the announcement of the price and the closure of the issue was far longer (in order to allow the council bills carrying the remittances used to purchase the stock on behalf of UK investors to reach India), and the Indian government until 1902 only revealed the minimum price after a flotation had occurred.[68]

In between issues, the banks and private investors would speculate on the expectation of a fall in London or Indian interest rates, which would make the dividends offered by rupee paper more attractive and increase demand/price, or an anticipated rise in the exchange that would increase the value of the dividends paid to UK investors and thus raise London demand/price.[69] Inevitably, they occasionally 'wrongly called the shots' and lost money, and, in the early 1880s, self-imposed limits on speculation were introduced. In 1881, for example, the Chartered Mercantile Bank bought for itself and clients over £0.77m of paper on the market and in a rupee flotation in the belief that the findings of the Second Monetary Conference on Bimetallism would lead to a recovery in the price of silver/the exchange. In the event, the Conference adjourned without coming to any practical conclusion and silver prices and the exchange tumbled.[70] The Chartered Mercantile Bank thus suffered an opportunity loss on the sums invested, which could have been lodged at the presidency banks at a rate of 4 or 5 per cent, plus an actual loss. The failure of the Conference precipitated a collapse in the market price of rupee paper, which accelerated when it emerged that the Bank's clients were refusing to pay for the stock bought. Expecting the Bank to dump its purchases onto the market, prompting a price collapse, existing holders offloaded their own investments causing the very price fall that they feared.[71]

Speculation on differences in London/Indian prices involved the banks and their fellow speculators buying paper in India and selling it in London when the Indian market price was lower than the market price in London and vice versa. Such price differentials and speculation occurred when there were exchange rate movements, with a fall or the expectation of a drop in the exchange precipitating a decline in London prices and the UK purchase and Indian sale of paper (and vice versa), or differences between London and Indian interest rates, relatively low Indian rates increasing the demand/price of paper and again prompting the UK purchase/Indian sale of stock.[72] Speculation also took place less regularly prior to new rupee issues,

---

68 *The Statist*, 10 May 1902, p. 953; *ibid.*, 30 June 1888, p. 728; *ibid.*, 2 Aug. 1902, p. 213.

69 *Ibid.*, 28 June 1902, p. 1272; *ibid.*, 6 July 1895, p. 2.

70 Muirhead, *Crisis Banking*, p. 114.

71 BL, L/F/5/64, Westland, 12 Jan. 1884, p. 4. More speculative losses were made the following year (*The Statist*, 15 April 1882, p. 424).

72 E.g. *The Statist*, 24 June 1893, p. 688; *ibid.*, 6 July 1895, p. 2; *ibid.*, 25 April 1896, p. 552; *ibid.*, 28 June 1902, p. 1272). Speculation on exchange rate movements virtually disappeared after 1898 (*ibid.*, 13 Dec. 1902, p. 1062).

when the Indian government in order to raise the price that could be obtained for a loan rigged market prices upwards through purchases by its 'banking and mercantile friends', and after conversions, when the price of the converted stock again rose to a premium in India.[73] Obviously, such price differentials existed for only a short period before the speculative purchases/sales caused them to disappear, and there was a danger that the banks, lacking the funds to make purchases, would have to waste valuable time borrowing them or would have difficulty buying stock because of the illiquidity of the market. To avoid such delays, they thus sought to keep both their London and Indian reserves well stocked with paper.[74]

Institutional purchasers included banks, brokers, insurance firms, European trading companies, the Bank of England and the Crown Agents, which acquired the stock for its colonial investment funds and especially for Ceylon and Mauritius.[75] The regulations of the Saving Bank Funds of both colonies required a large proportion of Fund investments to be kept in paper, and Ceylon found its holdings useful as security for advances from the Bank of England.[76] There was also some demand for the stock from France.[77] Lending to India was thought to be 'practically lending to England' and therefore safe, and the French had a preference for bond issues. The paper also often provided a higher return than French securities and could be used for remittances to India.[78]

Criticisms of purchase

Inevitably, the British purchase of rupee stock was the subject of much debate. Those in favour of the practice argued that it was highly beneficial both to the UK, which gained from the payment of relatively high dividends, and to India.[79] The investments reduced the call on Indian resources, from 1867 to 1913 by the equivalent of 0.03 per cent of National Product; allowed the government to raise more funds with lower yields than would otherwise have been possible; and avoided the high interest rates and fluctuation in rupee stock prices that would have occurred if the money had been raised exclusively in India. The withdrawal of funds from the market to pay for loans would have raised discount rates and Indian investors supposedly had a greater tendency than their English peers to sell during price downturns. It was also claimed with less justification that the purchase of council bills to transfer

---

73 *Ibid.*, 13 June 1896, p. 828; *ibid.*, 1 Sept. 1894, p. 262; PP 1898 [168], p. 14.
74 *The Statist*, 25 April 1896, p. 552; Muirhead, *Crisis Banking*, p. 208.
75 *The Statist*, 25 April 1896, p. 568; *ibid.*, 14 Sept. 1895, p. 308; PP 1920 [103], p. 81. See Goodhart, *The Business*, pp. 469, 473, 479–80.
76 NA, CAOG 9/147, CO to CAs, 18 April 1877; NA, CO 167/773/28358, CAs to CO, 9 May 1908; *ibid.*, Ommanney, 15 Aug. 1908, margin note ; NA, CO 54/667/35749, CAs to CO, 1 Nov. 1900.
77 E.g. BL, L/F/5/64, Westland, 12 Jan. 1884, p. 3; *The Statist*, 19 June 1880, p. 354.
78 *Ibid.*, 19 June 1880, p. 354; *ibid.*, 26 Jan. 1895, p. 119.
79 Banerji, *Aspects*, p. 104.

money to India for the purchase of new issues contributed to the maintenance of the exchange.[80]

Critics were less impressed by the practice. Purchases of paper dampened demand for sterling Indian government loans, the exchange risk premium was yet another example of British exploitation, and speculation by the 'birds of passage' who bought the loans could have a negative impact on the exchange.[81] There was also much criticism of the fee charged by the Bank of England for the management of the stock. The IO believed the initial charge of £300 per crore managed was excessive and was thus nonplussed when the Bank in 1905 demanded a fee of £500 per crore with a minimum payment of £7,000 pa, particularly as the reasons for the rise appeared weak.[82] The Bank claimed that its costs had been increased by greater holdings of the stock and by the introduction by the Indian government of promissory notes, which were not registered and the dividends of which were thus paid directly to holders who brought their notes into the Bank.[83] The IO accepted both points, but countered that the amount of stock managed had fallen by 35 per cent from 1896 to 1904 and that this decline was ongoing; that the stability of the exchange from 1898 had effectively increased the Bank's fee; and that its costs could be slashed overnight simply by combining its rupee stock and sterling loan management operations.[84] The Bank, however, remained obdurate and merely moderated its demands to £400 per crore with a minimum payment of £8,000. Having a legal duty to use its services, the IO had no alternative but to accept the compromise, though it continued to demand fee reductions in 1915 and 1917.[85]

By 1918, the amount of paper in London had fallen by a further 56 per cent, and the Bank's fee comprised the minimum payment of £8,000 pa – raising the fee per crore to over £900.[86] IO officials again requested a reduction and were again rebuffed.[87] The Bank would only lower its charges if promissory notes were replaced by cheaper-to-manage bearer bonds and if it was allowed to pay dividends in the

---

80 Goldsmith, *The Financial Development*, p. 41; *The Statist*, 24 July 1897, p. 141; *ibid.*, 21 Aug. 1897, p. 292; *ibid.*, 23 Feb. 1895, p. 232; PP 1898 [C.9037], q. 2869.

81 PP 1905 [167], p. 20; A. Bose, 'Foreign Capital', in V. B. Singh (ed.), *Economic History of India, 1857–1956*, London 1965, p. 497.

82 BL, L/AG/9/8/5, vol. 6, pp. 696–701, IO to B of E, no date; BL, L/F/7/164, f1372, note, 9 Jan. 1919.

83 BL, L/F/7/164, B of E Chief Accountant, 22 Nov. 1905. The average number of holdings per crore had risen from 353 in 1895, to 356 in 1905 (*ibid.*).

84 BL, L/AG/9/8/5, vol. 6, pp. 683–7, 696–701; BL, L/F/7/164, B of E Chief Accountant, 22 Nov. 1905.

85 BL, L/F/7/164, fol. 1372, note, 9 Jan. 1919; *ibid.*, fol. 6339, IO to Brunyate, 9 Dec. 1915; *ibid.*, fol. 430, note, 12 Jan. 1917.

86 *Ibid.*, fol. 124, note, Elkin, 3 Jan. 1918; *ibid.*, fol. 12121, Newmarch, 1915.

87 The IO also discovered that the Bank charged India a relatively high fee for the deduction of Indian income tax from stock dividends, but decided not to make a formal complaint owing to the small sums involved (BL, L/F/7/170, note, 1917; *ibid.*, note, 8 Dec. 1917; *ibid.*, note, 12 Dec. 1917).

form of drafts on India, conditions that it was well aware could not be accepted.[88] Relief came in 1923 with a proposal that the stock be managed by the Imperial Bank of India. This was welcomed with open arms by the IO, though also with some trepidation. It was feared that the loss of stamp duty exemption and perhaps the Stock Market quotation would reduce UK demand for the paper and that the Bank of England would either refuse to hand over its books and records to the Imperial Bank or use its power in the market to destroy future Indian sterling issues.[89] In the event, the Indian government agreed to pay stamp duty on the first transfer, the quotation was retained and the Bank of England reluctantly acquiesced to the changeover.[90]

Unfortunately, the joy of officials at their escape from the Bank of England's clutches was short-lived. The new agreement with the Imperial Bank reduced India's minimum annual payment to £4,000 pa if the UK rupee debt fell below 8 crores. In 1933, however, the IO auditor discovered that the Imperial Bank from 1927 to 1934 had deliberately moved rupee paper to London in order to keep its holdings above 8 crores and thus ensure the payment of the maximum annual fee. This behaviour was clearly improper. Nonetheless, the IO took no action against the Imperial Bank and provided an answer that was economical with the truth when a question relating to the management charges was asked in the House of Commons.[91] It was believed that the resulting scandal would have political implications in India and it had already been agreed that the management of the stock would be transferred to the Reserve Bank of India, the Governor of which had been the principal executive of the Imperial Bank during the period of the fraud.[92] Ironically, on taking over the management role in 1935, the Reserve Bank, which was paid a minimum fee of just £3,600 per annum, immediately subcontracted the work for the first year of the contract back to the Imperial Bank.[93]

Fall in demand

English demand for paper fell from the end of the First World War. British investors had fewer funds to spare for the purchase of the stock, which had become far less attractive. From 1914, dividends were taxed in both India and England; in 1923, transfers of inscribed stock after a first sale were subject to stamp duty; and, in the

88 BL, L/F/7/164, fol. 6339, IO to Brunyate, 9 Dec. 1915; *ibid.*, fol. 430, note, 12 Jan. 1917.

89 BL, L/F/7/172, IO to G of I, 20 July 1922; *ibid.*, fol. 4198, Financial Dept. to IO, 27 April 1922; BL, L/F/7/173, fol. 1848, memo, no date.

90 BL, L/F/7/173, fol. 1848, Kisch, 1 March 1923; *The Statist*, 20 Dec. 1923, p. 1095.

91 BL, L/F/7/813, Turner, 14 Sept. 1934; *ibid.*, Baxter, 23 Oct. 1934; *ibid.*, note, 5 Feb. 1935; *ibid.*, Ball, 28 March 1935; *ibid.*, Baxter, 27 April 1935; *ibid.*, Monday, 20 July 1936. It was stated that the 1933 underpayment was due to the temporary withdrawal of securities from London and this occurred after due consultation (*ibid.*, suggested answer, 18 July 1936).

92 *Ibid.*, Baxter, 27 April 1935.

93 BL, L/F/7/817, Finance Dept. to IO, 15 Feb. 1936; *ibid.*, note, 31 Jan. 1936; *ibid.*, Finance Dept. to IO, 23 Jan. 1936.

late 1920s, the returns offered by rupee loans were relatively low as compared to those of other securities available on the London market. There were also fears that India was close to political collapse and default.[94] To encourage purchase, the IO arranged for the paper to be sold in units of rs 1500, the equivalent of £100, rather than rs 1000, and sought, but failed, to allow tenders of new loans to be received in London, and, in 1922, to persuade the Stock Exchange to fix the exchange value of the rupee in dealings on the Exchange at 1s 4d rather than 2s.[95]

Luckily, the collapse in demand was offset by greater Indian purchase, both at issue and in the Indian and London markets.[96] Unable to find other employment for the vast profits made during the First World War, Indian merchants poured their surplus funds into paper. They were joined by insurance companies, banks, the native states and private investors, who were less suspicious of government securities, less inclined to hoard their savings, and again unable to find alternate outlets for their savings.[97] In the early 1920s, land prices were in free fall, and, later in the decade, the industrial stagnation engendered by credit restrictions and falling prices curtailed the number of corporate stock issues. Thus, by 1927, at least 60 per cent of rupee securities were to be found in Indian hands.[98]

War loan

The possibility of India raising funds for the British war effort was first proposed in 1915 by the UK Treasury, backed, for 'credit and kudos', by the Agha Khan.[99] The IO rejected the proposal. India was already making a significant contribution to the Empire's eventual victory and a loan would severely damage the country's finances. Giving the impression that the Imperial government was in financial difficulties and the war lost, it would encourage investors to hoard their cash, reducing Post

---

94 Dubey, *The Indian Public Debt*, p. 42; PP 1919 [Cmd.288, i–viii] *Royal Commission on Income Tax*, q. 1882, 1886; *The Statist*, 20 Dec. 1923, p. 1095; NA, T 172/238, Chamberlain, 6 July 1915.

95 BL, L/F/7/776, IO to B of E, 22 June 1922; BL, L/AG/4/12/1, no. 2, legal advisor, 9 July 1922. The Stock Exchange refused the request to fix the exchange, and the requirement that money could only be raised in England with Parliament's consent prevented the issue of London tenders (BL, L/F/7/776, IO to B of E, 8 Aug. 1922; BL, L/AG/4/12/1, no. 2, legal advisor, 9 July 1922).

96 PP 1914 [Cd.7069], q. 4228; *The Statist*, 11 June 1927, p. 1111.

97 PP 1920 [103], p. 81; PP 1914 [Cd.7069], q. 204. In 1923, 72 per cent of the reserves of India's forty-five insurance companies were invested in Indian government/municipal debt, though their holdings were comparatively small (P. A. Wadia and G. N. Joshi, *Money and the Money Market in India*, London 1926, p. 368; Goldsmith, *The Financial Development*, p. 116).

98 *The Statist*, 11 June 1927, p. 1111; NA, NA, T 160/474, Indian loans, 1932 and 1933, G of I to S of S, 12 Jan. 1903; Dubey, *The Indian Public Debt*, p. 43; Shah, *Sixty Years*, p. 406.

99 NA, T 172/238, Chamberlain to Chance, 7 July 1915; NA, T 1/11898, 19920, IO to Treasury, 20 Aug. 1915.

Office deposits and the demand for government paper and currency notes. Demand for government issues would be further damaged by the loan itself, particularly if it offered an attractive rate, and the remittance of the proceeds to London at a time of low council bill demand would have a negative impact on the exchange rate.[100] Needless to say, the Treasury was appalled and angered by the response and dismissed the arguments put forward in the 'discreditable document' as 'rubbish' and 'humbug'.[101] Nonetheless, it decided not to pursue the matter, though not before enacting its revenge. After considering forcing India to take on the cost of the Mesopotamian Expeditionary Force, Treasury officials informed the IO that it would have limited access to the London market and that any finance required should be obtained through the issue of rupee stock.[102]

The Indian government finally relented to pressure to make a contribution to the allied war effort in 1917. It was agreed that it would give HMG £35m and take over £65m of the 5 per cent British war loan 1929–47; to finance this liability, it would issue two rupee war loans in 1917 and 1918, and, in return, would be allowed to increase cotton import duties to 7 per cent.[103] To protect the exchange and to avoid the denudation of London capital markets, the loans were aimed at Indian rather than UK investors.[104] Nonetheless, a large proportion of the issues were taken up by Britons. By value, 52.78 per cent of the applications for the 1917 flotation came from Europeans, of which 55 per cent were from banks and 19 percent from commercial firms. Significant subscribers included Coutts, the Chartered Bank of India and Australia, the Eastern Bank and the Mercantile Bank of India.[105] The generosity of such institutional subscribers was no doubt partly motivated by patriotism, though self-interest also played a part. Involvement allowed them to curry favour with the Indian and British governments, and, to encourage subscription that damaged neither the exchange nor the liquidity of the London markets, the Treasury rescinded a previous order that required the proceeds of the sales of securities in India to be remitted to and retained in Britain, provided that they were used to buy the loans. Companies operating in India could thus offload underperforming investments and still keep the funds in the country.[106]

The loans were a tremendous success. In total, £68.915m was raised, allowing in 1919 a further £35m to be passed to the UK government, reducing India's liability

---

100 NA, T 1/11898, 19920, IO to Treasury, 20 Aug. 1915; *ibid.*, 24339, IO to Treasury, 14 Oct. 1915. The issue of a loan at an attractive rate would also create anger amongst existing government stock holders (*ibid.*, 19920, IO to Treasury, 20 Aug. 1915).

101 *Ibid.*, 19920, note, 15 Sept. 1915.

102 *Ibid.*, 19920, note, 30 Aug. 1915; *ibid.*, 19920, Treasury to IO, 29 Sept. 1915.

103 Husain, 'The Organisation ', pp. 95, 172–3. The cotton duty raised only £6m (*ibid.*, p. 95).

104 *The Statist*, 10 March 1917, p. 411.

105 BL, L/AG/14/17/1, no. 37, pp. 13, 14; *ibid.*, no. 21a, memo, 20 June 1917.

106 *The Statist*, 10 March 1917, p. 412.

for the British 5 per cent war debt to just £30.64m.[107] The issues also permitted the Indian government to finance the purchase of goods required for the allied war effort; by returning currency to government coffers, they minimised the shortage of coin caused by the fall in imports/the non-return of coin to the trading centres; and, as the proceeds were left in the presidency banks and lent to merchants and other banks, the operation had little impact on trade/interest rates.[108] To meet the liability for the 5 per cent British war loan, the Indian government, via the IO, paid the Treasury sums equal to the interest payments and a contribution to the issue's Sinking Fund, which was used to gradually buy and cancel the loan. From 1923, an annual payment to meet both dividends and the Sinking Fund contribution was made and the Fund's contribution was moved from March to November when the loan went ex-dividend and the market price fell, enabling more of the stock to be bought and cancelled.[109] Although financial difficulties occasionally precluded the Fund payment, the debt by 1934/5 amounted to just £16.72m, and, by 1939, £15m.[110]

Conclusion

The IO's presence in the London capital market was not confined to government stock. It was also involved in the issue of sterling bills, the loans of the part-nationalised guaranteed railway companies and the takeover of a proportion of the 5 per cent British war loan, and it closely monitored the purchase by UK investors of Indian rupee debentures. Raising the funds required by Indian guaranteed railway companies via the flotation of company loans rather than government securities freed the IO from the constraints of Parliamentary sanctions, and, as the loans were not counted as government liabilities and the interest payments not included in the home charges, respectively protected its London credit rating and minimised criticism of the size of the charges. As with Indian government loans, the sums raised were placed in the home balances until needed and thus helped to meet India's UK commitments, and, along with sterling bills, contributed to the recycling of funds.

Sterling bills were often issued explicitly to fund the home charges and were sold at the most propitious time of the financial year, though the IO was occasionally 'encouraged' to halt issues/renewals when they threatened liquidity/gold stocks. Officials usually complied, aware of the impact of high interest rates on their other

107 P. Budheswar, *India and the First World War*, Delhi 1996, p. 71; PP 1918 [61] *Return of Indian Financial Statement and Budget for 1918–19*, p. 6; PP 1924 [Cmd.2033], *East India (Statistical Abstract), 1911/12 to 1920/21*, p. 209, no. 104.
108 PP 1918 [61], pp. 7, 14, 15. The 1918 loan did slightly increase rates (PP 1918 [Cd. 9162] *East India (Progress and Condition), 1916–17*, p. 26).
109 BL, L/AG/14/17/2, IO to Governor General, 9 Nov. 1922; *ibid.*, IO to Treasury, 15 Nov. 1923; *ibid.*, note, 23 July 1929.
110 E.g. *ibid.*, Kisch to Treasury, 12 March 1930; PP 1924 [Cmd.2033], p. 209, no. 104; Dhar, *The Sterling Balances*, p. 10.

activities, but would negotiate a mutually agreeable solution if the loss from market withdrawal offset the gain from a lower base rate. A frame of mind similarly on display during the discussions with the UK government over a possible contribution to the allied war effort. Much to the disgust of the Treasury, the IO turned down an initial invitation to contribute, only relenting when it became clear that the flotation of securities and the takeover of a portion of a British war loan would help the Indian government finance the purchase of goods needed for the war effort and partly overcome coin shortages.

The London purchase of rupee loans and enfaced paper increased demand for and the price of rupee issues, reducing the amount of debt that needed to be raised in Britain and thus slowing the rise of the home charges. It also facilitated Indian trade by providing yet another means by which the exchange banks could move funds to India when council bills were expensive or unavailable. In both London and India, the paper also served as collateral for short-term loans and became an instrument for speculation, investors gambling on changes in the exchange and Indian/London prices and interest rates. Inevitably, the Bank of England charged excessive fees for the management of the stock, and although the IO eventually escaped its clutches, it subsequently discovered that its successor, the Imperial Bank of India, was similarly overcharging.

5

The Purchase of Silver and Other Currency Activities

From 1900 to 1925/6, the IO bought £132.96m of silver.[1] The metal was used for the minting of rupee coins, and, to a lesser extent, the pressing of medals, and purchases were therefore determined by Indian demand for coinage, which rose when exports were high and the economy buoyant.[2] After large acquisitions from 1857 to 1862, no further orders were placed until 1900.[3] Rather than leading to a dearth of currency, the 1893 closure of the mints caused hoarders of rupee coins to exchange their stashes for silver bars, the value of which was more secure, and, when this process came to an end, the maintenance of the exchange enabled the government to release some of its own reserves of rupees.[4] Shortages of coin thus only began to emerge in 1900 when £5.64m of silver was bought, followed by a further £4m in 1903/4, largely as a precaution against currency shortages.[5] The decision of the Secretary of State to sell council bills without limit and the reluctance of consumers to accept the gold sovereign then caused the demand for silver coin to soar. Unfortunately, after delaying silver purchases in 1905, the IO in 1907 bought and coined far too much specie, £29.63m from 1905/6 to 1907/8, in the expectation that the economy would continue to grow.[6] In fact, the failure of the 1907/8 harvests and the 1907 American financial crisis caused currency demand to plummet and coins to return to the reserves, partly through the sale of reverse council bills.[7] No further orders

---

1   PP 1906 [Cd.2754], no. 72; PP 1914–16 [Cd.7799], no. 72; PP 1922 [Cmd.1778], no. 72; PP 1928 [Cmd.3046] *East India (Statistical Abstract) 1916–17 to 1925–26*, no. 66.
2   PP 1920 [Cmd.528], q. 36; *The Statist*, 30 Nov. 1907, p. 1007.
3   BL, L/F/7/163, no. 22, file 2, fol. 1528, note, no date, 1906. In 1860/2, £1.099m was purchased (PP 1884–85 [352] *East India (Reduction of Expenditure)*, pp. 204–7).
4   *The Statist*, 15 Sept. 1900, p. 413.
5   BL, L/F/7/423; PP 1903 [151] *Indian Financial Statement for 1903–04*, p. 13. Purchases were also to increase PCR coinage holdings.
6   Keynes, *Indian Currency*, pp. 132–3; BL, L/F/7/423; PP 1914 [Cd.7069], q. 11502.
7   Keynes, *Indian Currency*, p. 133; PP 1914 [Cd.7071] *Royal Commission on Indian Finance and Currency: Appendices, Volume 2*, Howard, appendix 23, section 7, par. 45.

were therefore placed until 1912, when £7.059m was bought.[8] Thereafter, purchases occurred at regular intervals, peaking in 1918/19 at £43.7m.[9]

The specie was largely bought from the London silver market in the form of bars and spent foreign coins. The market could easily supply the large amounts of metal required by India and was dominated by four brokerage houses – Mocatta & Goldsmid, Sharps & Wilkins, Samuel Montagu & Co. and Pixley & Abell. Although there were claims that these firms charged their clients excessively high prices, the IO was convinced that they acted 'in a very high minded and honourable manner' and there is no evidence of the operation of a cartel.[10] The market was also infested by syndicates, groups of dealers who bought as much of the available specie as possible if they suspected that a government was about to make large purchases. They then sold their acquisitions to the administration at an excessive price, the whole operation being known as a 'corner'. India was targeted by a number of syndicates that closely monitored a variety of factors that could signal that the IO had or was about to enter the market. Syndicate members kept a close watch on Indian currency reserves and the movement of gold to India by the exchange banks, and, in the short term, on council bill sales, government gold shipments to England and large purchases of silver by the Bank of England's brokers.[11] The success of their operations is unknown. However, the IO paid on average 1.58d per ounce more than the Royal Mint on eleven of the thirteen occasions that it bought silver from 1902/3 to 1919/20, and, in 1906, a corner only failed when the Mexican government unexpectedly began to sell silver dollars on the market.[12]

An alternative to London was Bombay. Proponents of Indian purchase argued that it would reduce remittances to Britain, stimulate the development of the local specie market, prompt the release of hoarded silver and drastically reduce transport costs.[13] The use of the market, however, was not a realistic option. It was small, charged relatively high brokerage fees, often supplied impure silver and was home to numerous syndicates, which because of the market's size were difficult to circumvent through secret purchases. Nonetheless, when it was advantageous or UK interest rates were high and the Bank of England wished to maintain gold stocks,

---

8   BL, L/F/7/423.

9   In 1916/17, 1917/18 and 1919/20, £16m, £13.5m and £7m of specie was purchased (Figure 11 sources).

10 PP 1920 [Cmd.528], q. 5896; PP 1914 [Cd.7069] q. 11500.

11 *The Statist*, 24 Aug. 1912, p. 477; *ibid.*, 30 Nov. 1902, p. 593; *ibid.*, 8 July 1905, p. 45; *ibid.*, 25 May 1907, p. 1035; *ibid.*, 30 Nov. 1902, p. 593; PP 1920 [Cmd.528], q. 5194.

12 B. R. Ambedkar, *The Problem of the Rupee: Its Origin and its Solution*, London 1923, chap. 7; *The Statist*, 14 July 1906, p. 45. In 1903/4, it paid 3.5d per ounce more (Ambedkar, *The Problem*, chap. 7). High prices were also paid in 1916 and 1918/19 (PP 1920 [Cmd.529], p. 82; PP 1920 [Cmd.528], q. 5900).

13 PP [Cd.7069], q. 11122; PP 1920 [Cmd.528], q. 5187; PP 1920 [Cmd.529], p. 86; PP 1914 [Cd.7238] *Royal Commission on Indian Finance and Currency: Appendices*, p. 686, par. 85.

purchases were occasionally made there.[14] Other sources included China, which suffered the same drawbacks as Bombay, but was used in 1912; the Australian Baldwin mines and Perth Mint, to which the IO turned in 1920/1; and the US.[15]

At first, the silver was bought with gold shipped from India.[16] High transport costs and an awareness that the shipments made it obvious to speculators that specie purchases were about to occur then prompted the IO to turn to special issues of council bills, which officials argued helped to reduce the exchange, limited the movement of gold to India by the exchange banks and aided trade.[17] Others were unconvinced, claiming the policy was bad for both India and London. India was left with its large reserves of gold, occasionally a loss from the sale of the additional bills at low prices and an enlarged currency/inflation, and it also faced high London silver prices, as the additional bill sales again forewarned observant speculators that silver purchases were imminent. The withdrawal of large sums from the money market to pay for the bills, meanwhile, increased London interest rates.[18] The necessary funds thus began to be obtained from the home balances (though the consequent reduction in loans to City institutions reduced revenues and could again disturb the market) and via earmarking, gold being transferred from the London PCR to the home balances, with an equivalent payment made into the Indian PCR.[19] Earmarking was convenient; involved no opportunity costs; allowed more home balance loans to be made to the City, enhancing market liquidity and acting against high interest rates; and temporarily increased the amount of cash held in India's Bank of England current account, thus augmenting the Bank's gold stocks and minimising the need for an increase in base rate in the event of an outflow of gold.[20] Unlike the use of the home balances, however, it again indicated to speculators that India was about to enter the market. The finance required to purchase silver therefore occasionally came directly from the home balances, which then recouped the money from the London PCR, or straight from the London PCR, the gold spent being almost immediately replaced by the silver purchased.[21] In both cases, the London PCR was then replenished via

---

14   PP [Cd.7069], q. 11498; *ibid.*, q. 11150–1; *The Statist*, 24 Nov. 1906, p. 947. E.g. *The Statist*, 9 Jan. 1904, p. 53.

15   BL, L/F/7/421–2, Robinson to Franklin, 31 Aug. 1912; BL, L/AG/9/8/7, p. 1105; Ambedkar, *The Problem*, chap. 7.

16   PP [Cd.7069], q. 974. E.g. *The Statist*, 12 March 1904, p. 489; *ibid.*, 26 Oct. 1912, p. 199.

17   B. R. Tomlinson, *The Political Economy of the Raj 1914–47*, London 1979, p. 19; PP 1914 [Cd.7069], q. 1563.

18   PP 1914 [Cd.7069], q. 978, 981–9; *ibid.*, q. 1554–5. Given that sales were spread over an extended period, the impact of the withdrawal of sums from the money market was probably slight (*ibid.*, q. 1560–2).

19   *Ibid.*, q. 1558, 1560; BL, L/F/5/144, note for Baker, 18 Dec. 1912. A proposal that silver be bought using GSR funds, which were to be recouped from the GSR Indian silver reserve was rejected by the Indian government (BL, L/AG/37/4, IO to G of I, 20 July 1906).

20   PP 1914 [Cd.7069], q. 1666–71, 3559–60; PP 1906 [162] *Indian Financial Statement for 1906–07*, p. 17.

21   BL, L/AG/37/4, G of I to IO, 11 Sept. 1905; *ibid.*, IO to G of I, 11 Aug. 1905.

council bill sales, direct remittances of gold from India or the movement of funds into the Indian PCR.[22]

Silver was initially bought when the stock of rupee coins in the currency reserves on 1 October, the start of the trading season, was below 10m crores, later raised to 24 crores.[23] However, entering the silver market at roughly the same time each year and purchasing a large amount of specie over a relatively short period increased the cost of orders, as the resulting market shortages caused the price to rise, and syndicates, aware that a purchase was about to occur, prepared corners.[24] In 1904, therefore, a reserve of silver bullion was established in India that could be called upon if the stock of coin suddenly fell, and, in 1905/6, quarterly minimum holdings and, later, quarterly estimates of requirements were introduced.[25] At the start of each quarter, the amount of coin that would be needed during the following three months was calculated, taking into account the size of the reserves, predicted harvests and the likely demand for rupees, and this estimate was then checked and corrected weekly.[26] The result was that purchases were made in relatively small amounts over the whole year for either immediate delivery, or, if prices were low and expected to rise, for despatch at some time in the future.[27]

An alternate strategy was to purchase stocks well in advance of demand, particularly when prices were relatively low.[28] Speculators would find it more difficult to foresee purchases and prepare corners, there would be less price fluctuation (which damaged the international attractiveness of the market) and, in India, temporary shortages of coin/high interest rates would be avoided to the benefit of trade.[29] Some at the IO and in the Indian government, however, remained unconvinced and blocked such purchases. Not only was the strategy speculative, but it would lock up money that could be used for funding more economically or socially worthwhile projects, or for supporting the exchange, and, if the large purchases were funded via the issue of council bills or the home balances, could disturb the London market. Moreover, if the monsoon failed and demand for coin fell or more rupees returned from circulation than anticipated, the Indian government could be left with large stockpiles of silver that would earn no interest, or, if the metal was coined, result in an excess of money and inflation.[30]

---

22 PP 1906 [162], p. 20.
23 *The Statist*, 13 Aug. 1904, p. 282; *ibid.*, 12 Jan. 1907, p. 61.
24 PP 1914 [Cd.7069], q. 10869.
25 PP 1906 [162], p. 17.
26 PP 1914 [Cd.7070], appendix 5, pp. 197–8.
27 BL, L/F/7/421–2, MacKay to Abrahams, 25 Jan. 1911; *The Statist*, 14 Dec. 1912, p. 697. Agreements for delivery at some future date were known as forward contracts.
28 PP 1914 [Cd.7069], q. 10869–70.
29 PP 1914 [Cd.7070], appendix 8, p. 246, par. 39.
30 BL, L/F/5/144, discussion on Indian finance, 31 Jan. 1913; *ibid.*, note, no date, c.1914; PP 1914 [Cd.7069], q. 613.

Purchase through the Bank of England and the 1912 silver scandal

Purchases of silver were largely made through the Bank of England, the remuneration of which was much criticised by the IO. The Bank's role was to advise India on the state of the market, recruit the brokers who were to make the purchases, pay them the cost of the amounts bought and their ⅛ per cent fee, and arrange the insurance of the acquired metal. For these duties, it was paid ⅛ per cent of the cost of the silver procured, a commission that had been accepted by the Secretary of State without discussion in 1900, as it was believed that the purchase was a 'one-off' event that would not be repeated. The IO's objection to the fee was that it was 'a kind of toll exacted … for the right of access [to the silver market]' and 'out of all proportion to the work' undertaken. The Bank acted merely as 'a post office between the India Office and the brokers', writing a few letters and making a small number of telephone calls, for which from 1900 to 1906 it received £28,375.[31] It also performed its work 'less skilfully than might be expected'.[32] Silver bars purchased in 1904 were discovered to be of relatively poor quality, and, two years later, it was found to be making excessive insurance payments.[33] In 1906, a meeting with Bank officials was thus requested at which it was agreed that for the following seven years the Bank's and its brokers' fees would be combined and the joint commission would be ¼ per cent for the first £2m of silver ordered in any one year and ⅛ per cent on further amounts acquired.[34]

Towards the end of the agreement in 1912, the IO returned to the fray and was offered by the Bank a joint fee of 1/8 per cent for all purchases, which it rejected. In response, the Bank stated that it would accept a lower commission, but only if it was not financially responsible for the actions of the brokers it employed, a proposal that IO officials deemed ridiculous. They thus made a counter-offer – $^3/_{16}$ per cent on the first £2m bought in any financial year and ⅛ per cent on the remainder, with the right to purchase silver themselves in 'exceptional circumstances'. Fearing that it would be given none of the IO's business, the Bank rejected the proposal unless it continued to obtain the commission even when it had no involvement in purchases.[35]

Bemused by the Bank's response, the IO broke off the talks and decided to follow the practices of other government departments, such as the Royal Mint, and 'go it alone'.[36] The Office could easily perform the Bank's duties, and, besides saving money, would be able to draw up contracts more suitable to its own particular needs, closely

---

31   BL, L/F/5/144, Abrahams, 15 Oct. 1912; BL, L/F/7/163, no. 22, file 2, fol. 2573, note, no date, 1906; *ibid.*, no. 22, file 2, fol. 1528, note, no date, c.1906.

32   BL, L/F/7/421–2, fol. 1563, note, no date.

33   *Ibid.*; BL, L/F/7/163, no. 22, file 2, fol. 1528, note, no date, 1904.

34   BL, L/F/5/144, note for Baker, 18 Dec. 1912.

35   BL, L/F/7/426, memo, 29 Jan. 1913; *ibid.*, note, 19 Feb. 1913; *ibid.*, note, 12 March 1913; *ibid.*, Cole to Crewe, 25 March 1913.

36   BL, L/F/5/144, note for Baker, 18 Dec. 1912.

monitor the brokers employed and gain useful knowledge of how the silver market operated.[37] Moreover, it had already successfully made purchases, albeit from other financial institutions rather than the market. From 1905/6 to 1907/8, it had bought £4.137m of silver from the Russo-Chinese Bank and two exchange banks (the Hong Kong & Shanghai Banking Corp. and the Chartered Bank of India), and, in 1910, surplus colonial silver coins were acquired from the Crown Agents.[38] In 1906 and 1907, it had also entered into highly beneficial arrangements with the London City and Midland Bank and the Société Générale, both of which had stocks of silver in India. The IO bought silver from the banks for delivery in Bombay and exchanged specie, giving the banks 1m ounces of silver in London and receiving in return an equivalent amount of the metal in India. It thus saved the transport, insurance and interest cost of shipping the metal to India, and, in the case of purchases, the brokers' fees.[39]

Cost was not the only reason for the decision not to use the Bank of England. In 1910, the IO had become aware that a new syndicate had been formed and had begun to prepare a corner. Its existence was common knowledge in the City and the financial press, and Sir Felix Schuster was personally alerted of its intentions by the London Manager of Deutsche Bank and Ellis Franklin, a partner in Samuel Montagu & Co.[40] Managed by the Indian Specie Bank, it comprised Choonilal Saraiya, a prominent silver dealer, and a number of other Bombay speculators, and made its purchases through the London broker Sharps & Wilkins.[41] Pre-warned, the IO delayed coining, and, in December 1910, the syndicate 'lost heart' and began to offload its acquisitions, unable to meet the high interest payments on the money it had borrowed to finance its purchases. At first, prices remained relatively stable, as there was a large demand for silver from Chinese banks. However, when the Chinese discovered that they were helping to save a syndicate that had attempted to corner themselves the previous July, they halted all purchases and prices dived. This was the 'golden' moment for the IO to enter the market and it was urged to do so by Ellis Franklin. In the event, the Secretary of State blocked purchases and over the following few months prices recovered and the syndicate regrouped and again began to buy up stocks of silver, more confident than ever that India would eventually be forced into its trap.[42]

---

37 BL, L/F/7/426, Abrahams, 6 Feb. 1913; BL, L/F/7/163, no. 22, file 2, fol. 1528, note, no date, 1906.
38 BL, L/F/7/163, Financial Dept. collection 22, file no. 2, fol. 5700; NA, CO 129/370/11508, note, 19 April 1910. The two exchange banks provided 42 per cent of the £4.137m (*ibid.*).
39 BL, L/F/7/421–2, Deutsche Bank to IO, 27 Aug. 1912. The exchange was at an agreed price.
40 BL, L/F/5/144, Schuster's statement, 7 Feb. 1913; BL, L/F/7/421–2, Franklin to Abrahams, 7 Dec. 1910.
41 BL, L/F/7/421–2, Franklin to Abrahams, 7 Dec. 1910; BL, L/F/5/144, note, no date, c.1914; BL, L/F/7/214, financial collection 24, files 1–7, extract from *Capital*, 2 Jan. 1913.
42 PP 1914 [Cd.7069], q. 4148, 4158; BL, L/F/7/421–2, Franklin to Abrahams, 7 Dec. 1910.

If it wished to avoid being cornered by the syndicate, the IO had to keep its 1912 purchases secret. It therefore could not buy through the Bank of England, which was contracted to use as its brokers Sharps & Wilkins and Mocatta & Goldsmid, and, in 1910, had refused a request to use other dealers.[43] Any acquisitions made by these two companies would immediately alert the market that India had commenced purchasing, and both firms had connections to those attempting to corner India.[44] Sharps & Wilkins acted as broker to both the Indian Specie Bank and the syndicate.[45] Mocatta & Goldsmid had dealings with Choonilal Saraiya and had bought silver for the Indian Specie Bank, though it later claimed that it worked for the company only so that it could spy on its activities and relay any information discovered to IO officials.[46] Similarly, the IO decided to keep the operation secret from the Bank of England and failed to inform the Indian government of some of the larger purchases, fearful that officials would leak the information.[47]

As the silver market possessed only four brokers, with the removal of Sharps and Mocattas, the IO had the choice of using either Pixley & Abell or Samuel Montagu & Co. as its own broker. Montagus was picked for a number of reasons. The largest bullion trader in the City, it possessed the funds necessary to purchase the vast amount of silver required, and, unlike Pixleys, had never acted for the syndicate. More importantly, it could be trusted to perform its duties efficiently and honestly. The company had acted in a scrupulous manner in its previous dealings with the IO, was a keen supporter of Indian financial policy in its published weekly trade circulars, had privately alerted Schuster to the threat posed by the syndicate and was owned by a leading City figure with an unimpeachable reputation.[48] A leader of the United Synagogue and the Federation of Synagogues, Samuel Montagu was known as a man of utter probity, who eschewed speculation and possessed considerable financial skills and a strong sense of public duty.[49] Moreover, he was a personal friend of Abrahams and Schuster, who had done business with Montagus in his private capacity as a banker for over forty years and had 'always found them strictly honourable and absolutely reliable in their dealings'.[50] Both Abrahams and Schuster were no doubt further reassured by the fact that any dishonest behaviour

---

43 BL, L/F/5/144, note, no date, c.1914; BL, L/F/7/421–2, note, 25 May 1910.

44 BL, L/F/5/144, note for Baker, 18 Dec. 1912.

45 *Ibid.*; BL, L/F/7/421–2, Franklin to Abrahams, 7 Dec. 1910.

46 BL, L/F/5/144, Schuster's statement, 7 Feb. 1913; *ibid.*, Mocatta to Schuster, 29 Aug. 1912. No such information appears to have been passed to the IO.

47 *Ibid.*, Schuster's statement, 7 Feb. 1913; *ibid.*, Newmarch to Gillan, 27 June 1912.

48 *Ibid.*, note, no date, c.1914; *ibid.*, note for Baker, 18 Dec. 1912; *ibid.*, Schuster's statement, 7 Feb. 1913; Sen, *Colonies*, p. 124; M. de P. Webb, *Britain's Dilemma*, London 1912, pp. 42, 87.

49 M. Goodman, 'Vice Versa: Samuel Montagu, the First Lord Swaythling', *Jewish Historical Studies*, 40 (2005), pp. 75–103; E. Black, *The Social Politics of Anglo-Jewry 1880-1920*, Oxford 1988. p. 201; D. Hopkinson, 'Vintage Liberals', *History Today*, 28 (6) (1978), p. 365.

50 D. Gutwein, *The Divided Elite*, Leiden 1992, p. 358; Gutwein, 'Jewish Financiers', p. 183; BL, L/F/5/144, Schuster's statement, 7 Feb. 1913.

ical careers of Samuel Montagu's second
Secretary of State for India, and his two
e Postmaster General, and Herbert Louis
f the Jewish community that Montagu did

loyment of Montagus would reap rich divi-
k.[51] The company purchased and marketed
railway companies, bought and held Indian
government sterling debentu... .tock and sterling bills, and was one of the major
foreign exchange houses and buyers of Indian bills of exchange.[52] Samuel Montagu,
meanwhile, commanded great influence in both the City, and, as a former Liberal
MP, in politics; his other companies Keyser & Co. and Edward Lazard & Co. were
prominent players in respectively the foreign exchange and stockbroking sectors;
and his wife was related to the Rothschilds and the daughter of the prominent stock-
broker Louis Cohen.[53]

During the purchase of the silver, secrecy was maintained through a range of
'cloak and dagger' measures. All communications to Montagus were marked 'confidential' and directed to Ernest Franklin, Samuel Montagu's trusted brother-in-law,
who personally organised the operation.[54] The specie was sourced in London, but
also in China. Chinese purchases were less likely to be discovered, increased the
speed at which the silver required could be bought and reduced the amount of time
the secrecy had to be maintained, cut transportation costs (China being closer to
India than England), and allowed the payment of relatively low prices. Silver stocks
in Shanghai were high, and local speculators were eager to sell in order to regain
control of domestic demand/prices.[55] In London, the metal was bought in small
amounts of up to £500,000 at irregular intervals.[56] Purchases were placed in India's
Bank of England account, from which the payments for the London and Chinese
silver were made, preventing any suspicious rise in deposits, and the receipts sent
to the IO by a messenger with no connections to Montagus.[57] Only towards the
end of the operation was the silver shipped to India, and payment to Montagus for

---

51 BL, L/F/7/421–2, fol. 1563, note, no date.
52 Sen, *Colonies*, p. 124; BL, L/F/5/173, f ol. 7409/17; BE, C47/333; Gutwein, 'Jewish Financiers',
    p. 183.
53 *Ibid.*; *Oxford Dictionary*; Gutwein, *The Divided Elite*, pp. 53, 146. The Cohens were regu-
    lar purchasers of Indian guaranteed railway company loans and generous contributors to
    the Conservative Party (Sweeney, 'Indian Railroading', p. 70; R. F. Foster, *Lord Randolph
    Churchill*, Oxford 1982, p. 203).
54 BL, L/F/5/144, IO to Samuels, 4 March 1912; G. R. Searle, *Corruption in British Politics*,
    Oxford 1987, p. 208.
55 BL, L/F/7/421–2, Abrahams to Robinson, 27 Aug. 1912; *ibid.*, G of I to IO, 25 Aug. 1912.
56 BL, L/F/5/144, IO to Samuels, 4 March 1912.
57 Marshall Library, Cambridge, Keynes Papers, box 53a7, item 8, Schuster to Montagu, 9 Jan.
    1912.

both the London and Chinese acquisitions was made to Felix Schuster's Union and Smiths Bank and then passed to Montagus, only Schuster having knowledge of the reasons for the unconnected transactions.[58] In China, buy orders were placed by the Hong Kong & Shanghai Banking Corp. on its own invoices and then shipped to Bombay or Colombo. As the ships approached these ports, the Captains were cabled that there was a change of destination and the cargoes were offloaded at different seaports (Bombay or Calcutta) and then transferred to the local Hong Kong & Shanghai Banking Corp. branch, and, from there, to Indian government vaults.[59] A tempting ad hoc offer by the exchange banks to buy Chinese silver and deliver it free of charge to India was rejected. Although India would have saved transportation costs, the deal would have greatly increased the chances of the operation being revealed.[60]

By any measure, the IO's silver operation was a success. India obtained specie at relatively low prices, saving an estimated £500,000 to £885,000, and the syndicate was defeated.[61] Unable to sell his stockpiles and haemorrhaging cash in interest payments, Choonilal Saraiya in December 1912 offered to sell 2 lakhs to the IO at below market prices in return for a temporary loan of 50 lakhs.[62] The Secretary of State rejected the request, and, the following year, the syndicate collapsed when the Indian Specie Bank defaulted on £3m of forward purchase contracts.[63] Inevitably, the IO's activities were eventually discovered, though an impressive six months after the operation had begun and four weeks before it was due to end.[64] Mocatta's agents at the London railway stations and the Port of London reported suspicious movements of silver and the firm announced in its 9 August circular that there were rumours of Indian purchases, causing the price of silver to rise.[65] At the same time, it attempted to cut itself into the deal – offering to supply India with Chinese specie presumably in return for its support.[66] As the operation was almost at an end, the IO turned down the offer and the firm wrote an official letter of complaint regarding its non-employment, though it privately accepted that the strategy had resulted

58 *The Statist*, 24 Aug. 1912, p. 477; BL, L/F/5/144, Newmarch to Gillan, 27 June 1912; PP [Cd.7069], q. 11078.

59 F. H. King, *The History of the Hong Kong and Shanghai Banking Corporation, Volume 2*, Cambridge 1988, p. 76.

60 BL, L/F/7/421–2, Deutsche Bank to IO, 27 Aug. 1912; *ibid.*, Abrahams to Robinson, 27 Aug. 1912.

61 *Westminster Gazette*, 17 Feb. 1914; BL, L/F/5/144, Schuster's statement, 7 Feb. 1913.

62 BL, L/F/7/214, no. 24. files 1–7, *Capital*, 2 Jan. 1913; *ibid.*, *Times of India*, 28 Dec. 1912; *ibid.*, question raised Gwynne; BL, L/F/7/442, no. 42, file 2. A lakh was the equivalent of 100,000 rupees.

63 King, *The History ... Vol. 1*, p. 77. The contracts were with Sharps & Wilkins and were taken over by the Hong Kong & Shanghai Banking Corp. and a number of other banks (*ibid.*).

64 BL, L/F/5/144, note, no date, c.1914.

65 H. d'Avigdor-Goldsmid, 'The Little Marconi case', *History Today*, xiv (1964), p. 284; BL, L/F/5/144, discussion on Indian finance, 31 Jan. 1913.

66 BL, L/F/7/421–2, Mocatta to IO, 23 Aug. 1912.

in savings for India, and Edgar Mocatta met with the Assistant Unde
State.[67]

Aware that Mocatta would tell the Bank of England of its discov
informed the Governor of the IO's activities. His reaction was con
accepted that the Office 'could hardly have done anything else and th
have acted in precisely the same manner'. At a subsequent meeting,
Governor used 'very similar' expressions. [68] The Bank's attitude then cha
is not known. Possible reasons include a fear of permanently losing the
ness, pressure from Mocatta, and/or a wish to destroy the reputations of Samuel
Montagu and Felix Schuster, who had been harsh critics of the Bank's gold reserve
policy and had demanded that it be placed under greater political control.[69]
Whatever its motive, the Governor sent the IO 'a not very pleasant letter', in which
he claimed that the Office had broken a 1906 verbal and written agreement between
Lord Inchcape, a then member of the Finance Committee, and himself that all silver
would be bought through the Bank.[70] The following day, a question was asked about
the matter in the House of Commons, no doubt planted by Bank officials, which
exposed the 'scandal' to the media.[71]

To say the least, the IO doubted the veracity of the Governor's claims, even
though Inchcape supported his version of events. Inchcape had told neither the
Secretary of State nor the IO of the verbal agreement, failed to mention it in the oral
report of the meeting that he gave to the Finance Council, and the letter that the
Bank insisted implied exclusivity did no such thing.[72] Moreover, the Bank had made
not one reference to the arrangement in its voluminous post-1906 correspondence
with the IO, not even when the Office began to purchase silver from other financial
institutions, acquisitions that would have breached such a pact. After an exchange of
a series of increasingly hostile letters in which the Bank claimed that it had turned
a blind eye to the post-1906 orders, as the selling institutions had approached India
rather than vice versa and the acquisitions had not been made in the market, the
IO demanded that the conflict be passed to the Lord Chief Justice for arbitration.

67 BL, L/F/5/144, Mocatta to Schuster, 29 Aug. 1912; *ibid.*, Abrahams, 15 Oct. 1912.
68 *Ibid.*, Schuster's statement, 7 Feb. 1913.
69 Gutwein, 'Jewish Financiers', pp. 180, 183–4. The Bank's dislike of Schuster is discussed in
    Chapter 11.
70 BL, L/F/7/163, no. 22, file 2, note, 28 Nov. 1912; *ibid.*, no. 22, file 2, B of E to IO, 4 Nov. 1912;
    ibid., fol. 5942, IO to B of E, 19 Dec. 1912.
71 *Ibid.*, no. 22, file 2, Parliamentary question, Gwynne; *ibid.*, note, 28 Nov. 1912.
72 *Ibid.*, no. 22, file 2, B of E to IO, 24 Oct. 1912; *ibid.*, IO to B of E, 1 Nov. 1912; *ibid.*, no. 22, file
    2, fol. 2573, note, no date, c.1906; *ibid.*, no. 22, file 2, Abrahams, 2 Dec. 1912; *ibid.*, no. 22, file
    2, legal opinion; *ibid.*, fol. 5942, IO to B of E, 19 Dec. 1912. The IO's legal advisor concluded
    that the letter in no way bound India to the Bank (*ibid.*, no. 22, file 2, legal opinion).

The Bank rejected the call, as there was 'no room for doubt', and insisted that the agreement be honoured.[73]

Yet again, the IO backed down and returned to the Bank's fold. It did so partly for practical reasons. The market was now aware that any orders made by Montagus could be on behalf of India, the firm no longer wanted to act for the IO, and, in 1914, the Bank reduced its purchasing fees.[74] A far more important explanation, however, was that the whole silver operation had developed into a cause célèbre that threatened both the future of the IO and the reputations of its officials. From November 1912 to January 1913, 90 questions were tabled in the House of Commons on the topic, fifty by Rupert Gwynne MP, and the *Pall Mall Gazette* and *New Witness* both ran campaigns designed to bring the 'guilty' to justice.[75] Indignation was fuelled by the Marconi scandal of the previous year, anti-Semitism and anti-German sentiment. The Marconi scandal, in which it was claimed that Cabinet Ministers had gained from a contract awarded to the Marconi Company, had predisposed the public to further revelations, demonstrated to the press that government corruption sold newspapers and had involved Herbert Samuel, Samuel Montagu's nephew.[76] The scandal had also involved a number of Jews, and anti-Semite critics of the IO's silver purchases no doubt saw further opportunities to prove that the 'Jew wreckers' were destroying 'trade and business'.[77] *New Witness* was renowned for its anti-Semitism and the right wing Gwynne came from a family with a pronounced hatred of the Jewish race. Others depicted Schuster as a German–Jewish oligarch advancing Germanic interests.[78]

Critics of the silver purchases made a number of accusations. It was variously claimed that the Under Secretary of State for India, Edwin Montagu, had wished to enrich his own and his father's firm, that Montagus was given the contract as a reward for the family's past support of the Liberal Party, and that the company made excess profits from its operations.[79] In fact, Edwin Montagu had never been

73   *Ibid.*, no. 22, file 2, fol. 5942, IO to B of E, 19 Dec. 1912; *ibid.*, no. 22, file 2, IO to B of E, 20 Nov. 1912; *ibid.*, no. 22, file 2, B of E to IO, 10 Dec. 1912; *ibid.*, no. 22, file 2, fol. 5700, B of E to IO, 27 Nov. 1912.

74   BL, L/F/5/144, Abrahams, 15 Oct. 1912; BL, L/F/5/173, fol. 7409/17; BL, L/F/7/428, Abrahams, 19 Nov. 1915.

75   BL, L/F/5/144, discussion on Indian finance, 31 Jan. 13; *Pall Mall Gazette*, 31 Oct. 1912.

76   S. D. Waley, *Edwin Montagu: A Memoir and an Account of his Visits to India*, London 1964, p. 55.

77   *New Witness*, 8 Jan. 1914, pp. 308–9. The Head of Marconi was also Jewish (D. Feldman, 'Jews and the British Empire c.1900' *History Workshop Journal*, 63 (1) (2007), pp. 70–89).

78   R. Mathews, 'Prejudice: Anti-Semitism in the Distributist Weeklies', at http://racemathews. com/Assets/Distributism/1999%20Distributism&AntiSemitism.pdf (accessed May 2010); K. O. Morgan, *Consensus and Disunity: The Lloyd George Coalition Government 1918–1922*, Oxford 1979; *New Witness*, 10 Sept. 1914, p. 513; *ibid.*, 29 Oct. 1914, p. 626. Gwynne's sister, Violet, was an early admirer of Adolf Hitler and given to anti-Semitic rants (K. Ayling, *My Father's Family*, London 1979).

79   BL, L/F/7/224, extract from *Capital*, 20 Feb. 1913; Searle, *Corruption*, p. 202.

a partner of Montagus and had taken no part in its recruitment, recording in his personal diary when the allegations first emerged that he 'knew nothing of [the silver operation]'.[80] On his appointment, the Secretary of State, Lord Crewe, aware of his family connections with the City, had insisted that he saw no paper dealing with finance.[81] Moreover, he possessed a zeal for the development of India and was unlikely to do anything that would act against its advancement, and was out of the country during the period of purchase.[82] Depressed by 'a fine wave of anti-Semitism' that had descended upon him, he intended to sue the *New Witness* for libel, but was persuaded by his family not to do so.[83]

The claim that Montagus had 'piled up' silver prior to its recruitment and then sold these stocks to India at enhanced prices was equally absurd, and the firm 'protest[ed] most indignantly against such an imputation'.[84] Although it accepted that it had approached the IO and proposed that it should act as its broker, when the first order was made it held only £20,000 of silver, and, wishing to prove that it had no intention of cornering India, had offered to place its account books at the Secretary of State's disposal – an offer that was declined, as it would have implied 'a want of confidence for which there was no shadow of justification'.[85] The firm, however, refused to prove that it bought the silver by publicly identifying the names of the sellers and claimed that this information had not been divulged to the IO. It was the custom of the market that sellers' identities were kept secret, the disclosure of this intelligence would be commercially damaging, and, even if this was not the case, distinguishing which company provided the bars sold to a particular client would be like identifying 'a grape from which any given drop of wine had been obtained'.[86] In reality, in its day-to-day correspondence with the IO, sellers were identified, and it is clear that all of the silver supplied was either acquired on the London market or from China.[87]

Unable to prove their allegations against Edwin and Samuel Montagu, critics turned their attention to Sir Felix Schuster and Stuart Montagu Samuel. Accused of placing the contract with Montagus to benefit the Union and Smiths Bank, which acted as the firm's banker and obtained bullion from the company, Schuster pointed out that the bank, of which he was Chairman, acted for almost every institution in

---

80   Waley, *Edwin Montagu*, p. 55.
81   Searle, *Corruption*, p. 202.
82   H. F. Mooney, 'British Opinion on Indian policy, 1911–1917', *Historian*, 23 (2) (1961), pp. 191–210; Waley, *Edwin Montagu*, p. 54.
83   *Ibid.*, p. 56. Similar accusations were made against Montagu in 1921 by Moreton Frewen, who claimed that Indian finance was 'in the hands of a Jewish oligarchy' (Searle, *Corruption*, pp. 334–5).
84   BL, L/F/7/426, Montagu and Co. to IO, 13 Nov. 1912.
85   *Ibid.*; Searle, *Corruption*, p. 208; BL, L/F/5/144, Discussion on Indian finance, 31 Jan. 1913.
86   BL, L/F/7/426, Montagu and Co. to IO, 13 Nov. 1912.
87   E.g. BL, L/F/7/421–2, S of S to Comptroller General, 26 Oct. 1912. See also BL, L/F/5/144, Schuster's statement, 7 Feb. 1913

the City, its bullion business was shared with one of the other three brokers, and the contract with Montagus had severely damaged his own and therefore his bank's relationship with the Bank of England.[88] Schuster thus emerged from the scandal with his reputation intact. Stuart Montagu Samuel was less fortunate. A partner of the firm and a radical MP with many enemies, it was alleged that he had infringed the 1782 Contractors Act, which precluded MPs sitting and voting in the House of Commons whilst holding a government contract.[89] Although he had no knowledge of the legislation or Montagus' work for the IO, he was privately sued for contempt of the Act and investigated by a Select Committee and later by a Judiciary Committee of the Privy Council, which concluded that he had contravened the legislation, and, in doing so, had forfeited his Parliamentary seat. He thus had to seek re-election, and, in 1916, abandoned his Parliamentary career.[90]

Other currency activities

As well as purchasing silver, the IO bought gold and currency notes in London and sold silver, gold and nickel.[91] Paper currency was supplied by the Bank of England, which charged a fee of 15s per 1,000 notes for the 5 rupee note and 35s per 1,000 notes for other denominations. Fixed in 1872, the commission continued to be paid until 1913, when it was discovered that the Bank's charges to the Post Master General had halved over the period 1884–1913.[92] Further investigations revealed that the economies of scale reaped from the increase in the number of notes printed and savings from improvements in printing technology had probably reduced the Bank's costs by at least 42 per cent, and a lower fee was thus demanded.[93] The Bank's lofty response was that they were 'not trade printers and [could not]…be expected to work at trade prices'. The printing of currency notes required the employment of costly specialised staff and investment in expensive machinery, and, if the IO had the temerity to cut its commission, India would be required to simplify its note design and use thinner paper or forced to hold a larger minimum balance in its Bank current account. On hearing that the IO was prepared to take the business elsewhere, however, the Bank performed a volte face and offered to lower its fees. Although aware that further reductions were possible, IO officials accepted, wishing

88   *Ibid.*
89   Searle, *Corruption*, p. 206.
90   Avigdor-Goldsmid, 'The Little Marconi Case', pp. 284–5; *Financial Times*, 10 Feb. 1914, p. 4
91   Gold was shipped to India in 1860–62 (£1.1m) and 1919–22 (£34.5m) (PP 1884–85 [352], pp. 204–15; PP 1922 [Cmd.1778], no. 72; PP 1928 [Cmd.3046], no. 66).
92   BL, L/F/7/167, fol. 3386, IO to B of E, 2 July 1913.
93   BL, L/AG/9/8/6, pp. 867–8, B of E to IO, 11 July 1913; BL, L/F/7/167, IO to B of E, 29 April 1914; *ibid.*, report, Capt. G. H. Willis, 7 May 1914.

to maintain good relations with the Bank and to avoid the additional expense of switching suppliers.[94]

Sales of metals occurred mostly after 1900. Surplus PCR gold was disposed of through the Bank of England, which charged a commission of $^1/_{16}$, reduced to $^1/_{32}$ in 1901, and surplus nickel was sold either through the broker Mond Nickel, or directly to the War Office or purchasers in the US and France.[95] Silver began to be sold from 1928. Having adopted a proto gold bullion standard, whereby currency notes could be exchanged for gold, the Indian government began to sell off part of its PCR silver rupee holdings, even though the difference between the currency value of the coins and the silver content value meant that the specie was sold at a loss.[96] Over the period 1927/8 to 1937/8, 239m fine ounces of silver were disposed of (695m rupees at face value), generally at a rate of 25m to 30m ounces pa to 1934/5, after which only 10.7m ounces were sold.[97] The rupees were initially sent to the Bombay Mint where they were melted down and the residue sometimes refined, and the resulting ingots were then shipped to London.[98]

On arrival, the ingots were stored at the Bank of England or Royal Mint and then marketed through the brokers Mocatta & Goldsmid and Pixley & Abell, or, when London prices were low, sold direct to purchasers. Institutions that bought the silver included the Hong Kong & Shanghai Banking Corp., the Royal Mint, the German government and Johnson Matthey, which took delivery in both London and Hamburg. As regards sales on the market, in 1928 half the agreements were forward contracts (for the delivery of the specie some months hence), and the silver was sold at either the current (or 'spot') price or the spot price on the day of delivery. If the latter was the case, the contract usually contained a clause that freed the IO from the agreement if the price fell below a given level.[99]

To increase receipts, if the spot price of silver rose above the forward price after a forward contract had been signed, the IO would sell the contract specie a second time and use the proceeds to purchase an equivalent amount of metal on a forward contract with the same delivery date as the first contract, thus earning the difference between the spot and forward prices. So, for example, in mid July 1928 when the

94 BL, L/F/7/167, B of E to IO, 11 July 1913; *ibid.*, B of E to IO, 12 March 1914; *ibid.*, fol. 3326, note, no date ; *ibid.*, B of E to IO, 8 May 1914.

95 BL, L/AG/9/8/5, vol. 6, pp. 683–7; BL, L/F/7/164, fol. 7177, note; BL, L/F/5/10, no. 28, agreement between S of S and the Mond Nickel Co., 11 Dec. 1925; *ibid.*, nos 46, 49.

96 The PCR silver was to be replaced by gold. The currency value was 48.4 pence per ounce and the silver content value varied from 12 pence to 30 pence per ounce (*Report of the Controller of Currency*, 1929/30, p. 11). From 1927 to April 1932, the IO obtained £11.1m for the silver sold (BL, L/F/5/10, nos 57–6).

97 *Report of the Controller of Currency*, 1927/28 to 1934/5; *Financial News*, 6 (8), 26 Feb. 1938, p. 14. In 1933/4, 45m ounces were sold, 20m ounces of which were used to pay the British US war debt (*Report of the Controller of Currency*, 1933/4, pp. 14–15).

98 *Report of the Controller of Currency*, 1929/30, p. 11.

99 BL, L/F/5/10, nos 57–62, 139, 172; *ibid.*, nos 77–8, IO to G of I, 24 Sept. 1928; *ibid.*, no. 150, IO to G of I, 20 Aug. 1931.

spot selling price was ⅛ greater than the forward selling price, the IO sold 250,000 ounces of silver that had already been sold in May for delivery in November at the spot price, and used ⅞ of the proceeds to buy an equivalent amount of silver at the lower forward price, again for delivery in November. When the difference between the spot and forward price continued over an extended period, numerous purchases and sales would occur, the IO making a small gain on each transaction.[100] In the case of forward contracts for unrefined silver, further profits could be made by refining the silver, selling it at the higher refined price, and using the proceeds to purchase another forward contract for unrefined metal, with even greater profits being possible if the silver was refined during a slack period when the cost of refining fell.[101]

Conclusion

The 1912 silver scandal illustrates the sheer savagery of the London financial eco-system. In its purchase of silver and other metals, the IO clearly demonstrated its knowledge of the market and financial acumen, and its decision to employ Samuel Montagu & Co. made perfect economic sense. It enabled it to escape the Bank of England's excessive purchase commissions and to avoid a long prepared attempt to corner the market and force India to pay a high price for its silver. By any measure, the operation was a success. The Indian government saved a great deal of money, and the market was rid of a syndicate that had preyed and would have continued to prey on other purchasers of specie. To the denizens of the City, however, the affair provided an opportunity to advance their own interests. By conjuring up and perpetuating a scandal, Anglo-Saxon financiers hoped to weaken the IO's prefer-ence for dealing with Jewish owned/managed institutions; the Bank of England and Mocatta to regain India's specie business; and the Bank to display to the IO, other clients and the City in general both its power and its willingness to use it. The Bank also possessed a more personal motive, a wish to destroy the reputations of Schuster and Montagu and to weaken their campaign for the Bank to be stripped of its con-trol of the UK's gold stocks.

---

100   *Ibid.*, nos 77–8, IO to G of I, 24 Sept. 1928; *ibid.*, no. 227, IO to G of I, 7 Feb. 1935. From July 1930 to 1938, the IO made £16,758 profit on the sale/repurchase of silver (*ibid.*, no. 244).

101   *Ibid.*, nos 77–8, IO to G of I, 24 Sept. 1928; *ibid.*, no. 239, IO to G of I, 10 Aug. 1936. The silver was refined by Messrs Johnson Matthey and Messrs N. M. Rothschild & Sons (*ibid.*, Kitson to Johnson Matthey, 27 April 1936).

6

The Finance of Indian Trade

The finance of Indian trade was largely managed by the Indian exchange banks, which were based in Britain, but operated in India, and, in some cases, South East Asia and Australia. For much of the period there were five to seven such banks, the most important of which were the Oriental Banking Corp. (established in 1851, failed in 1892), the Hong Kong & Shanghai Banking Corp. (established 1865), and the Chartered Mercantile Bank of India, London & China (1858).[1] As reflected by their name, their main role was exchange dealing, and for the whole of the period they dominated this sector. The Indian joint stock banks lacked the necessary funds to enter the business, the Indian presidency banks possessed no London branches and were legally precluded from dealing in exchange, which was regarded as excessively risky, and any attempt to open up the market was fiercely resisted.[2] The banks also performed a variety of other financial activities – taking in current account and fixed deposits, providing overdrafts and short- and long-term loans against local bills of exchange and government securities, and underwriting Straits and Hong Kong loans.[3]

---

1   The other banks were the Agra & United Services Bank (1857), the Delhi & London Bank (1862), the National Bank of India (1863), the Commercial Bank of India (1864), the Asiatic Banking Corp. (1864), the Eastern Bank (1910), the P & O Banking Corp. (1920), and the Yokohama Specie Bank (J. McGuire, 'Exchange Banks, India and the World Economy: 1850–1914', *Asian Studies Review*, 29 (2005), p. 145; L. C. Jain, *The Monetary Problems of India*, London 1933, p. 105; Sayers, *Gilletts*, p. 95).

2   A. Krishnaswami, 'Capital Development of India, 1860–1913', University of London, PhD thesis, 1941; A. S. J. Baster, *The Imperial Banks*, London 1929, p. 177; Wadia and Joshi, *Money*, p. 338. Attempts to remove the exchange banks' monopoly in 1898 and 1904 failed (Baster, *The Imperial Banks*, pp. 173, 177).

3   PP 1898 [C.9037], q. 3473; Muirhead, *Crisis Banking*, p. 215; Crump, *The English Manual*, chap. 17, part 3; NA, CO 273/332/16226, CAs to Colonial Secretary, 3 May 1907; NA, CO 273/322/11688, CAs to CO, 2 April 1906.

The purpose of the banks' exchange dealings was to allow purchasers of Indian produce and UK goods to send payments respectively to India and the UK, and individuals and institutions to move funds between the two countries. To enable the transfer of money to India, they bought in India bills of exchange for rupees that were cashed in sterling in London and were commonly known as export bills/drafts; to permit the movement of money in the opposite direction (from India to the UK), they purchased in London bills of exchange (import bills/drafts) for sterling that were cashed in India in rupees (Appendix 2).

Export drafts were used by two groups. A small number were drawn up by individuals and institutions moving funds to India.[4] The vast majority, however, were created by British companies trading in India that exported to the UK a range of Indian raw materials, including cotton, jute, silk, indigo, tea, wheat, rice, hides and seeds.[5] The companies generally sold these products 'forward', for delivery two to six months hence, at a price based on the current value of the goods and the rate of exchange. They thus avoided the risk of the price of the goods or the exchange moving against them and had no money tied up in unsold stock.[6] After signing the contract of sale, they then drew up a usance export bill. This was a legal document that stated that the UK-based purchaser of the goods or his bank (known as the drawee) would pay the amount owed in sterling to the person/institution that held the bill at a specified future date, the period between the creation of the bill and its payment being known as its 'currency'.[7] Settlement was initially six months hence, and, after the construction of the Suez Canal, the arrival of the steamship and the telegraph, and the subsequent reduction in transit times, within a three month period.[8] The individuals/institutions wishing to transfer money to India, meanwhile, created and sold sight bills that were cashed immediately on arrival in London and named their own bank as the drawee.[9]

Having drawn up a bill, the exporter had two choices. He could send it direct to England where it would be paid in sterling and the money returned to India, or, if he also imported British goods, retained in England and used to purchase this merchandise. Usually, the bill was sent via an exchange bank, which 'collected' the payment

---

4   PP 1887 [C.5099], q. 3278.

5   *Ibid.*, q. 327. For example, Gaddum & Co., Rallis Bros, Ritchie Stuart & Co., etc. (D. Banerjee, 'Is There Overestimation of 'British Capital' Outflow?', *Indian Economic and Social History*, 41 (2) (2004), p. 154). The exporters' profit was the difference between the price at which they bought and sold goods (PP 1887 [C.5099], q. 1916).

6   PP 1887 [C.5099], q. 3271, 3273; PP 1887 [C.5099], q. 1906, 1940. The only major exception to forward sales was tea, the value of which could only be determined after a consignment had been delivered and tested *(ibid.)*. British importers of the goods also generally sold them forward, using the money obtained to finance the purchase (PP 1887 [C.5099], q. 1929).

7   *Ibid.*, q. 3300; G. F. Shirras, *Indian Finance and Banking*, London 1920, p. 382.

8   PP 1875 [351] *Report from the Select Committee on Banks of Issue*, q. 7040; Crump, *The English Manual*, chap. 17, part 6.

9   Muirhead, *Crisis Banking*, p. 206. In England, the sum owed was paid by the drawer's bank out of his account.

and returned it to India, and charged a small commission for the service, and, if the draft was for a small sum, the cost of postage. This method of payment was generally used by small merchants or those with poor reputations.[10] Alternatively and more usually, he could sell the bill in India to an exchange bank for rupees, using the proceeds either to purchase the goods to be exported (thus avoiding financing the deal from profits or debt) or to buy more Indian goods that were again sold forward.[11] If the drawee was European, either an appropriate European bank (Comptoir d'Escompte de Paris, Deutsche Bank) would be chosen or a UK-based bank, which would forward the draft to an agent in the relevant country.[12]

The bill was sold for an amount slightly less than its value, known as the discount rate, enabling the bank to cover its costs and to make a profit.[13] The necessary finance generally came from the bank's own resources, which comprised funds moved to India from London via the purchase of import or council drafts, its Indian deposits and loans. In some cases, however, it would advance money on behalf of the drawee (importer), or, more rarely, pass on an advance provided by the drawee's bank.[14] Prices depended on a range of factors including the exchange rate, lower prices being paid when the exchange was expected to rise; the bill's currency, the longer the currency the greater the discount; the month, discounts tending to fall in the middle of the trading season, when exports reached their zenith; and Indian interest rates, high rates resulting in large discounts, as the bank's opportunity cost during the time it held the bill was greater and the drawer could invest the draft proceeds at these rates. The intensity of exchange bank competition, the financial strength of the drawee (with drafts drawn on large trading companies, known as 'pictures', commanding a price premium) and the price of council bills were also influential.[15] In some cases, the price excluded the interest on the money advanced by the bank, which was charged separately and paid by the drawee and sometimes the drawer (exporter), who recovered the additional outlay by charging a higher price for his goods. If this was the case, the bank would provide a rebate if it sold on the bill or paid it early.[16]

10 W. F. Spalding, *Eastern Exchange, Currency and Finance*, London 1920, pp. 59–60; Crump, *The English Manual*, chap. 17, part 5.

11 PP 1887 [C.5099], q. 1901; PP 1887 [C.5099], q. 3288.

12 Crump, *The English Manual*, chap. 17, part 4. The transfer of the funds back to Britain, no doubt, benefitted the UK's Balance of Payments.

13 PP 1887 [C.5099], q. 3273; H. L. Chablani, *Indian Currency and Exchange*, Oxford 1925, p. 35.

14 Spalding, *Eastern Exchange*, pp. 60–1, 63. If the latter was the case, the bills were drawn on the bank providing the advance rather than the purchaser of the goods (*ibid.*, p. 63).

15 Crump, *The English Manual*, chap. 17, part 4; *The Statist*, 14 Sept. 1889, p. 286; Chablani, *Indian Currency and Exchange*, p. 35; PP 1887 [C.5099], q. 3278; *The Statist*, 20 Dec. 1902, p. 117. When a rise in the exchange was expected, traders sought to transfer funds before the rate movement occurred. The exchange rate used was based either on that for telegraphic transfers or for import bills, or the daily rate determined by the banks themselves (Spalding, *Eastern Exchange*, pp. 60–1).

16 *Ibid.*

Up to the early 1870s, purchase was 'clean', without collateral. The 1866–67 commercial crisis, the 1872 failure of Gledstanes & Co., and wider fluctuations in Indian produce prices then forced banks to demand as security the shipping documents drawn up by the exporter. These constituted proof of ownership, and, if the drawee (importer) failed to pay the amount owed, the bank could claim and sell the goods, keeping the sales proceeds. The only exception to the provision of such collateral was when the drawee was a large trading company, which was unlikely to go bankrupt and had probably itself obtained exporter security against non-delivery, or when the payment of the bill had been guaranteed by an acceptance house – a merchant bank, and, from the 1890s, increasingly a foreign financial institution.[17] Few Indian bills, however, were covered by such guarantees, as the commissions charged by the acceptance houses tended to be high and most banks/merchants regarded the provision of security to be sufficient.[18]

After buying the bill, the bank sent it to London, initially by ship but later by telegraphic transfer, and obtained the sum owed. This either was used to finance the purchase of import/council bills, gold and the other financial instruments used to send money back to India, or was placed on deposit or invested in short-term securities, deployment depending on the cost/availability of the various remittance methods, the demand for export bills and market interest rates.[19] On the bill's arrival, the bank's actions depended on the nature of the draft. Documents on Payment (DP) bills were held until they matured, i.e. until the date of payment.[20] Alternatively, Documents on Acceptance (DA) bills were immediately sold for an amount slightly less than their value, though they were sometimes held to maturity – for example, when the bank was well supplied with funds, when there was no immediate prospect of the proceeds being profitably employed or when London interest rates were dangerously high and taking money out of the market would worsen the situation.[21] Indian exports to the UK were therefore financed partly by the exchange banks and partly by the London discount market, in that from the arrival of a bill in London until the amount owed was paid, the cash received by exporters and used to finance

---

17   Crump, *The English Manual*, chap. 17, part 3; Kynaston, *The City … Vol.* 2, p. 9.

18   Sayers, *Gilletts*, p. 48. Bills discounted by Gilletts, which specialised in Indian bills, were occasionally guaranteed by Deutsche Bank, the Union Bank and the London City and Midland Bank (*ibid.*, p. 47).

19   Spalding, *Eastern Exchange*, p. 63.

20   BL, L/F/7/158, fol. 4544, Abrahams, 21 July 1916. With DP bills, the shipping documents, which gave title to the goods, were not delivered until the draft was actually paid, and financial institutions were therefore reluctant to buy the drafts before maturity (Spalding, *Eastern Exchange*, p. 61).

21   *Ibid.*, p. 63. With DA bills, the shipping documents were delivered when the draft was accepted by the drawee rather than when it was paid. Institutions that bought the bills thus had the documents/produce as collateral (*ibid.*, p. 61).

subsequent deals came from the exchange banks (DP bills) and the institutions that bought the DA bills.[22]

The main DA purchasers were discount houses and bill brokers, which either held the draft until the payment was made (their profit being the difference between the amount paid and the bill's value) or sold it on to a financial institution that held it in its short-term reserves and, if cash was needed, would use it as collateral for a money market loan or resell it to a discount house/bill broker or another financial institution.[23] Over its lifetime, a draft could be bought and sold several times, its price determined by the time it had to run (i.e. the days left before the amount owed had to be repaid), its currency, the financial standing of the drawee and short-term loan interest rates. As will be discussed in Chapter 11, the discount houses financed these purchases with short-term advances from joint stock banks, the IO and, in the case of Gilletts, merchant banks and railway companies, the collateral for which included Indian government securities and sterling bills, and Indian DA export bills.[24] Other purchasers were merchant banks, which from the turn of the century began to move into the discount sector; the Bank of England; the joint stock banks; and particularly Scottish banks, which placed the bills in their deposit-at-call reserves and also bought drafts from discount houses and bill brokers.[25] Fearful of acquiring bills that would not be paid, the joint stock banks tended to only buy those drawn on their own trading company clients or from banks with which they had a relationship.[26]

Import bills were used by individuals/institutions that wished to move money to England (in particular, government employees sending a portion of their income to their families), but mainly by trading companies that exported British manufactured goods and, in particular, cotton clothing, to India.[27] Like exporters of Indian raw materials, these firms sold their products forward at the current price/exchange rate, and, on shipping the merchandise, created a usance bill of exchange.[28] Drawn on the Indian purchaser of the goods, these had the same currencies as export drafts and were either sent to India for payment or more usually sold to the exchange banks for sterling, which was used to purchase more goods that were again sold forward.

22   Shirras, *Indian Finance*, p. 382; H. L. Chablani, *Indian Currency, Banking and Exchange*, Oxford 1929, p. 76.

23   Short-term reserves contained investments that circumstances could require to be sold at short notice. The holding of bills in reserves rose from the end of the century as the price of consols fell (Kynaston, *The City … Vol. 2*, p. 294).

24   Sayers, *Gilletts*, pp. 37, 52.

25   PP 1875 [351], q. 6886, 7089; Ball and Sunderland, *An Economic History*, p. 344. Deposits-at-call were deposits that clients could demand be repaid immediately.

26   PP 1875 [351], q. 7035, 7096, 7752.

27   Crump, *The English Manual*, chap. 17, part 4; *The Statist*, 13 July 1901, p. 45. Government employee transfers were known as 'family remittances'.

28   If prices were low, they purchased the goods before they had found an Indian buyer (PP 1887 [C.5099], q. 2240–1).

Individuals/institutions moving cash to the UK, meanwhile, sold sight bills, usually named their Indian bank as drawee.[29] Bank finance for the purchase of the bills came from the proceeds of the export drafts held to maturity or sold on the discount market, and, on those relatively rare occasions when these proved insufficient, from advances from the joint stock banks, the IO and discount houses.[30]

The price paid, again, was less than the final value of the draft and dependent on its currency, the financial viability of the drawee, the price of council bills, London interest rates, the exchange rate and exchange bank competition, with attempts in 1887 and 1890 to minimise rivalry via price-fixing agreements ending in disarray.[31] Some banks also charged interest on bills from their purchase to maturity, and, until 1899, provided a 1/4 per cent rebate if a company that both exported to and imported from India agreed to purchase their export bills.[32] After buying the draft, the bank then mailed and later telegraphed it to India, where it was held until it matured, the Indian discount market being relatively small.[33] The finance of the British export trade to India was thus wholly bankrolled by the exchange banks.

In an ideal world, the number of export bills arriving in London would have been equal to the import bills leaving the capital.[34] Unfortunately, exports from Britain to India were less than Indian exports to the UK, and the banks thus handled fewer import drafts than export bills.[35] It was to overcome this mismatch that the IO sold council bills, which, like import drafts, were bought in London for sterling and cashed in India by the Indian government in the form of rupee coin or notes.[36] On receipt of orders from their branches in India, these were purchased by the exchange banks' London headquarters with the proceeds of export bills and sent to India, though a small proportion were resold in London or not immediately despatched, but used as collateral for loans.[37] On arrival in India, they were presented to the Indian Treasury and the rupees received used to finance the purchase of more

29 Muirhead, *Crisis Banking*, p. 206. In India, the sum owed was paid by the drawer's bank out of their account.
30 PP 1914 [Cd.7069], q. 2811–12, 2817. The banks had close formal and informal links to City institutions (McGuire, 'Exchange Banks', p. 159). In 1897, Gilletts' loans to the exchange banks totalled £0.5m (Sayers, *Gilletts*, p. 51).
31 PP 1887 [C.5099], q. 3273; *The Statist*, 19 Jan. 1889, p. 62; *ibid.*, 16 July 1887, p. 58; *ibid.*, 5 March 1887, p. 250; *ibid.*, 7 June 1890, p. 668; PP 1887 [C.5099], q. 3296. High London interest rates increased the discount, as the banks suffered an opportunity cost, and the seller could lucratively invest the proceeds (PP 1887 [C.5099], q. 3298). The expectation of a fall in the exchange caused bill demand to rise and the prices paid to fall (*The Statist*, 5 March 1887, p. 250).
32 *Ibid.*, 5 Nov. 1904, p. 793.
33 Jain, *The Monetary Problems*, p. 108. The bills were therefore largely DP drafts. Occasionally, the bills were paid early (Spalding, *Eastern Exchange*, p. 61).
34 PP 1887 [C.5099], q. 3273.
35 Pandit, *India's Balance*, p. 144; Chablani, *Indian Currency and Exchange*, p. 64.
36 PP 1920 [Cmd.529], p. 121.
37 Muirhead, *Crisis Banking*, p. 210; *The Statist*, 14 Aug. 1897, p. 246.

export drafts. Without the bills, the banks would have moved funds to India in the form of specie or by various other means. In the event, these methods were used only when they proved cheaper than council bills.

Exchange banks and the exchange business

For the banks, the exchange business provided a reliable source of income, as traders had few alternatives to import/export bills. Prior to the 1870s, some importers/exporters used sight bills of exchange. Indian purchasers of UK goods, on the receipt and sale of the articles, bought in India from exchange banks and for rupees sight drafts, which the bank then transferred to London, where they were cashed for sterling by the exporter.[38] British importers of Indian produce, meanwhile, paid for the goods immediately a sale had been made by buying sight bills in London from exchange banks and for sterling, which were then sent to the Indian exporters, who cashed them for rupees.[39] To finance the manufacture of the goods exported to India and the purchase of the Indian produce, the British traders bought inland bills. On making the sale, a British exporter would sell a six month inland bill to a London or Manchester bank or to another trading company drawn on himself, giving as security the sales invoice. After the six months had passed, if he had received the sale proceeds from the Indian buyer (via the bill from India), he would then pay the inland bill, and, if the proceeds had not been paid, would renew the draft for a further three months, and, if necessary, for three more months.[40] Similarly, the British importer of Indian goods would finance purchase by buying a three month inland bill and repaying it on maturity, by which time the Indian produce would have arrived and been sold. The drawback of such bills, which emerged with the fall in silver prices, was that traders had no protection against exchange movements between the date of sale and the return of the sale proceeds/arrival of Indian produce, which was particularly damaging to exporters of cotton clothes to India who had slim profit margins.[41] The use of such drafts thus gradually diminished.

The same downside afflicted two other possible means of remittance – Indian exporters arranging for UK purchasers to send the amount owed to India via the purchase of council bills, and traders paying for goods with specie. Both practices were only adopted by large trading companies, particularly during the post-First

---

38   PP 1887 [C.5099], q. 1902, 3254.
39   S. Nishimura, *The Decline of Inland Bills of Exchange in the London Money Market, 1855–1913*, London 1971, pp. 33, 38.
40   PP 1887 [C.5099], q. 3253, 3263. The currency of the inland drafts eventually declined to four months, as the time it took for the goods to reach India and the proceeds to be remitted to England fell, and it was discovered that traders were using the cash obtained from the sale of six month bills for purposes other than the purchase of Indian produce (Nishimura, *The Decline*, pp. 36–8).
41   *Ibid.*, pp. 33, 36; *The Statist*, 21 Feb. 1891, p. 203

World War boom when the higher costs were offset by the high prices paid for Indian produce.[42] An alternative, payment for exports from India in the form of imports of UK manufactured goods and vice versa, especially popular with companies that both imported to and exported from India, led to delays in payment until the merchandise was sold, increased expenses and was not always feasible. Such exchanges therefore only took place when the cost of export/import bills was high.[43]

Although reliable, the banks' exchange business was far from lucrative. Profits comprised the difference between the prices banks paid for export and import/council bills, a mere ⅛d in the late 1880s.[44] To maximise returns, the banks usually retained relatively small amounts of funds in India and did not always remit the proceeds of export bills to India via council bills. When council bills were transported to India by ship, the banks had to keep relatively large sums in India to meet any sudden increase in the supply of export bills. Later, the telegraphic transfer of council bills permitted smaller balances to be held – £2.2m in 1901, £2.9m in 1910 and £5.2m in 1919, though reserves rose in the inter-war period.[45] The small size of the balances was the subject of some criticism. It was argued that they reduced exchange bank investments in Indian government securities, resulted in occasional shortages of money, which increased Indian interest rates, and meant that the banks would have no alternative but to seek support from the government in the event of a run on their deposits.[46]

The amount of funds retained was dependent on the exchange rate, London/Indian interest rates, rupee bond prices and the seasons. Some of the movements of money to and from the subcontinent were designed to gain additional profits and were speculative. As already discussed, sums were transferred to and from England to benefit from London/Indian interest rate differentials and actual and expected changes in the exchange rate, and funds were moved in the form of rupee government bonds to gain from differences in the London/Indian market price of these securities. A further influence was the season. Before the busy trading period, banks transferred cash to India in order to meet the rise in the supply of export bills when the season began and because exchange rates were low.[47] At the end of the trading year, sums were then returned to the UK, where they could generally earn a higher

42 PP 1920 [Cmd.528], q. 1803–4.
43 PP 1887 [C.5099], q. 4513–14; PP 1888 [C.5512] *Gold and Silver Commission*, q. 10176; PP 1887 [C.5099], q. 2870.
44 PP 1887 [C.5099], q. 3296.
45 BL, L/F/5/64, Westland, 12 Jan. 1884, p. 4; PP 1914 [Cd.7069], q. 2862; Wadia and Joshi, *Money*, p. 343; PP 1919 [Cmd.234, 235, 236, 237, 238] *Report of the Indian Industrial Commission, Evidence, Volumes 1–5*, p. 801.
46 PP 1898 [C.9037], q. 1815; BL, L/F/5/139, IO to Governor General, 1 March 1900; PP 1899 [C.9376] *Committee to Inquire into Indian Currency*, pp. 66–7; PP 1914 [Cd.7069], q. 2862.
47 *The Statist*, 15 Oct. 1904, p. 637; *ibid.*, 7 Jan. 1899, p. 3; PP [Cd.7069], q. 117.

return. As the repatriation of funds led to an exchange fall and increased costs, some cash was remitted prior to the end of the season.[48]

Non-council bill remittances

Despite the availability of council bills, the banks continued to transfer funds to India in the form of import bills, specie, rupee paper and railway bills, and financed exports bills via Indian deposits and loans. The banks were commercial operations in a competitive market and naturally chose the cheapest form of remittance. If they did not, their competitors and clients would do so.[49] The most significant alternate form of money transfer was specie. From 1870/1 to 1918/19, £475.6m net (£238.9m of gold and £236.7m of silver) was imported into India, and, in 1904/5–1910/11, gold and silver financed around a third of the country's trade surplus, council bills accounting for 50 per cent and the other modes of remittance the remainder (Figure 6).[50] Prior to the closure of the mints, remittance in the form of specie was largely by bar silver purchased mainly in London, but also in China, and, in 1885, in Austria.[51] On arrival in India, the specie was passed directly to trading companies, sold in the bazaars or sent to the mints, where it was transformed into rupee coins for a small seigniorage charge of 2 per cent.[52] Its use was dependent on its cost in relation to the price of council bills. The banks turned to the metal when the price, cost of transportation and the loss of interest during the voyage to India (during shipment, silver was not deposited in a bank and therefore earned no interest) was less than the price of council bills, which was generally the case in the busy trading period. A fall in London silver prices relative to Indian silver prices seems not to have prompted its use, as the banks could reap a profit from the price differences by sending telegraphic transfers to India.[53] There were, however, some speculative

48   *The Statist*, 17 June 1899, p. 936.
49   *Ibid.*, 20 Sept. 1890, p. 316; *ibid.*, 23 March 1889, p. 330.
50   Figure 6 sources; Tomlinson, *The Political Economy*, p. 20. Some of the specie will have been imported for non-trade purposes. In the five years leading to the First World War, specie financed 46 per cent of the trade surplus (Balachandran, *John Bullion's Empire*, p. 56).
51   Muirhead, *Crisis Banking*, p. 17; *The Statist*, 14 Oct. 1882, p. 428; *ibid.*, 16 May 1885, p. 534. From 1860/1 to 1880/1, total Indian silver imports amounted to £151.48m and gold imports £78.3m (PP 1882 [181], p. 259).
52   PP 1883 [135] *Financial Statement of Government of India, 1883–84*, p. 17; Crump, *The English Manual*, chap. 17, part 5; PP 1899 [C.9222, 9390], pars 4–10. Before the mass sale of consumer durables, many Indian exporters had little need for cash and demanded payment in precious metals (*The Statist*, 15 March 1913, p. 513). The banks made additional profit through the sale of the small amount of gold present in the silver bars and extracted during the minting process (PP 1871 [363], q. 6240).
53   PP 1887 [C.5099], q. 2578, 2584, 2589, 3117, 3120.

movements immediately prior to and after the closure of the mints, when it began to be stockpiled.[54]

Figure 6. Net private account imports of specie into India, 1870/1–1918/19

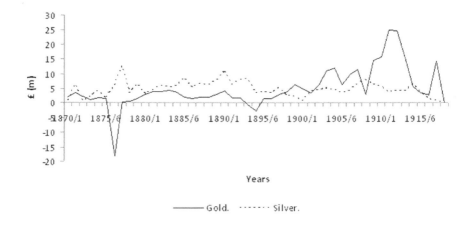

Sources. B. R. Ambedkar, *The Problem of the Rupee: Its Origin and its Solution*, London 1923, chap. 7, tables 51–2; PP 1920 [Cmd.528], p. 8, appendix 2.

After the mint closures and the banks' inability to coin imports, and the imposition of an import duty, the popularity of the metal as a form of remittance fell. It was used in preference to council bills only during times of Indian prosperity, when it was in demand for ornaments, and in 1902/3 and 1908 in anticipation of rumoured rises in Indian silver prices.[55] It was replaced by gold, which had been little used prior to 1893 owing to its unpopularity as a currency, and which was shipped as coin or bullion from London, Australia and various other countries by the exchange banks, and, to a lesser extent, by trading companies.[56] From 1909 to 1914, the metal financed 37 per cent of the trade surplus, with remittances reaching a peak in the early years of the First World War (when the sale of council bills was halted, silver imports prohibited and Indians sought a safe haven for their savings) before declining in the inter-war period.[57] Shipments again occurred when the gross price of the gold was less than the price of council bills, though if the price difference was slight,

54 McGuire, 'Exchange Banks', p. 156; *The Statist*, 10 Feb. 1894, p. 173.
55 *Ibid.*, 11 Feb. 1905, p. 221; *ibid.*, 22 Feb. 1908; PP 1903 [151], p. 13.
56 PP 1919 [Cmd.234–8], p. 801; *The Statist*, 27 Sept. 1913, p. 733.
57 *Ibid.*, 8 Sept. 1917, p. 395; Balachandran, *John Bullion's Empire*, p. 56; PP 1919 [Cmd.234–8], p. 801.

the banks would generally continue to purchase bills, as the use of specie could easily be increased by theft or loss at sea, and the export of London gold could trigger a rise in interest rates.[58] The gold was transported by British steamship, usually owned by P & O. The only exception occurred in 1912 when an urgent demand for money in India prompted the banks to send specie bought in England to Marseilles, where it was loaded onto steamers that sailed earlier than their London counterparts.[59] From 1901, some banks also sent the small bars of gold that were popular with Indian traders via parcel post, which was far cheaper than arranging carriage themselves.[60] Banned from using this mode of transport by the British and Indian Post Office under pressure from the shipping companies, they then began to use French parcel post until this practice too was outlawed in 1910.[61] On arrival in India, the gold was presented to the Indian government and exchanged for rupees or notes at the agreed/fixed price, and, in the early part of the period, passed directly to trading companies to be used for the purchase of goods.[62]

Ideally, the banks shipped gold from Australia, or, if money was urgently required, bought Australian gold in transit to London at Colombo.[63] The duration of the voyage from Freemantle/Colombo to India was less than that from London, and the banks thus enjoyed lower transport costs and lost less interest on their cargoes, and the purchase of Freemantle gold had less impact on London liquidity/interest rates. Such shipments, however, depended on the availability and cost of the metal. Little specie could be obtained in the October to February wool and wheat seasons, particularly when there was no drought and a large quantity of fleeces/grain were on sale, as large sums were required for the purchase of the wool/wheat, and its export caused the Australian exchange rate to rise.[64] Likewise, Australian banks were reluctant to sell gold to India if US or UK demand was strong and higher prices could be prised from American/British buyers, although when the price offered by UK purchasers was only slightly above that proffered by the exchange banks and London interest rates were high, the Australian banks would sell to India. Unlike their English counterparts, the exchange banks paid for their purchases in London prior to rather than on shipment, and, during periods of high interest rates, therefore, sales to India allowed the Australian banks to invest the proceeds and benefit from

58   BL, L/F/7/182, fol. 1536, minute, 23 Nov. 1910.
59   *The Statist*, 20 April 1901, p. 699; *ibid.*, 13 Jan. 1912, p. 51; *ibid.*, 3 Feb. 1912, p. 223.
60   BL, L/F/5/9, IO to Post Office, 4 Jan. 1901. Cost by parcel post was 3s per cent as against the 10s per cent charged by shipping companies (*The Statist*, 25 May 1901, p. 957).
61   *The Statist*, 1 Jan. 1920, p. 3; BL, L/F/7/182, IO to Governor General, 3 May 1901; BL, L/F/5/9, Abrahams, 9 Jan. 1910, p. 51. The Post Office only allowed gold worth less than £5 and in the form of ornament to be sent by parcel post (BL, L/F/5/9, Post Office to IO, 11 April 1901).
62   PP [Cd.7069], q. 114; *The Statist*, 15 March 1913, p. 513.
63   Chablani, *Indian Currency and Exchange*, p. 69.
64   PP 1914 [Cd.7069], q. 8327; *The Statist*, 17 Feb. 1912, p. 349; *ibid.*, 9 Oct. 1909, p. 777; *ibid.*, 18 Aug. 1906, p. 269; *ibid.*, 24 Sept. 1904, p. 501l; Spalding, *Eastern Exchange*, pp. 35–6.

the higher rates for a longer period than if they sold the gold to London dealers.[65] Over the longer term, the availability of the gold also depended on the amount mined, the Australian exchange rate and government fiscal policy – the construction of state railways and irrigation absorbing large amounts of surplus cash.[66]

Other sources of gold were Japan, Singapore, South Africa and Egypt.[67] Of these four countries, only small amounts were shipped from the Far East, which rarely possessed surpluses, or from South Africa, whose shipping service to India was unreliable. Far more came from Egypt, which was nearer to India than London (though further away than Australia), especially prior to the First World War, when its exchange rate fell.[68] The Egyptian autumn cotton crop was usually harvested and traded immediately before the Indian trading season, and Egyptian banks were more than happy to sell their excess holdings of gold to the exchange banks, the size of the surplus depending on whether the cotton crop had been good or bad.[69]

Far smaller amounts of funds were remitted in the form of Indian government rupee bonds, interest drafts and discharge notes. As discussed in Chapter 4, the securities were sent to India when market prices were or were expected to be higher than in the UK, and the interest drafts and discharge notes when respectively dividends were paid and loans were to be converted. Railway bills of exchange were similarly only available for limited periods. Drawn up by the Indian railway companies and used to transfer money to India, they were sold in London for sterling and cashed in India for rupees. The bills were often cheaper than council bills and were particularly popular with the banks in the late 1880s and early 1890s, their use being halted by the Indian government in 1898.[70]

Indian deposits and loans were used to purchase export bills in the early part of the period to cover temporary shortages of cash between the purchase of council bills and specie and their arrival in India, as well as during the First World War and at other times when the usual methods of remittance were not available. Deposits comprised current accounts and money repayable at short notice and earning a fixed interest rate, and they rose from relatively small amounts to £7.9m in 1901 and £36m in 1917, largely because of the banks' relatively good terms.[71] Loans were obtained from other exchange banks, mercantile firms and the bazaars, but largely from the presidency banks, which required collateral in the form of Indian government rupee securities, specie or council bills in transit to India, and, in the case of the Hong Kong & Shanghai Bank, sterling securities deposited with Coutts &

---

65   *The Statist*, 19 Sept. 1903, p. 497; *ibid.*, 26 Jan. 1901, p. 131.

66   BL, L/F/7/182, note, 4 May 1912; PP 1914 [Cd.7069], q. 7720.

67   E.g. *The Statist*, 26 Dec. 1903, p. 1179; *ibid.*, 22 Dec. 1906, p. 1153; *ibid.*, 26 Sept. 1903, p. 537.

68   *Ibid.*, 24 Nov. 1906, p. 947; *ibid.*, 20 Jan. 1912, p. 115; *ibid.*, 22 Nov. 1913, p. 403a.

69   Keynes, *Indian Currency*, p. 117; Spalding, *Eastern Exchange*, p. 35.

70   *The Statist*, 17 Sept. 1898, p. 403; *ibid.*, 19 Nov. 1887, p. 558; A. Banerji, 'Revisiting the Exchange Standard, 1898–1913: 2. Operations', *Economic and Political Weekly*, 6 April 2002, p. 1355.

71   PP 1914 [Cd.7069], q. 2861, 2863; Shirras, *Indian Finance*, p. 384; PP 1898 [C.9037], q. 3473; Wadia and Joshi, *Money*, p. 338.

Co. in London.[72] Occasionally, the banks also raised funds through the sale to the Calcutta banks of internal bills of exchange drawn on Bombay.[73] Attempts in 1898/9 to borrow short-term funds from the government or to gain access to the government advances to the presidency banks ended in failure.[74]

Conclusion

The finance of Indian trade involved the purchase of export and import bills. Exchange banks in India bought export bills for rupees from exporters of Indian goods; these export bills were sent to London and either held to maturity or immediately discounted. With the proceeds of the matured/discounted export drafts they then purchased in London import/council bills, or some other form of remittance, for sterling, which were cashed/sold in India, providing them with the rupees needed for the purchase of more export drafts. As the export/import bills were sold forward, the trade they represented was effectively financed, in the case of export bills, partly by the exchange banks and partly by the London discount market, and, in the case of import bills, wholly by the exchange banks. Bank profits from the exchange business derived from the differences between the rates at which bills were bought and sold, and from speculation on the movement of the exchange rate and London/Indian interest rates and rupee paper prices.

The importance of council bills lay in the fact that without them the banks would have had problems remitting funds to India, and that the IO, through their price, could control the price of export/import bills and thus to a great extent the exchange. Unfortunately, the system possessed a number of flaws. In India there was a possibility that the exchange banks would retain few reserves, which could have an impact on domestic interest rates, particularly at the start of the period when the shipment of council bills took weeks. In London, the banks and discount houses could lack the necessary funds respectively to purchase import/council bills and to discount DA export bills. To avoid such an eventuality, the IO lent portions of its home balances (which comprised the unspent proceeds of council bills and Indian government loans) to the exchange banks and discount houses, allowing them to buy respectively council/import bills and DA export drafts, and sold to these institutions Indian government securities that could be used as collateral for further advances from the discount market/joint stock banks (Appendix 1). There was also a danger that the banks would use a form of remittance other than council bills, which would weaken the IO's control of the exchange, and, in the case of gold, involve the outflow of London specie (diminishing gold stocks) and the shipment

---

72   PP 1898 [C.9037], q. 3473; Muirhead, *Crisis Banking*, p. 214; *The Statist*, 13 Feb. 1897, p. 244. Lack of funds occasionally caused the presidency banks to refuse advances (e.g. *The Statist*, 19 Jan. 1889, p. 62).

73   PP 1898 [C.9037], q. 3481.

74   Baster, *The Imperial Banks*, p. 174.

by the IO of the metal despatched back to England. The various solutions to this problem are discussed in Chapter 8 of this book.

7

Council Bills: Purpose and Nature

Council bills became one of India's main methods of remittance in 1862 and were unique; other Empire countries moved funds to the UK via commercial bills of exchange through the agency of local or UK banks.[1] They were issued for a number of reasons. The most important was to allow the Indian government to remit to Britain the money needed to meet a variety of commitments, commonly known as the home charges, without the despatch of gold. Total expenditure on these various outlays amounted to £920.94m from 1879/80 to 1925/6, to which should be added the £133m spent on the purchase of silver for the minting of coins.[2] The charges were much resented. Critics argued that they were excessive and that their payment increased taxation, reduced demand and had a strong deflationary impact on the economy.[3]

The largest and most controversial component was the loan interest and Sinking Fund payments made, and the annuities purchased on behalf of the various guaranteed railway and irrigation companies, which from 1879/80 to 1925/6 accounted for 36.6 per cent (£337.46m) of total expenditure (Figure 7).[4] Private companies built railways from 1849 to 1869 and 1882 to 1924. The initial decision to use the private

---

1   BL, L/F/5/139, remittance from India, 10 March 1881, p. 13; Doraiswami, *Indian Finance*, p. 108.

2   Figure 7 sources. Annual home charges rose from £4.43m in 1857/8 to £14.5m in 1879/80, £17.2m in 1900/1, and £28.2m in 1920/1, and then fell to £26.21m in 1930/1 and £23.44m in 1936/7. From 1860 to 1937, home charges totalled at least £1,220m (Figure 7 sources; PP 1884/5 [352], pp. 204–7; PP 1930–31 [Cmd.3882], no. 128; PP 1935–36 [Cmd.5158], no. 166). Payments tended to be 'lumpy', large outlays occurring on the dates loan dividend and annuities were due (early January, April, June and October), sterling bills had to be repaid, silver bought and GSR investments made (BL, L/F/7/167, IO to B of E, 9 April 1914).

3   Bhattacharayya, *Financial Foundations*, pp. 255–6; PP 1872 [327], q. 7678; BL, L/F/5/139, DB, 7 Feb. 1887; Banerji, *Finances*, p. 286.

4   Figure 7 sources. The percentage fell from 32.6 per cent in 1880/1 to 30.9 per cent in 1925/6 (*ibid.*).

115

sector was based on the government's lack of building and railway management experience/expertise (and the danger that this would increase the cost of and lead to delays in construction), and the attractions of private sector finance, which removed the need to pay for infrastructure up front, avoided the costly suspension of construction that would occur when public funds were not forthcoming and would stimulate the inflow of non-railway investment.[5] To encourage the establishment of companies for the construction of lines, lucrative inducements had to be proffered.[6] Firms were given land, and the government guaranteed to make up any shortfall in interest payments to shareholders (usually set at 5 per cent) if low profits prevented the company paying the full dividend, and to pay the full interest payment from the date the share capital was raised to when the railway became operational. Companies were also allowed to retain any excess profit after the dividend had been met, and the government agreed to take over lines and provide full compensation if working expenses failed to be covered by revenues.[7]

Figure 7. Home charges. Loan interest and military spending, 1879/80–1925/6

Sources. PP 1886 [C.4730], no. 4; PP 1890–91 [C.6502], no. 50; PP 1896 [C.8238], no. 50; PP 1906 [Cd.2754], no. 71; PP 1914–16 [Cd.7799], no. 71; PP 1922 [Cmd.1778], no. 71; PP 1928 [Cmd. 3046], no. 65.

5   PP 1872 [327] *Select Committee on Finance and Financial Administration of India,* q. 1883, 1890, 2972, 7528; PP 1878–79 [312], q. 22.
6   After receiving permission from the IO to build a line, a promoter would set up a company, raise the necessary funds through the issue of share capital and then employ a contractor to build the line, which would be operated by company personnel.
7   Bhattacharayya, *Financial Foundations,* p. 105; S. C. Ghose, *Lectures on Indian Railway Economics, Part Three,* Calcutta 1923, p. 7; PP 1872 [327], p. 1720.

The provision of such dividend guarantees was by no means unusual; they had been used in France and a number of British colonies with some success.[8] In the case of India, they permitted government intervention in the administration of lines and attracted large numbers of subscribers, ensuring the success of flotations and allowing issues to be sold at a premium, i.e. above par, which reduced the sum on which the government had to guarantee interest.[9] Without such guarantees, investors and particularly investment trusts would have been reluctant to buy stock, afraid that companies would fail to pay the agreed dividend. Such fears initially were based on the absence of knowledge of likely returns, and, later, the losses of the early lines, the stubbornly low market price of railway company securities, and the uncommercial nature of some of the projects, which were partly built for military/strategic reasons.[10]

The guarantees, however, were far too generous, and, in most years, the money could have been raised more cheaply through the issue of Indian government sterling loans (had this been permitted).[11] It was also argued that they 'debauched' subscribers, who became so used to government subsidy that they would refuse to invest even in potentially lucrative lines that lacked a guarantee, and reduced line profitability, making the payment of shortfalls inevitable.[12] Government subsidy encouraged the finance of unproductive infrastructure, provided companies with little incentive to economise on railway management expenses or to maximise railway business and led to the construction of costly lines, the payment of the guarantee on the capital outlay removing any need to economise on building costs.[13] Certainly, State construction proved far cheaper than company construction, and, by 1881/2, £34.25m of the capital raised was providing a return of less than 4 per cent. Nonetheless, some of these criticisms appear to have been somewhat overdone. A portion of the high construction costs were no doubt 'pioneer expenses', the result of Indian construction inexperience and the difficulty in transporting building materials. It also seems likely that the generous profit allocations would have incentivised companies to maximise returns. By the early 1880s, some lines were indeed highly

8   Prasad, *Indian Railways*, p. 51.

9   PP 1872 [327], q. 1733–6, 3074; BL, L/F/5/64, memo, 1889. The government did not guarantee interest on the additional sum raised by selling stock at above £100, the price at which the stock would be repaid.

10 Banerji, *Finances*, p. 22; PP 1878 [333], p. 353; BL, L/F/5/64, memo, 1889. From 1870 to 1913, Indian railways possessed the same risk adjusted returns as UK railway debentures (M. Edelstein, *Overseas Investment in the Age of High Imperialism*, New York 1982, p. 135).

11 PP 1872 [327], q. 1525. The guaranteed interest was generally 1 per cent higher than that on government securities (Bhattacharayya, *Financial Foundations*, p. 106).

12 PP 1878–79 [312], q. 653.

13 Ghose, *Lectures … Part One*, pp. 7, 21; Vakil, *Financial Developments*, p. 195.

profitable and the Acworth Committee found that private sector companies managed lines just as efficiently as the State railways.[14]

The high cost of the lines and the mounting guaranteed interest payments/home charges prompted the government to change its railway policy. In 1869, it was decided that all lines would forthwith be built and operated by the State, that the necessary funds would be raised by the public issue of rupee loans (except where a project was to relieve famine) and that a loan would only be floated if the associated railway was likely to be remunerative, that is, generate an annual income equal to the interest paid on the money raised. Infrastructure for the transport of food to areas likely to be affected by famine, meanwhile, was to be financed from annual government revenues and by flotations only if public funds were unavailable.[15] Unfortunately, the policy proved unsustainable. Indian loans were expensive as compared to those issued in London, and the government was unable to provide the funds required for the construction of much-needed famine relief lines. The government thus turned again to the private sector, allowing the establishment of new companies, which would raise the necessary capital, construct the lines and operate them for up to twenty-five years, after which the capital raised would be repaid at par and the government would take over their operations.

To encourage the formation of such companies, it again guaranteed the payment of the interest on the capital raised during the period firms operated lines, generally 3.5 per cent, and permitted the companies to retain a quarter of the profits after the payment of this interest.[16] As already discussed, when the contracts with the original guaranteed railway companies came up for renewal, the IO also either purchased their shares/debenture capital, financing the acquisitions via the issue of sterling government loans, or exchanged the share/debentures for annuities. Six of the purchased companies were permitted to continue to operate their lines and were allowed to retain their original share capital, on which 3 to 3.5 per cent interest was again guaranteed, and received up to a quarter of net profits.[17]

A further controversial component of the home charges was the purchase of Indian government stores, which from 1879/80 to 1925/6 made up 9.9 per cent (£91.06m) of the total (Figure 8).[18] The IO London stores department's main purchases were

14 PP 1882 [181], p. 124; PP 1878–79 [312], q. 63; Ghose, *Lectures … Part Three*, p. 8.The mutiny also raised costs. Some engineers estimated the cost of transporting construction materials increased expenses by £1,000 to £2,000 per mile (PP 1878–79 [312], q. 212).
15 Prasad, *Indian Railways*, pp. 53–4; Vakil, *Financial Developments*, p. 203.
16 L. E. Davis and R. A. Huttenback, *Mammon and the Pursuit of Empire: The Economics of British Imperialism*, Cambridge 1988, p. 100; Prasad, *Indian Railways*, pp. 59–60
17 PP 1921 [Cmd.1512], p. 61; Ghose, *Lectures … Part One*, p. 12.
18 Figure 7 sources. From 1860/1 to 1925/6, payments for stores amounted to £118.6m (Figure 7 sources; PP 1884/5 [352], pp. 204–7). Stores' percentage of the total fell from 12.6 per cent in 1880/1 to 9.9 per cent in 1925/6 (Figure 7 sources). In addition to its purchasing role, the department additionally paid for stores bought by the guaranteed railway companies, sold goods returned from India, and, in the 1920s, found technical training positions for Indian

engineering goods for the state railways, clothing and arms for the troops based in India, coal, liquor and stationery.[19] Critics claimed that the materials bought were too expensive and should have been sourced in India. The prices paid were indeed relatively high, though on average lower than those of the Crown Agents, which bought goods for the Crown colonies.[20] The primary culprits were the commissions charged by UK government suppliers and the department's high costs and purchasing practices.

Figure 8. Home charges. Other components, 1879/80–1925/6

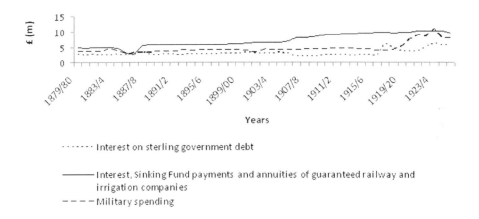

Sources. Figure 7 sources.

The department subcontracted many of its purchasing duties to other UK government departments. Military clothing and ordnances were acquired by the War Office, marine stores by the Admiralty, stamps by the Inland Revenue and stationery by the Stationery Office. All demanded high commissions for their services, which the department fought, and, occasionally, succeeded in reducing. In 1873, it simply refused to pay Admiralty fees that ranged from 8 to 35 per cent and obtained

---

students (PP1896 [C.8258], q. 2546; PP 1873 [311] *Select Committee on … the Purchase and Sale of Materials and Stores*, q. 7070; PP 1924–25 [201] *Report on the work of the India Store Department, 1924–25*, p. 3).

19   In 1896/7, 55.5 per cent of stores expenditure was spent on ordnance, 30 per cent on clothing, 7.7 per cent on miscellaneous articles for the commissariat and 5 per cent on medical items (PP 1898 [168], p. 91).

20   Sunderland, *Managing the British Empire*, chaps 2 and 3; Sunderland, *Managing British Colonial and Post-Colonial Development*, chap. 5.

reductions.[21] Likewise, the War Office in 1888 agreed to no longer include in its commission a charge for the interest paid on the capital equipment used to produce some of the goods supplied, and the Stationery Office in 1862 was persuaded to halve its charges given the large orders from India, though the subsequent fall in requisitions caused this decision to be reversed in 1886.[22]

As regards the stores bought by the department itself, prices were raised by a variety of additional costs/fees and its acquisition policies. The department's expenses ranged from 2 to 3.5 per cent of the value of the goods purchased, far higher than that of the Indian guaranteed railway companies, though lower than those of the Crown Agents.[23] Costs were relatively high as prices had to be communicated to India and various returns prepared; stores were largely bought from manufacturers rather than wholesalers, thus avoiding the latter's commission; and Indian requisitions for several goods were split into their constituent parts, there being a danger that if a company won an order for a number of items, it would subcontract those that it did not manufacture, for which it would charge a relatively high price.[24]

As well as the department's own expenses, India additionally had to pay inspection, shipping and insurance fees, and the remuneration of the consulting engineers who prepared engineering specifications and drawings and reported on tenders. Critics argued that inspection was unnecessary, given the use of reputable suppliers, who were conscious that criticism would damage their 'good name' and were willing to provide test certificates and/or written guarantees. The department disagreed. The goods supplied were often used in areas with few tools for repairs and situated a considerable distance from the nearest repair depot, which often kept small stocks of spare parts, and, if an article could not be mended, an order for a replacement would have to be made. The provision of faulty goods therefore could involve the loss of the use of equipment for a considerable period of time.[25]

There was similar criticism of the expenses and the remuneration earned by consulting engineers (though, where possible, the department used its own technical staff, and, for marine goods, the services of the Admiralty's technical branch) and of the fees paid to shipping companies for the transportation of orders.[26] Theoretically,

---

21   PP 1873 [311], q. 467, 6950, 7081. It was also claimed that the ships built by the Admiralty for India were relatively expensive (*ibid.*, q. 6949).

22   PP 1900 [Cd.130], p. 377; PP 1874 [263] *Report from the Select Committee on Public Departments*, p. 139; NA, T 20/6, pp. 89–90. War Office charges for clothing were 3 per cent and for ordnance 5 per cent (PP1896 [C.8258], q. 11733). The Inland Revenue fee for the supply of stamps was 3.7 per cent (PP1896 [C.8258], q. 11733).

23   Sunderland, *Managing the British Empire*, p. 76; PP 1924–25 [201], p. 9.

24   PP 1924–25 [201], pp. 10–11; BL, L/AG/9/8/6, pp. 4–6, memo, 8 Aug. 6.

25   PP 1924–25 [201], p. 3.

26   *Ibid.*, p. 12. From 1909 to 1915, consulting engineers' expenses (excluding their personal fee) were on average 0.68 per cent of the value of the contracts they oversaw, and, from 1919 to 1923, 1.14 per cent (PP 1924–25 [201], p. 27, appendix g). Personal fees in 1925 were fixed at £5,000 pa (*ibid.*, p. 12).

all shipments were publicly tendered and the contract awarded to the lowest bidder. In reality, there was no competition when delivery was urgent, and most of the tenders were won by the conference lines, which usually entered similar bids.[27] The chartering of vessels, which would have allowed the department to escape the clutches of the conferences was rarely adopted, as there was usually insufficient cargo to fill a single vessel, and the accumulation of goods until the chartering of a steamer became cost-effective would have led to delivery delays. The department further claimed that the conference rates were generally reasonable and lower than those offered to merchants, since the rings were well aware that excessive charges and the consequent loss of India's business would damage their profitability. Ships were thus only chartered when the conference rates were unusually high or they were unable to accommodate Indian cargoes.[28]

The prices paid for goods were further raised by the purchasing practices adopted – the lack of public tenders and the reluctance to cooperate with the Crown Agents or to acquire articles manufactured overseas. An analysis of the contracts published in the *Board of Trade Labour Gazette* from 1910 to 1914 shows that the department bought many products from just one firm, though to a far lesser extent than the Crown Agents (Table 2). Theoretically, all stores were obtained through public tenders advertised in popular newspapers. In reality, many quotes were rejected as the supplies were judged to be of inadequate quality, and a large proportion of goods were purchased via a more restricted tendering process involving a limited number of companies.[29] The department claimed that such tenders saved much 'useless expenditure of time and money'. Individual orders were often too small to be 'worthy of advertisement', others were for specialised or patented goods that could only be obtained from a small number of manufacturers, and the purchase of beer outside the London area would have increased inspection costs.[30] Advertisements also often failed to attract many tenders, potential applicants being put off by the bureaucracy and inspection involved in sales to India, and the use of a limited number of 'first rate people who have character to lose' lessened the likelihood of fraud and

27 PP 1909 [Cd.4670] *Report of the Royal Commission on Shipping Rings, Volume 3*, q. 9908, 9958, 10051–2, 10055.

28 *Ibid.*, q. 9909, 9927, 9943, 9950–1; PP 1909 [Cd.4685] *Report of the Royal Commission on Shipping Rings, Volume 4*, q. 14880. In such cases, the chartered ship filled up the unused space with coal (*ibid.* q. 10028–9).

29 PP 1873 [311], q. 7173; PP 1924–25 [201], p. 6. In 1924/5, 62 per cent of supplies were bought via public advertisement (PP 1924–25 [201], p. 7).

30 PP 1924–25 [201], p. 8; PP 1874 [263], p. xiv.

ensured the supply of quality products and the receipt of large trade discounts and favourable terms, the companies wishing to retain India's custom.[31]

Table 2. Purchases of stores by the Crown Agents and India Office, 1910–1914

	Crown Agents	India Office
Percentage of goods categories with three or more orders, of which 100 per cent were obtained from one supplier	16.1	10.8
Percentage of goods categories with three or more orders, of which 70 per cent were obtained from one supplier	31	18.7
Percentage of goods categories with three or more orders, of which 50 per cent were obtained from one supplier	60	55

Source. *Board of Trade Labour Gazette,* 1910–14.

Note. The CAs had 168 goods categories with more than three orders and the IO 203.

Departmental officials were similarly reluctant to 'club together' with other Imperial purchasing houses or to buy cheap foreign goods, though to a far lesser extent than the Crown Agents.[32] It was pointed out that the belief that the IO and the Crown Agents purchased the same stores and their competition drove up prices (and that greater trade discounts would be forthcoming if their orders were combined) was simply untrue. The goods ordered by the Crown colonies and India differed significantly.[33] Likewise, British manufacturers could often quote lower prices than their foreign competitors, and, where this was not the case, the price advantage of continental suppliers was often offset by higher inspection costs and delivery delays. In the 1920s, therefore, where there was foreign competition, a contract would only be awarded to the non-British company if the price difference between its and its UK rival's tenders was greater than 10 per cent.[34]

31 PP 1873 [311], q. 7073–6, 7174, 7190, 7274. To ensure that the prices charged were reasonable, the department and their inspectors compared those tendered with market rates. There is some evidence of price fixing in the railway engineering sector (J. F. Hargrave, 'Competition and Collusion in the British Railway Track Fittings Industry: The Case of the Anderton Foundry, 1800–1960', University of Durham, PhD thesis, 1992, p. 239).

32 In 1898/9, 1914/15 and 1924 the Department sourced respectively 1.6 per cent, 10 per cent and 12 per cent of supplies from countries other than the UK (PP 1904 [Cd.1915] *Review of the Trade of India, 1898/9 to 1902/3,* p. 87; PP 1908 [Cd.3969], *Review of the Trade of India, 1902/3 to 1906/7,* p. 105; PP 1913 [Cd.6783] *Review of the Trade of India, 1907/8 to 1911/12,* p. 88; PP 1916 [Cd.8343] *Review of the Trade of India, 1910/11 to 1914/15,* p. 144; PP 1924–25 [201], p. 6). In comparison, in 1911 and 1938/9 respectively £2,185 and £32,000 of Crown Agent orders were purchased overseas (CAS, 1913 report, file 53; NA, CAOG 12/97, CAs to CO, 27 Sept. 1939).

33 PP 1873 [311], q. 7012; PP 1874 [263], p. iv.

34 PP 1924–25 [201], p. 6; BL, L/F/7/224, p. 288.

Many critics, of course, claimed that the cost of the stores purchased was immaterial, arguing that they should rather have been sourced in India. Domestic purchase would diminish the home charges; promote the development and growth of industry and human capital; increase the wealth of the capitalist class, though many of the large engineering firms were actually owned and controlled by Europeans; weaken the impact of harvest failures by lessening the proportion of the population dependent on agriculture; and minimise the costly over-ordering of stores, a response to the long delivery delays of goods bought in England.[35] In 1883, a resolution was passed that allowed the Indian government to give preference to Indian manufactures where their price and quality was similar to that of UK goods.[36] The ruling, however, failed to slow British purchase. Indian administrators continued to send requisitions to England, often unaware of the availability of Indian goods, unwilling to take on the additional ordering work and fearful that supplies would be delivered late and/or be of poor quality. Many goods were also simply not manufactured in India, owing to inadequate demand, capital investment and skilled labour, and those that were produced were of relatively poor quality and expensive, and, even where this was not the case, were more costly at the point of delivery, due to the relatively high inland transport costs. A large number of engineering goods also comprised imported materials or components and were therefore not bona fide Indian manufactures, and, of course, the IO was well aware that the development of Indian industry would damage both British manufacturing and the triangular settlement system on which depended the prosperity of the City.[37]

In order to overcome these problems, in 1909 and 1913 the purchase of articles produced in India from imported materials was permitted, provided that 'a substantial part' of the manufacturing process had occurred in the subcontinent, and imported stores could be supplied by Indian firms involved in important construction works or if their rapid delivery resulted in an economy.[38] As a result of these initiatives, by 1900 India supplied all the government's beer requirements and a great deal of its military clothing.[39] Unable to obtain supplies from England during the First World War, the Indian government increasingly bought locally manufactured and imported materials, and, in 1922, an Indian stores department was established. This was permitted to buy domestically manufactured goods, if acquisition encouraged the development of domestic industries, and articles produced from imported

---

35 PP 1882 [181], pp. 125, 128; Bagchi, *Private Investment*, p. 40; V. Bahl, 'The Emergence of Large-Scale Steel Industry in India under British Colonial Rule, 1880–1907', *Indian Economic and Social History Review*, 31(4) (1994), p. 448; S. K. Sen, *Studies in Economic Policy and Development of India 1848–1926*, Calcutta 1966, p. 24.

36 *Ibid.*, p. 17.

37 Bagchi, *Private Investment*, pp. 299, 333–4, 336; PP 1883 [135], p. 100; PP 1896 [C.8258], q. 3957. The cost of Indian goods was raised by the relatively small production runs, which limited economies of scale.

38 Sen, *Studies*, pp. 22, 24.

39 PP 1900 [Cd.130], q. 14720, 15151.

materials, provided that neither the quality nor the price were 'unfavourable' and the goods were located in India at the time of the order or about to be shipped. To further encourage domestic purchase, Indian firms were given guaranteed orders, and the simultaneous tendering of orders in both India and the UK was introduced.[40]

Of the other home charges, from 1879/80 to 1925/6, 22.8 per cent (£210.35m) was military spending, 15.2 per cent (£140.4m) interest on Indian government London debt, and 10.9 per cent (£100.63m) expenditure on civil pensions/furloughs (Figures 7 and 8).[41] Civil pensions/furloughs comprised the pensions paid to former employees of the East India Company and British civil servants who had served at the IO and in India, and the allowances paid to Indian administrators during their annual leave in Britain. The Indian government believed them to be excessive; the Office countered that they were no greater than those paid to British civil servants.[42] Payments to the army encompassed effective charges (£88.6m) – a 'capitation' fee of £10 and, from 1891, £7 10s for every British soldier serving in India or defending its interests elsewhere to cover the cost of recruitment, training and maintenance until embarkation, and a contribution to the Chelsea and Kilmainham military hospitals – and non-effective charges (£115.9m), largely the pensions paid to officers and non-commissioned officers and their widows/families. Naval expenses (£5.88m), meanwhile, included an annual contribution of £117,000 (lowered, from 1901, to £100,000) to the Admiralty to cover the cost of the squadron that patrolled Indian waters, plus the payment of the local expenses of these vessels and the salaries of British officers manning Indian government defence vessels.[43]

All the military payments were believed to be excessive. Critics thought the effective charges to be extortionate and strongly objected to having to pay for Indian troops, even when they were deployed outside the country. It was argued that such military spending was only necessary because of India's membership of the Empire, that the cost of recruiting and training the soldiers was too high and that the unilateral decision by the War Office to introduce short service (the enlistment of soldiers for seven rather than ten years) had greatly increased transportation costs. As for the contribution to the Royal Navy, this was again immoderate, particularly as the vessels were often employed outside Indian waters. The 1896/1900 Welby Commission, established to investigate the whole issue, remained unconvinced, though it did recommend that the British Treasury pay half the troop transportation costs. There was no evidence that India would have been less susceptible to external attack had

40 *The Statist*, 17 Dec. 1921, p. 1078; Sen, *Studies*, pp. 28–9; PP 1924–25 [201], p. 21.
41 From 1860/1 to 1925/6, dividend payments amounted to £182.4m (Figure 7 sources; PP 1884/5 [352], pp. 204–7). Military spending's percentage of the total fell from 24.1 per cent in 1880/1 to 22.8 per cent in 1925/6. The percentages for interest payments in the same years are 16.2 per cent and 19.1 per cent, and for civil pensions/furloughs 11.2 per cent and 7 per cent (Figure 7 sources).
42 H. M. Hyndman, *The Bankruptcy of India*, London 1886, p. 132.
43 Figure 7 sources; Bhattacharayya, *Financial Foundations*, p. 97; PP 1900 [Cd.131] *Indian Expenditure Commission, Volume 4*, pp. 137–40.

she been independent, and soldiers had only been deployed to areas where unrest would damage the country's interests; where this was not the case, as in Afghanistan, the additional expenses had been recompensed. Service in Egypt was essential to keep open the Suez Canal; in East Africa, China and the Malay Peninsula to protect trade with these regions; and in Afghanistan, to defend India's frontiers. The capitation charge was similarly regarded as reasonable, given the need for high calibre troops, the rise in recruitment costs and India's failure to contribute her fair share to the expenses of the two military hospitals; and it was discovered that short service would result in long-term savings by reducing pension costs. As regards India's contribution to its naval defence, this was modest, equal to that paid by the Australian and Cape governments, and no vessels were employed outside the country's waters without Indian government permission.[44]

Bringing up the rear of the home charges was expenditure on the administration of the subcontinent, which was relatively moderate. Civil administration in England, largely the salaries of those who worked at the IO, the costs of Coopers Hill Civil Engineering College and the fees paid to the Bank of England for the issue and management of loans and other work accounted from 1879/80 to 1925/6 for just 1.1 per cent of the total (£10.15m) and civil administration in India for 1.7 per cent (£15.45m) (Figure 8).[45] Inevitably, India resented the payments. It was claimed that the salaries of the London and India based civil servants were overgenerous, that the long home leaves, early retirement and lavish amenities of Indian administrators were unnecessary and that the payment of the costs of the Coopers Hill College was unfair, as many of its graduates never worked in India. The UK government disagreed, though the Welby Commission recommended that the cost of civil arbitration in England be shared with the British Treasury, the 1924 Retrenchment Committee required IO expenditures to be cut by £48,700, and, in 1931, the salaries of new recruits to the Indian civil service were reduced.[46] It was also unsympathetic to allegations that India's subsidisation of various communications projects was unfair, pointing out that the country greatly benefitted from their existence; however, over time, it reduced diplomatic expenses included in the Indian civil administration charges.[47] The contribution to the cost of the administration of the

---

44 PP 1900 [Cd.131], pp. 137–42; Bhattacharayya, *Financial Foundations*, pp. 139, 258. See also Pandit, *India's Balance*, p. 64; Sen, *Colonies*, pp. 36–7.

45 In 1880/1 and 1925/6, Civil Administration (England) accounted for respectively 1.1 per cent and 0.74 per cent of the total, and Civil Administration (India) for respectively 1.73 and 6.9 per cent of the total (Figure 7 sources).

46 Maddison, *Class Structure*, chap. 3; Husain, 'The Organisation', pp. 314–15; Sen, *Colonies*, pp. 37–8. The Indian government also grumbled that the Coopers Hill College was established without its consent and it had no involvement in the determination of the budget, which was excessive (PP 1896 [C.8258], q. 11940–2).

47 India variously subsidised the Euphrates & Tigris Steam Navigation Co., the Peninsular and Oriental Steam Co., the Red Sea Telegraph line and the Zanzibar-Mauritius cable (Pandit, *India's Balance*, p. 61; PP 1900 [Cd.131], p. 136).

Straits Settlements and the military and political expenses of Aden ceased in the 1860s, and, in 1901 and 1903, the stipends paid towards the expenses of the consular missions to respectively Persia and China came to an end.[48]

Overall, the home charges consumed just 0.9 to 1.3 per cent of India's National Domestic Product (1868 to 1930), generally financed services that the country was unable to supply itself and bestowed valuable benefits.[49] The most important of these was the maximisation of Indian exports, which enabled the country to develop, aided British industry through the provision of cheap raw materials, increased Indian incomes and demand for British imports, and permitted the triangular settlement system that allowed the overseas lending that was so crucial to the prosperity of the City and to India. The loans on which guaranteed and other interest was paid financed the construction of the railways that opened up new areas for development and transported produce out and capital equipment/imports into the country, and a portion of Indian government loans was used for the maintenance of a stable exchange, of crucial importance to exporters. Likewise, the various civil and military charges ensured internal peace and protection from foreign aggression, both important for development; the administration provided by the British was arguably superior and cheaper than any Indian alternative and greatly benefitted the commercial sector; and, as discussed, many of the stores purchased in the UK were simply not available in India and partly comprised various railway materials.[50]

The sale of council bills also maximised Indian exports in their own right. They gave the IO control over the exchange rate, ensuring that it remained stable, and reduced the costs of trade. Any attempt by the exchange banks to 'squeeze' merchants could be halted by a rise in council bill prices that would be immediately matched by the banks, which were well aware that they would lose clients if their import/export bills were relatively more expensive than council bills.[51] Likewise, the council bills allowed the banks to hedge exchange risks, with any loss suffered from the fall in the exchange on export bills being offset by the gain on councils bills (and vice versa). Without such 'cover', banks would have passed the cost of the risk onto their clients and charged an export bill discount rate similar to that on drafts sent

48 King, *The History ... Vol. 1*, p. 260; Pandit, *India's Balance*, p. 61. India contributed a third of the cost of the China mission, and, from 1891, £12,500 (King, *The History... Vol. 1*, p. 260; PP 1900 [Cd.131], p. 136).

49 Maddison, *Class Structure*, p. 87.

50 T. Morrison, *The Economic Transition in India*, London 1911, pp. 238–9; L. Rai, *England's Debt to India*, London 1917, pp. 81, 83; C. Cristiano, 'Keynes and India, 1909–1913: A Study of Foreign Investment Policy', *European Journal of the History of Economic Thought*, 16 (2) (2009), pp. 308–9.

51 PP 1887 [C.5099], q. 3277. Exporters of goods from India would arrange for the UK purchaser to send the amount owed to India through the purchase of a council bill. Those moving funds to India would buy council bills in preference to import bills (PP 1887 [C.5099], q. 3273, 3277). The relationship between council bill and import bill prices only broke down when the banks lacked funds in India to meet import drafts and thus wished clients to switch to council bills (*The Statist*, 19 Jan. 1889, p. 62).

from India to China and Japan, which in 1887, at 12 per cent, was double that of bills bound for the UK.[52]

As discussed below, the bills additionally halted the flow of gold into and out of India, helping to keep London interest rates low, to the benefit of both the UK and India, and assisted the Imperial economy in other ways. The drafts shackled Indian trade to London based financial, shipping, trading and insurance networks and thus maximised the profits of all these sectors, and, by increasing the number of export bills handled by the discount market, contributed to the growth of that financial bazaar and enhanced its liquidity, allowing interest rates to be kept low, again insulating Bank of England gold stocks.[53]

The nature of bills

From 1850/1 to 1924/5, £994.1m of council bills were issued (Figure 9).[54] The drafts were sold through tenders, which ensured high prices, but through the resultant publicity drew attention to the size of the home balances, and, in the early part of the period, had a greater impact on the exchange than if the number of bills sold and prices charged had been kept secret.[55] The auctions were organised by the Bank of England, the cost of its duties being met from the remuneration it received from the maintenance of the IO's current account.[56] Tenderers could thus be confident that the process would be fair, and, from 1898, the Bank could monitor the number of bills issued and determine likely remittances to India via gold. Auctions were held initially on the first Wednesday of each month, then on two Wednesdays per month, and, from 1876, every Wednesday, an innovation much criticised by some in the City who argued that the more regular sales would amplify exchange fluctuations and increase costs. At each auction, a previously announced specified number of bills were offered for sale. The IO, however, was not bound to allot the full amount, and, until 1878, those left unsold/withheld were carried forward to the following

52   PP 1914 [Cd.7069], q. 6600; PP 1887 [C.5099], q. 3273–83. Like the UK, China and Japan's exports from India were greater than their exports to the continent. Merchants, in turn, would then have passed the extra cost on to the native producer of the produce sold, reducing Indian incomes (*The Statist*, 6 Sept. 1890, p. 272).

53   G. Balachandran, 'Introduction', in G. Balachandran (ed.), *India and the World Economy, 1850–1950*, Oxford 2003, pp. 12–14. It was also suggested that, prior to 1898, the IO and the Bank of England used council bill sales to control the price of silver on the London market. High bill prices increased the amount of the metal shipped to India and its price in London and vice versa. Some further claimed that, in the late 1880s, bill/silver prices were kept low in order reduce the competitiveness of American wheat/cotton relative to that produced in India (Senate of the United States, Speech by Hon. William M. Stewart, 1 May 1888).

54   Figure 9 sources.

55   PP 1878–79 [312], q. 562, 564; BL, L/F/5/64, memo, 7 Aug. 1880, p. 4.

56   BL, L/F/7/164, B of E to IO, 19 Aug. 1887. The Bank only charged the IO for the payment of stamp duty (PP 1871 [363], q. 9379).

Wednesday.[57] The minimum tender was rs10,000, which reduced issue costs and precluded applications from small traders (who were left with little option but to use the exchange banks), though, in 1888, this rule appears to have been temporarily suspended in an attempt to force the banks to resume bill purchase.[58]

Figure 9. Sales of council and reverse council bills, purchase of sterling and exports, 1850/1–1939/40

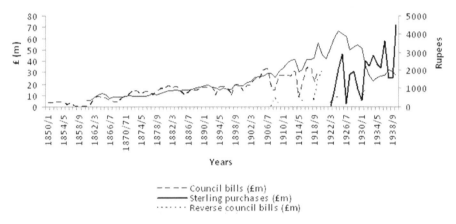

Sources. PP 1929–30 [Cmd.3386], p. 19; PP 1930–31 [Cmd.3670]; PP 1931–32 [Cmd.3969]; PP 1931–32 [Cmd.4161]; PP 1932–33 [Cmd.4416]; PP 1933–34 [Cmd.4695]; PP 1930–31 [Cmd.3882], no. 113; PP 1938–39 [Cmd.6079], no. 150; PP 1942–43 [Cmd.6441], no. 140; PP 1887 [C.5210], no. 57; PP 1896 [C.8238], no. 61; PP 1899 [C.9376], p. 139; PP 1914–16 [Cd.7799], no. 84; PP 1922 [Cmd.1778], nos 84, 84a; PP 1930–31 [Cmd.3882], nos 113–14; B. R. Mitchell, *International Historical Statistics: Africa, Asia and Oceania, 1750–2000*, London 2003, p. 537.

On arrival in India, bills were presented to one of three Indian treasuries, and the purchaser received their value, though, to avoid the payment of forgeries, only after the Indian authorities had received the counterfoil, which the IO despatched separately. The sums paid out were recorded and the accounts theoretically sent to the IO where the London and Indian payments were compared, again to counter fraud. In reality, in 1860, such comparisons had not been made for twelve to fourteen years, and, for many years thereafter, monitoring was made difficult by the incompleteness and inaccuracy of the Indian accounts and the practice in London of two different officials recording sales in two sets of account books.[59]

Bills could be drawn in Calcutta, Madras or Bombay, though initially only 10 lakhs could be obtained in each of the centres to prevent the depletion of their treasuries.

---

57 BL, L/F/5/139, remittance from India, 10 March 1881, pp. 13–14; Chablani, *Indian Currency and Exchange*, p. 66; Crump, *The English Manual*, chap. 17, part 5.

58 PP 1899 [C.9376], p. 24; BL, L/F/5/59, note, 28 March 1883; *The Statist*, 11 Aug. 1888, p. 152.

59 PP 1873 [354], q. 4136–9; *ibid.*, q. 2692–7, 2707.

Little demand for funds in Madras caused the restriction on that city to be abolished in 1864, and, as their Treasury funds increased, the limits on Calcutta and Bombay were also lifted, though the heavy demands on the Bombay Treasury caused by the Abyssinian campaign forced drawings on this centre to be suspended from 1867 to 1870.[60] Repeated attempts to add Karachi and Rangoon as places of encashment were unsuccessful.[61] The use of both cities would require the establishment of reserve treasuries, lose the government the commission paid on the internal drafts used to transfer cash between the presidency towns and these conurbations, and reduce the sums held in Bombay/Calcutta and thus increase the possibility of currency shortages/high interest rates. Furthermore, there was little exchange bank demand for drafts drawn on either city, as any money not used in the purchase of export bills either lay idle, earning no interest, or had to be returned to Bombay/Calcutta.[62]

Three types of council bill were offered/drawn – the basic council bill, the telegraphic/deferred telegraphic transfer, of which £76.73m were issued from 1919/20 to 1934/5, and intermediates.[63] The basic council bill was sent to India by ship and thus had a currency of sixty days, and, on the arrival of the telegraph, was gradually superseded by telegraphic transfers.[64] These were introduced in 1876, suspended in 1877 and reinstated in 1882. The transfer of money by telegraph allowed the immediate movement of funds, enabling banks to hold smaller reserves and to meet sudden upturns in trade/increased supplies of export bills without having to remit London gold/intercept gold bound for London. There were thus fewer currency shortages and hikes in Indian interest rates and less likelihood of a fall in London gold stocks/higher London interest rates.[65] Moreover, they saved the Indian government money. Less cash sat in its Treasury awaiting the arrival of council bills and earning no interest, and the IO could charge a higher price for the transfers.[66] There were, however, drawbacks. There were dangers that excessive use would deplete Treasury balances, the transfers would increase exchange destabilising speculation on interest rate differentials/exchange rates, and the exchange banks would reduce the size of their reserves (with all that entailed) or use the interest savings that resulted from the use

---

60 PP 1899 [C.9376], pp. 24–5.
61 Calls were made in 1894, 1898 and 1899–1900 (Rangoon) and 1912 (Karachi) (PP 1896 [166] *Financial Statement of Government of India, 1896–97*, p. 89; PP 1900 [225], p. 148; BL, L/F/7/178, note, no date, 1912).
62 PP 1896 [166], pp. 89–90; BL, L/F/7/178, note, no date, 1912. The banks financed both centres from Calcutta/Bombay.
63 PP 1929–30 [Cmd.3386], p. 19; PP 1930–31 [Cmd.3670]; PP 1931–32 [Cmd.3969]; PP 1931–32 [Cmd. 4161] *East India. Accounts and Estimates 1932–1933*; PP 1932–33 [Cmd.4416] *East India. Accounts and Estimates 1933-1934*; PP 1933–34 [Cmd.4695] *East India. Accounts and Estimates 1934–1935*; PP 1934–35 [Cmd. 5000] *East India. Accounts and Estimates 1935–1936*.
64 PP 1899 [C.9376], **p. 24.**
65 PP 1914 [Cd.7069], q. 1370.
66 PP 1898 [C.9037], q. 4351.

of the drafts to provide unfair competition in the Indian deposit market.[67] To avoid the latter, the IO sold the transfers at a premium of at least $^3/_{32}$d above the minimum price fixed for basic bills in the preceding week, and, later, $^1/_{32}$d above the maximum price. Both premiums took account of the amount, based on an Indian interest rate of 5 per cent, that the exchange banks would gain by receiving the money in India immediately rather than 15 days hence.[68] If Indian interest rates rose above 5 per cent, the premium rose to $^2/_{32}$d, and, in 1904, this practice was formalised – $^2/_{32}$d being charged when either the Calcutta or Bombay rates rose above 6 per cent; from 1906, over 9 per cent; and, after 1925, above 8 per cent, though in 1916, fear that the perceived rise in the cost of the transfers would lead to further Indian stringency caused the additional payment to be waived.[69]

Deferred telegraphic transfers were first sold in 1915 when shipping difficulties had greatly increased the time it took to transport basic council bills to India. The obvious solution to the problem, encouraging the use of telegraphic transfers by reducing their price, would have rapidly depleted the Indian Treasury. The next best option was therefore chosen, which was to sell at the same price as council bills telegraphic transfers that were payable in India sixteen days after issue rather than immediately.[70] Remitters thus obtained the funds required and the Indian Treasury was given time to accumulate the money needed to cash the bills.

Intermediates, or 'specials' if they took the form of telegraphic transfers, were sold on a first come, first served basis between the Wednesday tenders.[71] Only a limited amount were offered for sale, unless, after 1898, the price reached the gold import point, and they were sold at a premium of 1/32d above the minimum price obtained at the previous Wednesday auction.[72] An attempt in 1886 to sell the drafts at the tender minimum was abandoned, as it was thought unfair to those who had bid above this price, and an experiment nine years later to sell at the highest allotment price and thus strengthen the exchange failed to attract a sufficient number of applicants.[73] The bills benefitted both the remitters and India. Remitters obtained the exact amount of drafts required, having to worry about neither the size of allocations nor minimum applications.[74] The IO ensured that any sudden increase in

---

67 *The Statist*, 14 Dec. 1889, p. 664; BL, L/F/5/139, IO to Governor General, 1 March 1900; *ibid.*, IO to G of I, 19 July 1901.

68 BL, L/F/5/59, note, 28 Nov. 1882; Chablani, *Indian Currency and Exchange*, p. 66.

69 *The Statist*, 21 Oct. 1899, p. 619; BL, L/F/5/139, IO to G of I, 19 July 1901; BL, L/F/7/182, note, 20 March 1913; *ibid.*, minute, 18 Jan. 1916; *ibid.*, fol. 1140, minute, 19 Jan. 1916; Chablani, *Indian Currency and Exchange*, p. 66. An above 5 per cent interest rate would allow the banks to make a profit from the use of the bills.

70 BL, L/F/7/188, cutting; *The Statist*, 27 Feb. 1915; *ibid.*, fol. 719, note, no date, 1915; *ibid.*, B of E, 22 Feb. 1915; BL, L/F/5/80, note, 12 Dec. 1916.

71 Ambedkar, *The Problem*, chap. 7; PP 1898 [C.9037], q. 4308–9.

72 PP 1914 [Cd.7069], q. 1342–3; BL, L/F/5/59, note, 28 Nov. 1882. The gold import point is discussed in the following chapter.

73 *The Statist*, 29 May 1886, p. 580; *ibid.*, 12 Jan. 1895, p. 35.

74 BL, L/F/5/170, Indian Tea Association to IO, 21 Dec. 1916.

demand for remittance was met through drafts rather than gold, minimised the fall in the exchange that often occurred between auctions and obtained a price premium, though some claimed that Wednesday applicants were encouraged to put in low tenders in the knowledge they could buy low priced intermediates if their applications were unsuccessful.[75]

The main purchasers of council bills in all their various guises were the exchange banks and trading companies. In the three months from April to June 1920, 72 per cent of the drafts issued were bought by banks and 27 per cent by merchants, the former making more and larger purchases than the latter.[76] Of the bank acquisitions, 40 per cent were bought by exchange banks and the remainder by non-British institutions (16.6%) and UK joint stock/merchant banks (10.3%). Other purchasers included non-guarantee railway companies moving funds to India, the four bullion dealers that dominated the London specie market and, in the 1860s, the Crown Agents, which used the bills to move funds to India and thence to Ceylon and Mauritius, either in the form of gold, or, if the rate of exchange was favourable, through commercial bills of exchange.[77] There were also sales in China (£0.310 in 1856/7 and 1866/7–1867/8) and, from 1918 to 1920, in America.[78] To pay for silver HM Treasury had purchased from the American government on India's behalf, the IO sold bills via the Federal Reserve Bank of New York to the US Treasury, which then sold them on to merchants and the exchange banks, transferring the dollar proceeds to the UK government's New York account from whence they were used to pay Britain's US dollar debts.[79] Further US sales were then made through the Bank of Montreal and the Ottawa Mint, and the proceeds shipped to India in gold.[80]

75 BL, L/F/5/139, memo 1043, Hamilton, 1 Dec. 1876; *The Statist*, 14 Dec. 1912, p. 709; PP 1914 [Cd.7069], q. 1344–5.

76 The average number of purchases and the average value of each purchase per company were respectively 35.2 and £29,030 for the exchange banks; 12.5 and £27,372 for the foreign/joint stock/merchant banks; and 6.65 and £12,921 for the trading companies. The exchange bank buyers were the Chartered Bank of India, Australia & China (9.89%), the Eastern Bank (7.2%), the Hong Kong & Shanghai Banking Corp. (6.72%), the Mercantile Bank of India (7.97%) and the National Bank of India (7.87%). The largest merchant purchasers (of thirty-two companies) were E. D. Sassoon (5.74%), Mitsui & Co. Ltd (4.68%) and Cox & Co. (5.23%). The main UK joint stock/merchant banks (of seven) were Coutts & Co. (3.54%), the London Joint City and Midland Bank (2.5%) and Barclays Bank (2.5%). The largest foreign bank buyers (of seven) were the Bank of Taiwan (4.19%), the Yokohama Specie Bank (3.6%) and the International Banking Corp. (3.6%) (BL, L/AG/24/36).

77 *The Statist*, 26 Oct. 1895, p. 488; BL, L/AG/24/36; NA, CO 167/444/8393, CAs to CO, 23 Aug. 1862; NA, CO 54/429/4764, CAs to Ceylon, 26 Mar. 1867.

78 PP 1884/5 [352], pp. 204–7.

79 NA, T 120/2, Treasury to IO, 18 May 1920; *The Statist*, 9 Feb. 1918, p. 217. Later rupee credits were placed at the disposal of the Federal Reserve Bank and drawn by the US Treasury (NA, T 120/2, Treasury to IO, 18 May 1920).

80 PP 1920 [Cmd.529], p. 103; *The Statist*, 26 July 1919, p. 132.

Supply and demand of bills

Like all commodities, sales of council bills and the prices charged for them were determined by a combination of supply and demand. The number of bills offered for sale was dependent on the size of India's UK commitments, which rose over time; ad hoc events, such as the GSR 1908 support of the exchange and the need in 1909/11 to replenish its contents; the ability of the Indian Treasury to cash the bills; and, as discussed in the following chapter, from 1904, the prices paid for the drafts.[81] The amount offered also tended to rise on the eve and after the flotation of rupee loans. The higher sales allowed UK applicants to cheaply remit to India down/full payments for debentures purchased, steadied the exchange and reduced Indian interest rates, encouraging Indian applications for debentures.[82]

Demand can be split into trade and non-trade factors. Trade determinants included the level of Indian exports/imports and sales of export/import bills, the time of year and the extent of the trade imbalances between India, the UK and the Far East. If exports were high, the exchange banks would need rupees in India to purchase export bills, and, through their encashment in England, would have sufficient sterling to buy council drafts.[83] The level of exports, in turn, was primarily dictated by the appearance of the monsoon, the state of Indian harvests and a variety of lesser factors, such as European demand for Indian produce, World commodity prices, the availability of shipping and exporter speculation.[84] Merchants dealing in non-perishable goods would speculate by holding back exports if they believed that prices would rise in the near future or the exchange rate would fall, financing future purchases of produce from their own cash resources or via exchange bank and other bank loans, for which the undelivered goods served as collateral.[85] Such holdbacks often occurred towards the end of the trading period when prices sometimes rose and the exchange fell, and, in the case of early/mid-season exchange rises, caused the exchange to right itself via the fall in the demand for and price of council bills.[86]

---

81 PP [Cd.7069], q. 478; PP 1914 [Cd.7236] *Royal Commission on Indian Finance and Currency. Final Report*, paras 10, 31, 32, 143, 144, 174–6; British-Indian, *Finance*, p. 300. In 1909/10, £6.63m of bill sales were for the GSR (PP 1910 [169] *Return of Indian Financial Statement and Budget for 1910–11*, p. 272).

82 *The Statist*, 10 July 1897, p. 46; *ibid.*, 21 July 1906, p. 87.

83 A Pearson product moment correlation of net exports and council bill sales from 1870/1 to 1918/19 gives a coefficient of 0.727046 (net export figures from Ambedkar, *The Problem*, chap. 7, table 52). Occasionally, when the future exchange was likely to move against them, the banks would refuse to buy export bills (PP 1887 [C.5099], q. 2823, 2829).

84 PP 1898 [C.9037], q. 2681. E.g. *The Statist*, 28 May 1898, p. 861; *ibid.*, 14 May 1898, p. 786; *ibid.*, 20 April 1901, p. 699. When harvests failed, some council bills would be sold for the transfer of famine relief funds raised in London (*ibid.*, 30 Jan. 1897, p. 112).

85 *Ibid.*, 18 April 1896, p. 516; *ibid.*, 22 Jan. 1898, p. 120; PP 1898 [C.9037], q. 4276.

86 *The Statist*, 28 May 1898, p. 861; *ibid.*, 9 May 1896, p. 624; *ibid.*, 6 Feb. 1897, p. 206. Merchants would expect an early/mid-season exchange bubble to burst and would thus hold back produce.

By contrast, if imports into India were high, more money could be moved via import bills and less by council bills and vice versa, the level of imports depending on Indian demand/prosperity and the exchange rate. When the rate was low, UK merchants would hold back exports until there was a rise, financing the future purchase of goods with loans from the exchange banks. On at least one occasion, though, when merchants were 'speculating in the exchange', halting exports in the expectation of a rise, the exchange banks forced them to return to trading by withdrawing these loans.[87]

As regards the influence of time and trade balances, demand rose prior to holidays and in the weeks leading up to and during the trading season (October to March).[88] To meet this demand, the IO increased its supply of bills, stockpiling money for when purchases fell in the low-trade months, but refused to make all or most its sales during this period, even though such a policy would reduce the number and cost of council bill auctions and avoid the sale of the bills at low prices during the slack season.[89] Such a strategy would be risky in that a poor harvest would severely restrict receipts, high sales would depress prices, and the later non-availability of drafts in the non-trading period would inconvenience and damage the goodwill of the banks and force them to ship specie.[90]

The trade imbalances between India, Britain and the Far East were significant because they were offset through the purchase of council bills. India's exports of opium and cotton yarn/goods to China, Japan, Manila and Singapore were far greater than its imports from these countries. Alternatively, Britain's exports to the Orient were miniscule, but its imports, mainly of silk, were relatively large. To offset these imbalances, the exchange banks bought in India and for rupees the bills of exchange drawn by Indian exporters on the Far Eastern purchasers of their goods and sent them to China/Japan, etc. Their Far Eastern branches then used the payments made on these drafts to buy bills drawn by Oriental exporters of produce on British importers, which were sent to London. Here, their London headquarters used the sterling payments on these drafts to buy council bills, and their Indian branches then employed the rupees paid in India on these bills to finance the purchase of the Indian drafts drawn on the Far East. The process avoided the banks moving specie to the Orient and thus protected London gold stocks and also increased the demand for council bills.[91]

---

87 *The Statist*, 11 May 1901, p. 853; *ibid.*, 22 Aug. 1903, p. 341; *ibid.*, 4 Sept. 1886, p. 252; *ibid.*, 9 Dec. 1893, p. 652.

88 During holidays, demand fell (*ibid.*, 19 Nov. 1904, p. 909).

89 PP 1898 [C.9037], q. 5537; BL, L/F/5/139, memo 1043, Hamilton, 1 Dec. 1876. From 1894/5 to 1912/13, 44 per cent more bills were sold from October to March than from April to September (PP 1914 [Cd.7070], appendix 7, table 3, p. 233).

90 PP 1914 [Cd.7069], q. 1481; PP 1898 [C.9037], q. 4346; BL, L/F/5/139, IO to G of I, 14 Dec. 1869.

91 *The Statist*, 14 Oct. 1882, p. 428; Crump, *The English Manual*, chap. 17, part 3.

Sales of council bills on the Far Eastern 'account' were dependent on the amount of goods exported from India to China/Japan, etc., and from the Orient to Britain, as well as on Far Eastern and UK demand for respectively Indian and Chinese/Japanese merchandise.[92] Sales peaked in 1895 on the payment in silver of a large war indemnity by China to Japan and the later issue in London of a Chinese loan. The indemnity prompted speculators to buy bills in the belief that China would source some of the silver from India, and Japan would increase its imports of Indian goods. There was also some buying by the Chartered Bank of India, acting on behalf of its Japanese agent, and by the Japanese government, which remitted some of its balances in London to India, where they were lent to Japanese merchants wishing to buy Indian produce, the merchants eventually repaying the advances in Japan. Later in the year, a £1m Chinese loan floated in London led to further purchases by speculators, who believed that a portion of the issue would again be used to buy Indian goods. Sales on the China account were also exceptionally great in 1902, 1909 and 1911; they were similarly high, on behalf of Japan, in 1904, owing to large Japanese imports of Indian goods as a result of the Russo-Japanese War, and again in 1906, when the failure of the domestic rice crop increased imports of Indian rice, and the Japanese government used the bills to transfer some of the proceeds of that year's London loan issue to India, where they were again lent to Japanese merchants.[93]

Non-trade determinants of demand included the level of capital investment in India, the price of bills, the availability and relative price of other forms of remittance, and the amount of cash held in the exchange banks' Indian reserves: if reserves were high, less money would be brought over and vice versa.[94] Demand was also influenced by a myriad of disparate factors. For example, sales rose in 1892, owing to the imminent failure of the New Oriental Bank Corp. and fears of a run on other exchange banks; in 1896, because American purchases of Indian silver prompted domestic speculation in the metal; and in 1902, when the possibility of conflict in Afghanistan caused Indians to increase their hoards of rupees.[95]

Of more significance were London and Indian interest rates and the exchange rate. High London rates lessened the demand for Indian produce, and the exchange banks were less willing and able to purchase bills. The banks reaped a greater return from investing their export bill proceeds than by using them to buy council bills or import bills, and they obtained a lower price when discounting DA export bills and had to pay a high rate for the London bank loans sometimes used to finance bill purchases. Their Indian branches were consequently deprived of funds and either purchased fewer export drafts, which again reduced the demand for council bills,

---

92   *The Statist*, 31 Aug. 1895, p. 265; *ibid.*, 12 Sept. 1885, p. 282, *ibid.*, 16 Oct. 1886, p. 422.

93   *Ibid.*, 30 March 1895, p. 405; *ibid.*, 13 July 1895, p. 43; *ibid.*, 5 Oct. 1895, p. 414; *ibid.*, 1 March 1902, p. 3; *ibid.*, 24 April 1909, p. 823; *ibid.*, 15 July 1911, p. 107; *ibid.*, 13 Feb. 1904, p. 277; *ibid.*, 17 Feb. 1906, p. 274.

94   *Ibid.*, 25 Feb. 1905, p. 323. A Pearson product moment correlation of average annual prices and the annual amount of council bills sold from 1850/1 to 1924/5 gives a coefficient of 0.54.

95   *Ibid.*, 11 June 1892, p. 652; *ibid.*, 27 June 1896, p. 918; *ibid.*, 18 Feb. 1905, p. 273.

or borrowed the necessary finance, both actions increasing Indian interest rates and further damaging trade and the demand for export/council bills.[96]

High Indian interest rates, alternatively, increased bill demand. Facing costly Indian bank loans, exporters were less willing to hold back their produce and fund future business with debt, and the exchange banks were more likely to finance the purchase of export bills with money remitted from England rather than Indian loans. The banks also indulged in speculation.[97] While relatively high British interest rates caused them to shift cash to London, relatively high Indian rates prompted a movement of their UK reserves and money borrowed from British joint stock banks in the opposite direction.[98] Such transfers particularly occurred after the issue of rupee loans and during the trading season when Indian rates tended to rise. After the issue of rupee debentures, money left the Indian money market to pay for allocations of stock, and the government deposits placed in the presidency banks prior to flotations to dampen rates and to maximise demand for the bonds on offer were withdrawn. In the busy season, the need for rupees to purchase produce from farmers and to finance exports inevitably led to currency shortages, exacerbated by tax demands and the unwillingness of the Indian government and IO respectively to increase presidency bank deposits or to allow these banks to purchase council bills or to borrow funds in London.[99] Such speculative movements of cash also became more common over time. The introduction of telegraphic transfers allowed advantage to be taken of rate differentials before they narrowed, and the stability of the exchange after 1898 minimised the possibility that interest gains would be offset by exchange losses.[100]

High exchange rates, again, reduced the demand for bills, as bankers would make less or no profit when the bills were exchanged for rupees. Purchases would thus be postponed until rates began to fall, and fewer export bills would be bought or their purchase financed from Indian reserves or loans.[101] As with interest rates, banks also speculated on the exchange. If the exchange rate was high, cash would be remitted

---

96 *Ibid.*, 27 Oct. 1906, p. 727; *ibid.*, 5 March 1887, p. 250; *ibid.*, 23 Sept. 1905, p. 491; PP [Cd.7069], q. 179, 248, 289; BL, L/F/7/182, fol. 1536, minute, 23 Nov. 1910. In addition to ad hoc spikes, rates temporarily rose each December (*The Statist*, 20 Dec. 1902, p. 117). Those banks that did not halt import bill purchase paid a lower price for them, curtailing supply. To the extent that the decline in trade slowed the movement of gold to India, the system was self-righting (*ibid.*, 15 March 1913, p. 513).

97 PP 1887 [C.5099], q. 5096–7; PP 1914 [Cd.7069], q. 1519, 2854; *The Statist*, 8 March 1902, p. 509.

98 PP 1898 [C.9037], q. 3502; *The Statist*, 21 Oct. 1899, p. 619.

99 *The Statist*, 16 Oct. 1886, p. 422; *ibid.*, 16 Jan. 1904, p. 93; PP 1898 [C.9037], q. 3502; PP 1901 [171] *Indian Financial Statement for 1901–02*, p. 168. Higher government deposits would restrict the Indian Treasury's ability to meet any sudden increase in the sale of council bills, and presidency bank purchase of bills and/or London borrowing was believed to be excessively risky (PP 1901 [171], p. 197; PP [Cd.7069], q. 241–2).

100 *The Statist*, 18 March 1905, p. 463; *ibid.*, 21 Oct. 1899, p. 619.

101 *Ibid.*, 28 Nov. 1896, p. 808; PP 1899 [C.9222, 9390], q. 9845–6.

to London in order to gain the profit, and, if there was an expectation of a rise, additional council bills would be purchased in anticipation of future Indian needs and to permit the retransfer of the funds back to the UK when the rise occurred.[102] Reverse transfers took place if the exchange was low or a fall anticipated.

Conclusion

Council bills had two roles. They firstly promoted trade by handing the IO some control of the rate of exchange and allowing the exchange banks to remit funds to India and to hedge currency transaction risks. They also enabled the Indian government to transfer cash to England for the payment of its UK commitments. It cannot be denied that portions of these home charges were excessive – the guarantees provided to the companies that built the early railways were undoubtedly overgenerous, government stores could have been sourced more cheaply and some of the administrative expenses were unfair. The charges, however, were the inevitable consequence of and directly contributed to the development of India, providing the country with the essentials for development – peace, efficient and honest administration, and effective infrastructure.

Bill sales were determined by a combination of supply and demand factors. The amount offered in the Wednesday auctions depended on the size of the home charges, ad hoc events, the ability of the Indian Treasury to cash the bills, and, from 1904, the prices offered for the drafts. Demand, meanwhile, was dictated by trade, most significantly the level of Indian exports/imports, the time of year and the trade imbalances between India, the UK and the Far East, as well as non-trade influences, such as capital investment in India, the price of the bills, the availability/price of alternate forms of remittance and exchange bank Indian cash reserves.

---

102 PP 1914 [Cd.7069], q. 6597–8; *The Statist*, 30 May 1896, p. 748. Before making such transfers, banks also took into account Indian/London interest rate differentials (*ibid.*, 5 March 1887, p. 250). Occasionally, forecast rate movements failed to occur and the banks suffered losses, as happened in December 1882 and 1887 (*ibid.*, 15 April 1882, p. 424; *ibid.*, 21 May 1887, p. 537).

8

Council Bills: Price

In the setting of bill prices, the IO had two goals. It wished to sell its bills at or above the rate at which they were exchanged for rupees in India, sales below this figure leading to losses that had to be recouped by higher taxes, more borrowing or less capital expenditure.[1] Secondly, it wanted stability. Fears that the exchange would fall and money would be returned to the UK at a loss discouraged the arrangement of forward contracts and trade, inward capital investment and English investors' purchase of rupee debt, and weakened the credit of India in the London capital market, investors being aware of the impact an unstable exchange rate had on trade.[2] It also prompted exchange banks to maintain small Indian reserves, which reduced liquidity and increased Indian interest rates, with rates remaining high for longer than otherwise, as speculators were less willing to transfer funds to India to benefit from the London/Indian rate differential.[3]

Whether the IO always obtained the highest possible return from the sale of bills was the subject of some debate. Many believed that the banks agreed the day before each tender the price at which they would bid.[4] Officials had little knowledge of the demand for import and export bills and did not expect the size of tenders to accurately reflect trade needs.[5] As allocations were made pro rata, to be sure of obtaining sufficient bills, purchasers tended to apply for more than they required, often the full amount on offer, and made applications through agents and in the names of directors, staff and relatives. Tenders were thus often over a hundred times oversubscribed, and this continued to be the case even after a 1903 ruling that the bids

1 Keynes, *Indian Currency*, p. 107; PP 1887 [C.5099], q. 1646–9.
2 PP 1898 [C.9037], p. 578; PP 1899 [C.9222, 9390], q. 9109; PP 1889 [123], p. 86; Cristiano, 'Keynes', p. 304.
3 PP 1898 [C.9037], q. 574, 576; PP 1889 [123], p. 86.
4 Doraiswami, *Indian Finance*, pp. 100, 107; BL, L/F/5/139, memo 1043, Hamilton, 1 Dec. 1876; *The Statist*, 28 June 1902, p. 1273.
5 BL, L/F/5/59, note, 16 Nov. 1882.

submitted by or on behalf of any one applicant should not exceed the total amount offered.[6]

In fact, there is no evidence for collusion, and the denials of secret deals by both the banks and the IO appear credible. Bank owners pointed out that low bill prices made a relatively small contribution to their profits, which were largely determined by turnover, and that the fierce competition within the sector acted against cooperation.[7] IO officials, meanwhile, argued that the banks had always acted with 'conspicuous trustworthiness', largely because they were managed by honourable individuals who had little need to 'take advantage' and would refrain from any behaviour that would damage their reputation in the City on which their ability to attract business depended.[8] They and the banks also had an 'honourable bilateral understanding on the basis of which all big business is done in the City'. Any institution that was discovered to be involved in collusion, broke an agreement or acted badly 'would be in our black books for a very long time' and no doubt would find their access to bills restricted and their applications for advances from the home balances rejected.[9]

The history of council bill prices can be split into two distinct periods – the early 1870s to the end of the First World War, which saw the introduction of a fixed 1s 4d exchange rate, and the immediate inter-war years when an attempt was made to introduce a 2s fixed rate.

Pre-First World War prices

The adoption of a fixed rate of exchange was made necessary by the fall in World silver prices from the early 1870s. While the supply of the metal increased with the opening of new American mines, demand fell as countries such as Germany, Scandinavia and the Latin Union (France, Belgium, Italy and Switzerland) abandoned or restricted silver coinage, and the exchange banks increasingly used council bills rather than silver to remit funds to India.[10] Since council bills were cashed in silver rupees, the value of which was dropping, the prices banks were prepared to pay for drafts similarly declined, from 1s 10 1/4d in 1870/1 to just 1s 2 5/8d in 1892/3, and the cost to the Indian government of paying its home charges increased (Figure 10).[11] European

---

6   BL, L/F/7/184, fol. 5943, note, no date; *The Statist*, 28 June 1902, p. 1273. The ruling, which proved impossible to police, followed an attempt by the banks themselves to restrict multiple applications and the additional costs these imposed on them (*ibid.*, 1 Aug. 1903, p. 201).

7   *The Statist*, 8 May 1897, p. 700; PP 1914 [Cd.7069], q. 2828.

8   BL, L/F/7/192, Abrahams, 2 Jan. 1917; PP 1920 [Cmd.528], q. 5255.

9   PP 1920 [Cmd.528], q. 5257–8.

10 Fawcett, *Indian Finance*, pp. 49, 132–3; Banerji, *Finances*, p. 248; Vakil, *Financial Developments*, p. 324.

11 If an exchange rate of rs10 to the pound is adopted, the Indian government from 1861/2 to 1898/9 made a loss of £141.6m from the sale of bills (Figure 10 sources).

residents in India, largely civil servants, also suffered, finding it more expensive to move funds home. At first, the additional cost of the home charges was offset by the rise in tax revenues; the falling exchange rates reduced the price of and increased exports and raised import prices, leading to some import substitution and a more prosperous manufacturing sector. The extra expense of government stores, meanwhile, was counterbalanced by the fall in World commodity prices.[12] Over time, however, exporters' Indian rupee costs adjusted upwards, and the continued decline of the exchange forced the introduction of higher taxation, which threatened to increase support for the emerging nationalist movement.[13] Attempts by the IO to reverse the fall through the rejection of low priced tenders ended in abject failure, as the banks merely turned to other forms of remittance, particularly silver, and the need to meet the home charges limited the amount of time sales could be suspended.[14] Moreover, such action usually prompted a barrage of criticism from the trading community, angry at the resultant fluctuation in the exchange and the rise in Indian interest rates.[15]

Figure 10. Council bill rates and gains/losses and reverse council bill rates, 1850–1939/40

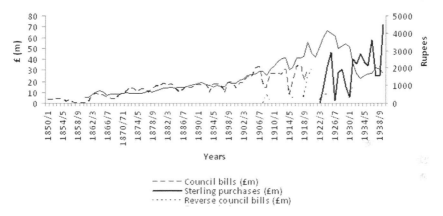

Sources. Figure 9 sources; PP 1886 [C.4730], no. 57.

Notes. 1861/2–1898/9 losses at exchange 10rs = £1. 1899/1900–1919/20 losses/gains at exchange 1rs = 14d.

12   Leavens, *Silver Money*, p. 74; P. J. Cain and A. G. Hopkins, *British Imperialism, Volume 1: Innovation and Expansion, 1688–1914*, London 1993, p. 344
13   Ambedkar, *The Problem*, chap. 7, table 51; PP 1893–94 [C.7060, C.7060.I, C.7060.II] *Indian Currency Committee*, pp. 155–9; Cain and Hopkins, *British Imperialism, Vol. 1*, p. 345. In particular, a tax on salt was introduced (de Cecco, *The International Gold Standard*, p. 66).
14   Attempts were made to raise prices in 1876, 1877, 1878, 1882 and 1886 (BL, L/F/5/139, HW, 1881; *ibid.*, remittance from India, 10 March 1881, p. 14; PP 1899 [C.9376], p. 25; *The Statist*, 8 May 1886, p. 496).
15   BL, L/F/5/139, IO to G of I, 13 July 1876.

A solution to the problem emerged in 1893 when the recommendations made by the Herschell Committee were put into effect. The Committee had concluded that India should eventually have a gold currency, but, in the meantime, silver coin should continue to circulate and the value of the rupee should be raised to that of gold (1s 4d).[16] To achieve this, the Indian government, as recommended by the Committee, announced that it would only exchange gold for rupees at the rate of 1 rupee = 1s 4d, halted its own silver coinage and prohibited the minting of silver coin by the private sector. Cutting the supply of new coin would cause the value of the rupee to rise and the closure of the mints, and the setting of a 1s 4d gold/rupee exchange rate would allow the IO through its control of the supply of council bills to raise the bill price/exchange to 1s 4d – banks having no alternative but to remit via council bills, as they were unable to coin silver and had no financial incentive to ship gold until the price reached 1s 4d.[17]

From June/July to November 1893, the IO thus suspended all bill sales.[18] Unfortunately, 'a more unfavourable time [for taking on the banks] could hardly have been selected'. Sales were halted in the middle of the 'slack' (non-trading) season and an expected surge in remittances on the issue of the rupee loan of that year failed to materialise. When trading recommenced, exports were much reduced, owing to the closure of the mints, and could easily be met by the large speculative remittances of bills and silver that had been made by the banks in anticipation of closure and by alternative modes of remittance, all of which were widely available.[19] Although the speculative pre-mint closure remittances and an early London issue of a £1.3m loan for the repayment of railway debentures had inflated the IO's balances, these rapidly evaporated.[20] Officials were thus forced to reduce some of India's UK commitments, obtain a £4.75m loan from the Bank of England and turn to the London capital market, issuing £1.386m of debentures in September and £6.25m of sterling bills from October to January 1894.[21]

16 S. L. N. Simha and G. Balachandran, *History of the Reserve Bank of India*, Bombay 1970, pp. 45–6.

17 A. Banerji, 'Revisiting the Exchange Standard, 1898–1913: 1. Steps to the Exchange Standard', *Economic and Political Weekly*, 1 Dec. 2001, p. 4491; *The Statist*, 22 Jan. 1887, p. 110; Simha and Balachandran,*History*, p. 46. 1s 4d rather than the 1s 6d preferred by the Indian government was chosen, as the market rate of exchange was then 1s 2d, and it was feared that a higher rate would fuel deflation (Leavens, *Silver Money*, p. 76).

18 PP 1898 [C.9037], q. 56, 1265.

19 *The Statist*, 19 Aug. 1893, p. 207; *ibid.*, 22 July 1893, p. 86. The closure of the mints stimulated imports and sales of import bills, which could be bought at a relatively low price (*ibid.*, 16 Dec. 1893, p. 693; *ibid.*, 14 Oct. 1893, p. 422). There was also plenty of silver, gold and Indian railway company bills of exchange available (*ibid.*, 16 Sept. 1893, p. 306; *ibid.*, 18 Nov. 1893, p. 566).

20 PP 1894 [92], p. 12. The loan was due to be issued in October, but was actually floated in July. On 30 June, the balances reached £4.17m (*ibid.*).

21 PP 1894 [92], pp. 12, 22, 48.

The Office capitulated in January 1894, despite advice to the contrary from the Indian government, which was convinced that the exchange banks were about to run out of funds.[22] The home balances could meet neither India's UK commitments nor the repayment of the sterling bills issued, and the renewal of these bills and further flotations would destroy India's credit and further increase its loan interest payments. The suspension of council bill sales had also caused India's Treasury balances to reach a record rs23.8m, none of which was earning interest.[23] On 30 January, the IO thus began to sell bills at 1s 2³/₈d, well below the minimum, and the price eventually slumped to 1s 1 ½d before recovering to 1s 2d.[24]

Gradually, over the following six years, the restriction of coinage and the expansion of trade caused bill prices/the exchange to gradually rise, attaining the long hoped for 1s 4d in January 1898.[25] In the same year, on the recommendation of the Fowler Committee, it was decided that India would be placed on the gold standard, and an attempt was made to introduce gold coin. Unfortunately, the gold sovereigns and half sovereigns put into circulation were rejected by consumers, partly because their value was too high for everyday use, and the whole project was opposed by powerful Treasury officials and City figures. These wished to scotch the bimetallic campaign in Britain before it threatened the gold standard and worried that an Indian gold currency would increase the independence of the Indian authorities, raise the World price of the metal and reduce the Bank of England's gold stocks, which had recently been diminished by the second Boer War (1899–1902) and the disappearance of South African gold.[26] The initiative was thus abandoned, it was decided to retain the status quo and the IO set about ensuring that the trade-friendly fixed rate was maintained – succeeding from 1901/2 to 1912/13 in restricting its fluctuations to an annual average of just 0.239d.[27]

22   PP 1898 [C.9037], q. 2585. Even if the IO had held out, rates would probably have collapsed in the slack trading season (*ibid.*, q. 2586).

23   PP 1894 [92], pp. 12, 22. The Treasury had possessed large amounts of rupees before the new policy had been implemented, owing to the large silver imports in anticipation of the closure of the mints (PP 1898 [C.9037], q. 3006).

24   PP 1894 [92], p. 12.

25   The protracted nature of the rise was due to the large hoards of silver, which were slowly released into circulation.

26   Cristiano, 'Keynes', pp. 306–8; Simha and Balachandran,*History*, pp. 47–8; A. M. Carabelli and M. A. Cedrini, 'Indian Currency and Beyond: The Legacy of the Early Economics of Keynes in the times of Bretton Woods II', *Journal of Post Keynesian Economics*, 33 (2) (2010/11), p. 264; de Cecco, *The International Gold Standard*, p. 347; PP 1914 [Cd.7070], appendix 3, pp. 96–7. The Bank of England's gold reserve had plummeted to an all-time low (M. de Cecco, *Money and Empire*, London 1974, p. 69).

27   The average fluctuation between the annual maximum and minimum price obtained (Keynes, *Indian Currency*, p. 123).

Minimisation of gold flows to India

Since the price of bills was now close to the gold/rupee exchange rate (1s 4d), the exchange banks had a financial incentive to remit funds to India in the form of gold if the price of council bills exceeded this rate plus the expense of transporting the specie to India (1/8d). The IO, however, opposed such transfers, which would not only make it more difficult for it to meet India's UK commitments (fewer council bills would be sold), but lead to higher London interest rates and require it to ship the gold remitted back to Britain. The possible rise in London interest rates prompted by an outflow of gold in 'an inconvenient week' would damage both the City and India.[28] The higher borrowing charges would reduce demand for Indian government debentures/stock and sterling bills and the securities floated by the guaranteed railway companies, forcing higher yields to be offered, and, as discussed, apply 'the brake to the wheels of India trade'.[29] Moreover, a rise in UK rates caused by fewer council bill sales would disturb the delicate mechanism of trust and reciprocity on which the successful operation of the IO's activities rested and damage the reputations of its financial advisors on which India free rode.[30]

Yet more problems were created by the arrival of the metal in India. As there was little demand for gold sovereigns, the specie was exchanged by the Indian government for rupee coins or notes and placed in its Treasury and the PCR.[31] These stockpiles earned no interest and the increase in the proportion of gold relative to silver held in the PCR could create problems if there was a run on notes.[32] The gold therefore had to be shipped back to England, where it was used to pay for the minting of new coins.[33] Replacing council bills, these shipments reduced the amount of bills available for sale, increasing the cost of Indian trade; alerted speculators on the London silver market that the metal was about to be purchased, enabling them to buy up stocks that they then sold to the IO at inflated prices; and, in 1912, cost 3/16d per rupee in freight, insurance and packing, plus an unknown sum for gold lost or stolen in transit.[34]

To discourage exchange bank movement of gold to India, the IO determined that if the price of council bills reached the price at which it was cheaper to ship gold

28 G. Balachandran, 'Britain's Liquidity Crisis and India 1919–1920', *Economic History Review,* 46 (3) (1993), pp. 575–6.

29 BL, L/F/5/7, Newmarch to Comptroller-General, 24 Jan. 1913; BL, L/F/7/182, fol. 1536, minute, 23 Nov. 1910; PP [Cd. 7069], q. 179.

30 BL, L/F/7/182, fol. 1536, minute, 23 Nov. 1910.

31 PP 1914 [Cd.7069], q. 1507, 1529; PP 1920 [Cmd.528], q. 4521; Chablani, *Indian Currency and Exchange,* p. 67.

32 BL, L/F/7/182, fol. 5941, minute, 18 Dec. 1912. In a run, holders would demand their notes be exchanged for silver coin. It was also claimed that the bullion depreciated the value of precious metals and fuelled inflation (PP 1872 [327], q. 7661, 7668).

33 Chablani, *Indian Currency and Exchange,* p. 68.

34 PP 1914 [Cd.7069], q. 1392; *The Statist,* 21 Oct. 1905, p. 677; *ibid.,* 23 Feb. 1901, p. 317; *ibid.,* 14 Dec. 1912, p. 709.

(1s 4 ⅛d and known as the gold import point), it would sell an unlimited amount of bills at or below that price, thus causing the banks to continue to remit via bills. At the same time, it began to purchase Australian and Egyptian gold being transported to India by the exchange banks and to redirect the shipments to London. Selling bills without limit was much criticised. Indian nationalists argued that taxation and inflation would have been lower, fewer rupee loans would have been issued and more money ploughed into economic development if the funds transferred had been retained in India.[35] However, there is little evidence that the additional sale of bills was a major cause of inflation, it appears unlikely that domestic investment would have risen had the policy not been pursued and the lending of the surplus balances to the City, by assisting the London market, greatly benefitted the Indian government.[36] Unlimited sales also facilitated the finance of trade, built up the home balances, reduced the sterling debt, and facilitated the transfer of funds to the GSR and the London branch of the PCR.[37]

Sales in aid of trade were important, as, after a period of stagnation caused by the currency problems created by the closure of the mints, two famines and the 1895 Sino-Japanese war, Indian exports had finally begun to take off, growing by 255 per cent from 1897 to 1913.[38] To ensure that this boom continued, it was essential that merchants could sell the export bills required to finance shipments at a relatively high price and that there were no shortages of rupees that could lead to higher Indian interest rates, which would damage trade directly and indirectly through exchange bank speculation.[39] It was equally important that additional home balances be accumulated to prevent the IO being 'caught short' and unable to meet UK commitments.[40] Such an eventuality was far more likely than previously and could occur if Indian trade fell, reducing sales of council bills or forcing the payment of low prices; government sterling loans failed or high London interest rates precluded their flotation; or there was an unexpected rise in commitments.[41] 'Mak[ing] hay whilst the sun shines' would also enable the Office to continue to finance the railway programme in poor trading years and prevent the overselling of bills that often occurred after a fall in their demand, which invariably led to a further drop in the exchange.[42]

---

35   Mukherjee, *Imperialism*, p. 96; PP 1914 [Cd.7069], q. 1570; H. F. Howard, *India and the Gold Standard*, London 1911, pp. 118–34.

36   S. E. Harris, *Monetary Problems of the British Empire*, New York 1931, pp. 381, 411; D. Banerjee, 'Is there Overestimation of 'British Capital' Outflow? Keynes' Indo-British Trade and Transfer Accounts Re-examined with Alternate Evidence', *Indian Economic and Social History*, 41 (2) (2004), p. 43.

37   BL, L/F/5/144, discussion on Indian finance, 31 Jan. 1913.

38   McGuire, 'Exchange Banks', p. 156.

39   Doraiswami, *Indian Finance*, p. 36; PP 1914 [Cd. 7069], q. 1395.

40   PP 1914 [Cd. 7069], q. 10194.

41   BL, L/F/5/144, Memorandum on IO balances, no date; PP 1914 [Cd.7069], q. 1361.

42   PP 1914 [Cd.7069], q. 1336, 1360; PP 1914 [Cd. 7071] , appendix 23, p. 578, par. 9.

A further advantage of a large reserve and not living 'hand to mouth' was that the IO would not be 'compelled to borrow in an unfavourable market', allowing money to be raised at a cheaper rate; could reduce the size and number of loans and sterling bills issued specifically to meet UK commitments; and could even begin to pay off liabilities. Interest payments and the amount of money to be remitted to London would thus be reduced and India's credit in the market would be improved, allowing loans for other purposes to be successfully issued at a relatively low cost.[43] In the event, the IO reduced the size of loans issued to meet its UK commitments by less than it hoped. The most propitious time for flotations was early in the year (i.e. prior to the end of the trading season) during which most of the additional council bills were sold. Unaware of the amount of money it would obtain from the sale of council bills by the end of the season, the IO tended to act on the side of caution and issue loans that in retrospect were excessive.[44]

Unfortunately, the gold import point was hopelessly inaccurate. No account was taken of fluctuations in the price of the metal, falls in London interest rates (which reduced transit interest losses) and the decline over time of insurance premiums and shipment costs, caused by the use of English and French parcel post and cuts in steamship tariffs.[45] The price also assumed that the banks sourced all their gold from London and thus overlooked the lower cost of sending gold from Australia and, to a lesser extent, Egypt, and it appears that the IO initially failed to monitor the availability/price of London/Australian/Egyptian specie.[46]

Aware that the import point was incorrect, officials nonetheless decided against lowering it. It was pointed out that small imports of gold were necessary to meet Indian demand for sovereigns; the banks' use of specie was not based on cost factors alone and had not in the past significantly reduced council bill sales; and the banks' transfers of Egyptian and Australian gold (if redirected to the UK) could prove beneficial to India.[47] The IO was also well aware that speculation stabilisation mechanisms would eventually reverse any appreciation of the exchange/outflow of gold. A rise would advance short-term money rates – the fall in the home balances would limit the number of loans made to the City and the IO's issue of sterling bills to meet the home charges would soak up money – and the higher interest rates would halt the outflow of gold and cause the exchange banks to move funds to

43 PP 1914 [Cd.7070], appendix 1, section 7, p. 14; PP [Cd. 7069], q. 1358, 11050, 11194.
44 BL, L/F/5/144, note for Baker, 18 Dec. 1912.
45 PP 1914 [Cd.7069], q. 1499; BL, L/F/7/182, fol. 5941, minute, 18 Dec. 1912. Insurance costs fluctuated, rising even at a hint of military conflict (*The Statist*, 9 Jan. 1904, p. 53).
46 PP 1914 [Cd.7069], q. 1497; BL, L/F/7/182, Hong Kong & Shanghai Banking Corp. to IO, 14 March 1914; Balachandran, *John Bullion's Empire*, p. 28. In 1914, the gold import points for Australian and Egyptian gold should have been respectively 1s 3 15/16d and 1s 4 1/16d (Keynes, *Indian Currency*, p. 117). The IO insisted that it was always fully aware of the availability and price of gold from whatever source (PP 1914 [Cd.7069], q. 1500).
47 BL, L/F/7/182, fol. 1536, minute, 23 Nov. 1910; *ibid.*, fol. 5941, minute, 18 Dec. 1912; PP [Cd.7069], q. 114–6.

London to reap the higher returns available. A slight rise in the exchange would also induce the banks to purchase additional council bills to permit the retransfer of the funds back to the UK in order to gain the profits from the continuation of the rise, and the very purchase of these bills would again trigger an exchange fall.[48]

Occasionally, the IO deliberately allowed the price of bills to drift above the gold point, especially at the start of the busy season when the demand for the drafts peaked, there were profits to be made and the urgency of the banks' need for rupees discouraged the shipment of bars and sovereigns.[49] Prices were similarly permitted to rise if the IO was short of money or wished to increase the gold holdings of the Indian PCR and when there was little metal available to buy on the London market or the Bank of England held large stocks.[50]

The banks' shipment of Australian and Egyptian gold to India was solved by simply purchasing and redirecting the specie to England. Australian gold was purchased from 1905 to 1913. On discovering that a shipment was being made, the IO sold the bank or trading company involved telegraphic council bills at 1s 4d against the specie, required a bill of lading to be made in its favour, and instructed the ship's captain to deliver his cargo in London, or, in 1906, in Egypt, where the gold was resold to the Anglo-Egyptian Bank for payment in London.[51] Purchases were made only nine or ten days after a ship had left Freemantle, preventing firms with no intention of moving specie to India taking advantage of the scheme, and the cost of freight and insurance to London was covered by the bank/trading company involved, bringing the cost of the remittance to just below 1s 4 ⅛d, the gold import point.[52] To reduce the risk of non-delivery, purchases were made from a relatively small number of firms that had Head Offices in the Empire, though agreements were occasionally entered into with foreign companies that provided a guarantee from an approved English bank.[53] The diversion of Egyptian gold to London occurred from 1906 to 1910. The acquisition process was the same as with Australian gold, except that some purchases were made before the gold had left Egypt, and, when this occurred, the specie theoretically had to be moved to England by the City, Papayanni or Ellerman shipping lines. In reality, other companies were used, and, in 1907, to fulfil the seller's agreement with its insurance company, gold was transported to Trieste, overland to Bremen and thence by steamer to London.[54]

---

48   Officer, 'Gold Standard'.

49   PP 1902 [187], p. 13.

50   PP 1914 [Cd.7069], q. 1341, 1499; *The Statist*, 20 Nov. 1909, p. 1117; *ibid.*, 27 April 1907, p. 827.

51   BL, L/F/5/9, p. 26, note, 1 May 1906; BL, L/F/5/79, note, 29 July 1905.

52   BL, L/F/5/79, note, 29 July 1905; BL, L/F/5/9, p. 41, note, 22 Feb. 1907; *ibid.*, p. 26, note, 1 May 1906.

53   *Ibid.*, p. 35, IO to International Banking Corp., 30 Nov. 1906. In 1907, the IO refused to accept a deposit of first-class English bank bills at the Bank of England in lieu of this guarantee (*ibid.*, IO to Credit Lyonnais, 9 March 1907).

54   *Ibid.*, IO to Chartered Bank of India, Australia & China, 10 March 1910; *ibid.*, p. 40, note, 7 Feb. 1907.

The scheme had a number of advantages. It helped to stabilise the exchange, reduced the amount of specie reaching India, increased London gold stocks and avoided the decline in these holdings that occurred when Australian and Egyptian gold was transferred to India. Some of the Australian gold shipped would otherwise have been purchased by Egypt, which would have been forced to buy the specie required in the London market.[55] Egyptian banks, after selling the specie to the exchange banks for a premium, would meet internal demand through direct or indirect purchases in the London market, and, when internal demand was low, some of the gold sent to India would have gone to London.[56] The purchases also constituted a remittance of Indian government funds to the UK, which, unlike council bills and earmarking, had no impact on Bank of England gold stocks; if the specie was bought to replenish the gold holdings of the London PCR in preference to the transfer of gold from India, the purchases resulted in freight and insurance savings; and, when the specie was sold to the Anglo-Egyptian bank, the purchases allowed the IO to earn a commission of ⅛ per cent.[57] Finally, the bills used in payment for the gold were not included in official council bill sales figures, abating criticism of the size of the home charges/remittances.[58]

Although the policy was first developed in 1898, it was only put into practice in 1905/6.[59] From December 1905 to June 1906, £3.39m of gold sovereigns were purchased, saving £17,000 in repatriation costs. The depletion of the specie portion of the Indian PCR then caused the scheme to be temporarily shelved, an IO proposal to resume purchases in November 1906 being blocked by the Indian government, which feared a run on notes and requested a further delay until PCR gold stocks had reached £4.5m. Acquisitions recommenced in January 1907, continued until gold stocks dipped below £4.5m in March 1907, and restarted in March/August 1910 when holdings rose above the new £5m limit and the IO needed to build up the gold stocks of the GSR, which had been denuded by the 1907/8 financial crisis.[60] The scheme was then used just once more – in 1913 to avoid the transfer of £2.1m coinage profits to England via council bills/earmarking. Given the low Bank of England

55 PP 1906 [162], p. 69; *The Statist*, 19 Oct. 1912, p. 131; PP 1914 [Cd.7069], q. 1349; Spalding, *Eastern Exchange*, p. 35.
56 *The Statist*, 27 Jan. 1912, p. 168; *ibid.*, 4 Dec. 1909, p. 1221. The exchange banks paid a premium price because Egypt was closer to India than London (*ibid.*, 20 Jan. 1912, p. 115). Some Egyptian bank London purchases were made via France (*ibid.*, 14 Dec. 1912, p. 697).
57 BL, L/F/5/7, Newmarch to Comptroller-General, 24 Jan. 1913; PP 1914 [Cd.7069], q. 1349, 1441; BL, L/F/5/9, IO to Anglo-Egyptian Bank, 17 April 1906. Earmarking and the impact the practice and the sale of council bills had on Bank of England gold stocks are discussed in Chapter 9.
58 *The Statist*, 31 March 1906, p. 565.
59 *Ibid.*, 29 Jan. 1898, p. 172.
60 BL, L/F/5/9, p. 26, note, 1 May 1906; *ibid.*, IO to G of I, 13 July 1906; *ibid.*, G of I to IO, 5 Nov. 1906; *ibid.*, S of S to G of I, 8 Nov. 1906; *ibid.*, S of S to G of I, 5 Jan. 1907; *ibid.*, S of S to G of I, 21 March 1907; *ibid.*, G of I to IO, 12 Aug. 1907; *ibid.*, S of S to G of I, 8 March 1910; PP 1914 [Cd.7069], q. 1445.

gold reserves, the remittance would have prompted a rise in London interest rates that would have damaged that year's intended Indian government loan issue and the renewal of guaranteed Indian railway debentures.[61]

Measures to prevent a fall in the exchange

The upper limit of the price of exchange/sale of bills was 1s 4d, the rate at which gold would be exchanged for rupees in India, or 1s 4 ⅛d if the cost of transporting the specie was taken into account. However, there was no lower limit – the IO was not legally required to sell bills for 1s 4d. Officials, nonetheless, were reluctant to allow the price to fall too far below this level as India would make a loss on all bills sold, and there would be problems in meeting the home charges and criticism of the exchange banks' profits; the resulting instability of the exchange would damage trade and lose the Office the trust of the merchant community; and, at below 1s 3 29/32d, it became financially beneficial for the banks to move gold from India to the UK, which could leave the subcontinent dangerously short of specie.[62] It thus set a lower price limit (the gold export point) of 1s 3 29/32d, below which it would not sell. Many believed that a 1s 4d minimum price would have been more appropriate, removing exchange fluctuations and thus aiding trade, a view rejected by the IO, which pointed out that a 1s 4d lower limit would reduce sales in the slack trading period, and that the disappearance of the end-of-trading season exchange fall would prompt banks to repatriate more of their funds to England, with all the problems this entailed, and to return the money at the start of the following season, thus increasing the demand for council bills and causing the price to rise.[63]

On prices falling towards the gold export point, the IO would sell fewer bills at the Wednesday auctions, forcing the banks to buy the more expensive intermediate bills, and, if there was a fall below the export point, reverse council bills would be issued, which would staunch the outflow of gold.[64] Reverse council bills were sold by the Indian government in India for rupees and cashed in sterling in London by the IO. From 1861/2 to the start of the Second World War, £105.9m of bills were issued as ordinary bills and as telegraphic transfers (Figures 9 and 10). The proceeds were placed in the Indian silver branch of the GSR or the PCR, and the funds used to cash the drafts theoretically came from the GSR, though in reality other sources were tapped – in 1908, 1915/16 and 1919/20 the home balances, overflowing with money; the PCR in 1919/20; in 1908, when sales of GSR securities could not keep pace with liabilities, the issue of sterling bills and a Bank of England loan; and in

---

61   BL, L/F/5/7, S of S to Finance Dept., 26 Nov. 1913.
62   The profit from the purchase of the bills (the 1s 4d obtained in India minus the lower price paid) was large enough to offset the cost of buying and shipping the gold to London (PP 1914 [Cd.7070], appendix 1, section 6, par. 26). From 1899/1900 to 1919/20, the Indian government made an overall profit from the sale of council bills of £12.5m (Figure 10).
63   PP 1914 [Cd.7069], q. 6589; *ibid.*, q. 2958, 6606.
64   E.g. *The Statist*, 28 Oct. 1899, p. 653; *ibid.*, 4 July 1903; *ibid.*, 23 Jan. 1904, p. 134.

1915, advances from HM Treasury and the sale of more sterling bills.[65] Any profits from the sales were credited to the GSR, if its contents had been used to meet the bills, or, otherwise, to the home balances.[66] Unable to meet the vast amount of bills issued in 1916, the IO instructed the Indian government to sell deferred reverse drafts, which were payable sixteen days from the date of issue rather than on receipt, thus giving itself more time to find the necessary funds. To encourage take-up, the bills were cheaper than non-deferred drafts and free of stamp duty, and an arrangement was made with the Bank of England whereby the Bank would buy the bills at a discount to their full value a day after their receipt.[67]

The bills were brought into play to a significant extent in 1907/8 and 1914/16 when respectively £8.058m and £13.893m were sold.[68] In 1907/8, their deployment was prompted by the low sales and prices of council bills due to a poor harvest and the collapse of a number of US trust companies. Fearing for their savings, American investors bought gold, much of which came from the UK, denuding London stocks and forcing the Bank of England to raise interest rates to 7 per cent. Demand for Indian exports thus fell, and the exchange banks began to move funds to the UK, where, along with the proceeds of export bills, they could be profitably invested.[69] In 1914/16, the culprit was war. Panic-stricken investors transferred funds to London and were joined by patriots wishing to invest in the UK government's war loans and the dislocation of trade, and the Wheat Scheme lowered the demand for council drafts.[70]

On both occasions, the IO's intervention was the subject of criticism. It was claimed that in 1907 officials hesitated before announcing that they would issue drafts and that this delay 'very nearly ruined the country', generated much bitterness amongst the Indian business community and forced the sale of more drafts

65   PP 1909 [122] *Indian Financial Statement for 1909–10*, p. 19; PP 1920 [Cmd.529], p. 38, appendix 2, par. 2; BL, L/F/5/8, S of S to Governor General, 22 Oct. 1915; *ibid.*, Abrahams, 17 July 1915; PP 1920 [103], p. 396; BL, L/F/5/5, note, 5 Aug. 1908; *ibid.*, note, 19 Jan. 1909; NA, T 1/11898, 4821, confidential memo.

66   BL, L/F/5/8, S of S to Governor General, 22 Oct. 1915.

67   BL, L/F/7/190, fol. 6274, Newmarch to Fraser, 13 Jan. 1916; *ibid.*, notice, 9 Aug. 1916; *ibid.*, Newmarch, 2 Dec. 1915; *ibid.*, IO to G of I, 21 April 1916; *ibid.*, fol. 3165, note, 31 May 1916. The Bank then held the bill to maturity, at which time it received the full value from the IO. If the rate of discount was lower than the price difference and the stamp duty saving, purchasers gained a slight profit by buying a deferred bill (*ibid.*, IO to G of I, 21 April 1916).

68   PP 1914 [Cd.7069], q. 1415; Ambedkar, *The Problem*, chap. 7, table 45; PP 1920 [Cmd.529], p. 122; BL, L/F/7/189, Abrahams to Meyer, 6 May 1916. In 1909/10, a further £0.156m were disposed of (BL, L/F/7/188, fol. 4981, note, Abrahams, no date, 1916).

69   PP 1908 [170], pp. 22–3.

70   PP 1914–16 [233] *Return of Indian Financial Statement and Budget for 1915–16*, p. 4; PP 1916 [80] *Return of Indian Financial Statement and Budget for 1916–17*, p. 30; B. Eichengreen, *Golden Fetters: The Gold Standard and the Great Depression, 1919–39*, Oxford 1992, pp. 68–70.

the following year than would otherwise have been necessary.[71] Privately, the IO accepted censure, blaming the time it took to put a policy that had never previously been used on any great scale into operation and its reluctance to sell at a loss GSR investments.[72] Similar criticisms were made in 1915.[73] It was also argued that in 1914/16 some of the money was brought to the UK for speculative purposes, and, in 1908, that their use had seriously depleted the GSR (prompting the IO to later sell council bills at a relatively low rate to replenish it), forced the sale of some of its investments at a loss and led to Indian currency shortages.[74]

Introduction of the 2s exchange

While the fixing of the 1s 4d rate was prompted by the fall in silver prices, the 2s rate set in 1920 was the result of a rise from approximately 1917 in the price of the metal, largely caused by shortages. Within India, the war saw the return of hoarding and disrupted shipments of specie, and, in the wider World, there were falls in Mexican output, large purchases at high prices by the US to restore its depleted stocks, and greater demand for silver coinage fuelled by the post-war boom.[75] By September 1917, the bullion value of the silver rupee exceeded its exchange value, and the Indian government, unable to reduce the silver content of the rupee for fear of political unrest that could damage the war effort, linked council bill prices to those of silver.[76] It thus prevented speculators buying drafts and melting down and selling the rupees obtained, which would have had political implications, increased the amount of bills sold, and led to currency shortages and losses when the rupees withdrawn from circulation were replaced with newly minted coins.[77] The price/exchange rise also enabled the Indian government to make large profits

71   PP 1914 [Cd.7069], q. 2715, 2940, 7725; PP 1920 [Cmd.528], q. 4203. Some claimed that the IO deliberately delayed issuing bills until London interest rates had fallen from their highs (Banerji, 'Revisiting the Exchange Standard', p. 4500). There is no evidence of this in the IO files.

72   BL, L/F/7/188, fol. 4981, note, Abrahams, no date, 1916; PP 1920 [Cmd.528], q. 4205.

73   PP 1920 [Cmd.528], q. 4203; Ambedkar, *The Problem*, chap. 7.

74   BL, L/F/7/186, fol. 6746, Abrahams to Finance Dept., 10 Aug. 1914; PP 1909 [122], p. 19; Keynes, *Indian Currency*, p. 140; PP [Cd.7069], q. 928. The IO stated that the need to replenish the Reserve only had a 'slight effect' on bill prices (*ibid.*).

75   PP 1920 [Cmd.529], p. 121; PP 1917–18 [94] *Return of Indian Financial Statement and Budget for 1917–18*, p. 10; PP 1920 [Cmd.529], pp. 39–40; PP 1919 [Cmd.442] *Report on the Conditions and Prospects of British Trade in India at the Close of the War*, p. 20. Government war-time restrictions on gold imports into India prevented the metal from being used as currency or currency backing and thus partly abating silver shortages (PP 1920 [Cmd.528], q. 107, 3518). At the end of the war, India also imported large amounts of silver for coinage (Balachandran, 'Britain's Liquidity Crisis', p. 578).

76   PP 1918 [61], p. 26; PP 1920 [Cmd.529], p. 40; PP 1920 [Cmd.528], q. 173–4, 232–6, 407–49.

77   PP 1920 [Cmd.528], q. 2936.

on the sale of bills, effectively reducing the cost of meeting India's UK commitments, and reduced the size of its sterling debt, strengthening its credit.[78] As regards
trade, imports were cheaper, cooling inflation, increasing currency circulation and
benefitting the British manufacturer/merchant to the detriment of their foreign and
Indian counterparts. Theoretically, exports were more expensive and should have
fallen. In reality, they held up relatively well. The high World demand for commodities and the lack of competition in sectors such as linseed, oil seeds and hides
allowed exporters to raise prices without loss of sales, and the lower cost of import-
ing machinery/employing Europeans reduced expenses.[79] Having said that, exports
would undoubtedly have been greater without the exchange rise, though so would
the shortage of currency/inflation.[80]

In January 1920, on the recommendation of the Babington-Smith Committee,
the exchange was linked to gold and fixed at 2s, far too high given that World prices,
including that of gold, were on the slide.[81] Instead of immediately supporting the
exchange, the IO again hesitated, leaving the 'fate [of the country]...in the hands of
a God named "chance"'.[82] It then began to aggressively sell reverse council bills, £55m
in the first nine months of 1920, cashed with funds taken from the home balances
and the London PCR.[83] However, although the sales helped to deflate the Indian
economy and returned to India the money that had accumulated in the London PCR
during the war, they failed to slow the collapse in the exchange, which by September
had fallen to 1s 3d.[84] Moreover, they induced trade-damaging fluctuations in the
exchange and currency shortages; led to the loss of 35 crores from the forced sale of
depreciated sterling securities in the PCR; and resulted in 'objectionable' speculation.[85] Speculators were able to 'snatch a considerable profit' in a number of ways.
Those who had remitted money to India at 1s 4d returned it to the UK at 2s, at a
loss to the Indian government of an estimated £25m.[86] Others purchased the bills to
obtain the difference between the market rate at which they were bought, based on

78   PP 1919 [104] *Return of Indian Financial Statement and Budget for 1919–20*, p. 327; PP 1923
      [128], p. 10.

79   PP 1920 [Cmd.528], q. 842, 855, 4501, 4503, 4505, 4512–14; PP 1919 [Cmd.442], p. 21.

80   B. F. Madon, *Exchange Fallacies Exposed: Being India's Exchange Problem, Part 2*, Bombay
      1925, p. 3; PP 1920 [Cmd.528], q. 855. Lower exports also reduced the price of raw materi-
      als/labour for Indian manufacturers and the price of previously exported food (*ibid.*, q. 865,
      881).

81   Mukherjee, *Imperialism*, p. 80; Bagchi, *Private Investment*, p. 63. The Committee believed
      that silver prices would remain high for some years and that the 2s rate was necessary to
      counter inflationary pressure in India and to maintain a silver currency (Balachandran,
      'Britain's Liquidity Crisis', pp. 584, 586; PP 1920 [Cmd.529], pars 33–60).

82   Ambedkar, *The Problem*, chap. 7; PP 1921 [153], p. 76.

83   Ambedkar, *The Problem*, chap. 7, table 47; PP 1920 [103], p. 396.

84   Mukherjee, *Imperialism*, p. 81; PP 1920 [Cmd.528], q. 1035.

85   PP 1920 [103], p. 72; PP 1921 [153], p. 105; BL, L/F/7/199, Finance Dept. to IO, 15 Sept. 1920;
      Balachandran, *John Bullion's Empire*, p. 91.

86   PP 1920 [103], pp. 74, 106; Mukherjee, *Imperialism*, p. 81.

the falling sterling-dollar exchange, and the 2s received in London, which could be as much as 3 ¾d, or bought the bills and then immediately sold them for a smaller profit in the Indian market. A minority, expecting the fixed exchange to be eventually abandoned, sent the money to England intending to transfer it back to India when the exchange fell, thus making a further profit. Appalled at the greed of remitters, the IO sought to halt the speculation by requiring the Indian government to force tenderers for reverse council drafts to provide deposits and to purchase at least £10,000 of bills, and to reject bids from suspected speculators. The government's efforts, however, had little impact and often halted transfers by genuine remitters.[87]

The 2s fixed rate was finally abandoned in September 1920, creating more casualties. Indian importers who had sold merchandise at 2s saw its value plummet, many refusing to take delivery and thus passing the loss onto their British trading partners.[88] With World prices sliding further, the exchange fell to 1s 3d in March 1921, and, in the autumn, the IO sought to appreciate the rupee through the suspension of council bill sales, at which point the City's involvement in the exchange effectively came to an end.[89] Gradually, Indian exports and the exchange recovered, regaining the 1s 4d level towards the end of 1924. But rather than accepting this price as the new ratio, it was decided to appreciate the exchange further to 1s 6d, a level reached in June 1925, and, in 1927, following the recommendations of the Hilton-Young Commission, this became the official fixed rate.[90] Supporters of the initiative argued that wages and prices had already adjusted to the ratio, which had brought stability to the exchange and would raise real incomes, reduce import prices and cut the cost of meeting the home charges, thus easing government finances and improving India's credit to foreign investors. Others regarded it as a cynical attempt to boost UK exports to India and to allow British Indian officials to profit from the remittance of their salaries. They argued that a lower ratio would promote the expansion of Indian domestic manufacturing and exports, and the income thus generated would enable the government to easily meet the home charges and enhance the demand for UK manufactured goods.[91] In the event, the controversy was interrupted by the 1930 World recession and accompanying fall in commodity prices, which devastated Indian exports, and, along with an anticipation of a lower exchange and disquiet over the emergence of the civil disobedience movement, led to an outflow of foreign capital. Calls for devaluation, however, again fell on stony ground. Fearing that this would be the start of a slippery slope leading to further depreciation and even default, the fixed rate was supported via a deflationary budget and heavy calls on

87   Balachandran, *John Bullion's Empire*, p. 96; PP 1920 [103], pp. 239, 241, 288; PP 1921 [153], p. 105.
88   Sir V. Chirol, *India: Old and New*, London 1921.
89   Balachandran, *John Bullion's Empire*, p. 97; Balachandran, 'The Sterling Crisis', p. 15.
90   Hilton-Young recommended the creation of a Gold Bullion Standard (PP 1926 [Cmd.2687] *Royal Commission on Indian Currency and Finance*, pars 35–53).
91   Mukherjee, *Imperialism*, pp. 81–2, 91; Bagchi, *Private Investment*, pp. 64–5; Cain and Hopkins, *British Imperialism, 1688–2000*, p. 554.

government gold reserves, and, in September 1931, on Britain's abandonment of the gold standard, the rupee was linked to sterling, again at 1s 6d, causing exports in the years leading up to the Second World War to fall further and forcing imports and the home charges to be financed with gold.[92]

---

92 Simha and Balachandran,*History*, p. 57; Cain and Hopkins, *British Imperialism, 1688–2000*, p. 556. The impact on Indian exports of the abandonment of the gold standard and depreciation of sterling/the rupee was offset by falling World prices.

9

Indian Government Difficulties in Cashing Bills and Other Methods of Remittance

A major drawback of council bills was that, on occasion, the Indian government simply lacked the funds to cash them, particularly after 1904. This state of affairs was partly due to the difficulties faced by the government in the early part of the period in determining the size of Treasury balances at any one time and in predicting the amount of coin that would flow back to its Treasuries, which often caused shortages of funds towards the end of the trading season.[1] A further factor was the unpredictable nature of the Indian climate and harvests. Good crops and high exports led to unexpectedly heavy sales of council bills, and crop failure resulted in famine, low receipts and high expenditure on relief measures.[2] Another imponderable was war. During the First World War, the Indian administration spent £200m on behalf of the UK government and had to meet £103m of council bills, sales of which had risen owing to the heavy demand and high prices paid for Indian raw materials needed for the war effort and to a series of good harvests.[3]

The inability of the Indian Treasury to meet council bills was solved via reverse earmarking, the restriction of bill sales and loans from the GSR. The Indian government also issued larger than usual rupee loans, which offered purchasers discounts for early payment; in 1919, obtained advances from the presidency banks and issued additional currency notes; and, in 1926, raided its Post Office Savings Bank deposits.[4] Reverse earmarking involved the IO transferring the proceeds of council bill sales from the home balances to the London PCR, and the Indian government moving an equal amount of gold or rupees from the Indian PCR into its Treasury balances or issuing currency notes to the same value, and using the gold, rupees or notes

---

1   PP 1873 [354], q. 2807, 2810.

2   Famine, for example, denuded the Indian Treasury in 1868/9, 1896/7 and 1900/1 (BL, L/F/5/139, Remittance from India, 10 March 1881, p. 14; PP 1897 [193], p. 12; PP 1901 [171], p. 59; PP 1914 [Cd.7070], appendix 5, p. 197).

3   PP 1920 [Cmd.529], pp. 82, 121; PP 1920 [Cmd.529], p. 38, appendix 2, par. 4.

4   *The Statist*, 14 Aug. 1897, p. 246; PP 1920 [103], p. 6; Wadia and Joshi, *Money*, p. 355.

to cash the council bills arriving in India. Although quick and cheap, the practice was much disliked by the London market. The movement of funds from the home balances caused less money to be lent to the City, reducing liquidity and tending to raise interest rates, and the amount of cash held in India's Bank of England current account temporarily fell, making the Bank more vulnerable to outflows of gold and more likely to react to such effusions via higher base rates.[5]

To avoid such eventualities, the IO tended to reverse earmark in December/January when the market was replete with funds, abandon the practice when interest rates were relatively high, and, if market stringency caused by reverse earmarking would directly impact on India, transfer funds in anticipation of a fall in Treasury balances.[6] In 1911, for example, officials decided to earmark in April rather than during the autumn of that year, as high London interest rates would have an impact on the September/October issue of East Indian Railway Co. debentures.[7] In normal times, it also heeded Bank of England requests to abandon operations or to delay them until the market improved, though often with a distinct lack of grace, and, in 1915, developed a strategy that allowed it to continue to reverse earmark without denuding London gold stocks.[8] Arranging the passage of an ordinance that allowed a larger portion of the London PCR to be invested in securities, it continued to transfer the proceeds of home balance sales to the Reserve, but then invested them in UK Treasury bills, thus releasing the money back to the Bank of England.[9]

When unable to earmark because of the state of the London markets, the IO restricted the amount of council bills sold, and, to avoid the exchange banks remitting specie to India, increased sales when the price reached the gold import point, the price at which it was cheaper for the banks to use London gold than bills.[10] The restriction of council bill sales reached its apex during the First World War, when the ban on imports of gold into India prevented the exchange banks turning to specie. The IO initially withdrew its offer to sell bills without limit, suspended intermediates and reduced the amount of bills available each Wednesday.[11] To further curtail sales, it then introduced fixed minimum prices and drew up a list of eight exchange banks and three trading companies to which bills would be sold, and, to prevent any one firm obtaining a large proportion of those bills on offer through

5   BL, L/F/5/7, Financial Secretary, 16 Dec. 1912; *ibid.*, note, 24 Oct. 1913; PP [Cd.7069], p. 11506.
6   *The Statist*, 29 Dec. 1906, p. 1203; BL, L/F/5/7, memo, 24 Oct. 1913.
7   BL, L/F/5/6, S of S to Viceroy, 27 April 1911; *ibid.*, note, 6 Sept. 1911. In the event, no earmarking occurred (*ibid.*, Viceroy to S of S, 16 May 1911).
8   BL, L/F/5/7, note, 24 Oct. 1913; BL, L/F/7/592, no. 2, Abrahams, 3 Jan. 1916. In 1913, for example, officials grumbled that the Bank 'ought to manage their managed currency system well enough to avoid these frequent appeals for mercy' (BL, L/F/5/7, note, 24 Oct. 1913).
9   PP 1916 [80], p. 30.
10 BL, L/F/5/7, Financial Secretary, 16 Dec. 1912; BL, L/F/5/6, note, 6 Sept. 1911.
11 Chablani, *Indian Currency and Exchange*, p. 73; *The Statist*, 16 Dec. 1916, p. 1261; PP 1917–18 [94], p. 10.

large applications at high prices, restricted the maximum amount that each institution could purchase.[12] The eleven approved purchasers were also required in the first instance to use the proceeds of council bills to finance export bills that covered goods that were essential for the war effort and to keep the price of export bills close to that of council drafts; later, they were also required to comply with a schedule of rates.[13]

Needless to say, there was much criticism of these actions – restrictions on bill sales contributed to the fall in exports, and those institutions not included on the approved purchaser list questioned their exclusion and claimed that the eight exchange banks used their position to maximise their own and their clients' returns. Export bills were supposedly sold at prices below those of council bills and only to those British trading companies with which the banks had long and lucrative business relationships, enabling these firms to 'make vast profits', the demands of war and the halting of other country supplies having caused World prices of Indian produce to soar.[14] Such criticism fell on deaf ears. The large number of exchange banks on the list was a reward for their support during past and future crises, and the IO turned a 'blind eye' to any contravention of the rules laid down.[15] The restrictions thus stayed, and the IO's wish to slow or reverse the rise in the exchange caused them to be retained even after hostilities had come to an end. Eventually, however, officials were forced to surrender to the inevitable. Exporters of British goods to India began to hold back their merchandise, convinced that the rise in the exchange rate would continue. Fewer import bills were thus available, and the eight exchange banks had more difficulty financing Indian exports, and, less able to use import drafts to hedge the exchange risks of export bills, lowered the prices paid for these drafts.[16] In September 1919, therefore, all restrictions were withdrawn and the pre-war tender system was reintroduced.[17]

The Indian government obtained several loans from the GSR. The first was in 1906 when, although the Indian Treasury lacked sufficient silver currency, the IO was reluctant to undertake a reverse earmarking operation, which would increase UK interest rates that were already excessive. Even higher rates would not only lose India 'the goodwill of the market', but also increase the cost of a guaranteed railway company loan that was about to be floated in London.[18] Officials therefore proposed that the Indian government borrow £4m of silver from the silver branch of the Indian GSR at an interest rate of 3.5 per cent and transfer the ingots to the Indian PCR,

12   BL, L/F/5/80, note, 3 Jan. 1917; *The Statist*, 6 Jan. 1917, p. 3; BL, L/F/7/192, Abrahams, 2 Jan. 1917.
13   PP 1920 [Cmd.528], q. 218; BL, L/F/7/192, Abrahams to Chartered Bank, 18 Jan. 1917; *The Statist*, 20 Sept. 1919, p. 498.
14   PP 1920 [Cmd.528], q. 1741, 1825–6, 1828, 3665.
15   BL, L/F/7/192, Abrahams, 2 Jan. 1917.
16   BL, L/F/7/193, Viceroy to S of S, 19 June 1919.
17   BL, L/F/7/198, note, 18 Sept. 1919.
18   BL, L/F/5/4, G of I to S of S, 21 Feb. 1907; *ibid.*, Baker to Abrahams, 21 Feb. 1907.

which would allow an equivalent amount of rupees to be moved from the Reserve to the Treasuries. To plug the gap in the silver branch of the GSR, gold would then be moved from the home balances to the London branch of the GSR, where, to prevent the transfer reducing the Bank of England's gold stocks, it would be invested in Treasury bills.[19] Unfortunately, the Indian government refused to sanction the proposal on the grounds that it was 'made exclusively in the interests of the City and not of India', the loans contravened the true purpose of the silver branch of the Indian GSR and reverse earmarking was a more straightforward method of replenishing its Treasury.[20] A compromise was therefore reached by which the Indian government simply borrowed £3m of silver from the silver branch at an interest rate of 3.5 per cent, which was to be repaid through the purchase and shipment of London silver when finances allowed.[21] When, in February 1907, the government was able to repay the loan, however, the IO proved reluctant to purchase the necessary silver. Officials pointed out that there was no pressing need for immediate repayment, and that the balances could be needed for earmarking in the coming trading period and, in any case, were lent to the City at 4.5 per cent as against the 3.5 per cent owed on the loan. These arguments were dismissed by the Indian government, which again accused officials of acting only in the interests of the City and successfully insisted that the debt be repaid.[22]

The silver branch of the Indian GSR was again called upon in 1908 (£3m), September 1909, and 1913, when the borrowing process reverted to the IO's original conception of the policy.[23] Fearing that further loans would 'create distrust in the management of the Reserve', officials, in the face of stiff resistance from the Indian government, insisted that the advance of that year be accompanied by a transfer of an equivalent sum from the home balances to the UK branch of the GSR.[24] All subsequent advances then came exclusively from this Reserve, the Indian silver branch having been dismantled in 1914, and the proceeds were transferred to India via reverse council bills. Initially, the IO was loath to permit such borrowing, which was not 'a proper employment of the fund' and 'very risky'.[25] The run on the Indian Post Office Bank at the outbreak of war, however, forced a rethink, and, in 1914, it allowed £7m to be borrowed (fully repaid in 1917) and, in 1915/16, a further £11m.[26]

19   BL, L/F/5/9, S of S to G of I, 30 Oct. 1906.
20   BL, L/F/5/4, Baker to Abrahams, 21 Feb. 1907; *ibid.*, Finance Dept. to S of S, 21 Feb. 1907; Banerji, 'Revisiting the Exchange Standard', p. 4496.
21   BL, L/F/5/4, fol. 9006/6. Reverse earmarking may have been used to transfer the remaining £1m (Sen, *Colonies*, p. 91).
22   BL, L/F/5/4, Abrahams to Baker, 15 March 1907; *ibid.*, Baker to Abrahams, 21 Feb. 1907; PP 1914 [Cd.7070], appendix 5, p. 197.
23   BL, L/F/5/5, note, 19 Jan. 1909; *ibid.*, p. 199, note, no date.
24   PP [Cd.7069], q. 580; BL, L/F/5/7, Financial Secretary, 16 Dec. 1912.
25   PP 1920 [Cmd.528], q. 4238, 5625; BL, L/F/7/460, S of S, 30 Sept. 1916.
26   BL, L/F/7/460, Abrahams, 12 Sept. 1916; PP 1917–18 [94], p. 271; PP 1922 [Cmd.1778], no. 83.

Non-council bill methods of meeting UK commitments

Advances, export bills, specie and earmarking

Non-council bill remittances were made via advances, export bills, specie and ear-marking, from funds already in Britain and by the purchase of sterling in India (Appendix 2). Advances were used in the early part of the period. The East India Company made loans in India to merchants, who repaid them in England in sterling, providing as collateral the exports bought with the money lent.[27] The remittances were more secure, faster and cheaper than those using specie, and, from 1834/5 to 1846/7, accounted for 32 per cent (£12.79m) of the funds moved to London.[28] The loans, however, were much criticised by Chambers of Commerce, which claimed that their irregular provision created uncertainty and led to speculation, and that they acted as unfair competition to export bills and entwined merchants in a 'vicious system of credit'.[29] In 1843, the Indian government thus recommended their abandonment, though this did not occur until the 1850s and they continued to be viewed as a potential alternative to bills.[30] In 1866, when other methods of remittance became problematical, the IO proposed supplying merchants with loans worth either three-fifths of the export bill given as collateral or 90 per cent of the Indian government securities provided as security.[31] In the event, an improvement in council bill sales meant that only one advance of rs3.00.000 (£28,750) was provided to the French company Comptoir d'Escompte de Paris.[32] Ten years later, the idea was resurrected once more, and, in 1879, it was proposed that advances be given to opium exporters.[33]

The transfer of money via export bills involved the Indian government purchasing bills from exchange banks and despatching them to London, where they were discounted or held to maturity by the IO. The bills were used only very occasionally, as they were only available in large quantities in the trading season, and there was the 'dangerous' risk that the drawee would fail to pay the amount owed, forcing the IO to sell the associated produce and to become involved in bankruptcy proceedings that could generate bad publicity and damage its market credit. It was also believed not to be within the Indian government's remit to become involved in trade, and purchases in 1878 led to 'something like panic in the [Indian] market'.[34]

---

27   Ambedkar, *The Problem*, chap. 7.
28   McGuire, 'Exchange Banks', p. 144; PP 1899 [C.9376], p. 24.
29   Ambedkar, *The Problem*, chap. 7; McGuire, 'Exchange Banks', p. 144.
30   BL, L/F/5/139, Remittance from India, 29 Jan. 1883. £1.39m of advances were made in 1850/1–1851/2 and 1853/4–1854/5 (PP 1899 [C.9386], p. 139).
31   BL, L/F/5/139, IO to G of I, 26 June 1866; *ibid.*, telegram IO to G of I, 15 June 1866.
32   *Ibid.*, Remittance from India, 10 March 1881, p. 16; *ibid.*, G of I to IO, 21 June 1866; *ibid.*, financial letter to India, 26 June 1866.
33   PP 1899 [C.9376], p. 25.
34   BL, L/F/5/139, Mallet, 13 Dec. 1876; *ibid.*, Cassels, 19 Feb. 1877; PP 1899 [C.9222, 9390], q. 9094.

Nonetheless, the use of such bills was reconsidered in 1898 when it was suggested that they be bought by the presidency banks from merchants. Supporters of the proposal pointed out that remittances were made through the banking sector in the Crown colonies and that purchases could prove more profitable than the sale of council bills, lower the exchange rate and diminish criticism of the home charges by making it more difficult for critics to determine the amount of money actually transferred to the UK.[35] The IO was less convinced. Such an initiative would create uproar from the exchange banks, which would be less able to buy council bills, and there was little evidence that purchases would either increase returns or lower the exchange.[36] The proposal was consequently dropped, as was an earlier suggestion that some money could be remitted through the sale by the IO of import drafts. Obstacles to the use of such bills included insufficient and irregular exchange bank demand and the negative impact sales would have on trade.[37]

From 1854/5 to 1919/20, the Indian government sent £1.4m of silver and £20.1m of gold to London (Figure 11).[38] Specie was commonly used as a mode of remittance prior to the arrival of the council bill, but then fell out of favour. Its transportation was costly, slow and involved the risk of theft and loss at sea.[39] Silver was thus only despatched in 1915/16 to 1916/17, and gold when there was little demand for bills, to increase GSR or PCR London bullion stocks or to purchase silver for minting into coin when the use of council bills or earmarking would have a negative impact on London interest rates.[40] Gold exports peaked in the early 1930s – the Indian government had difficulty securing remittances, there was a surplus of gold in India due to forced sales by the rural population and deflation had pushed Indian gold prices below the World price. By improving the balance of payments, strengthening sterling and helping the repayment of US war debts, the exports were also of benefit to Britain.[41]

---

35 PP 1898 [C.9037], q. 4176–7, 4257, 5512.

36 BL, L/F/5/170, p. 55.

37 BL, L/F/5/139, Remittance from India, 10 March 1881, p. 15. Sales would reduce the banks' capacity to absorb bills drawn up by merchants.

38 PP 1906 [Cd.2754], no. 72; PP 1914–16 [Cd.7799], no. 72; PP 1922 [Cmd.1778], no. 72; PP 1928 [Cmd.3046], no. 66; PP 1899 [C.9376], p. 139.

39 McGuire, 'Exchange Banks', p. 144.

40 PP 1922 [Cmd.1778], no. 72; BL, L/F/5/7, Comptroller to Newmarch, 13 Feb. 1913. A Hong Kong & Shanghai Banking Corp. 1932 proposal for the Bank to purchase silver from the Indian government and pay for it in England was rejected (BL, L/F/7/806, S of S to Finance Dept., 21 Dec. 1932).

41 A. Mukherjee, 'The Depression Years: Indian Capitalists' Critique of British and Monetary Financial Policy in India 1929–39', in A. K. Bagchi (ed.), *Money and Credit in Indian History from Early Medieval Times*, New Delhi 2002, pp. 149–50, 157.

Figure 11. Specie remittances and railway company net receipts/withdrawals, 1850/1 –1920/1

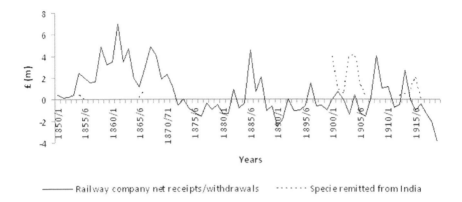

Sources. PP 1906 [Cd.2754], no. 72; PP 1914–16 [Cd.7799], no. 72; PP 1922 [Cmd.1778], no. 72; PP 1928 [Cmd.3046], no. 66; PP 1930–31 [Cmd.3882], no. 66; PP 1938–39 [Cmd.6079], no. 115; PP 1935–36 [Cmd.5158], no. 64; PP 1899 [C.9376], pp. 139–40.

A related method of remittance was the purchase and sale of gold in transit to and from India. As discussed in Chapter 8, the IO bought Australian and Egyptian gold that the exchange banks were remitting to India and redirected the shipments to London. At the same time, it sold for payment in London Indian government gold headed for the UK. In 1905/6 and 1908, specie was sold to the Anglo-Egyptian Bank, Credit Lyonnais and the London City and Midland Bank, and offloaded at Port Said, Egypt. The sales benefitted the banks, the IO and the Bank of England. The banks saved the cost of transporting gold from the UK to Egypt, and the IO charged a 1/8 per cent commission for the sales and was relieved of the expense of insuring the cargo during the latter part of its journey to London and the interest loss it would have suffered during this leg of the voyage. The reduced outflow of specie from London to Egypt, meanwhile, helped the Bank of England in its management of market gold stocks.[42] In 1906, gold about to be shipped to Britain was sold via the Yokohama Specie Bank to the Japanese government and instead exported to Japan, and, in 1914, gold in transit to the UK was bought by the War Office and again delivered to Port Said.[43]

---

42   BL, L/F/5/9, note, 13 April 1905; *ibid*, p. 26, note, 1 May 1906. In 1905, the P & O Steamship Navigation Co. refused to give the IO a rebate for the shortened voyages (*ibid*., p. 16, IO to Indian Financial Sect., 14 Nov. 1905).
43   BL, L/F/5/8, Treasury to IO, 7 Aug. 1914; BL, L/AG/37/4, B of E to IO, 22 Feb. 1906; *ibid*., note, no date, 1906; *ibid*., note, 22 Feb. 1906; *ibid*., IO to G of I, 22 Feb. 1906.

Earmarking involved the IO transferring gold from the London PCR into the home balances, from where it met India's UK commitments, and the Indian government either moving an equal amount of gold or rupees from its Treasury balances into the Indian PCR or cancelling currency notes to the same value.[44] The practice was adopted when council bill remittance and later sterling purchases were not possible, most significantly in 1907–8, 1914–15, 1919–25, 1927, 1931 and 1933. It allowed money to be moved from India to the UK rapidly and cheaply, and, if it was placed in the IO's Bank of England account, increased the Bank's gold stocks.[45] It was also seen by the Bank of England as a possible solution to crises. In 1906, wishing to rapidly reduce interest rates, the Bank proposed that £500,000 of Australian gold being shipped to India and about to be purchased by the IO and redirected to London be allowed to continue to Calcutta and placed in the Indian PCR, allowing a simultaneous release of gold from the London PCR into the IO's Bank of England account and the immediate relief of interest rates. In the event, the situation in London eased and the operation was abandoned.[46] In 1916/17, however, a similar stratagem went ahead. Unable to ship £7m of South African and New Zealand gold to Britain because of the war in the Atlantic, the Bank transported the specie to India, where it was placed in the Indian PCR, allowing an equal amount of gold to be released from the London PCR to the home balances and the Bank.[47] The IO permitted the operation to go ahead for patriotic reasons, but also because it allowed a large remittance to be made, and the sale of some of the gold in India helped to relieve that country's currency shortages.[48]

Use of UK funds and purchase of sterling

Within Britain, India's UK commitments were met through borrowing on the capital market and from City institutions and the GSR, the deposits of Indian railway companies in the home balances and the payments in London of money owed to India by the UK government. As discussed in Chapters 1 and 4, the proceeds of Indian government loans issued in the London markets and placed in the home balances were used to meet UK commitments until needed, and some loans and sterling bills were raised specifically for this purpose. From 1922/3 to 1924/5 and 1931/2 to 1935/6,

---

44 PP 1914 [Cd.7069], q. 1379, 1384. The IO were said to 'earmark' the PCR gold as belonging to the home balances.

45 *Ibid.*, IO to G of I, 7 April 1905; Keynes, *Indian Currency*, p. 137; PP 1914–16 [233], p. 4; PP 1924 [115] *Return of Indian Financial Statement and Budget*, p. 157; PP 1926 [108] *Return of Indian Financial Statement and Budget*, p. 86; *The Statist*, 11 June 1927, p. 1111; Kale, *India's National Finance*, p. 90; Harris, *Monetary Problems*, p. 377.

46 BL, L/F/5/9, p. 34, IO to Meston, 23 Nov. 1906; *ibid.*, IO to G of I, 21 Nov. 1906.

47 BL, L/F/5/8, S of S to Finance Dept., 5 Feb. 1916; *ibid.*, Finance Dept. to S of S, 7 Feb. 1916; NA, T 120/1, Treasury to IO, 25 April 1917.

48 A. Pope, 'Australian Gold and the Finance of India's Exports during World War I: A Case Study of Imperial Control and Coordination', *Indian Economic & Social History Review*, 33 (2) (1996), p. 117; PP 1917–18 [94], p. 11. The remaining gold was shipped to Ottawa for refining (NA, T 120/1, Treasury to IO, 7 Sept. 1917).

the sterling proceeds of loans floated in London by Indian public bodies (£5.7m) were also used to meet the home charges, an equivalent rupee sum being paid to the public bodies concerned by the Indian government.[49] In 1917, subscription to the India war loan by UK investors had to take the form of HM Treasury bills, which were placed in a special account at the Bank of England until they matured, when the proceeds were again transferred to the home balances.[50] Institutional loans were obtained from a number of organisations, including Coutts & Co. (in 1872), the Bank of England, the Treasury and the Imperial Bank.[51] The Bank of England allowed the IO to run overdrafts on its current account, but if these continued for some time would require the Office to take out an advance.[52] From 1866 to 1914, at least twelve such loans were obtained from the Bank worth a total of £14.9m and lent at either base rate or ½ per cent below this rate – a rate of return higher than that charged to HM Treasury, but below that paid by the Crown Agents for their advances from the Bank.[53] The advances were made in £250,000 instalments for one month to three years (though generally for six months), ranged from £250,000 to £4.75m and were secured on collateral in the form of Indian government debentures.[54]

Imperial Bank and Treasury loans were far less common. The London branch of the Imperial Bank lent India £6m in 1930, and there were Treasury loans in 1879 and 1915.[55] The 1879 advance to help pay for the Afghanistan War was freely given by the Treasury, which charged no interest, gave the IO seven years to pay it back and accepted specially created 3 per cent annuities as collateral.[56] Treasury officials were more reluctant to come to the IO's aid in 1915, finally relenting only because the dominions had obtained similar loans, India was providing men and resources for the war effort and there were no feasible alternative sources of finance. Borrowing on the London market would absorb badly needed funds, loans from the GSR would reduce India's defences if there was a run on the rupee and a rise in taxation could have political implications.[57] The Treasury thus agreed to make an advance of £2m for three months from the Wheat Scheme at an interest rate of 4.5 per cent, which

49 PP 1923 [128], pp. 150, 160; PP 1930–31 [Cmd.3882], no. 113.
50 BL, L/AG/14/17/1, no. 23, IO to B of E, 9 June 1917; *ibid.*, no. 37.
51 BL, L/F/5/139, IO to G of I, 1 Aug. 1872.
52 PP 1871 [363], q. 9363.
53 BE, F11/3/4123/3, memo, 5 July 1866; PP 1878–79 [312], q. 844; BE, G23/66/249; BE, G23/67/33; BE, G23/67/94; BE, G23/67/264; BE, G23/68/162–3; BE, G23/68/224–5; PP 1897 [193], p. 59; BL, L/AG/9/8/7, p. 79, IO to B of E, 17 June 1914; PP 1894 [92], p. 48; PP 1896 [C.8258], q. 2433; Sunderland, *Managing the British Empire*, pp. 196–8.
54 BL, L/AG/9/8/5, vol. 5, p. 121, memo, no date; *ibid.*, vol. 5, p. 843, IO to B of E, 11 Aug. 1893.
55 The Imperial Bank borrowed the £6m from the Bank of England on the security of Indian government rupee loans (BL, L/F/7/813, Ball, 28 March 1935; *ibid.*, Kelly, 20 Feb. 1935). The loans were repaid in April/June 1931 (PP 1931–32 [Cmd.3969] *Explanatory Memorandum, of the Accounts and Estimates for 1931–32*, p. 14).
56 NA, T 1/16802, IO to Treasury, 11 Feb. 1879; *ibid.*, IO to Treasury, 21 Aug. 1879; *ibid.*, note, 14 Sept. 1879.
57 NA, T 1/11898, 4821, confidential memo.

the IO charged to the scheme's profit and loss account, and credit of up to £1m to March 1916 and £3m to March 1917 to be called upon when needed.[58]

The GSR and Indian railway company deposits met UK commitments at either end of the period under review. The GSR provided funds from 1902. Its receipts were available to pay for disbursements until invested; from 1908 to 1919, an annual average of £2.667m of its contents were placed in the home balances; and it was itself regarded as a source of money if the IO could only sell council bills or purchase sterling at unacceptably low prices – drawings being made in 1901 (£500,000), 1915/16 (£7.5m), 1927, 1929 and 1930/1 (£12m).[59] Railway company deposits were a major source of funds only in the 1850s and 1860s. The deposits comprised the capital raised by London share issues and loans, which was placed in the home balances by the guaranteed railway companies and refunded to them in England and India when needed (Figure 11).[60] For some years, the amount of money entering the home balances tended to be greater than that leaving it, and the IO could use the funds to meet India's UK commitments. The railways' share issues and loans tended to be floated when market demand was high, which was often some time before work on lines was due to commence, and companies sometimes overestimated their capital needs.[61] Moreover, rather than paying the money required in India to the companies in England and then selling them council bills for its remittance, these sums were paid in India by the Indian government, and the companies' deposits were adjusted accordingly. The remittance of such funds therefore had no impact on sales of council bills or the exchange.[62] The contribution of the deposits to the home balances, however, was short-lived, beginning to wane from the early 1870s. The first phase of infrastructure construction had come to an end and less capital was required, and, from 1869, lines were increasingly built by the State and financed by rupee loans raised in India.[63] Thus, although the IO received £41.5m of deposits from 1850/1 to 1919/20, by 1872–77 average annual net capital receipts had fallen to £0.023m from a high of £5.7m in 1863–68.[64]

The payment in London of money owed by HMG to the Indian government amounted to £479.34m from 1850/1 to 1925/6 and can be divided into military and

---

58   BL, L/F/5/8, Abrahams, 3 Aug. 1915; *ibid.*, minute, 4 Aug. 1915; NA, T 120/1, Treasury to IO, 12 Aug. 1915; NA, T 1/11898, 24339, Treasury to IO, 7 Dec. 1915. The Wheat Scheme is discussed below.

59   PP 1908 [170], p. 65; PP 1914–16 [Cd.7799], no. 83; PP 1922 [Cmd.1778], no. 83; PP 1920 [Cmd.528], q. 5618; PP 1902 [187], p. 13; PP 1916 [80], p. 30; BL, L/AG/29/1/153, 138, no. 3, note, 3 April 1928; *ibid.*, 138, no. 4, note, 3 Oct. 1929; *ibid.*, 138, no. 5, note, 2 April 1931; *ibid.*, 138, no. 6, note, 5 April 1932.

60   BL, L/F/5/139, Remittance from India, 10 March 1881, p. 15.

61   PP 1890–91 [225] *Financial Statement of Government of India, 1891–92*, pp. 33, 45.

62   PP 1898 [C.9037], q. 2633, 2684.

63   Banerji, *Finances*, pp. 62, 206.

64   PP 1906 [Cd.2754], no. 72; PP 1914–16 [Cd.7799], no. 72; PP 1922 [Cmd.1778], no. 72; PP 1928 [Cmd.3046], no. 66; PP 1899 [C.9376], p. 140; Banerji, *Finances*, p. 231.

non-military receipts (Figure 12).[65] Military payments rose during wars and largely comprised deferrals for the use of Indian troops and their equipment in non-Indian conflict zones such as Labuan (1869/70), Abyssinia (1867–70), Suakim (1884/5), South Africa (1899/1900), China (1900/1), Somaliland (1904/5), Europe (1914–18), East Africa (1917/18), Persia (1916/17) and Mesopotamia (1916/17 and 1922/3).[66] Other recoveries included military pensions paid in India, goods supplied to HMG ships operating around its coasts, and, during the First World War, military supplies purchased in India and the employment of enemy ships.[67] Debts reached their peak from 1914/15 to 1920/1, when a total of £342.2m was recovered, and, although the payments 'led to a sea of [administrative] troubles', they provided a cheap and rapid means of meeting the home charges.[68]

Figure 12. Repayment in London of money owed by HMG to Indian government, 1850/1–1925/6

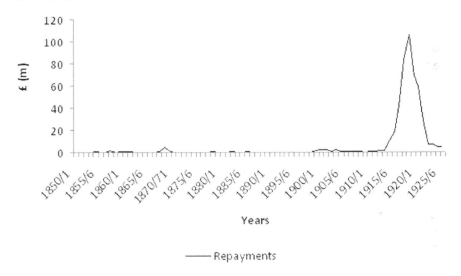

Sources. Figure 11 sources.

65   PP 1906 [Cd.2754], no. 72; PP 1914–16 [Cd.7799], no. 72; PP 1922 [Cmd.1778], no. 72; PP 1928 [Cmd.3046], no. 66; PP 1899 [C.9376], p. 139.

66   PP 1871 [363], q. 10298, 10303; PP 1884–85 [151] *Financial Statement of Government of India, 1885–86*, p. 25; PP 1900 [225], p. 13; PP 1901 [171], p. 59; PP 1905 [167], p. 63; PP 1914–16 [233], p. 4; PP 1918 [61], p. 282; PP 1923 [128], p. 160; PP 1899 [254], p. 39.

67   PP 1871 [363], q. 10300–1; PP 1914–16 [233], p. 204; PP 1916 [80], p. 284.

68   PP 1906 [Cd.2754], no. 72; PP 1914–16 [Cd.7799], no. 72; PP 1922 [Cmd.1778], no. 72; PP 1928 [Cmd.3046], no. 66; PP 1920 [103], p. 96.

Non-military receipts comprised the recovery of debts expended by a host of colonies, protectorates and dominions, including Uganda for Indian government loans to Zanzibar, Mauritius for advances made to coolies prior to their emigration to the colony, and, from 1881 to 1886, Ceylon and Hong Kong for bills of exchange drawn on the Indian Treasury.[69] Empire money and postal orders drawn on and paid in India were also recouped in London.[70] During and after the First World War, these countries were joined by a host of others. Ceylon, unable to buy council bills, received rupees from the Indian government, the value of which was retrieved in the UK.[71] Egypt paid for gold and coins, China for opium, and Australia and the East Africa Protectorate for a range of goods.[72] Post-war recoveries were made, among others, by Iraq, Mesopotamia, Hong Kong, the Straits and Siam.[73] As for the repayment of debts owed by the UK government, these again rose during the First World War, three of the largest items being the £2m of gold sold to the Bank of England in 1915/16, the Mauritian sugar purchased on behalf of the UK government, and the Wheat Scheme, under which the Indian administration bought grain in India on behalf of Britain and received payment in London. Over its lifetime, the IO received £20.4m from the scheme, though from June to September 1915 £4.7m of these funds were repatriated to India through the sale of reverse council bills in order to reverse the depletion of the Indian government's Treasury balances.[74]

The Indian government began to purchase sterling in India in 1923, and, by 1939/40, had bought £549.18m, though in most years and especially in the early and late 1930s, the majority of UK commitments were met through other means (Figure 9).[75] Initially, purchases were made by the Imperial Bank of India at fixed prices from exchange banks/trading companies that needed rupees to finance the purchase of export bills/exports and were on an approved list.[76] Criticism that such transactions restricted competition and prices then led in 1927 to the introduction of weekly public tenders held each Wednesday simultaneously in Calcutta, Bombay,

69 PP 1896 [166], p. 55; PP 1871 [363], q. 10295; BL, L/F/5/139, Treasury to IO, 1 Feb. 1886. Adopted to reduce the number of council bills sold, the payment in London of bills drawn on India by Ceylon and Hong Kong was abandoned when the price of these bills exceeded that of council bills (*ibid.*).

70 PP 1896 [C.8258], q. 2581–2.

71 NA, T 120/1, Treasury to IO, 20 Jan. 1917. From 1919, the value of the rupees was recouped from HMG Treasury chest in Ceylon (NA, T 120/2, Treasury to IO, 23 Nov. 1918; *ibid.*, Treasury to IO, 29 April 1919; *ibid.*, Treasury to IO, 2 Aug. 1919).

72 PP 1914–16 [233], p. 204; PP 1917–18 [94], p. 268; PP 1918 [61], p. 283.

73 PP 1923 [128], pp. 158, 160; PP 1926 [108], p. 238. In addition, in 1929, non-government purchasers of Hong Kong dollars minted in India paid for their acquisitions in London (*Report of the Controller of Currency*, 1929/30, p. 11).

74 NA, T 120/2, Treasury to IO, 6 Dec. 1918; PP 1916 [80], p. 30.

75 PP 1929–30 [Cmd.3386], p. 19; PP 1930–31 [Cmd.3670]; PP 1931–32 [Cmd.3969]; PP 1931–32 [Cmd.4161]; PP 1932–33 [Cmd.4416]; PP 1933–34 [Cmd.4695]; PP 1930–31 [Cmd.3882], p. 113; PP 1938–39 [Cmd.6079], no. 150; PP 1942–43 [Cmd. 6441], no. 140.

76 *India Finance*, 7 April 1928; Simha and Balachandran, *History*, p. 61.

Madras and Karachi.[77] The IO, at first, objected to the new procedure, which reduced its control over the exchange and was strongly opposed by the exchange banks that feared for their profits.[78] Gradually, however, it relented. In 1923, the purchase of sterling had a less depressive impact on the exchange than an increase in council bill sales, and officials began to appreciate the benefits of acquisitions over the sale of bills.[79] Not only were administrative costs lower, but the greater involvement of merchants increased competition and resulted in the payment of better prices, and the government could more accurately and rapidly assess market conditions and the factors influencing the exchange, and, through its purchases, thus maintain a more stable exchange.[80] By giving India some control of its own currency, the purchases also reaped political dividends, and the acquisition of rupees by merchants direct rather than through the exchange banks reduced the cost and promoted the expansion of trade.[81] The only drawback was that during periods of low exports insufficient amounts of sterling became available, and the rate of exchange that could be obtained fell, though from 1931 the depreciation of the rupee as a result of the abandonment of the gold standard and the associated increase in gold exports somewhat increased sterling availability. The government therefore had to make large purchases when exports were resurgent, building up reserves that could be called upon when the state of trade worsened.[82]

Conclusion

Prior to the arrival of the council bill, funds were remitted via the provision in India and the repayment in London of trading company loans, the purchase of export bills and the movement of specie. Later, when the issue of council bills was not possible or feasible, the IO again turned to specie and to earmarking (particularly if there was a rise in London interest rates in the offing), or used money raised in the UK via Indian government or guaranteed railway company loan issues, or British government debt created in India but paid off in London. When the Indian government simply lacked the funds necessary to cash council bills, it restricted sales, occasionally permitted the government to borrow from the Indian silver branch of the GSR or transferred money to India via reverse earmarking, though it took care not to denude the London market of gold, ever fearful of the impact of high London interest rates on its own financial activities.

---

77   J. C. Sinha, *Indian Currency Problems of the Last Decade*, Delhi 1938, p. 66; BL, L/F/5/37, circular, 21 April 1927; Chablani, *Indian Currency, Banking and Exchange*, p. 111.
78   Tomlinson, *The Political Economy*, p. 72; Balachandran, *John Bullion's Empire*, p. 116.
79   Balachandran, 'The Sterling Crisis', p. 19.
80   Sinha, *Indian Currency Problems*, p. 65; PP 1926 [Cmd.2687], p. 22.
81   Balachandran, 'The Sterling Crisis', p. 18; Sinha, *Indian Currency Problems*, p. 65.
82   *The Statist*, 23 April 1938, p. 617; *ibid.*, 17 Nov. 1934, p. 665; *Report of the Controller of Currency*, 1931/2, pp. 12–13.

10

Gold Standard and Paper Currency Reserves

Created in 1899 on the recommendation of the Fowler Committee, the Gold Standard Reserve (GSR) was initially intended to support the establishment of a gold currency.[1] With the abandonment of an Indian gold standard, its purpose then became to underpin the exchange and to provide a pool of money that could be used to cash the reverse council bills sold in India and cashed in London when the exchange rate fell below the gold export point and as an alternate source of funds when council bills/sterling could not be sold/bought at sufficiently high prices. It also provided temporary loans to the Indian government when it lacked the funds to meet council bills; helped to minimise Indian inflation; by ensuring the stability of the exchange, improved Indian credit in the London capital market; and, con-troversially, in 1907 financed the repayment of £1.1m of railway debentures, which the IO was unable to renew owing to a dearth of money in the City.[2] Indian critics denounced the raid.[3] The repayment of the debentures should have been financed via the issue of sterling bills, a solution rejected because officials wished to avoid acting against their City friends, and the use of the Reserve for 'purposes...wholly foreign to its object' would 'shake public confidence' in India's determination to maintain the exchange, threatening its stability. Accepting that the initiate was con-trary to the declared aim of the GSR, the IO argued that it was large enough, at £25m, to withstand such a withdrawal, which had no impact on confidence, as it was recorded in such a manner that it did not appear in the accounts. As for the issue of sterling bills, the securities would have had to have carried an unaccept-ably high interest rate to attract buyers, the resultant increase in India's debt would have weakened both the country's credit and confidence in its ability to support the

---

1 Sen, *Colonies*, p. 88.
2 Harris, *Monetary Problems*, p. 396; Dubey, *The Indian Public Debt*, p. 57.
3 BL, L/F/5/5, minute, 2 July 1909.

exchange, and the resultant greater London stringency/higher interest rates would have negatively affected its own operations in the City.[4]

The contents of the Reserve largely came from coinage profits. Since the rupee was worth more than its bullion content, the Indian government made a small gain on the issue of coins, which was initially paid into revenues.[5] From 1900 to 1917, this sum (£21.39m) was transferred to the GSR via the sale of council bills, and, if demand for bills was low, the shipment of gold, the purchase of Australian/Egyptian specie in transit to India, and earmarking.[6] The payment of coinage profits into the Indian Paper Currency Reserve (PCR) and the simultaneous earmarking or movement of an equivalent sum from the London PCR to the GSR had the additional advantage of enabling the money transfers to be rapidly invested.[7] Ideally, the profits were remitted as they accrued rather than in large accumulated amounts, as otherwise the GSR lost interest, and there was a possibility that large investments would be made during periods of high security prices.[8] Other income streams came from GSR investments – dividends, trading profits and price appreciation – though the fall in the price of consols led to a 1900/1–1928/9 overall depreciation loss of £2.032m.[9] The Reserve also received, in 1907, a £0.5m advance from the London PCR to enable the advantageous purchase of exchequer bonds, and, in 1932, the £9.34m raised in that year's government sterling loan.[10] The Reserve had been denuded by the recent financial crisis, its restoration improved India's credit in the London market, and the home balances had little need of the loan proceeds.[11]

The growth of the Reserve was rapid (Figure 13). By 1905/6, it had reached £12.25m.[12] Denuded by £9.11m during the 1907–09 exchange crisis, its size was rapidly restored, even though many claimed it would have made more financial sense to pay off the sterling bills issued during the emergency on which an interest rate of 2.75 per cent was paid, as compared to the 2 per cent that was received from the Treasury bills in which funds flowing into the GSR were invested.[13] The reason for the decision was simple; the IO feared further exchange weakness and needed to rebuild its defences. It had also determined to fight a future crisis wholly with GSR funds, and thus avoid the damage to its credit wrought by the issue of sterling bills,

---

4   BL, L/F/5/4, Baker to Abrahams, 18 July 1907; *ibid*, Abrahams to Baker, 7 Aug. 1907; *ibid.*, Scott, 5 July 1907; *ibid.*, Abrahams to Baker, 28 June 1907.

5   Tomlinson, *The Political Economy*, p. 19. Profit was net the cost of coinage, transport of coin to India and incidental expenses (PP 1901 [171], p. 25).

6   PP 1906 [Cd.2754], no. 83; PP 1914–16 [Cd.7799], no. 83; PP 1922 [Cmd.1778], no. 83; PP 1901 [171], p. 25; BL, L/F/5/7, Newmarch to Comptroller General, 24 Jan. 1913.

7   BL, L/F/5/7, Newmarch to Gillan, 21 Feb. 1913; PP 1906 [162], p. 20.

8   PP 1901 [171], pp. 25, 198.

9   PP 1929–30 [Cmd.3386], p. 18.

10 BL, L/AG/37/4, IO to G of I, 6 June 1907; *ibid.*, G of I to IO, 13 June 1907; NA, T 160/474, Indian loans, 1932 and 1933, S of S to G of I, 28 April 1932.

11 *Ibid.*, Indian loans, 1932 and 1933, G of I to S of S, 24 April 1932.

12 PP 1911 [155], p. 305.

13 BL, L/F/5/7, Newmarch, 16 Dec. 1912; BL, L/F/5/5, note, 19 Jan. 1909.

and believed that an announcement that the bills were to be repaid could trigger a further exchange fall, signalling to the market that the restoration of the Fund was considered a secondary matter.[14] Having restored the Reserve to its previous value, it then, in 1910, set a maximum size of £25m, later raised to £30m, and, in 1920, £40m, arguing that the 1907–09 crisis had clearly demonstrated inadequate resources.[15] On reaching these maximums, coinage profits and investment returns were diverted to other uses, and, from 1921, were channelled into the PCR to replace the rupee Treasury bills that had been purchased during the war, £2.86m being transferred for this purpose.[16] Thereafter, returns were credited to revenue (£9.5m from 1923/4 to 1929), thus improving India's rupee and sterling credit rating, and, from 1928/9, partly paid into a Revenue Equalisation Fund.[17] Established to guard against the depreciation of the Reserve's investments in the turbulent markets of the late 1920s/ early 1930s, the Fund received the whole of the excess of returns up to £1.6m and half of any remaining surplus, and could transfer up to £1.6m into the GSR in any one year.[18]

On the change of its primary purpose from supporting the circulation of gold to the maintenance of the exchange, the Reserve in 1902 was moved from India to London, and the gold that made up its contents was sold and invested in UK securities. The reasons for both initiatives were perfectly logical. If the Reserve had been located in India and invested in specie, gold would have had to have been transported to London during an emergency, increasing costs and leading to delay.[19] Also, securities earned interest, which reduced the amount of money that had to be transferred to London to increase/maintain the size of the Reserve; short term Treasury bills were as marketable as gold; and, in the event of a crisis and difficulties in offloading longer term stock, cash could always be obtained from the home balances or from the PCR.[20] Moreover, UK securities earned a higher return than their Indian counterpart and were unlikely to decline in value, and their purchase helped to finance British public expenditure; in the case of Treasury bills, they increased Bank of England gold stocks at times of gold outflows, lessening base rate rises; and

14 BL, L/F/5/5, note, 19 Jan. 1909.

15 *Investors Review*, 24, (Jan./July 1910), p. 406; Doraiswami, *Indian Finance*, appendix; PP 1920 [Cmd.529], appendix 1, p. 30, par. 6; Tomlinson, *The Political Economy*, p. 23. Critics in 1920 pointed out that exchange crises over the previous eighteen years had denuded the GSR by just £9m and that its existing resources were more than adequate (PP 1920 [Cmd.529], p. 124).

16 PP 1913 [130], p. 232; BL, L/F/7/596, fol. 6567/21, note, no date, 1921; PP 1929–30 [Cmd.3386], p. 18.

17 PP 1923 [128], p. 18.

18 PP 1930–31 [Cmd.3670], p. 20. In 1929/30 and 1930/1 respectively, £422,709 were transferred to and £33,748 from the Fund (PP 1931–32 [Cmd.3969], p. 21).

19 PP 1920 [Cmd.529], p. 124.

20 PP 1905 [167], p. 19; PP 1920 [Cmd.528], q. 5228–9; PP 1914 [Cd.7069], q. 1384, 1390. By 1912, the Reserve had earned £3.25m of interest (£2.5m if depreciation losses are taken into account) (Keynes, *Indian Currency*, p. 125).

Figure 13. Gold Standard Reserve, 1901–1935

Sources. PP 1906 [Cd.2754], no. 83; PP 1914–16 [Cd.7799], no. 83; PP 1922 [Cmd.1778], no. 83; PP 1930–31 [Cmd.3882], no. 110; PP 1938–39 [Cmd.6079], no. 149.

Note. Amounts as of 31 March.

they supported gilt prices, the level of which influenced the market price of Indian government loans, which, in turn, had an impact on the demand for and the price of new issues of these securities.[21]

Indian nationalist opposition to both policy changes straddled a range of positions. Some questioned the very need for a Reserve, arguing that it had rarely been used for its proper purpose, that the sums required to cash reverse councils could easily be raised via the issue of a loan or sterling bills, and, in 1920, that the resultant greater circulation of gold within India if the Reserve was abolished would dampen inflation and the rise in silver prices.[22] Such assumptions ignored the difficulty of raising funds in the UK, particularly during an emergency, the impact of debt on credit, the minimal demand in India for gold as a currency and the myriad other factors behind the rise in silver prices.[23] Others accepted the need for the Fund, but urged that it be kept in India and in gold. An Indian Reserve would make it easier for the Indian government to borrow its contents, and the costs and delays involved in transporting specie could be overcome through the sale of London PCR investments and the transfer of the proceeds to the GSR with a simultaneous reverse

21 PP 1920 [Cmd.528], q. 5228–9; Balachandran, *John Bullion's Empire*, p. 30; *Financial Times*, 3 Nov. 1922, p. 1.

22 PP 1920 [Cmd.529], p. 124; BL, L/F/5/5, Finance Dept. to IO, 19 Aug. 1909; PP 1920 [Cmd.528], q. 5154–6.

23 BL, L/F/5/5, p. 7, minute, no date; PP 1920 [Cmd.528], **q. 5157.**

movement of funds in India, though this would involve the expansion of the PCR/
note circulation.[24]

Still others promoted an Indian Reserve deposited in the presidency banks (thus
reducing Indian interest rates and interest rate fluctuations in the trading season,
and leading to the development of a money market) or invested in Indian government rupee securities (the resultant fall in supply and rise in market prices of which
would permit issued stock to be offered at a lower yield and more money to be available for capital investment).[25] Such arguments discounted the relatively low demand
for capital in India, particularly outside the trading season, the relative scarcity of
government securities and the likelihood that during an exchange crisis the price
of such investments would plummet to such an extent that they could become
unsalable.[26] A small minority, meanwhile, accepted the logic of a London Reserve,
but campaigned for a larger gold component, drawing attention to the Fowler and
Chamberlain Committees' recommendations that respectively the whole and half
its funds should be held as specie, which could easily be sold in times of crisis and
would not depreciate in value.[27]

Needless to say, the IO held firm against the repatriation to India of any part of
the Reserve, pointing out that the sale of UK securities would severely disrupt the
London market and its own City operations, and, in 1920, that the movement of
funds transferred to England at 1s 4d back to Calcutta at 1s 10d would involve large
losses.[28] Nonetheless, it kept small amounts of specie in India; in 1906, the PCR
Indian silver reserve, discussed below, became part of the GSR; and, prior to the
abolishment of the Reserve in 1935, gold stocks in the country rose dramatically.[29] In
1912, it also agreed to invest up to £5m in gold in the UK, a U-turn prompted by difficulties in obtaining suitable securities, the depreciation in consol prices described
below and a wish to give supporters of gold 'innocent pleasure at not too great an
expense'.[30] On the outbreak of war, this policy was abandoned, but readopted in
1927/8, when £1.73m and, from 1928/9 to 1934/5, £2.15m was held as specie.[31]

24 PP 1920 [Cmd.529], q. 4240; *ibid.*, appendix 1, p. 31.
25 PP 1918 [61], p. 92; Krishnaswami, 'Capital Development'.
26 BL, L/F/5/144, discussion on Indian finance, 31 Jan. 1913; PP 1914 [Cd.7069], q. 1407;
    Krishnaswami, 'Capital Development'.
27 BL, L/F/5/7, Newmarch, 16 Dec. 1912; PP 1920 [Cmd.528], q. 5228–9; BL, L/F/5/144, note for
    Baker, 18 Dec. 1912.
28 PP 1914 [Cd.7069], q. 2741; PP 1920 [Cmd.529], p. 126. See also PP 1918 [61], p. 120.
29 The IO had £417 of gold in India in 1904, £21,725 in 1907, £5.24m in 1915, £238,734 in 1916,
    £103,000 in 1917, and £6.25m, £27.15m and £11.62m respectively in 1931, 1932 and 1933 (PP
    1906 [Cd.2754], no. 83; PP 1914–16 [Cd.7799], no. 83; PP 1922 [Cmd.1778], no. 83; PP 1930–31
    [Cmd.3882], no. 110; PP 1938–39 [Cmd.6079], no. 149).
30 BL, L/F/5/144, note for Baker, 18 Dec. 1912; BL, L/F/5/7, Newmarch, 16 Dec. 1912; BL, L/
    F/7/166, financial, no. 76, 28 June 1912; Sen, *Colonies*, p. 131; PP 1920 [Cmd.528], q. 5630. In
    1913, 1914 and 1915, the GSR held respectively £1.62m, £4.32m and £1.25m of gold (PP 1914–16
    [Cd.7799], no. 83; PP 1922 [Cmd.1778], no. 83).
31 PP 1930–31 [Cmd.3882], no. 110; PP 1938–39 [Cmd. 6079], no. 149.

Investment policy

From 1901/2 to 1935, on average 93 per cent of the Reserve was invested in securities, the IO over the period acquiring £66.9m worth of stock.[32] Of the remainder, small sums awaiting investment were kept on deposit at the Bank of England; from 1909 to 1914, £1m to £3m was held in the home balances, from whence it was lent out at short notice to City institutions or deposited at call in London banks; from 1917 to 1921, miniscule amounts were advanced to UK banks; and, in 1915/16, there were loans to the home balances and the Bank of England.[33] The 1915/16 advances to the home balances, regarded by the Secretary of State as 'wrong in principle and dangerous in practice', amounted to two £2m six month 4 per cent loans to help repay £7m of sterling bills.[34] The Bank of England loans, meanwhile, were at a fortnight's call and sought to increase the liquidity of the Reserve in the face of an expected run on the exchange.[35]

The stock bought can be roughly divided into UK government securities (which comprised consols, Treasury bills and Treasury bonds) and a variety of other debentures and bills. To ensure that cash could be obtained rapidly and with little capital loss, it was crucial that the Reserve held a certain proportion of investments that had relatively short lives (currencies), were highly marketable and could be easily sold at little loss in times of crisis. Liquidity ratios were thus laid down that determined the currencies of the securities that the Reserve should hold, which varied over time depending on the perceived likelihood that funds would be called upon, required yields and the ease with which investments with the correct maturities could be obtained. In 1923 and 1925, for example, £10m was to be held in securities with maturities of respectively less than ten years and two to five years, and, in 1928, £20m was to be invested in stock with lives of two to ten years, and half this amount in investments with less than five years to run.[36] To ensure that these ratios were complied with, the IO had to obtain the permission of the Finance Council before making acquisitions. In reality, if speed was of the essence, it would obtain retrospective approval for purchases, and, if a stock offered particular benefits, a case would be put forward for circumventing the ratio limits.[37]

32 PP 1906 [Cd.2754], no. 83; PP 1914–16 [Cd.7799], no. 83; PP 1922 [Cmd.1778], no. 83; PP 1930–31 [Cmd.3882], no. 110; PP 1938–39 [Cmd.6079], no. 149; PP 1914 [Cd.7070], statement c, pp. 99–102.

33 de Cecco, *The International Gold Standard*, p. 71; BL, L/AG/14/14/3. From 1920 to 1935, an average of £1,971 was held at the Bank of England (PP 1922 [Cmd.1778], no. 83; PP 1930–31 [Cmd.3882], no. 110; PP 1938–39 [Cmd.6079], no. 149).

34 BL, L/F/7/460, S of S, 30 Sept. 1916; *ibid.*, f ol. 7809/16, Badock ; *ibid.*, note, no date.

35 BL, L/F/7/189, Abrahams to Meyer, 6 May 1916.

36 BL, L/AG/29/1/153, 138/1, note, 6 Nov. 1923; *ibid.*, 138/1, Kisch to G of I, 1 July 1925; *ibid.*, 138, no. 3, note, 11 June 1928.

37 E.g. *ibid.*, 138, no. 4, Kisch, 24 Feb. 1930; BL, L/F/5/6, note, 7 Dec. 1911. See also BL, L/F/7/460, fol. 12320, note, 8 Nov. 1921.

Surprisingly, money was initially ploughed into consols, a long-term security with no repayment date and a falling price – the result of overissue to finance the Boer War and the appearance in the market of a plethora of more attractive foreign stocks. The IO saw the security as a 'one-way' bet.[38] The eventual reversal of the price fall would reap the Fund a useful profit and the stock paid a higher interest rate than short-term securities and, given the vast amounts in the market, would be just as realisable during a crisis.[39] The Indian government was less convinced, suspecting that large disposals during a crisis would cause the already falling price to plummet. IO officials were thus urged to buy a wider range of long-term securities, the crisis sale of which would have less impact on price, and which, in some cases, paid a higher dividend than consols.[40]

The IO began to accept the error of its ways in 1907/8, by which time it had bought £7m of consols. The expected price recovery had failed to occur, and, in that year, the exchange fell and the GSR was needed to cash reverse council bills. Aware that large sales would decimate prices, lead to large losses, reduce market demand for the securities and have a knock-on effect on all gilt prices, reducing its ability to issue sterling bills (another potential source of funds), the IO delayed the sale of reverse councils. When this strategy became unsustainable, it obtained the necessary cash from GSR investment dividends, the proceeds of maturing Treasury bills, the portion of the Reserve that had been transferred to the home balances and the sale of its non-consol longer term investments, keeping as much as possible of its relatively small stockpile of short-term securities in reserve to be employed only if the exchange continued to fall, by which time the prices of long-term stock would have collapsed to levels that precluded sales.[41] It also procured a £0.862m loan from the Bank of England, discounted £1.24m of Treasury bills at the Bank, issued sterling bills and took temporary advances from its home balances.[42]

When eventually it had no choice but to offload consols, it sold £0.536322m to the PCR and, believing that any approach to the Bank of England would be rebuffed, then turned to the Treasury. Mindful that large market sales would damage current and future consol prices and depress other gilt values, and that the acquisition of the securities would reduce government interest payments, Treasury officials permitted

38   de Cecco, *The International Gold Standard*, p. 70; Kynaston, *The City ... Vol. 2*, p. 542. There is no evidence in the files to support the claim that officials wished to help the UK government finance the Boer War or to slow down the price fall (J. G. Balachandran, 'Power and Markets in Global Finance: The Gold Standard, 1890–1926', *Journal of Global History*, 3 (2008), pp. 313–35; Simha and Balachandran, *Indian Currency and Finance*, Bombay 1913, p. 4).

39   BL, L/F/5/3, fol. 8506, note, 28 Nov. 1906; Vakil, *Financial Developments*, p. 79; PP 1920 [Cmd.529], appendix 1, p. 31, par. 9.

40   BL, L/F/5/3, G of I to IO, 30 July 1903; *ibid.*, IO to Governor General, 11 Sept. 1903.

41   BL, L/F/5/5, memo, 28 July 1908; *ibid.*, fol. 3530, note, 10 June 1908; *ibid.*, note, 30 Sept. 1908; *ibid.*, Council minute, 25 March 1908; PP 1909 [122], p. 61.

42   BL, L/F/5/5, note, 5 Aug. 1908; *ibid.*, note, 30 Sept. 1908; *ibid.*, note, 19 Jan. 1909; *ibid.*, note, 9 Sept. 1908.

the National Debt Commissioners (NDC) to buy £1m of consols for the UK government's Sinking Fund at the average market price of the day.[43] These disposals were then followed by sales of £300,000 of local loans, Transvaal stock and Treasury bonds, and £1.163m of National War loan, the NDC acquisition of which was funded by a special issue of Treasury bills, purchase being again designed to curb market instability.[44]

Believing that in a future emergency either the 'British Cabinet' would prohibit sales of consols or 'City magnates' would simply refuse to buy them, after the 1908/9 crisis the IO halted purchases, offloaded more of its holdings over the next few years onto the PCR at the price of the day and made disposals in the market, though only when the price rose above a stated minimum.[45] Sales, however, were slow and any resultant fall in prices had a domino effect on gilt-edged securities, including Indian government loans, making the issue of new stock more difficult and costly.[46] When the UK government in 1915 offered war loan consol conversion rights, the IO thus launched a complex operation to once and for all rid itself of its purchases.

The terms of the war loan allowed investors who bought £100 to convert £75 of consols into an additional £50 of the security.[47] The IO thus purchased £0.1396m of the loan for its various discount Sinking Funds, which then sold the conversion rights to the GSR at a price of 5s per £75 of rights, and bought a further £1.39m of the loan from the UK government.[48] The latter acquisition was financed with £0.396m of GSR investment interest and dividends, and by the movement of almost £1m from the PCR to the GSR, with a corresponding reverse transfer occurring in India – an operation strongly opposed by the Indian government, which argued that given the fragility of the exchange it was important that the PCR remain as liquid as possible.[49]

At the same time, the IO theoretically bought £2.0667m of war loan in the market, appropriated the conversion rights and then resold the security ex-rights. In reality, on each sale the stock was purchased from and resold to the same institution; the purchase/resale occurred simultaneously and there was no exchange of money between the IO and the institution beyond the difference between the rights price at which the loan was bought and the ex-rights price at which it was resold. The

---

43   *Ibid.*, note, 30 Sept. 1908; *ibid.*, fol. 3530, note, 10 June 1908; *ibid.*, memo, 28 July 1908; *ibid.*, Council minute, 25 March 1908; *ibid.*, Abrahams to Hervey, 21 March 1908. £0.075m of the £1m was used to buy Treasury bills (*ibid.*, note, 25 April 1908). India made a loss of £0.04m on the deal (*ibid.*, note, 18 March 1908).

44   *Ibid.*, note, 25 June 1908; *ibid.*, fol. 3530, note, 10 June 1908; *ibid.*, note, 30 July 1908; *ibid.*, Blain to Abrahams, 31 July 1908.

45   PP 1920 [Cmd.529], appendix 1, p. 31, par. 9; Doraiswami, *Indian Finance*, p. 104; BL, L/F/5/7, Abrahams, 12 Dec. 1912; *ibid.*, note, 18 Feb. 1913; BL, L/AG/37/4, note, 14 April 1908.

46   BL, L/F/5/7, note, 11 Feb. 1914.

47   BL, L/F/5/8, Newmarch, 24 June 1915.

48   *Ibid.*, note, 5 Oct. 1915; *ibid.*, note, 9 Oct. 1915.

49   *Ibid.*, S of S to IO, 16 July 1915; *ibid.*, minute, 28 Aug. 1915; *ibid.*, Viceroy to S of S, 3 July 1915.

operation only occurred when the rights/ex-rights price difference amounted to 3/8 per cent per £100 war loan, and was initially to be financed through profits from the sale of war loan stock obtained through the use of the conversion rights, as the Finance Council refused to allow the GSR to fund the procedure. But in the light of its success, this ruling was relaxed and the necessary funds were procured from the early payment discount received when the IO paid for the £1.39m of loan stock it had bought from the UK government.[50]

Even more conversion rights were obtained through the Bank of England and the Bank of Bengal, both purchases being free from market commissions. The Bank of England sold rights on £0.4718m of war loan at 5s per £100. Initially, the Bank of Bengal was to buy £0.15m of consols, convert them into war loan using their own rights, and then sell the converted stock back to the IO for a fee of 1 per cent of the value of the consols converted. The Bank was then persuaded to simply sell its rights to the IO, thus simplifying the operation, but refused to reduce its fee, even though the market price of conversion rights had fallen in the meantime.[51]

On the abandonment of consols, the IO began to purchase Treasury bonds (also known as exchequer bonds), which carried a fixed date of repayment, usually a few years hence, and Treasury bills, repayable within three to six months. Although both securities paid relatively little interest, they were widely available, easily realisable with little risk of loss and were unlikely to drastically fall in value, though pessimists in the Office questioned the marketability of bonds and glumly predicted that both would follow the same price trajectory of consols.[52] Their purchase also helped to shore up public finances and thus allowed the IO store up goodwill with the government. By 1912, the GSR held £4.7m of bonds, and, by 1929, £32m (80 per cent of the Reserve).[53] They were bought at issue by tender, direct from the NDC and in the market.[54] Direct purchases began in 1907 when the Treasury offered the IO Irish Land stock, which it wished to avoid selling to the public at a 'ruinous' price. After declining the offer on the grounds of their newfound enthusiasm for securities with short maturities, IO officials suggested that they be allowed to buy bonds/bills from the NDC, which would in turn permit the Commissioners to buy the Irish stock. In the event, purchases from the NDC of bonds close to their maturity date and at the ruling market price became a regular feature, as they carried a number of benefits for India. The costs associated with buying such securities at issue or in the market were saved, any accrued interest was reaped, market shortages/rises in prices were avoided and, by reducing the amount of time the bonds were held until repayment, the dangers of depreciation were dissipated.[55]

---

50 *Ibid.*, note, 20 Aug. 1915; *ibid.*, note, 9 Oct. 1915; *ibid.*, minute, 28 Aug. 1915.
51 *Ibid.*, note, 9 Oct. 1915; *ibid.*, Viceroy to IO, 30 July 1915; *ibid.*, S of S to Finance Dept., 3 Sept. 1915.
52 BL, L/F/5/3, fol. 1940, note, 11 April 1905; *ibid.*, Abrahams to Baker, 11 Nov. 1904.
53 Keynes, *Indian Currency*, p. 126; PP 1929–30 [Cmd.3386], p. 18.
54 BL, L/AG/29/1/153, 138, no. 3, note, 3 April 1928.
55 BL, L/F/5/4, Treasury to IO, 7 May 1907; *ibid.*, IO to Treasury, 9 May 1907; *ibid.*, note, 15 June 1907.

Bonds purchased in the market were generally acquired in small amounts to avoid any rise in price.[56] Apart from criticism of its broker's commission, which some regarded as excessive, the IO's acquisitions appear to have been exemplary, only attracting attention in 1915, when the IO accepted that it had been a mistake to purchase five year bonds that were subsequently discovered to be difficult to realise at short notice, and, more significantly, in 1925 when £4.125m of bonds were acquired immediately prior to a rise in interest rates and a fall in security prices.[57] The government auditor expressed surprise that the rate rise had not been foreseen and questioned the apparent lack of any discussion of the matter. Commenting that it was 'easy to be wise after the event', IO officials declared that they had been well aware of and had discussed the rumours, but had decided not to delay purchase. There was always 'talk about the likelihood of a rise or fall in the bank rate', and, if 'we … tried to be too clever in anticipating the course of markets, we should incur serious risks, and, when luck was against us, we should expose ourselves to losses and justifiable criticism'. The expected rise in interest rates had also been factored into the market price of the bonds, which had slumped in the week prior to the rate rise, and the losses, estimated by the broker at £8,000, were therefore relatively minor.[58]

After purchase, the bonds acquired were either held to maturity or sold early. Premature sales occurred when the funds were needed to meet an emergency; agreed liquidity ratios had to be restored; the Treasury was expected to repay bonds at the first redemption date, which would cause the price to fall to the redemption value; or the price rose to a premium, prompting the IO to sell at a profit and to reinvest the proceeds in another bond issue.[59] The securities were offloaded onto the market, ideally after the most recent interest payment had been made, or sold at the market price to the Bank of England, which often allowed the IO to retain the interest coupon and thus obtain any remaining dividends, but, in return, sometimes required all or some of the proceeds to be reinvested in Treasury bills.[60] If an offer of

56 BL, L/F/5/5, note, 19 Jan. 1909.

57 BL, L/F/7/189, Abrahams to Meyer, 6 May 1916; PP 1914 [Cd.7069], q. 2098–9. To encourage him to obtain the best prices possible, the broker obtained ¼ per cent of the value of the securities bought/sold up to £1,500 pa. This was the commercial rate for the work. The UK government broker received a fixed fee (PP [Cd.7069], q. 1891, 2100–1). The Crown Agents' broker earned ¼ per cent, half of which was passed to the Agents in payment for their work on the trades (CAAL, L 266, CAs to Brunei, 28 Sept. 1950).

58 BL, L/AG/29/1/153, 138/1, ag/12639/25, note, no date ; *ibid.*, auditor, 8 Jan. 1926; *ibid.*, Kisch, 14 Jan. 1926.

59 *Ibid.*, 138, no. 9, note, 18 April 1935; *ibid.*, 138, no. 4, note, 15 April 1929. See also *ibid.*, 138, no. 5, note, 21 July 1930; *ibid.*, 138, no. 7, note, 11 April 1933. In 1929, the IO exchanged £4.5m of bonds (*ibid.*, 138, no. 4, note, no date). In the case of the 3 per cent bonds 1933/42, 10 per cent of which were redeemed each year, the decision to sell was related to a fear that India's holdings would be redeemed and it would lose the price premium that then ruled (*ibid.*, 138, no. 9, transactions statement for 1933/4).

60 E.g. BL, L/F/7/460, fol. 12320, note, 8 Nov. 1921; BL, L/AG/29/1/153, 138, no. 4, IO to B of E, 14 Nov. 1929.

conversion was made, the IO generally converted in order to avoid the cost of rein-vestment and to benefit from any additional redemption yield offered.[61] The only exception was in 1930, when the currency of the new loan would have disrupted the Reserve's liquidity ratios, and the IO wished to increase its Treasury bill holdings in anticipation of the coming financial storm.[62]

War bonds were purchased at issue in 1903 (£1m) and in 1915/16 (£3.5m).[63] The motivation was patriotism mixed with a heavy dose of financial self-interest. The securities offered a higher yield than consols and possessed a repayment date, and, in the case of the 1915 loan, the sheer amount of the stock sold made it highly mar-ketable. In addition, as already discussed, its conversion rights provided the IO with a perfect opportunity to reduce its consol holdings.[64] Purchases also occurred post-war in 1921/2 and 1930, when IO officials found it difficult to buy Treasury bonds of the required currency and the securities offered a relatively high return. In 1930, there was also an expectation that Treasury bill rates were about to fall. As with ordinary bonds, the stock was bought by tender and in the market, but also from Nivisons, acting on behalf the British Linen Bank.[65] To ensure low prices were paid, the IO, in 1909, agreed to inform the NDC when it intended to enter the market to avoid both institutions buying simultaneously and thus driving up the price, and, in 1918, allowed the Treasury to make purchases on its behalf each time the price slipped, which gave the UK government more control of market prices.[66]

The various war bonds permitted investors to convert their holdings into further war securities before a given date. As the market price rose prior to the conversion date and thereafter fell, the IO, in 1922, sold its £6.4m holdings immediately before the deadline, turning down an offer from the Treasury, which wished to maintain market prices, to swap its holdings for Treasury bills at a fixed price. Although this would have saved India sales commission, and there was a possibility that the bills could be sold at a good price before maturity, more immediate profit could be made via market sales. The same decision was made in 1927, though officials considered converting and pressuring Nivisons to share a portion of the 0.41 per cent commis-sion it received for arranging conversion – the small return, the relatively long life of the new stock and fears of a post-conversion price fall causing the plan to be aban-doned. In 1932, however, the IO opted for conversion, even though the new loan had a long currency and alternative government investments were available. Given the UK government's desire for India to convert, the help provided by the Treasury in

61   E.g. *ibid.*, 138, no. 3, note, 2 April 1929.
62   *Ibid.*, 138, no. 4, note, 24 Feb. 1930; *ibid.*, 138, no. 4, Kisch, 24 Feb. 1930.
63   BL, L/F/5/3, fol. 3220; PP 1916 [80], p. 32.
64   BL, L/F/5/3, fol. 5339, note, 19 Aug. 1903; PP 1916 [80], p. 32.
65   BL, L/F/7/460, fol. 12320, note, 8 Nov. 1921; BL, L/AG/29/1/153, 138/1, note, 17 Oct. ; *ibid.*, 138, no. 4, S of S to G of I, 26 Feb. 1930; *ibid.*, 138, no. 4, note, no date; *ibid.*, 138/1, note, 27 March 1923. £1m was purchased from Nivisons (*ibid.*).
66   BL, L/F/5/5, Hervey to IO, 20 Feb. 1909; *ibid.*, Abrahams to Hervey, 4 March 1909; NA, T 120/1, Treasury to IO, 14/318; *ibid.*, Treasury to IO, 14 Jan. 1918.

the immediate past and the likely future assistance required, it was decided politic to convert and to then dispose of the stock at a favourable opportunity.[67]

Like bonds, Treasury bills were bought at issue by tender, in the market and from the NDC, the PCR and the home balances. Although the IO usually chose the maturity of the securities obtained from the NDC, it was occasionally 'privately' informed 'what we would prefer', and a wish to pay the Commissioners the average price of the last public issue during the preceding fortnight was summarily turned down, as such an arrangement would 'act unfavourably either for them or for us'. The price was thus set by the Bank of England.[68] After purchase, the bills were either allowed to mature, when they were usually automatically renewed by the Treasury, and, in 1917, replaced by older bills for which India paid a proportionately lower price, or sold on the market or to the PCR/home balances at the market price.[69]

The popularity of the bills as a GSR investment waxed and waned according to the amount of economic turbulence buffeting India. Holdings rose in 1916 in the expectation of a 'bad financial panic' and the need to issue large amounts of reverse council bills, though critics claimed the true purpose was to help finance the British war effort, and, at the end of hostilities, drew attention to the fall in bill prices, which they insisted must have been foreseen by the IO.[70] A further upswing in purchases occurred in 1927, followed by sales and the acquisition of Treasury bonds – a response to a fall in bond prices and a need to buy more long-term securities.[71] Unfortunately, bill sales were overdone, and the 1930 financial crash forced the newly purchased bonds to be offloaded at a loss and bills to be bought with the proceeds. A fall in bill prices, a feeling that they had been 'over cautious' in building up large holdings of longer currency securities and the issue of bonds redeemable by annual drawings, which increased their liquidity, then prompted IO officials to re-embrace bonds.[72]

Other securities held by the GSR included local loans stock (securities issued for local authorities by the Treasury), Irish Land stock and securities placed on the market by the Corporations of London and Birmingham, the Metropolitan Water Board and various colonial and commonwealth governments – all acquired when

---

67 BL, L/AG/29/1/153, 138/1, note, 13 Sept. 1922; *ibid.*, 138/1, 2 Oct. 1922; *ibid.*, 138/1, note, 17 Oct. 1922; *ibid.*, 138/1, note, 17 Oct. 1922; *ibid.*, 138/1, note, 3 Jan. 1927; *ibid.*, 138, no. 7, note, 7 July 1932; *ibid.*, 138, no. 7, note, 13 Sept. 1932.

68 NA, T 1/11261, 12865, note, no date, 1910; *ibid.*, 12865, IO to Treasury, 7 Oct. 1910; *ibid.*, 12865, note, 11 July 1910; *ibid.*, 12865, Treasury to IO, 11 July 1910.

69 BL, L/F/5/7, Newmarch to Chalmers, 4 Jan. 1912; NA, T 120/1, Treasury to IO, 8 Jan. 1917.

70 BL, L/F/7/189, Abrahams to Meyer, 6 May 1916; PP 1920 [Cmd.528], q. 2065; PP 1920 [103], p. 96.

71 BL, L/AG/29/1/153, 138/1, Kisch to Brayne, 14 April 1927; Shah, *Sixty Years*, p. 400. Bonds in the Reserve purchased many years previously had just two years to run, disturbing the liquidity ratio (BL, L/AG/29/1/153, 138, no. 3, note, 11 June 1928).

72 BL, L/AG/29/1/153, 138, no. 4, note, 3 Oct. 1929; *ibid.*, 138, no. 4, note, 9 Aug. 1929; *ibid.*, 138, no. 9, note, 20 June 1933; *ibid.*, 138, no. 7, Kisch, 13 Sept. 1932.

UK government securities were scarce or provided a relatively low yield.[73] The British Empire stock comprised both long- and short-term investments. Longer term securities issued by the Transvaal, Nigeria and Queensland were generally purchased when they were within two and a half years of being repaid and were bought in the market.[74] Three or six month bills issued by the Commonwealth of Australia, New South Wales, Southern Australia, New Zealand, Canada, South Africa and Natal were bought at issue, often from Nivisons (the broker usually employed to place the securities in London), and, when they came to their end of their lives, were often renewed.[75] As already discussed, the IO also acquired on the market Indian sterling bills close to maturity, though the bills were occasionally more expensive than their Treasury equivalent.[76] It drew the line, however, at long-term Indian government or guaranteed railway stock. Although both often offered a relatively high yield and purchase would have further increased India's credit, it was thought that during a crisis they would be unsellable or able to be offloaded only at a large price discount, damaging credit and leading to falls in all gilt prices.[77]

Paper Currency Reserve

The PCR was established in 1861 when the government transferred the right to issue notes from the presidency banks to the government in an attempt to overcome shortages of coin during the busy trading period and the tax collection season.[78] Its raison d'être was to provide financial backing for the notes issued, ensuring that holders could at any time exchange them for coin, and its size thus determined the amount of notes in circulation and vice versa.[79] Initially having a maximum size of 4 crores, this upper limit was increased to 10 crores in 1896, 12 crores in 1905 and 14 crores in 1911. During the First World War, further enlargement occurred, and, by 1918, its ceiling had reached 100 crores.[80]

73 E.g. *ibid.*, 138/1, memo, 29 July 1922; *ibid.*, 138/1, Turner, 29 July 1922; BL, L/F/5/4, Treasury to IO, 7 May 1907; BL, L/F/5/5, note, 2 March 1909; BL, L/F/5/3, fol. 316, note, 29 Jan. 1904.

74 BL, L/F/5/3, fol. 5807, note, 25 Aug. 1904; BL, L/F/5/6, note, 7 Dec. 1911; BL, L/F/5/70, note, 30 Sept. 1913; *ibid.*, note, 27 May 1913.

75 E.g. BL, L/AG/29/1/153, 138/1, Nivisons, 1 April 1924; *ibid.*, 138/1, note, 22 Dec. 1924; *ibid.*, 138/1, 31 Jan. 1925; *ibid.*, 138/1, note, 23 Oct. 1922; BL, L/F/5/6, note, 13 July 1911; BL, L/F/5/5, minute, 2 July 1909; *ibid.*, note, 5 Oct. 1909; BL, L/F/5/7, note, 30 Sept. 1913.

76 BL, L/AG/29/1/153, 138, no. 3, extract from weekly statement, no date.

77 BL, L/F/5/3, G of I to IO, 30 July 1903; *ibid.*, G of I to IO, 30 July 1903; *ibid.*, IO to Governor General, 11 Sept. 1903. The purchase of foreign government loans was similarly ruled out (*ibid.*, fol. 8506, note, 28 Nov. 1906).

78 Banerji, 'Revisiting the Exchange Standard', p. 4497; *Investors Review*, 8 (July/Dec. 1896), p. 237.

79 Keynes, *Indian Currency*, p. 127.

80 Sen, *Colonies*, p. 82; BL, L/AG/37/4, IO to G of I, 14 Oct. 1904; Howard, *India*, p. 13; BL, L/F/7/596, fol. 13856/18, note, 7 Dec. 1918.

To ensure that exchange could occur immediately, the Reserve was initially located in India and contained silver rupees, bullion and securities. The UK off-shoot appeared at the turn of the century in order to allow earmarking and reverse earmarking (discussed in Chapter 9) to occur. Earmarking was used when the IO was unable to sell council bills during periods of poor trade, needed funds to cash reverse councils, or wished either to raise the exchange through the restriction of council bill sales or to transfer funds to the UK for the purchase of silver or for purposes officials wished not to become generally known. From 1905 to 1912, for example, £0.945m was moved to reduce London interest rates and thus cut the cost of renewing Indian railway debentures, £0.92m to purchase investments for the GSR, and £0.85 to repay gold transferred to India in 1905/6.[81] Reverse earmarking was adopted when the Indian Treasury lacked sufficient funds to cash council bills.

The UK reserve spluttered into life. The Gold Note Acts of 1898 and 1900 permitted some of the Reserve to be held in gold and in London, and, from 1899 to 1900, £1.6m of specie was bought by the Bank of England and placed in a special account.[82] In 1901, however, the whole amount was transferred to the home balances and used to buy silver for coinage, and a permanent UK Reserve only appeared with the passage of the 1905 Paper Currency Act, which required £5m of the Indian Reserve to be held in the UK as gold or securities (Figure 14).[83] Inevitably, Indian nationalists criticised the Act, calling it 'a most fantastic and ridiculous step', and campaigned for the return of the funds to India. As with the GSR and the home balances, it was argued that the investment of money in England rather than in India damaged the Indian money market and trade and also weakened note convertibility, the funds being unable to be rapidly transferred to India in a crisis.[84] In response, the IO again pointed out that there was little demand for the money in India and that the Indian Reserve contained sufficient funds to meet a run on notes. It also highlighted the benefits of a London subsidiary – UK securities could be more rapidly sold than their Indian equivalent, allowing the Reserve to rapidly respond to increases in note circulation; more secrecy in silver purchases was possible, lowering the prices paid for the metal; and the Reserve constituted a second line of defence if the exchange fell below the gold export point and reverse councils needed to be cashed.[85] Faced in 1919/20 with further demands for repatriation, it argued that such a move would be extremely costly given the relatively high exchange rate, would involve the sale of large numbers of Treasury bills, would raise London interest rates (damaging

---

81   BL, L/AG/37/4.

82   PP 1906 [162], p. 18; BL, L/AG/37/4, IO to B of E, 8 Oct. 1903; *ibid.*, note, no date, 1900.

83   BL, L/AG/37/4; Doraiswami, *Indian Finance*, p. 15. Owing to the excessive quantities of gold in the Indian government PCR, the money was transferred to London in the form of gold ingots.

84   *Investors Review*, 5 (Jan./June 1900), p. 263; PP 1920 [Cmd.528], q. 5783; PP 1920 [Cmd.529], p. 109.

85   Doraiswami, *Indian Finance*, p. 105; BL, L/F/5/144, Baker, 18 Dec. 1912; PP 1914 [Cd.7069], q. 1390.

India's financial operations in the UK) and would not, as claimed, lower Indian silver prices.[86]

Figure 14. Investments of the London PCR, 1905/6–1934/5 (crores)

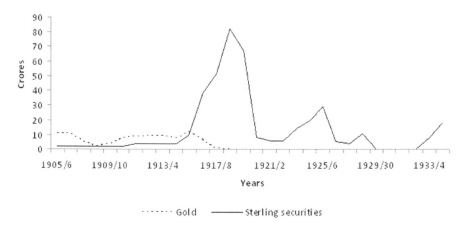

Sources. PP 1914–16 [Cd.7799], no. 89; PP 1922 [Cmd.1778], no. 89; PP 1930–31 [Cmd.3882], no. 128; PP 1938–39 [Cmd.6079], no. 166.

Investment in securities

Up to the First World War, there was no limit on the proportion of the Reserve that could be invested in securities, though from 1905 and 1911 only two crores and four crores respectively could be held in sterling debentures/stock. In practice, the invested portion varied from 20.3 per cent of the total in 1913 to 44.9 per cent in 1872, reaching a high of 61.5 per cent in 1874.[87] The amount of securities held then took off owing to the greater wartime issue and use of currency notes, the result of a rise in the demand for currency and shortages of both rupee and gold coin. A series of good harvests, the heavy demand and high prices paid for Indian raw materials needed for the war effort, and the payment in India of the costs of military operations in Mesopotamia, Persia and East Africa all increased the need for silver rupees. Unfortunately, there was less coin in circulation due to a fall in the purchase of imports, the rise in silver prices and shortages of gold sovereigns. Pre-war, the coin issued to finance the purchase of exported produce in the provinces returned to the main trading centres when producers used the proceeds from the sale of their wares to purchase imported goods. During the war, these transfers dried up. Farmers

86 PP 1920 [Cmd.529], pp. 109, 126. See also PP 1920 [Cmd.528], q. 3671, 3681.
87 PP 1920 [Cmd. 529], pp. 154–5. Investment dividends were transferred to government revenues (BL, L/AG/37/4, fol. 1998, note, 15 April 1908).

fearing a German victory and the collapse of British rule were more inclined to hoard revenues rather than spend them on imports. In addition, shipping difficulties and the transference of Western manufacturing capacity to the production of armaments restricted the availability of imports and raised their price, again damaging demand.[88] The rupees that were moved 'up country' thus stayed there.

Currency shortages were exasperated by the rise in the price of silver and a dearth of gold sovereigns. The rise in silver prices caused the bullion value of rupee coin to exceed its exchange value and forced the government to temporarily halt coinage and prompted recipients to either hoard coins in anticipation of further price rises or to melt them down and sell the silver. A 1917 ban on silver imports, an attempt to slow the price rise, only succeeded in making the shortage of currency even worse, though the impact was offset by the prohibition of the export and melting down of coin and its use for non-currency purposes, as well as by the Indian government's purchase of silver from the US government at a relatively low price.[89] Gold bullion and sovereigns were in similarly short supply. Shipping and other difficulties reduced imports from Australia and Egypt, and many gold standard countries, including Britain, France and America, restricted outflows in an attempt to conserve supplies. The price of gold in the bazaars thus rose, and any specie that managed to make it into India was rapidly melted down and sold as bullion.[90] To ensure that this did not occur, the Indian government required all imported gold to be sold to its Treasury at a fixed price based on the exchange rate rather than the higher bazaar price, prohibited the melting down of sovereigns, and, from 1919, bought limited amounts of the specie from New York and London.[91]

Faced with a dearth of coin, the government greatly increased the amount of notes in circulation, and, to encourage their acceptance, issued them in smaller 1 and 2.5 rupee denominations and required their use for the purchase of certain crops.[92] The greater issue of notes, in turn, forced the expansion of the Reserve, which, owing to the shortage of specie, was achieved by increasing holdings of securities and especially UK government stock, thus helping the war effort. [93] The maximum size of the invested portion was increased in 1915 to 20 crores (£13.3m), the 4 crores sterling limit remaining unchanged, and to 26 crores in 1916, of which 10 crores (£6.6m) could be in sterling securities and of this 6 crores in Treasury

---

88 PP 1920 [Cmd.529], p. 38, appendix 2, par. 5; PP 1920 [Cmd.528], q. 164; PP 1920 [Cmd.529], p. 82; PP 1920 [Cmd.529], pars 9–10.

89 *The Statist*, 8 Sept. 1917, p. 395; PP 1920 [Cmd.528], q. 1818; *ibid.*, p. 6.

90 Chablani, *Indian Currency and Exchange*, p. 72; PP 1920 [103], p. 288; R. L. Nash, *A Short Inquiry into the Profitable Nature of Our Investments*, London 1880, p. 61.

91 PP 1920 [103], p. 288; PP 1920 [Cmd.528], q. 73, 112; Balachandran, *John Bullion's Empire*, p. 74. The government may also have wished to protect London gold stocks.

92 Previously, 5 rupees had been the lowest denomination issued (PP 1920 [Cmd.529], pars 24, 28).

93 PP 1920 [Cmd.529], p. 39; PP 1920 [Cmd.528], p. 6; *ibid.*, q. 5656.

bills.[94] By 1919, the maximum invested portion had reached 100 crores – up to 10 crores of which could be in Indian government rupee securities, 80 crores in UK Treasury bills and 10 crores in either Indian or British government stock. The result of these changes was that the proportion of the Reserve held in securities rose from 21.1 per cent in 1914 to 64.2 per cent in 1919.[95]

Investment in UK securities

The reasons for the increase in the proportion of British government securities that could be held by the PCR were the same as those for the purchase of such stock for the GSR. As with the latter Reserve, the IO initially had a penchant for consols and exchequer bonds, later transferring its affections to Treasury bills. Proposals that the Fund be invested in municipality and colonial stock or deposited in London banks were all rejected.[96] The IO's enthusiasm for consols cooled as the price depreciated. It was decided, however, not to include the PCR's holdings in the conversion operation undertaken to offload the GSR's securities. The Paper Currency Act prohibited the implementation of the scheme, and, in any case, the IO lacked the necessary funds to purchase sufficient war loan. Instead, the holdings were sold on the market – slowly, taking advantage of any price upturns, and in small amounts to prevent sales forcing the price down further. To avoid 'absurd and extravagant' losses, a minimum price was set, though this did not prevent losses occurring, which were written off using appropriations from revenue, coinage profits and a depreciation fund.[97] Established in 1917, this last was worth £0.891m by June 1919 and comprised Treasury bills bought with Indian government revenues and reinvested bill interest.[98] In 1920, much to the disgust of the Indian government, the IO also transferred £0.85m of consols to the GSR at cost price, receiving Treasury bills at market price in return, the loss to the GSR being made up via the transfer to the Reserve of £0.033m from the PCR depreciation fund and £0.1m from Indian government revenues.[99]

The money released from the sale of consols was invested in exchequer bonds and, from 1916, in Treasury bills. By 1920, however, the Reserve contained £55m of Treasury bills, and there was a feeling within the IO that its enthusiasm for the

---

94 Howard, *India*, p. 13; BL, L/F/7/592, no. 2, fol. 208/16, note, 19 Jan. 1916; PP 1920 [Cmd.529], p. 154.

95 PP 1920 [Cmd.529], appendix 1, p. 31, pars 8, 155.

96 BL, L/AG/29/1/153, 138/1, Turner, 29 July 1922; BL, L/F/7/597, fol. 8227, IO to Finance Dept., 1920. Colonial stock had relatively long maturities and it was feared that bank deposits would lead to Indian claims that the IO was propping up the British banking system (PP 1914 [Cd.7069], q. 1809; PP 1920 [Cmd.528], q. 5672).

97 BL, L/F/7/593, no. 3, Newmarch, 27 Jan. 1916; *ibid.*, no. 3, fol. 1897, note, 22 March 1917; *ibid.*, no. 3, fol. 7499, Abrahams, 24 Nov. 1916; *ibid.*, no. 3, fol. 6988/17, Lucas, 21 July 1917; PP 1920 [Cmd.528], q. 5667; BL, L/F/7/597, Viceroy to Finance Dept., 10 Aug. 1920.

98 BL, L/F/7/593, statement, 30 March 1917; PP 1920 [Cmd.529], p. 156.

99 BL, L/F/7/597, Viceroy to Finance Dept., 10 Aug. 1920; BL, L/F/7/593, no. 3, fol. 10301, telegram, 10 Sept. 1920; *ibid.*, no. 3, Howard, note, 2 Sept. 1920.

securities had been somewhat overdone.[100] Not only was the price of the bills beginning to fall, but the rise in the exchange rate reduced the value of the sums that could be remitted to India. If there was a run on notes, there was thus a distinct possibility that the Reserve would be unable to meet holders' demands for coin and notes would be inconvertible, with all the consequences described below. A restructuring of the Reserve, however, would be even more catastrophic – the sale of bills/halting of their purchase would cause the price to plummet further and decimate UK government finances, prompting a rise in interest rates and damaging India's operations in the market. The IO thus chose a strategy of 'wait and see', which eventually bore fruit when the exchange fell and the price of bills recovered. Thereafter, bills continued to make up the bulk of the Reserve, with the IO in 1930, when the price of bills suffered a further fall, again coming to the rescue of the UK Government and protecting India's market interests by increasing purchases.[101]

Investment in Indian securities

The invested portion of the Indian PCR comprised Indian government rupee loans and Treasury bills, as well as commercial bills of exchange. Government rupee loan stock was bought at issue, on the market, and, during the First World War, it was specially created for and then sold to the Reserve along with Treasury bills.[102] The money obtained from these wartime sales of stock and bills enabled the Indian government to cash the enlarged number of council bills arriving in India, and the enlarged PCR holdings permitted the expansion of currency notes.[103] By the early 1920s, however, the IO was becoming concerned at such 'printing press finance' and the size of these stock/bill holdings, which comprised twenty per cent of the Indian invested portion, and determined that stock/bills had 'to be wiped out as soon as practicable'.[104] The securities, rather than representing 'real value', were essentially government of India 'credit' and would be difficult to offload in the event of a crisis.[105] Initially, it required the interest on the securities to be reinvested in the PCR, allowing an equal amount of stock/bills to be withdrawn.[106] Unfortunately, in 1921, difficulties in issuing sterling and rupee loans forced this income stream to be redirected to government revenues in an attempt to strengthen Indian credit in the London and Indian capital markets, and the IO was forced to find an alternate

---

100   PP 1920 [103], p. 19.
101   NA, T 160/472, Indian government securities, note, 23 Jan. 1930.
102   PP 1871 [363], q. 6429; BL, L/F/7/597, S of S to Finance Dept., 25 Aug. 1920; PP 1872 [327], p. 498, appendix 1, budget estimate. Specially created Treasury bills were held from 1918 (BL, L/F/7/596, fol. 14396, Viceroy to S of S, 24 Dec. 1918).
103   PP 1916 [80], p. 30.
104   Goldsmith, *The Financial Development*, p. 114; PP 1920 [Cmd.528], q. 5711; BL, L/F/7/598, CHK, 2 June 1921.
105   BL, L/F/7/597, fol. 8227, IO to Finance Dept., no date, 1920.
106   BL, L/F/7/596, fol. 6567/21, Kisch, no date, 1921.

source of funds.[107] After dismissing the use of surplus home balances as impracticable, it turned to the GSR.[108] Although the redirection of GSR income to the PCR was counter to the recommendations of the Chamberlain and Babington-Smith Committees and could set a dangerous precedent, it was eventually decided that all coinage profits and interest on investments should be transferred to the PCR when the value of the GSR breached £40m.[109] From 1921 to 1923, £2.866m of specially created stock/bills were replaced using this income and more of the securities were retired via the reinvestment in the PCR of the interest earned on commercial bills and, in 1926, the profits made on sales of PCR silver.[110]

The holding of Indian domestic commercial bills was first considered in 1920. Fears were that the value of the bills could plummet during a crisis, purchase would be administratively complex and costly, and the government's lack of expertise in the sector could result in the acquisition of bills that were not paid. Conversely, purchases made in the busy season when money was scarce would provide cultivators of export goods with much-needed finance and allow the government to temporarily increase the issue of currency notes, and the bills would restore confidence in the Reserve, following its acquisition of specially created stock/bills.[111] Believing the pros of purchase outweighed the cons, the IO in 1921 permitted up to rs5 crores of such financial instruments not exceeding ninety days' maturity to be held.[112]

Specie holdings

The 1861 statute setting up the Reserve permitted the Indian government to hold against notes issued silver bullion and rupee/other government coin, as well as gold bullion or coin. In the event, gold made an appearance only in 1865 (20.5 lakhs), and, after 1875, disappeared completely, only to make a comeback in 1902 (1,054 lakhs).[113] Prohibited from holding rupees, the London branch of the Reserve contained 1,056 lakhs of gold in 1905/6 (84 per cent of its total holdings). The amount then fell to 1919/20, after which the metal ceased to be held, though there continued to be small amounts in the Indian Reserve.[114]

The proportion of silver in the Reserve initially ranged from 55.1 per cent (1872) to 57.7 per cent (August 1914), but during the First World War it plummeted to just 10.8 per cent (March 1918), and, by June of 1918, it appeared that any large demand

---

107 PP 1923 [128], pp. 18, 27.
108 BL, L/F/7/598, 4902, minute, no date, 1921.
109 BL, L/F/7/597, CHK, note, 9 July 1920; *ibid.*, fol. 8899, Howard, 14 July 1920.
110 PP 1930-31 [Cmd.3882], no. 110; BL, L/F/7/596, fol. 6567/21, Kisch, no date, 1921; BL, L/F/7/601, S of S to IO, 19 Aug. 1926.
111 PP 1920 [Cmd.528], q. 3271, 3312-3, 5659-61, 5711.
112 BL, L/F/7/599, fol. 11654, note, no date.
113 PP 1920 [Cmd.529], p. 153.
114 PP 1920 [Cmd.529], p. 155. For holding the gold, the Bank of England obtained a fee of 1/32 per cent of the value of the specie held (BL, L/AG/9/8/6, p. 871).

for the exchange of notes for coin would not be met.[115] The economic and political consequences of inconvertibility were alarming. Economically, there would most probably be a run on the Post Office Savings Banks, a slowdown in the circulation of money and rise in prices (increasing the cost of war supplies), a collapse of exports, and less demand for Indian government rupee loans and, in particular, the war loans. The loss of trust in notes, meanwhile, would make the further expansion of paper currency out of the question. Politically, inconvertibility would lead to a backlash against British rule, which many feared would damage the loyalty of Indian soldiers serving on the various fronts and force British troops to be moved from the trenches to India to quell any resultant civil unrest.[116] In the event, inconvertibility was averted by the United States government, from which £26m of silver (1918–20) was bought by HM Treasury acting on behalf of the Indian authorities.[117]

In the longer term, the Chamberlain Commission and Indian government urged that specie holdings be raised to the equivalent of a third of note circulation (plus the notes held in government treasuries) and half of the average note circulation over the previous three years respectively.[118] The continued increase in the amount of notes issued would naturally raise the number returned to the Treasury for exchange for coin, and, having avoided inconvertibility in 1918 'by a hair's breadth', neither wished to face the same crisis again.[119] Moreover, if the exchange fell and there was little market demand for securities or pressure was placed on the IO by the Bank of England to avoid sales for the sake of the City, a UK PCR comprised almost wholly of investments would be unable to help the GSR cash reverse bills.[120] The IO was undecided. The Indian government no longer had to exchange rupees for gold sovereigns, and there was no evidence that greater note circulation increased encashment; indeed, there was some indication that the Indian trader was finally beginning to accept notes as a substitute for coin. Greater specie holdings would also reduce dividend income and damage relations with the City.[121] On the other hand, another crisis would prompt yet another re-evaluation of India's currency system and the possible introduction of a gold standard, which would divert gold to India, increasing its World price and diminishing London holdings, with the inevitable consequences on interest rates.[122] Eventually, the IO plumped for a greater specie portion, and, in 1923, required at least half of the Reserve to be in precious metals.[123] In an attempt to establish a proto-Gold Bullion Standard and to permit the exchange of notes for gold, from 1927/8 large portions of the silver holding were

115 PP 1920 [Cmd.529], p. 155; PP 1920 [Cmd.529], p. 39; Leavens, *Silver Money*, p. 170.
116 PP 1920 [Cmd.528], q. 348–50, 384–9, pp. 81–8.
117 NA, T 120/2, Treasury to IO, 24 March 1920.
118 PP 1920 [Cmd.529], appendix 1, p. 32, par. 12; PP 1920 [Cmd.528], q. 5650.
119 BL, L/F/7/597, fol. 8899, Howard, 14 July 1920; PP 1920 [Cmd.528], q. 2069.
120 PP 1914 [Cd.7069], q. 1388; Doraiswami, *Indian Finance*, p. 33.
121 BL, L/F/7/597, fol. 8227, IO to Finance Dept. 1920; PP 1920 [Cmd.528], **q. 5656.**
122 Balachandran, 'Britain's Liquidity Crisis', p. 579.
123 Vakil, *Financial Developments*, p. 80.

sold off and replaced by gold, though the return of rupees from circulation to the Reserve was so great that by 1935 it contained more silver than when the policy was inaugurated.[124]

Indian silver reserve

To supplement the Indian silver holdings, in 1904 an additional reserve containing 3 crores (£2m) of assayed silver ingots was established.[125] The recent rapid growth of exports had created a great demand for coin, and the reserve allowed any sudden upsurge to be met, prevented overpurchase of silver and coinage if the upturn proved temporary, and reduced the need to earmark during periods of London stringency. The purchase of large amounts of specie at short notice, which could lead to the payment of high prices, was also avoided, and, in 1906 and 1913, the reserve controversially provided the Indian government with loans, enabling it to meet heavy council bill sales.[126]

In 1906, the reserve was doubled in size, was required to hold rupee coin rather than ingots and was transferred to the GSR.[127] A sudden demand for coin in November 1905 had almost exhausted its contents, and coined rupees allowed any shortages to be almost immediately countered.[128] Initially, the additional funds were to be drawn from the PCR via the sale of its sterling securities. Fearful that this would weaken India's ability to earmark, the IO then considered transferring rupees from the Indian Treasury and replacing these with newly printed currency notes. Aware that the increase in note circulation could stoke inflation, it then mulled over obtaining the money from the home balances or the GSR, or issuing a special loan. As a transfer from the home balances would greatly reduce its advances to the City and a special loan damage India's credit, it eventually opted for the GSR. The GSR was considered excessively large, and the siphoning off of 3m crores of coinage profits and the loss of interest from the specie tied up in the silver reserve would slow its growth.[129] To resolve any dearth of coin during the trading season, it was agreed that rupees would be moved from the silver reserve to the PCR, and an equal amount of gold earmarked from the PCR to the GSR in London in the event of shortages.[130]

The reserve came to an end just before the First World War. There had been criticism of its use in the 1907/8 crisis when it had received the proceeds of the sale

---

124 *Report of the Controller of Currency*, 1926/7, 1934/5.
125 Banerji, 'Revisiting the Exchange Standard', p. 4495.
126 *The Statist*, 16 March 1907, p. 527; PP 1914 [Cd.7070], appendix 5, p. 198; PP 1914 [Cd.7069], q. 11506.
127 Banerji, 'Revisiting the Exchange Standard', p. 4495; BL, L/F/5/7, Newmarch, 16 Dec. 1912.
128 PP 1906 [162], p. 17.
129 PP 1907 [140] *Indian Financial Statement for 1907–08*, p. 24; BL, L/F/5/7, note, 13 Jan. 1913; *ibid.*, note, 28 Dec. 1912; *ibid.*, Newmarch, 16 Dec. 1912; PP 1907 [140], p. 24.
130 BL, L/F/5/7, note, 28 Dec. 1912.

in India of reverse council bills, causing its size to balloon to £10.58m before the recovery of the exchange permitted the excess funds to be transferred to London and invested.[131] Later, both the Chamberlain Commission and the Secretary of State questioned its presence in the GSR, pointing out that silver located in India was of little use during an exchange crisis. Others argued that unexpected demands for coins should be met by increasing the amount of rupees kept in the PCR.[132] In July 1914, the reserve was therefore abolished and its £4m contents transferred to the PCR.[133]

Conclusion

The GSR and the London portion of the PCR primarily existed for the maintenance of the exchange and the support of trade. The contents of the GSR were available for the encashment of reverse council bills, and the PCR permitted earmarking and reverse earmarking. Both also performed other roles. The GSR occasionally provided temporary loans to the Indian government and the IO, and funded India's UK commitments, and the PCR furnished financial backing for currency notes. The reserves were largely invested in UK government securities, which provided a reasonable return, carried no risk of default, and, as regards consols, held out the possibility of price appreciation and a capital profit. Alas, the expected price rise failed to occur and the IO thus had little choice but to offload the securities at a loss, though in the case of the GSR this was minimised via the conversion of the securities into war loan – an operation that demonstrates both the financial ingenuity of officials and the importance of trust relationships and the reciprocal exchange of favours.

Having divested itself of consols, the IO opted for safety and, thereafter, invested the reserves in short-term Treasury bonds and bills, the purchase of which in times of gold outflows increased the Bank of England's gold stocks. Again, India obtained preferential treatment from the Bank/Treasury, a reward for past and future favours. Bonds close to their maturity date were purchased from the NDC, and the IO was permitted to draw the interest on bonds sold back to the Bank of England before their repayment date. The exchange of favours, however, was not a given. If the interests of India outweighed any possible gains, UK government overtures would be rejected. A Treasury request in 1922 for the IO to swap its holdings of war securities for Treasury bills, for instance, was summarily turned down in favour of the immediate profits available from market sales. Likewise, as will be seen in the following chapter, the Bank of England was equally willing to sacrifice India, if, in doing so, its own interests were advanced.

131   *Ibid.*, Newmarch, 16 Dec. 1912.
132   Simha and Balachandran, *History*, p. 50; BL, L/F/5/7, Abrahams, 28 Dec. 1912.
133   BL, L/F/5/8, minute, 7 July 1914.

11

Home Balances

Theoretically, the home balances were used to meet India's UK commitments. In reality, they often far exceeded the country's liabilities, from 1860/1 to 1939/40 averaging £6m, and rising to £18m in 1910/11 and £16.6m in 1917/18 (Figure 15).[1] This excessive size was partly designed to allow the IO to make loans to the City and to increase the Bank of England's gold holdings, which directly benefitted Indian finance, and was partly the result of poor budgeting and an aversion to risk. The uncertainty of the monsoon and unexpected external 'shocks' caused estimates of expenditure and receipts to be highly inaccurate (Figure 15) and officials were well aware that India's failure to meet its liabilities, especially interest payments, would severely damage its credit. It thus kept a generous minimum balance of £3m, reduced to £2–2.5m in 1908 and then raised to £4m in 1913/14.[2]

These minimums were substantially exceeded from 1904, largely due to the decision to sell council bills without limit, and, to an even greater extent, from 1909/10 to 1912/13, for which a myriad of factors was responsible. In India, there was a series of good monsoons, which increased exports/government revenues and reduced famine relief expenditure, a rise in opium exports to China, relatively little capital expenditure and an unexpected increase in Savings Bank deposits.[3] In the UK, relatively little silver was purchased for coinage, loans were issued in advance of need to avoid market upturns, and there were fewer transfers to the PCR and GSR and less guaranteed railway company expenditure. The preparation and sanctioning of railway orders appears to have slowed, and the railway mania that gripped much of the World and a series of railway strikes caused many manufacturers to

---

1   Figure 15 sources.
2   PP 1871 [363], q. 9336; PP 1909 [Cd.4474], q. 774; PP 1914 [232] *Return of Indian Financial Statement and Budget for 1914–15*, p. 27.
3   BL, L/F/5/144, Discussion on Indian finance, 31 Jan. 1913. Taxes remained high as the additional opium revenue was regarded as a temporary windfall (*ibid.*).

Figure 15. Home balances, 1860/1–1939/40, and excess/deficiencies of council bills drawn as compared to budget estimates, 1872/3–1917/18

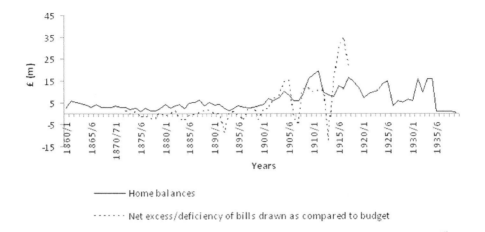

Sources. PP 1878 [C.2147], no. 33; PP 1887 [C.5210], no. 59; PP 1896 [C.8238], no. 62; PP 1906 [Cd.2754], no. 85; PP 1922 [Cmd.1778], no. 85; PP 1930–31 [Cmd.3882], no. 115; PP 1935–36 [Cmd.5158], no. 112; PP 1938–39 [Cmd.6079], no. 146; PP 1942–43 [Cmd.6441], no. 136; Ambedkar, *The Problem*, chap. 7, tables 51–2.

struggle to meet deadlines and payments to drift across financial years.[4] The size of the balances then fell, only to rise again (until the mid 1920s) with the outbreak of the First World War, the repayment in London by the War Office of money spent in India and greater economy in Indian UK expenditures.[5] Indeed, such was the size of the additional balances that a special reserve of £20m was set up. Established to avoid Indian criticism and demands for the money to be repatriated, the fund was invested in UK government securities (and thus helped the war effort), and was intended to meet an expected post-war upturn in railway expenditure.[6]

Inevitably, there were demands from Indian nationalists that surplus balances be returned to India and lent to the presidency banks. These proposals were disparaged by the IO, which pointed out that the Indian government would be reluctant to lend the money, as default would lead to the sale of the Indian rupee paper held as collateral, causing prices to fall and reducing subscriptions for the annual rupee loan issue; institutions receiving such advances would reduce their own lending by a pro rata amount; and, even if this did not occur, the dumping of vast amounts of cash by the banks on the relatively small Indian money market would simply cause

4   *Ibid.*, Schuster's statement, 7 Feb. 1913; PP [Cd.7069] q. 76, 133.
5   NA, T 120/1, Treasury to IO, 7 Dec. 1915.
6   PP 1920 [Cmd.528], q. 5594, 5605–6.

interest rates to plummet.[7] Moreover, it was unlikely that any funds so invested could be rapidly retrieved if urgently needed in London, and any such withdrawal of funds would harm financial markets.[8] The balances were thus wholly invested in the UK and variously placed on deposit at the Bank of England (and, for a brief period, at joint stock banks), lent to City institutions and used to buy UK government securities.

Bank deposits

The Bank of England deposit account contained an agreed minimum of £0.5m, which met unanticipated or unexpectedly large UK commitments, avoiding recourse to expensive Bank of England loans, and ensured that India was not without funds if council bill sales collapsed.[9] As the account did not pay interest, the IO monitored its contents daily to ensure that the minimum was not breached, but was powerless to halt its growth in periods of low City demand for the loans that it made from its remaining balances or when heavy payments were due – the Bank insisting that sums to be withdrawn the following day be deposited the previous evening at the latest.[10] At certain times of the year, deposits thus exceeded £0.5m – in December 1879 and 1912 by over £1.5m.[11] Aware that the minimum deposit alone was costing it around £11,000 to £16,500 pa in lost interest, IO officials repeatedly and 'on bended knee' appealed to the Bank to either reduce the minimum balance or provide some return, but to no avail. There was a legislative requirement that the Bank hold the account, and its Governor stoutly defended the status quo, reminding the IO that a similar no-interest policy was adopted for other government clients (including HMG), the account aided the defence of the gold standard, and the Bank provided a range of services for India for which it received no remuneration. Not only did it manage the account, plus those of the GSR, PCR and various pension funds, but it also organised the weekly council bill tender, checked and held the collateral lodged by City institutions borrowing from the balances, and provided much valuable advice and information on trading and borrowing conditions.[12] The IO was

---

7   BL, L/F/5/144, Memorandum on IO balances, no date; Doraiswami, *Indian Finance*, appendix; PP [Cd.7069], q. 11183.

8   PP [Cd.7069], q. 356, 10534–6.

9   *Ibid.*, q. 1935; PP 1896 [C.8258], q. 2433. The minimum balance was agreed upon in 1859 (BL, L/AG/9/8/6, pp. 869–70, memo, 16 July 1913).

10 PP 1871 [363], q. 9348, 9370; PP 1896 [C.8258], q. 2439; PP 1914 [Cd. 7069], q. 2025–6. By comparison, the Crown Agents until 1912 monitored its Bank of England account only once per fortnight (NA, CO 323/591/9213, CAs to CO, 23 Mar. 1912).

11 BL, L/AG/9/8/6, pp. 869–70, memo, 16 July 1913; PP 1871 [363], appendix 11, p. 710, cash balances; PP [Cd.7069], q. 2049–50.

12 PP 1914 [Cd.7069], q. 2027, 2048, 2054, 11097; PP 1871 [363], q. 9346, 9379; BL, L/F/7/164, B of E to IO, 19 Aug. 1887.

unconvinced. The cost of these services was almost certainly less than the interest lost, and the Bank additionally earned a hefty return when it re-lent the deposits, estimated in 1912 at from £8,250 to £16,500 pa.[13]

IO anger at the situation intensified in 1887 and 1914, when the Bank sought to increase the minimum balance on the basis that the turnover and the cost of managing the account had greatly increased and it rarely held more than £0.5m; the magnitude of the IO lending to the City and the workload associated with its unremunerated services had grown; and, in 1914, the Bank's fee for organising the printing of currency notes was to be cut.[14] The IO strongly resisted the demand. Although it accepted that the Bank's unremunerated workload had expanded, it continued to maintain that the estimated cost of completing these tasks was grossly overestimated and more than covered by the lost interest/re-lending return.[15] Unfortunately, as discussed below, a separate dispute with the Bank regarding the right of India to loan money to the City forced the IO, in 1914, to relent and to permit the minimum balance to be increased to £1m.

This agreement, however, did not halt its attempts to throw off the Bank's shackles. In 1921, the Finance Council considered abandoning its 'false' relationship with the Bank and opening an account with the Imperial Bank of India, only deciding not to do so because the 1914 agreement was legally binding until 1929.[16] Two years later, the High Commissioner's account was transferred to the Imperial Bank, and, on the conclusion of the 1914 agreement, many at the Office called for either the minimum balance to be cut or all the Bank's duties to be transferred to the Imperial Bank. Proponents of a lower minimum balance reminded colleagues that many of the Bank's account management duties had been taken over by the High Commissioner, that the disappearance of the council bill and City loans had drastically reduced its unremunerated workload, and that high market interest rates had made its re-lending of India's deposits even more lucrative. Supporters of the wholesale transfer of duties, meanwhile, highlighted the positive political consequences of such a move, which was 'a natural and desirable line of development'.[17]

Others were less enthusiastic, arguing that the Bank now made no charge for the purchase and holding of gold; its expenses had almost certainly risen since 1914; and, having to hold $^{15}/_{16}$ per cent of its holdings as cash, it probably lent out as little as £20,000 of the £1m minimum. As for a transfer of duties, the Imperial Bank was simply incapable of efficiently delivering some of the services, and their relocation would provide it with an unfair commercial advantage. More importantly, given the likely turmoil of the coming years, the IO would need the Bank of England's help

---

13   BL, L/F/5/64, Currie, 8 Dec. 1887; BL, L/AG/9/8/5, vol. 6, p. 683–7.

14   BL, L/F/7/167, B of E to IO, 12 March 1914; *ibid.*, B of E to IO, 11 July 1913; BL, L/F/7/164, B of E to IO, 19 Aug. 1887.

15   BL, L/AG/9/8/6, pp. 869–70, memo, 16 July 1913.

16   BL, L/F/7/169, note, ESM, 30 May 1921; *ibid.*, fol. 5596, note, 26 May 1921.

17   BL, L/F/7/173, fol. 1848, Kisch, 1 March 1923; *ibid.*, fol. 1394, note, no date; *ibid.*, fol. 1394, Turner, 24 Jan. 1930.

even more than ever.[18] No changes were therefore made to the relationship, a 1938 suggestion by the government auditor that India pay for the unremunerated services in return for the payment of interest on the account being summarily rejected. The minimum balance was reduced to £0.5m in 1935 (though only because the Reserve Bank of India kept £0.5m of the deposits at the Bank), and to £0.48m in 1937 when Burma separated from India and set up its own account with its own minimum.[19]

Depositing surplus balances in joint stock banks began May 1909 and ended in November 1912, though similar deposits had occasionally been made in the past. The practice was introduced because the City institutions to which the bulk of the balances were lent were unable to absorb the vast sums accumulating in London, and the IO wished to avoid lending to weaker establishments. It ended when the purchase of silver for the minting of coin and the discharge of debt had greatly diminished balances. Rather than leaving the funds at the Bank of England, where they would earn no interest, the IO thus decided to follow the practice of the Crown Agents and foreign governments and to deposit some of the cash, £29.6m from 1909 to 1912, with joint stock banks.[20] Officials were also no doubt aware that some of the deposits would be lent to discount houses and brokers, helping them to discount Indian DA export bills. To maximise returns, three, six (1911) and, from 1912, seven banks were used, the London County & Westminster obtaining the largest slice of the total amount lent (31 per cent), followed by the National Provincial (28 per cent) and the Union (25 per cent).[21] All were UK owned, under British legal jurisdiction and had large capital assets – important factors as the IO received no security for its deposits. Unwilling to create preferential creditors, the clearing banks were reluctant to provide collateral and would have paid far lower interest rates had it been demanded.[22]

Opponents accused the IO of cant and hypocrisy, claiming that the choice of bank was determined purely by the self-interest of current and past Finance Council

18 *Ibid.*, fol. 1394, memo, no date; *ibid.*, fol. 1393, Cecil Kisch, 31 Oct. 1930.

19 BL, L/F/7/177, fol. 1326, Ball, 26 Jan. 1938; *ibid.*, IO to B of E, 4 Jan. 1937; BL, L/F/7/177, Baxter to Nixon, 23 Feb. 1937.

20 Doraiswami, *Indian Finance*, appendix; BL, L/F/5/144, Discussion on Indian finance, 31 Jan. 1913; *ibid.*, Inchcape, no date; *ibid.*, Draft passage on deposits with banks, 6 Feb. 1913; PP 1909 [Cd.4474], q. 1207, 1210; PP 1914 [Cd. 7069], q. 10690; BL, L/AG/14/14/3; BL, L/AG/14/14/5.

21 BL, L/F/5/144, Draft passage on deposits with banks, 6 Feb. 1913; *ibid.*, Discussion on Indian finance, 31 Jan. 1913; BL, L/AG/14/14/3; BL, L/AG/14/14/5. The first three banks were the National Provincial, the London County & Westminster and the Union (PP 1914 [Cd.7069], q. 10692). The other borrowers were the London Joint Stock, the London City & Midland, Glyn Mills Currie & Co., and Barclays (PP [Cd.7069], q. 1968). The London County & Westminster, the Union and the London Joint Stock were also used by the Crown Agents (e.g. NA, CO 48/439/9353, CAs to Cape, 21 Sep. 1867; NA, CO 247/111/4604, CAs to CO, 23 Apr. 1869).

22 BL, L/F/5/144, Draft passage on deposits with banks, 6 Feb. 1913; PP [Cd.7069], q. 170, 1107, 1940.

members.[23] Schuster was the Governor of the Union Bank, which, in 1887, had merged with his father's bank, Schuster Son & Co., and had been a director of the Imperial Bank, later absorbed by the London Joint Stock Bank.[24] Lord Inchcape and a previous Committee member, Francis Le Marchant, were directors of the National Provincial Bank, and a further past member, Bertram Currie, was a partner of Glynn Mills Currie & Co. Given the make-up of the Finance Council, it is perhaps surprising that there were not more connections between members and the banks employed, and, as the IO pointed out, not using the banks would have 'prejudiced the interests of Indian revenues', and their employment almost certainly benefitted India.[25] The Council members could use their influence to ensure that deposits were repaid on time and the highest possible interest obtained, Inchcape claiming that he 'squeezed the very last penny' from the National Provincial. The IO was also well aware of the potential conflict of interests. The increase in the number of banks engaged was an attempt to forestall criticism, and deposits at the Union Bank were sanctioned by Inchcape without any reference to Schuster.[26]

To reduce risk and accusations of impartiality, each bank received a similar number of deposits, the average size of which was £230,000.[27] Money was placed for between one and three months depending on India's future UK commitments, a relatively long period as compared to the Crown Agents' seven to ten days.[28] Even longer deposit periods, as proposed by critics, may have increased returns, but would have led to losses if rates had risen during the time funds were lodged. If the money was not required, the deposit was renewed for a further time period at a new interest rate. Such extensions encouraged the banks to take India's cash and avoided the impact on the money market of withdrawals, though this was cushioned by banks covering deposits with the purchase of three month bank bills that matured on the date a repayment was due, and by the IO's one week warnings of withdrawals.[29] Over the period during which deposits were made, 355 were renewed with an average of 3.25 extensions per bank – the London County & Westminster, National Provincial and Union accounting for 85 per cent of the renewals and the greatest number of per bank extensions.[30]

23   BL, L/F/5/144, Draft passage on deposits with banks, 6 Feb. 1913.
24   S. Chapman, *The Rise of Merchant Banking*, London 1984, p. 136; *Financial Times*, 15 May 1936, p. 6.
25   BL, L/F/5/144, Draft passage on deposits with banks, 6 Feb. 1913.
26   PP [Cd.7069], q. 1949, 10707, 10692; BL, L/F/5/144, Inchcape, no date.
27   PP [Cd.7069], q. 2250, footnote; BL, L/AG/14/14/3; BL, L/AG/14/14/5.
28   BL, L/F/5/144, Draft passage on deposits with banks, 6 Feb. 1913; PP 1909 [Cd.4474], q. 1207, 1210.
29   PP [Cd.7069], q. 10713, 11002, 10702, 10744-5. The withdrawal of a deposit would force the bank to obtain the money lost from the money market.
30   BL, L/AG/14/14/3; BL, L/AG/14/14/5. Two deposits ran for over three years and three for almost three years (*ibid.*).

The interest rates obtained were far from the 'give-away rates' described by critics, though, in 1907, they were slightly less than those achieved by the Crown Agents, and were occasionally lower than those the IO paid to purchasers of sterling bills.[31] They were determined by the five brokers the IO employed over the period, all of whom were members of the Scott family, the owners of a brokerage house, and who, from 1905, were required to become partners of Nivisons, the stockbroking firm that handled the issue of India's sterling loans.[32] The members of one family were employed to reduce the likelihood of dishonesty, and the Nivisons partnership benefitted both the company and India.[33] Nivisons obtained a proportion of the broker's fees, improved its standing in the City and its ability to attract business, and, it was suggested, channelled loans to its own clients. The broker gained access to the formal and informal information possessed by the firm and could thus make better deals for the IO, and Nivisons, not wishing to lose its broking role, was no doubt encouraged to perform its loan issue work competently and honestly.[34]

The deposit rates obtained were ¼ to ⅛ per cent less than that of the three month bank bills that the banks purchased to cover deposits, the discount constituting the banks' very slim profits. A proposal that the IO simply buy the bank bills itself was rejected as 'it was not the business of any government to go into commercial banking', purchase would be 'difficult and cumbersome', and it was thought unlikely that the Bank of England would be willing to take on the role unless an excessive fee was paid. On fixing the rate, the broker then offered the deposit to the bank most likely to meet this return, and, if it rejected the deal, made the same offer to other banks until the money was taken up. 'Practically liv[ing] in the money market', the broker was well aware of current rates, and, prior to placing the money, obtained the sanction of the Chairman of the Finance Council. He also passed details of deposits made and the rates obtained to the Finance Council for monitoring at the end of each week/month, and details of the deposits/rates were published in the financial press, with

31 Doraiswami, *Indian Finance*, p. 131; PP 1909 [Cd.4474], q. 732, 1208; BL, L/F/5/144, Memorandum on IO balances, no date.
32 BL, L/AG/9/8/5, vol. 6, p. 597, Sheppards Pellys Scott & Co. to IO, 31 March 1905; PP 1914 [Cd.7069], q. 10732. John Guilliam Scott (who shared the role with Anthony Hammond), appointed in 1844, was succeeded by Henry Scott, Hubert Scott, Willie Amherst Winckworth Scott (employed from 1888 and Hubert's nephew) and Horace Hubert Scott (appointed 1904) (PP 1842 [409] *Exchequer Bills Forgery*, q. 4117; BL, L/AG/9/8/5, vol. 6, p. 465; *ibid.*, vol. 5, p. 301, IO to Scott, 2 Feb. 1888; *ibid.*, vol. 6, p. 483). In 1888, Messrs Scott, Corthorn and Scotts merged with Messrs Sheppards Pelly and Allcard to become Messrs Sheppards Pelly Scott & Co. and later Sheppards & Co. (*ibid.*, vol. 5, p. 301, IO to Scott, 2 Feb. 1888; *ibid.*, vol. 6, p. 597).
33 Long relationships generate trust, and dishonesty by one broker would have reduced the chances that the next generation of the family would inherit the role and would thus have carried a heavy familial cost (see Sunderland, *Social Capital*, pp. 7–8).
34 PP [Cd.7069], q. 10733, 2043–4, 10735, 1902. Also in the broker's absence, his work could be completed by another Nivisons partner (*ibid.*, q. 1975).

the result that 'if we go wrong, everybody knows it'.[35] Open tenders were not used as they would have been administratively costly to organise, resulted in money being lodged with undercapitalised banks, and disclosed the size of the balances to be deposited, lowering the rates offered. Tenders from just the banks employed would again have reduced rates and disrupted the even distribution of deposits.[36]

Loans and securities

Loans were provided to City institutions, the Bank of England and the GSR if the Reserve wished to purchase a particularly alluring security but lacked the funds to do so.[37] Taking into account the £0.5m kept at the Bank of England and using end of financial year balance figures, from 1860/1 to 1914/15 when the lending slowed, £244.43m was lent to financial institutions, £3,177.62m, assuming an average loan period of four weeks.[38] The advances were arranged by the broker and the money lent only to firms on a list of approved borrowers, which, prior to 1906, contained forty-three companies, and, by 1913, sixty-two firms, and included the five exchange banks, the discount houses handling DA export bills and a number of stockbrokers.[39] To gain access to these hallowed ranks, companies had to make a formal application to the Finance Council; the Chairman and, later, all the members of the Finance Council then made enquiries in the City as to suitability.[40] Successful applicants had to possess a 'first class' reputation for 'trustworthiness' and considerable resources, be able to provide the necessary collateral, and be domiciled in the UK and thus covered by the British legal system.[41] Critics of the list complained that it was 'somewhat arbitrary', excluding many well-known high calibre institutions; its existence and the accompanying application procedure were unknown in the City; fifteen or sixteen members were never offered loans; and no attempt had been made to attract new borrowers on the expansion of the home balances.[42] Some also questioned the inclusion of Samuel Montagu & Co. and Messrs A. Keyser, firms

35   *Ibid.*, q. 1931, 2214, 2219–23, 2228–30, 2238, 10692, 11002–3, 11090–4; BL, L/F/5/144, Draft passage on deposits with banks, 6 Feb. 1913.

36   PP [Cd.7069], q. 11238, 10742, 2258, 2250, footnote.

37   E.g. BL, L/F/5/6, note, 7 Dec. 1911. A proposed 1910 loan of £1m to the Treasury, to be repaid in Treasury bills, did not go ahead. The 'few days' loan was required because the necessary legislation for the issue of the bills had been delayed. In the event, the arrangement proved unnecessary (BL, L/F/5/5, note, 15 March 1910).

38   Figure 15 sources.

39   BL, L/F/5/144, Discussion on Indian finance, 31 Jan. 1913; *ibid.*, Memorandum on IO balances, no date; BL, L/F/7/167, p. 315.

40   PP 1914 [Cd.7070], p. 309, par. 2; PP 1914 [Cd.7069], q. 533.

41   PP 1909 [Cd.4474], q. 726; PP [Cd.7069], q. 533; BL, L/F/5/144, Discussion on Indian finance, 31 Jan. 1913.

42   PP [Cd.7069], q. 1956–7, 10680–2, 2033, 10495.

part-owned by the family of Edwin Montagu, the Under Secretary of State, and Sheppard & Co., part-owned by the broker's family.[43] The exclusivity, of course, was deliberate; the IO wished to avoid default and only lend to organisations it could trust, and, as discussed below, to channel money just to firms that could help its own operations. As regards the reluctance to solicit new borrowers, the rapid growth of the balances was thought to be a temporary occurrence, if officials 'approached a firm, we should be obliged to accept them', and the use of new unknown companies increased the risk of default.[44] On the realisation that large balances were becoming a permanent feature, however, a quarterly review of the list was inaugurated and an additional fourteen firms added.[45]

Money was lent to list firms in multiples of £50,000, which reduced bookkeeping costs, but meant that occasionally there were sums of less than this amount not lent.[46] Each company had a maximum borrowing limit, related to its standing, willingness to pay high interest rates and ability to deposit the necessary securities, and this was regularly reviewed and increased/decreased according to the financial situation of each firm and the size of the home balances.[47] As regards the period April 1909 to July 1914, the only one for which records are available, 1,291 loans were made worth just over £120m. The average size of each advance was £1.8m and each borrower received an average of 25.3 loans.[48] Distribution, however, was inequitable. Just ten companies received 57 per cent of the advances by value, with the three largest recipients receiving almost a quarter of the loans.[49] By sector, brokers received the most money and the greatest number of loans, followed by discount houses and the five main exchange banks (Table 3).

Table 3. Home balance loan borrowers, April 1909 to July 1914

Sector	Number of list companies	Value of loans received and percentage of total	Number of loans received and percentage of total
Brokers	30	£38.5m (42%)	581 (45%)
Discount houses	11	£36.02m (39.3%)	48 8 (37.8%)
Exchange banks	5	£12.05m (13.2%)	141 (10.9%)
Non-exchange banks	5	£5.05m (5.5%)	81 (6.3%)

Source. BL, L/AG/14/14/1.

43   Searle, *Corruption*, p. 202.
44   PP [Cd.7069], q. 2038–9.
45   PP 1909 [Cd.4474], q. 726.
46   PP [Cd.7069], q. 1854, 1856.
47   BL, L/F/5/144, Baker, 18 Dec. 1912; *ibid.*, Inchcape, no date.
48   BL, L/AG/14/14/1.
49   *Ibid.* The largest borrower was the National Discount Co. (£8.65m), followed by the Union Discount Co. (£7.4m) and Samuel Montagu & Co. (£4.7m) (*ibid.*).

The cash was lent for three to five weeks, and occasionally six weeks, reducing the likelihood that the IO would be caught up in the collapse/bankruptcy of a borrower and enabling all the balances advanced to be recalled within three to six weeks if needed.[50] Reimbursement dates were arranged so that a small sum became available each day and other repayments occurred immediately before expenditure had to be met.[51] 'The entire game [was thus] for safety' – to allow the IO to fulfil both unexpected and anticipated commitments. To others, it was 'over cautious'. Critics argued that, from 1906, commitments could easily have been met from the increased council bill sales or the issue of government/guaranteed railway company loans, and sums thus lent for longer periods, allowing a higher return to be reaped. The IO begged to differ, pointing out that low council bill demand, postponement of bill payments or poor market conditions that precluded the issue of securities sometimes forced a reliance on loan repayments, and, if these were unavailable, India would be forced to procure costly loans from the Bank of England, increasing the Bank's control of its finances.[52]

On the arrival of the repayment date, if the money was not required, the loan would be extended at the current ruling interest rate for a further three to six week period, or, if no longer required, repaid and lent to another institution.[53] Renewals were extremely common. During the eight months from May to December 1913, 714 advances were renewed, over a quarter were 'turned over' four or more times, and the average currency was sixty-three days and the longest five years.[54] Borrowers thus received long-term loans at interest rates normally paid on short-term advances.[55]

To obtain the loans, list companies had to provide collateral in the form of short-term debentures or securities registered at the Bank of England, on which they received an interest rate similar to and sometimes greater than that paid for the IO funds.[56] These comprised UK government Treasury bills and bonds; the bills of the London County Council and Metropolitan Water Board; Indian government sterling short-term stock, bonds and bills and enfaced rupee paper; Indian guaranteed railway company debentures; and, by 1914 when guaranteed railway company debentures were in short supply, the Treasury bills and bonds of colonial governments.[57]

---

50   BL, L/F/5/144, Memorandum on IO balances, no date; PP [Cd.7069], q. 1858; PP 1914 [Cd.7070], p. 310. In 1842, the smaller UK home commitments allowed money to be lent for an average of two months (PP 1842 [409], q. 4139).

51   PP 1909 [Cd.4474], q. 725; BL, L/F/7/167, IO to B of E, 9 April 1914.

52   PP [Cd.7069], q. 1997, 10902, 10609, 10614; PP 1914 [Cd. 7070], pp. 309–10.

53   PP 1909 [Cd.4474], q. 725; PP [Cd.7069], q. 1859. If borrowers refused to renew at the current interest rate, the loan would be recalled (*ibid.*).

54   BL, L/AG/14/14/2; PP [Cd.7069], q. 5447.

55   PP 1914 [Cd.7071], p. 553.

56   PP [Cd.7069], q. 2085–7. If collateral interest rate was greater than that of the borrowed funds, the borrower gained a profit.

57   PP [Cd.7069], q. 1921, 2034, 3363; PP 1909 [Cd.4474], q. 727; BL, L/F/5/139, memo, 4 June 1894; PP 1914 [Cd.7070], p. 310, par. 5. In 1842, the collateral comprised exchequer bills (PP 1842 [409], q. 4124).

Inevitably, some believed the choice of security inappropriate. City figures insisted that only UK government securities should be accepted, as these would be relatively easy to sell at a high price in the event of default, and such a requirement would increase demand for British government debt to the benefit of public finances and the management of the gold standard. Others argued that the range of securities taken was far too limited and should be extended to include colonial and corporate stocks registered at joint stock banks and even bills of exchange. The demand for such investments would thus be increased, and more companies would apply to join the IO's list of borrowers and request loans, enabling higher interest rates to be secured, and, from 1908, removing the need to deposit a proportion of the balances with joint stock banks. The IO again disagreed. The securities accepted were usually widely available; the requirement that collateral should be debentures/stock registered at the Bank of England allowed the Bank, acting on its behalf, to satisfy itself that the holder of the investment actually owned it, and, in the case of stock, facilitated its transfer to the Secretary of State's stock account, thus reducing costs; and, if the borrower defaulted, short term securities could be easily sold or held until maturity.[58] More importantly, as discussed in Chapter 2, the acceptance of Indian government and guaranteed railway company securities increased demand at issue and the price at which they were sold, and, by increasing their liquidity, helped to maintain market prices.[59]

To further increase the use of and demand for Indian government and guaranteed railway company debentures/stock/bills, they were accepted as collateral at their par value (£100), even if this was above their market price.[60] All other securities were taken at their market value, or, if it was believed that this could fall during their lifetimes, from 1896 at 5 per cent below this price, though this too was a generous valuation given that other lenders set margins of 10 per cent and of up to 25 per cent in the case of mining securities.[61] The Bank of England believed the policy as regards Indian securities to be simply 'bad business'. The difference between the par value and the market price ranged from ½ to 2 per cent and allowed 'a man with £99,000 [of stock to]…get £100,000 immediately' and make an unjustified profit. In addition, if the borrower defaulted, India would suffer a loss on the sale of the loans, as had occurred on two prior occasions.[62] For the IO, however, any borrower profit was more than justified by the resultant increase in demand/market prices of the securities. Officials also disputed the claim that the two previous defaults had led to losses and promised that when a further default occurred they would hold the

---

58   PP [Cd.7069], q. 1875–7, 103365, 1920, 11222, 10720–4, 1862, 1864, 1871, 3507–8. A proposal that stock inscribed at joint stock banks provided as collateral should be accompanied by a certificate from the bank guaranteeing ownership was rejected by the IO, which was doubtful that such guarantees would be forthcoming (*ibid.*, q. 10726, 3509).

59   BL, L/F/5/144, Schuster's statement, 7 Feb. 1913.

60   PP 1914 [Cd.7070], p. 310, par. 5.

61   *Ibid.*; BL, L/AG/9/8/5, vol. 6, p. 11, memo, 1 Oct. 1896; Kynaston, *The City … Vol.* 2, p. 280.

62   PP [Cd.7069], q. 3364, 2077–80; Doraiswami, *Indian Finance*, p. 101.

security, drawing the interest, until it matured.[63]

As with the joint stock bank deposits, many claimed that the interest rates obtained for the loans were relatively low and pointed out that some of recipients of the advances re-lent them at a slightly higher interest rate, failing to realise that this was standard practice. In fact, the rates achieved varied over the year, higher returns being procured at the end of the financial year when money was in demand, and were generally just slightly below bank rate, a return even the Bank of England believed acceptable.[64] To ensure that this was the case, lists of the loans made and the rates obtained were submitted each week to the Finance Council, and, from 1913, to the Secretary of State and each month to the Indian government auditor.[65] Higher rates could certainly have been secured, but this would have involved the risk of default, which would have led to politically embarrassing losses that would have severely damaged India's credit and ability to raise funds at a relatively low cost. Moreover, the primary goal of the loans was not to maximise returns, but to increase demand for Indian government securities and to provide funds to those institutions that would use them for the benefit of India.

Critics, nonetheless, insisted that inadequate rates were secured, highlighting as the main culprits the restricted number of borrowers, the limited range of collateral securities, the short loan periods, the supposed inadequacies of the lending process, and, in particular, the way in which the broker was remunerated and his method of distributing money.[66] Criticisms of the broker's fees were that they were excessive and gave him little incentive to obtain the highest interest rates. His remuneration was certainly lucrative when set against that of Civil Servants, but the commissions were relatively low when compared to the rates charged by other brokers, owing to the relatively large size of India's lending operations; the prestige he and his family firm gained from his position, which attracted business from other City institutions; and, in the case of Horace Hubert Scott, his share of Nivisons' profits.[67] The commission also fell over time as the amount of money lent increased, dropping by 9 per cent in 1888 and a further 60 per cent in 1911.[68] As regards incentives, the broker initially received a sliding scale fee, which increased as the interest rates paid for the

---

63   PP [Cd.7069], q. 1961. In 1906, the IO had sold the collateral at a profit, and, in 1907, the loss on sale a few months after the default was offset by the interest earned prior to realisation, which was higher than that obtained for its loans (PP 1914 [Cd.7070], p. 312, par. 15).

64   PP [Cd.7069], q. 2154, 3420; PP 1909 [Cd.4474], q. 732; BL, L/F/5/144, Discussion on Indian finance, 31 Jan. 1913; de Cecco, *The International Gold Standard*, pp. 71–2; BL, L/F/5/144, Schuster's statement, 7 Feb. 1913.

65   BL, L/F/5/144, Discussion on Indian finance, 31 Jan. 1913; PP 1914 [Cd.7070], p. 8. There appears to have been no criticism of the rates secured.

66   PP [Cd.7069], q. 3420, 1932.

67   From 1893/4 to 1912/13, the broker earned £105,737, giving him an annual salary far higher than Cabinet Ministers and most bank higher executives (PP 1914 [Cd.7070], p. 330, supplementary statement 3; PP [Cd.7069], q. 1929).

68   BL, L/F/5/139, memo, 4 June 1894; PP [Cd.7069], q. 2184.

IO's loans rose to an upper limit of 3 per cent plus.[69] He thus had no motivation to obtain rates above this maximum, though such rates were rarely seen except during periods of stringency. This problem was rectified in 1888 when a fixed rate of 5 per cent of the interest received was introduced, which both gave him an incentive to maximise returns and rewarded him when rates were excessively high. This rate in 1911 was then reduced to 2.5 per cent of the interest on loans with collateral of up to £5,000, and, thereafter, 1.25 per cent.[70]

Criticisms of brokers' lending procedures are also unconvincing. At the start of each day, the broker was told the amount of new money that had to be placed and the loans that had to be renewed. He then determined the interest rate at which he would lend (basing his decision on the current money market charge and discussions with City contacts, the Accountant General and, occasionally, the Chairman of the Finance Council) and offered loans at this rate to those list firms he knew were in search of funds.[71] If a company rejected the rate, he moved on to the next potential borrower, only reducing the charge and re-offering the loans if all or a large proportion of list companies rejected it, though the latter situation rarely arose. The option of 'sitting on the money' until the rate was accepted was only permitted if less than £0.5m remained to be placed and the broker was confident that rates would rise significantly the next day, as the resultant slight gain in return would be offset by the loss of one or more days' interest, and the loans when eventually taken would not be repaid on the date required. Likewise, borrowers were not retrospectively required to increase the amount paid for loans if the rate had risen by the end of the day, as such behaviour would lead to accusations of unfairness, and a similar offer to reduce charges would have to be made if interest rates fell.[72] Putting the loans out to tender to list companies, meanwhile, was rejected because it was unnecessary given the broker's knowledge of institutional needs, and would be administratively costly, have little impact on returns and prevent the broker directing funds to institutions that would use them to the benefit of India. A further proposal that the Bank of England should take over the broker's role was similarly dismissed. The Bank would perform the task in a very similar manner, but would charge a higher fee, and, as the work would compete with its own operations, would have little incentive to obtain the best rates available.[73]

For the IO, the loans to the City generated relatively high returns (£3.06m from 1888/9 to 1912/13), gave it financial patronage that it could use to India's advantage,

69 He received $^1/_{16}$ per cent for interest up to 1.5 per cent pa, $^2/_{16}$ per cent for interest of 1.5 to 3 per cent pa, and $^3/_{16}$ per cent for interest above 3 per cent pa (BL, L/F/5/139, memo, 4 June 1894).

70 PP [Cd.7069], q. 2182, 2176–7; PP 1914 [Cd.7070], p. 311, par. 7.

71 PP 1914 [Cd.7070], p. 310, pars 6–7; PP [Cd.7069], q. 2161–3; PP 1896 [C.8258], q. 2426.

72 PP [Cd.7069], q. 2165, 2171, 2174, 10603, 10743–4, 2031, 2167, 2192. If during the day, a firm offered more than his required rate, however, the broker would accept it, though only if all subsequent borrowers were prepared to borrow at that rate (*ibid.*, q. 2192).

73 *Ibid.*, q. 10742, 10924, 11023–4, 10511.

and had a benign impact on money market interest rates, causing them to be lower than otherwise (again to the benefit of India), particularly prior to the First World War when the market was plagued by the seasonal outflow of short-term capital to the United States to finance wheat and corn harvests.[74] More importantly, they had a positive impact on the sale of Indian government and guaranteed railway company loans/bills and council bills (Appendix 2).[75] The inclusion of Indian securities in the list of accepted loan collateral increased demand and issue/market prices, and many of the brokers that received advances used them to purchase sterling bills and to make the down and instalment payments for Indian government debentures/stock, which they then offloaded onto the public. Of the sixteen institutions that purchased the 1 December 1911 sterling bill issue, for example, 75 per cent received loans from the IO, and the number and size of advances made often peaked immediately before and after issues of stock/debentures/bills, with the institutions receiving them presumably simultaneously buying the securities on offer.[76] Advances to exchange banks and discount houses, likewise, directly and indirectly increased council bill demand, helping to maintain the exchange and facilitate trade. The five exchange banks that obtained advances bought up to 40 per cent of the IO's council bills, and the provision of funds to discount houses enabled these institutions to buy DA export bills and the exchange banks to use the proceeds to purchase further council drafts.

Unaware of or unwilling to accept the advantages of short-term lending, opponents highlighted the interest rate disparity between the IO's short-term advances and the money it borrowed via stock/debenture/bill loans, which cost India far more than it received from its City lending, and claimed that the bankers sitting on the Finance Council professionally benefitted from the low interest rates generated by the advances. This accusation was strongly denied by Schuster, who pointed out that Indian lending competed with bank advances and that low interest rates tended to reduce banking profits.[77] The Bank of England adopted an alternate line of attack. To its Governor, the IO 'acted against the interests' of Britain and its loans were 'bad money', which weakened the Bank's control of the money markets and could lead to domestic and international financial Armageddon.[78] The sheer amount lent and the supposedly relatively low rates at which it was placed drove down the discount rate, leading to a greater than otherwise outflow from the country of gold, and often acted against the Bank's attempts to staunch leakages through higher interest rates. More importantly, demands for the repayment of large numbers of loans in order

---

74 BL, L/F/5/144, Schuster's statement, 7 Feb. 1913; Balachandran, *John Bullion's Empire*, p. 31.

75 BL, L/F/5/139, memo, 4 June 1894; PP 1914 [Cd.7070], p. 318; Doraiswami, *Indian Finance*, pp. 35, 37.

76 BE, C47/333; BL, L/AG/14/14/1. See also the 28 Sept. 1914 issue (C47/334; BL, L/AG/14/14/1; C47/333; BL, L/AG/14/14/1). The loans to the broker J. & A. Scrimgeours appear to have been used to purchase Crown colony loans (Sunderland, *Managing the British Empire*, p. 174).

77 BL, L/F/5/144, Discussion on Indian finance, 31 Jan. 1913; *ibid.*, Schuster's statement, 7 Feb. 1913; PP [Cd.7069], q. 11015.

78 BL, L/F/7/167, B of E to IO, 16 April 1914; PP 1914 [Cd.7069], q. 10382.

to allow bulky UK commitments to be met damaged market confidence, and the calling in of all advances in the event of an Indian financial crisis similar to that of 1907/8 could devastate the London market, especially if there was a simultaneous UK financial emergency.[79] Borrowers would either fail to make repayments, forcing the IO to offload the collateral onto the market, which would trigger a devastating plunge in security prices, or, in order to repay the loans, would present the collateral securities to the Bank of England and demand and obtain advances that would reduce the Bank's gold holdings. The gold repaid to the IO, meanwhile, would be moved to the GSR or PCR and cease to be part of the Bank's reserves.[80]

The IO was bemused by these fears. India's UK commitments were moderate and largely known in advance, its investment practices ensured that loans matured as payments became due, and the non-renewal of a few advances to meet the payment of dividends/annuities or to discharge sterling bills was hardly likely to dent market confidence. As for a financial crisis, this was unlikely to occur over a short period of time, and gold would flow out of the country whether or not the balances were lent to the City.[81] Officials thus speculated that the Bank was launching its attack for purely self-interested reasons. Given that the IO advances competed with the Bank's own loans to the City and weakened its ability to secure high returns for its clients, the dismantling of Indian City lending made commercial sense, particularly as the IO would be forced to keep far larger sums in its Bank deposit account, which paid no interest.[82] It also seems more than likely that the Bank saw an opportunity to demonstrate its power ahead of the negotiation of its government sterling loan management charges, to punish Schuster for his perceived temerity to suggest to the Indian Commission that the IO should be cut loose from its legal requirement to use the Bank, and to undermine the very public campaign waged by Schuster in his private capacity to strip the Bank of its powers.[83] Schuster's anti-Bank argument was that it disregarded the needs of British industry and trade, and actively conspired against the growth of the joint stock banking sector, in particular by depriving the banks of funds in its role of lender of last resort. More significantly, he maintained that the Bank held insufficient gold reserves and that its control of outflows via higher interest rates created instability that harmed both the money market and the banking system. Opposed to an expansion of joint stock bank reserves at the

79 PP [Cd.7069], q. 3349, 10338, 10361, 3348, 3371; BL, L/F/7/167, B of E to IO, 1 April 1914; *ibid.*, B of E to IO, 16 April 1914.

80 BL, L/F/7/167, B of E to IO, 16 April 1914; *ibid.*, B of E to IO, 12 March 1914.

81 *Ibid.*, IO to B of E, 9 April 1914.

82 de Cecco, *The International Gold Standard*, p. 74.

83 BL, L/F/7/167, Cunliffe to Schuster, 30 April 1914; *ibid.*, Bardock, 16 July 1913. The 1905 loan management fee agreement expired in 1915 (BL, L/F/7/164, fol. 1372, note, 9 Jan. 1919). The Bank's dislike of Schuster may also have been related to the animosity it felt towards the joint stock banks for which he acted as spokesman. Although the capital of these banks had increased by £15m from 1881 to 1891, the 1844 Bank Act had placed no obligation on them to keep their reserves with the Bank of England, and they thus lodged less than two per cent with the Bank (de Cecco, *The International Gold Standard*, p. 95).

Bank, which would benefit its shareholders at the expense of those of the joint stock banks, he proposed the establishment of a second gold reserve composed of joint stock bank deposits and managed by committee comprised of representatives of the banks, the government and the Bank of England. Such sacrilege naturally infuriated Bank officials, and it is more than conceivable that its claim that much market instability was caused by the IO, effectively led by Schuster, was an attempt to weaken his critique of its activities.[84]

In November 1913, the Bank's criticisms were translated into action. The Governor threatened that unless India's lending activities were restricted to two-thirds of its surplus balances and loan collateral took the form of securities that City custom deemed could not be used as collateral for its own emergency loans, it would no longer check the IO's collateral securities and provide compensation if these proved worthless. Although legislatively bound to use the Bank, and, in any case, reluctant to take on financial liability for security fraud, the IO rejected the proposal, pointing out that it was legally bound to accept British and Indian government securities as collateral, the Bank treated no other client in this manner, and the lending restrictions would reduce its income while increasing that of the Bank, which would benefit from the greater sums held in India's deposit account. Instead, it proposed that Schuster and the Governor and Deputy Governor meet to thrash out a mutually acceptable agreement. To say the least, the meeting went poorly. The Bank alleged that Schuster stated that there was no legislative requirement for the IO to use the Bank for the checking of security and that it intended to employ other financial institutions to carry out this function and to continue with its loan programme. Schuster denied that he had said any such thing, claiming that he had merely mentioned that using 'other channels' was a 'contingency the India Office had the least desire to entertain', and demanded that the Governor alter his written version of the meeting. The Governor refused, effectively calling Schuster a liar, and raised the stakes by refusing to issue any Indian government sterling loan until the matter was settled and threatening to no longer accept Indian government securities as collateral for its own loans or to provide advances to the IO if lending continued.[85]

The IO reaction was one of shock. The Bank's refusal to float securities or provide advances would 'seriously prejudice' that and following years' budgets, and an issue after the ban was lifted could prove costly if the market had become unfavourable. More importantly, the refusal to accept Indian securities as collateral for emergency loans, 'a very striking and sensational act', would decimate 'India's power of borrowing' and would 'strike a very harmful blow at the position of Indian securities', triggering a collapse of market prices. Officials sought a compromise – that only balances over £3.5m be lent – which was summarily rejected, and, after much soul-

---

84   Gutwein, 'Jewish Financiers', pp. 180, 182–3; *Financial Times*, 16 Jan. 1907, p. 5.

85   BL, L/F/7/167, IO to B of E, 1 May 1914; *ibid.*, B of E to IO, 27 Nov. 1913; *ibid.*, B of E to IO, 16 April 1914; *ibid.*, IO to B of E, 5 Dec. 1913; *ibid.*, Schuster to Newmarch, 5 May 1914; *ibid.*, fol. 3326, note, no date; *ibid.*, Schuster to Cunliffe, 1 May 1914; *ibid.*, Cunliffe to Schuster, 30 April 1914; *ibid.*, Abrahams, 7 May 1914; *ibid.*, B of E to IO, 6 May 1914.

searching, they accepted the Bank's counterproposal. It was agreed that loans to the City would not exceed £10m and that a minimum balance of £1m would be kept in India's current account at the Bank, plus a quarter of any amount up to £6m lent to City institutions and a fifth of lending of between £6m and £10m. Balances in excess of £10m were to be invested in securities, or, again, added to India's account. In addition, liability was accepted for any collateral security passed by the Bank that was subsequently discovered to be fraudulent, and the IO agreed to immediately comply with any request that lending be reduced or cease.[86]

Although loans to the City continued after the agreement, the sums placed were much diminished and far more cash was invested in Indian guaranteed railway company debentures, UK Treasury bills, war bonds and, from the early 1930s, Treasury bonds.[87] As with the GSR, during and after the First World War the Bank of England pressed the IO to purchase Treasury bills, offering as a lure its willingness to discount holdings at any time.[88] The bills were bought at tender, in the market or from the NDC, GSR and PCR, which allowed investments to be made when there was no public issue but the IO had funds to invest; they were then either allowed to mature, or sold in the market or to the GSR, PCR or, on two weeks' notice, the Bank of England at rates more favourable than those obtainable on the market.[89]

Loans to the Bank of England were made in 1890, 1893, 1915/16 and March/April 1932, though there is some evidence that advances occurred prior to 1878, and were designed to increase the Bank's gold stocks and to strengthen the effectiveness of its base rate rises at times of high gold outflow.[90] The 1890 £3.2m loan, made at the height of the Barings crisis, additionally helped to finance the Bank's bailout operation and was provided at a generous interest rate.[91] In 1915/16, the IO initially wished to move a portion of its excessive balances into the GSR, where it would be available to cash reverse councils.[92] Both the Bank and the Treasury demurred, arguing that such a transfer would reduce the Bank's gold holdings and be against 'the interests of the Empire', and, after permitting at least one transfer to occur, persuaded the IO to lend its surplus funds (plus the GSR funds temporarily transferred

86   *Ibid.*, Abrahams, 7 May 1914; *ibid.*, Abrahams, 8 May 1914; *ibid.*, IO to B of E, 1 May 1914; *ibid.*, B of E to IO, 6 May 1914; *ibid.*, fol. 3326, IO to B of E, 25 June 1914.

87   BL, L/AG/14/13/1, p. 83; BL, L/F/7/173, fol. 2047, note, no date.

88   In 1921, Treasury bills accounted for 56 per cent of the balances (BL, L/AG/14/13/1, pp. 22–30). The IO strongly suspected that in an emergency the Bank would decline to discount if it was not in the City's interest (BL, L/F/5/8, Abrahams, 5 Nov. 1915).

89   BL, L/AG/14/13/1, pp. 22–30; BL, L/F/7/173, fol. 1394, memo, no date; BL, L/AG/14/15/1, IO to G of I, 6 Oct. 1932; NA, T 1/11261, 12865, IO to Treasury, 7 Oct. 1910.

90   PP 1878 [C.2157], q. 859; Sayers, *The Bank of England 1891–1944*, p. 38. The loans to the Bank reduced the funds lent to the market, which would otherwise have tended to lower interest rates. £1.85m was advanced in 1932 (BL, L/AG/29/1/153, 138, no. 7, note, no date).

91   BE, G23/68/277–8, B of E to IO, 13 July 1890; PP 1887 [C.5099], p. 16. The interest rate was 1 per cent below Bank rate when the rate was 3 per cent or below, and 1.5 per cent at a higher rate (BE, CT39, 18 June 1890).

92   BL, L/F/5/8, Abrahams to Ramsay, 6 April 1915; PP 1916 [80], p. 284.

to the home balances) to the Bank for periods of seven and fourteen days and one and three months.[93] The balances would thus be easily realisable in the event of an exchange crisis and the money would earn interest, which initially was higher than that offered by City institutions or Treasury bills.

Over time, however, the arrangement became less financially lucrative. There were two reasons. Market/Treasury bill interest rates rose above that offered by the Bank and resulted in losses of £159 per week.[94] Abrahams thus met with representatives of the Bank and, using the threat of a return to the policy of transferring surplus balances to the GSR, persuaded them to raise rates. Yet more losses stemmed from the Governor's insistence on treating the advances as market loans for the purpose of the 1914 agreement, which pushed the amount of balances lent to the City to over £4m and thus triggered the requirement that the IO hold a larger sum in its non-interest bearing current account. After unsuccessfully remonstrating with the Bank to alter its definition of the advances, which could not remotely be regarded as market loans as no collateral was provided, or to recompense India for the losses via higher interest, the IO began to reduce the sums lent and invest the money released in three month Treasury bills.[95] Aware that it could only tie up a small proportion of its funds in these relatively illiquid securities, it also asked the Treasury to consider selling it one month Treasury bills. Although the request was turned down, the Treasury came back with a counter-offer – that the IO lend its surplus balances at seven days' notice to the credit of the Ways and Means Account at 4.5 per cent, a rate far higher than that received from the Bank.[96]

In the event, no money was lent, as the Bank on learning of the Treasury's proposal performed a volte face and offered to maintain the minimum balance at £1m, even if market loans exceeded £4m, and to temporarily cancel the 1914 agreement's £10m limit on City advances, though only if the loans were made exclusively to the Bank. After calculating the financial consequences of the proposal, the IO found that it would still be better off lending to the Treasury, but nevertheless accepted the Bank's offer, largely out of fear.[97] A refusal would result in a 'quarrel' similar to that of 1914, which it could 'not afford', the Bank would almost certainly seek to persuade the Treasury to withdraw its proposal, and, if it succeeded, punish the IO with a far

---

93 BL, L/F/5/8, Abrahams, 11 Dec. 1915; *ibid.*, Abrahams, 24 March 1915; *ibid.*, B of E to IO, 26 March 1915; *ibid.*, B of E to IO, 14 May 1915; *ibid.*, Newmarch to Treasury, 22 March 1915; BL, L/F/7/169, LA, 5 Nov. 1915; *ibid.*, LA, 15 March 1916; *ibid.*, note, Abrahams, 25 Feb. 1915; *ibid.*, fol. 6619, Abrahams, 17 Dec. 1915; *ibid.*, Abrahams, 14 March 1916.

94 BL, L/F/7/169, Abrahams, 25 Feb. 1915.

95 BL, L/F/5/8, Abrahams, 5 Nov. 1915; *ibid.*, note, 15 Dec. 1915; *ibid.*, Abrahams, 17 Dec. 1915; *ibid.*, Abrahams to Schuster, 23 Dec. 1915; *ibid.*, note, 16 Feb. 1916; BL, L/F/7/169, Abrahams, 25 Feb. 1915.

96 BL, L/F/7/169, LA, 15 March 1916; BL, L/F/5/8, Treasury to IO, 10 March 1916.

97 BL, L/F/7/169, B of E to IO, 14 March 1916; *ibid.*, IO to B of E, 16 March 1916; *ibid.*, LA, 15 March 1916. The difference between the two offers was £25,000 pa on each £10m lent (*ibid.*, Abrahams, 15 March 1916).

worse deal. Even if it failed, the Treasury could easily pull out of its arrangement after a few months, again leaving India at the tender mercy of the Bank.[98]

Conclusion

The home balances were the lynchpin of the IO's financial operations. Not only did they meet India's UK commitments, but their loans to the City reduced the funds that had to be remitted from India, contributed to a generally low interest rate environment in which the IO could perform effectively, allowed the recycling of resources and constituted the subcontinent's contribution to the City's gift economy. Critics were ignorant of the true reasons for the advances. Unaware that the exclusive use of list companies, rejection of tenders, restriction of collateral securities, low valuations of Indian government and Indian railway company collateral, and the short currencies/renewals of loans were essential if these purposes were to be achieved, they severely criticised the IO's investment practices. Having little knowledge of the customs of the City, they additionally attacked procedures that were common and widely accepted in financial circles.

The exception was the Bank of England, which was cognisant of the reasons for the policy, but claimed that it threatened the stability of the market, although it probably had more self-interested motives for its opposition – the maximisation of its profits and the weakening of its critics. In its modus operandi of bringing the advances to an end, it again displayed its power and the sheer savagery of the City. By warning that unless India agreed to its demands it would withdraw from the issue of government loans and no longer accept them as collateral for its own advances, it effectively threatened to bring the whole edifice of Indian finance crashing down. The IO, having no alternative, capitulated and heavily restricted its lending and began to invest surplus balances in UK government securities, but, in doing so, contributed to the later demise of the council bill and to the eventual disappearance of Indian government sterling loans.

---

98   *Ibid.*, Abrahams, 15 March 1916; *ibid.*, JWH, 16 March 1916; *ibid.*, Abrahams, 16 March 1916; BL, L/F/5/8, note, 15 March 1916.

Conclusion

Like nature's ecosystems, Indian finance at first appears highly complex, a perception exploited by IO officials, who 'delight[ed] in the lucidity of mystification', aware that the financial labyrinth that constituted their work acted as a cloak, shrouding their activities from criticism.[1] In reality, the world of Indian finance was a surprisingly small one, comprising no more than a hundred individuals and institutions, and relatively straightforward. It can perhaps be best understood through the prism of principal-agent theory and the concepts of trust, the gift economy and enlightened self-interest. Principal-agent theory postulates that all agents possess two interests – that of their principal, which is to fulfil the task for which they were retained, and their own self-interest – and argues that many agents are tempted to pursue their own interests to the detriment of those of their principal, a practice termed moral hazard.[2] One way principals can counter this self-interested behaviour is through the employment of agents they already know through family, social, network or business connections and with whom they establish close long-term trust relationships. Such agents will be less willing to act selfishly, as, in doing so, they will not only lose the emotional pay-offs they gain from their relationship with their principal and any future gains from the association, but will also damage their family, social, network or business reputations, reducing the chances that others will trust/associate with them.[3] One method of building trust relationships is through the provision of gifts. In a gift economy, participants exchange gifts at a cost to themselves in the knowledge that they will receive rewards in return, either from the recipient or another member of the community, and the act of giving will increase their social status and reputation for trustworthiness. This concept is extended in the theory of

---

1   *Investors Review*, 10 (July to Dec. 1897), p. 80.
2   P. Milgrom and J. Roberts, *Economics, Organisation and Management*, Princeton 1992, chaps 5–6.
3   Sunderland, *Social Capital*, pp. 6–9. The theory assumes that the principal will break off the relationship with the agent and will inform others of the agent's duplicity.

enlightened self-interest, which contends that people will act in the interests of the wider community and against their own immediate advantage if, as a member of that society, they too gain over the longer term.[4]

All the participants in Indian finance were agents obliged to act in the interests of their principals. The duty of the Indian government and the IO was to protect the fortunes of India, that of the Bank of England and Treasury to safeguard the British economy, and that of the IO's service providers to meet their contractual obligations. In reality, all of these agents had their own self-interests: the survival and growth of their organisations and the maximisation of their income, power and status. They also served a number of principals with contradictory interests. For example, the Indian government and the IO were ultimately agents of the UK government that ruled India; the Indian government represented the local business community, whose goals were often at variance with those of the country as a whole; the IO and their brokers were the agents of the investors who bought Indian government loans; and the Bank of England acted on behalf of the City of London.

The self-interested goals of IO officials comprised the survival and growth of their Office, which, in turn, depended on limited Indian and City criticism of their activities and the expansion of the Indian economy, while those of the Finance Council's City members encompassed the protection and advancement of their reputations for competence and honesty, and the self and social esteem gains they would garner from aiding the development of the subcontinent. It was thus in the IO's self-interest to meet the objectives of the Indian government rather than that of the UK and to perform its duties in a highly competent, honest and conservative/risk-free manner. To ensure that India's goals were met, it sought to minimise the self-interest of its service providers through the establishment of long-term trust relationships. It also provided these institutions with gifts, allowing them to obtain large short-term gains, and acted in the immediate interests of the City and against those of India, in the knowledge that the subcontinent, as part of this financial community, would gain in the longer term. The Office furthermore allowed brokers to act in a manner that harmed their secondary principals (the general investing public), and itself occasionally operated in ways that were detrimental to its own secondary principals (the UK government and, again, the investing public).

The IO had two official inter-related goals – the maximisation of Indian exports and the payment of India's UK commitments. High Indian exports benefitted both of its principals, increasing the wealth of India and advancing Britain's industrial, trading and financial sectors. High exports ensured that British industry obtained the cheap raw materials required for the manufacture of its goods, and the income earned by Indians increased their demand for UK imports. At the same time,

---

4   R. L. Trivers, 'The Evolution of Reciprocal Altruism', *Quarterly Review of Biology*, 46 (1971), pp. 35–57; A. Offer, 'Between the Gift and the Market: The Economy of Regard', *Economic History Review*, 50 (3) (1997), pp. 450–1; G. D. Keim, 'Corporate Social Responsibility: An Assessment of the Enlightened Self-Interest Model', *Academy of Management Review*, 3 (1) (1978), p. 34.

the trade generated benefitted the country's mercantile community, fuelled the expansion of the discount market and permitted the triangular settlement system described in the Introduction on which the City's domination of the international monetary system rested.

The maximisation of exports was achieved through the expenditure that constituted and contributed to the home charges, and the transfer of funds from India for the payment of these commitments. The charges financed the prerequisites of development. The loans on which guaranteed and other interest was paid funded the construction of an extensive and reliable railway system, the various military and civil charges ensured internal/external peace and efficient and effective administration, and a portion of the proceeds of Indian government sterling loans ensured the maintenance of a stable exchange rate. The payment of the charges, similarly, facilitated trade. Council bills permitted the exchange banks to transfer funds to India and to purchase the export bills that financed shipments, and, by allowing them to hedge exchange risks and controlling the price charged for export/import bills, reduced the cost of Indian trade. From 1893, they also ensured exchange stability, which facilitated the arrangement of forward contracts, inward capital investment and English investor purchase of rupee debt, all of which boosted commerce.

The home charges, however, were both a boon and a threat. IO officials were well aware that failure to meet India's UK commitments, owing to failed harvests or any other event, would have a devastating impact on the Indian and British economies, seriously disrupting Indian trade and inward investment, and causing government and guaranteed railway company debenture/stock prices to plummet. Moreover, it would destroy their professional and social reputations, and threaten the very survival of the Office. The IO's second goal was thus to avoid default at all costs. This was achieved in a variety of ways. To protect the home charges from falling silver prices, India in 1893 adopted the gold exchange standard, and, to maximise receipts, council bills where possible were sold at a relatively high price – from 1904, above 1s 4d, the rate at which they were exchanged in India for gold. When the Indian Treasury was unable to cash the bills, a predicament that additionally threatened exports, reverse council drafts were issued, bill sales restricted and the Indian government permitted to obtain loans from the GSR. Sums were also borrowed from the London market/institutions, and drawn from the home balance deposits of the guaranteed railway companies and money owed by HMG to the Indian government and paid in London.

Key aspects of the IO's payment of the home charges and the maximisation of exports were its operations in the London market, specifically the raising of loans, the lending of the home balances, its support of the gold standard and its attitude towards moral hazard. To ensure that government loans were fully subscribed, the IO maximised demand and avoided credit-destroying loan failures. It thus chose appropriate issuing houses and brokers, widely advertised flotations, and issued short-term bonds, known as floaters, which could be used as collateral and further increased demand for government securities as well as facilitating exports. The advances obtained from the discount market with the floaters were used by brokers to bankroll further purchases of government debentures/stock and by the exchange banks to buy council drafts/import bills, enabling them to finance Indian trade. The sums procured by the discount houses from joint stock banks, meanwhile, were used to discount DA export bills, permitting further exchange bank council draft/import bill purchases. To offload the debentures/stock, the IO additionally offered extremely generous yields. Much criticised, these boosted demand and avoided underwriters being left with large amounts of unsold securities that they would dump onto the market, which would lead to a collapse of market prices and a downgrading of Indian credit that would force the IO to offer even better terms when it next entered the market.

A similar strategy was adopted as regards the money lent from the home balances. At first sight, these loans also appear to have benefitted recipients and disadvantaged India. The advances were bestowed at relatively low interest rates to a small coterie of favoured institutions. In reality, the loans were part of a further benign cycle that ultimately helped India, again by enhancing the demand for government securities and facilitating Indian exports. The sums advanced were used by brokers to purchase sterling bills and Indian government debentures/stock; by exchange banks to buy the council drafts/import bills needed to finance export bills; by discount houses to underwrite Indian government loans and to discount DA export bills, thus enabling the exchange banks to purchase more council drafts/ import bills; and by joint stock banks to finance their own loans to the discount houses, again facilitating the discounting of DA export bills. Moreover, the acceptance on very generous terms of Indian government debentures/stock as collateral for the advances further increased demand for these securities, and the loans acted as gifts to the City that were reciprocated in the form of favours, market information and help during periods of crisis.

In its support of the gold standard, the IO demonstrated enlightened self-interest. Officials were well aware that the outflow of gold and the resultant rise in bank rate would have a negative impact on India. Higher borrowing charges would curtail the demand for sterling bills and Indian government and guaranteed railway company loans, leading to the failure of issues or the provision of higher yields, and would lessen exports. High rates and the non-availability of funds would make it more difficult for UK importers to finance purchases of Indian produce, and the exchange banks would be less able and willing to buy council drafts/import bills. The lower prices obtained when discounting DA export bills would encourage them to hold council drafts to maturity, and the higher interest rates would dissuade them from financing the purchase of drafts/import bills with bank loans and spur them to invest export bill proceeds in London and to transfer Indian funds to the UK to enable even greater returns to be made. Deprived of finance, the exchange banks' Indian branches would thus variously pay lower prices for export bills, reducing merchant and farmers profits; purchase fewer export bills, further reducing the take-up of council drafts/import bills; or borrow the necessary finance locally, which, along with lower export bill purchase, would raise Indian interest rates and further damage export/council bill demand.

The IO was additionally conscious that it would be subjected to intense pressure from other financial institutions if it failed to support the gold standard, and that coming to the aid of its City brethren strengthened its reputation for trustworthiness and generated much goodwill, particularly with the Bank of England and the Treasury, both of which were aware of India's crucial role in the survival of the gold standard and the impact default of the home charges/Indian government loans would have on the City/the UK economy. They thus reciprocated the gift of the support of gold proffered by the IO and sought to prevent any form of default. Over the period, the Bank variously supplied much useful market information, accepted Indian government stock as collateral for its own advances, possibly brought forward interest rate cuts to boost demand for the 1897 and 1904 issues, helped excess consol holdings to be offloaded in the war loan conversion, permitted current account overdrafts, provided £14.9m of loans (1866–1914), and, in 1916, agreed to buy reverse council bills at a discount. The Treasury, meanwhile, came to the IO's aid in 1908 by allowing the NDC to buy GSR UK government stock; in more normal times, permitted Treasury bills to be bought/sold directly from/to the Commissioners; from 1915 to 1916, provided India with credit; and, in 1931, extended its embargo on market issues to ensure a good reception for a loan that the IO had at the height of the financial crisis agreed to postpone.

The IO underpinned the gold standard via the home balances, earmarking and the issue of council bills. The home balances loans to the discount market increased liquidity and kept down interest rates and the portion of the balances kept in the IO's Bank of England current account supplemented the Bank's gold stocks, as did the advances to the Bank at times of gold outflow, which additionally strengthened the impact of any base rate rise by depriving the market of funds. The later investment of the balances, along with the GSR and the UK portion of the PCR, in UK government securities again increased gold stocks, but was largely designed to limit risk, facilitate the defence of the exchange and maintain the market prices of Indian government loans, which were highly sensitive to gilt prices. As for earmarking and the issue of council bills, the remittance of Indian government funds via earmarking increased the Bank's gold stocks, and, from 1904, the unlimited sale of council bills when the price reached 1s 4 ⅛d, the level at which it was cheaper for banks to remit funds to India in the form of specie, slowed gold outflows, and the purchase and redirection to the UK of Australian and Egyptian gold in transit to India increased London gold stocks and eschewed the fall in holdings that occurred when Australian/Egyptian specie was shipped to India.

Not all of the IO's activities, however, supported the gold standard. The issue of council bills and Indian government loans took money out of the market, though the latter drain was offset by the inflow of Indian funds to meet dividend payments, and reverse earmarking reduced the amount of gold held in the IO's Bank of England current account. To mitigate the possible repercussions of these actions, flotations were timed to avoid clashes with other loan issues or postponed when interest rates were high, and, where possible, reverse earmarking was undertaken in December/ January when the market was replete with funds and the practice avoided during periods of stringency. The IO was also not prepared to buttress the gold standard where the loss to India was far greater than any possible gain. It thus resisted all attempts by the Bank of England to increase the portion of balances kept in the Bank's current account and stoutly defended its right to lend to the discount market and issue sterling bills, disparaging the Bank's claims that the sudden recall of IO advances could initiate a liquidity crisis and that sterling bills took money out of the market and reduced the demand for UK Treasury bills.

Although willing to acquiesce to the self-interest of others when there was a gain to be made, the IO sought to prevent self-seeking behaviour that damaged India. Indian government proposals designed to aid a local business elite or political group at the expense of the country's economy were simply rejected. Service provider moral hazard was lessened via trust and power. The Office worked with a small number of high status companies of good repute managed by executives who had similar social and, in some cases, ethnic backgrounds to IO officials, with whom they formed close working relationships/friendships. There was thus much trust between the IO and the financial institutions that did its bidding, and the managers of these organisations were well aware that acting against the interests of India would end their friendships with IO staff, damage their own and their firm's reputation for trustworthiness (a valuable asset in the City), and lose them a great deal of future Indian business. The exception was the Bank of England, the self-interest of which could be constrained by neither trust nor power. The Bank fought to maximise its commission income, and, in 1914, attempted to eliminate the competition posed by the IO's home balance advances to its own market loans, to weaken the campaign led by Sir Felix Schuster for it to be stripped of its powers and to reap revenge on Schuster for his temerity to utter such blasphemies. Lacking a trust relationship with the Bank and having a legal duty to use its services, the IO had no option but to succumb to its demands.

Strangely, while insisting that its service providers treat itself fairly, the IO had no objection to them committing moral hazard against their own agents, the investing public, provided it was in India's interests and the public/media were oblivious of the behaviour. Purchases of securities by the Office's syndicates/underwriters on the announcement of an issue and during flotations benefitted the brokers involved by increasing the demand for and the price at which they could sell their allotments, and, in the case of the rigging of the grey market, allowed them to make large profits. The IO, similarly, gained. The market manipulation raised the prices obtained for loans, reduced the likelihood of undersubscription, and, as regards grey market dealings, helped to defeat attempts by non-syndicate brokers to drive down prices. For the private investors 'suckered' into buying expensive debentures/stock, however, such actions could be disastrous. If demand proved to be low, the immediate post-issue price of their purchases would plummet, and, even if this failed to occur, the market price of the loan would inexorably fall until it reached its true value.

If it benefitted India, the IO was similarly willing to act against the interests of its own principals. In order to maximise its Parliamentary borrowing powers, and, in 1933, to increase subscription, it was 'economical with the truth' in its prospectus descriptions of the purposes of loans, and, immediately before and after flotations, planted positive news stories about India and made announcements designed to rally support. As a government department, it was under an obligation to follow public sector rather than private sector ethical norms.[5] It presumably occasionally pursued the latter, as it was highly unlikely that the UK/Indian governments or media would learn of the moral hazard, it dealt with private companies on a day-to-day basis and thus absorbed the sector's values, and its adoption of these norms helped it to form stronger ascribed trust relationships with service providers – demonstrating that it was 'one of them'.

The widely accepted view that the IO in its financial dealings was a 'puppet' of the financial magnates that bestrode the City can thus be seen to be a gross falsehood.[6] In reality, it was a crucial component of a financial ecosystem composed of self-interested institutions and individuals, which survived and prospered through mutual dependency. Although they sought to maximise their principals' and their own self-interests, the IO, the Bank of England, the Treasury and City institutions were well aware that they stood or fell together. They were thus willing to provide costly favours on the understanding that these would eventually be reciprocated and to act in the interests of the City and against their own immediate advantage – aware that as members of the financial community they too gained over the longer term.

---

5   See R. Chapman, *Ethics in Public Service for a New Millennium*, Aldershot 2000, pp. 219, 227.

6   Doraiswami, *Indian Finance*, p. 64.

Appendices

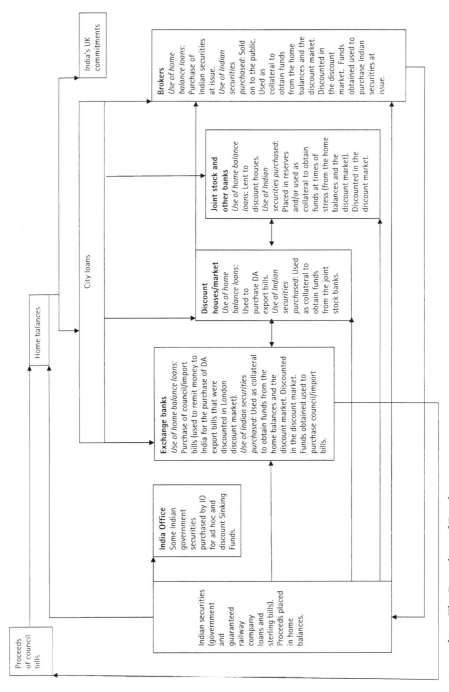

Appendix 1. The Recycling of Funds

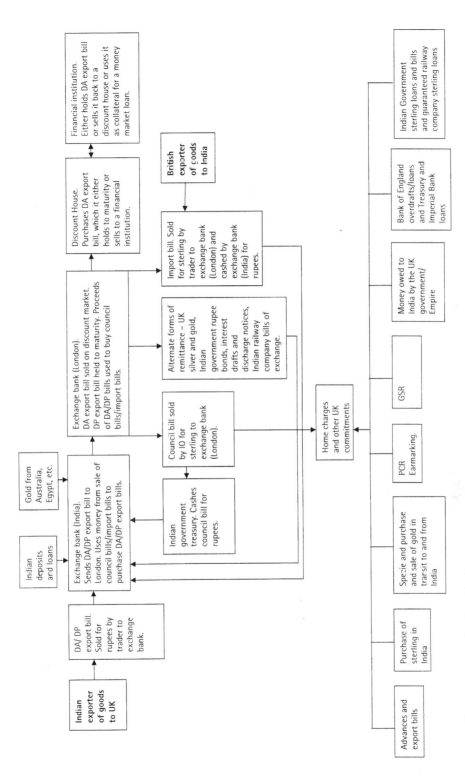

Appendix 2. Finance of Indian Trade

Bibliography

Bank of England Archive, London (BE)

AC 14/14; AC 30/121; AC 30/471; ADM 19/7; C 40/289; C 47/333; C 47/334; CT 39; F 11/3/4123/3; G 1/323; G 1/411; G 8/48; G 23/66/249; G 23/67/33; G 23/67/94; G 23/67/264; G 23/68/162–3; G 23/68/224–5; G 23/68/277–8

British Library, London (BL)

India Office. Accountant-General's Records, c.1601–1974:
L/AG/4/12/1; L/AG/9/8/5; L/AG/9/8/6; L/AG/9/8/7; L/AG/14/10/1; L/AG/14/11/1; L/AG/14/11/2; L/AG/14/11/3; L/AG/14/11/4; L/AG/14/11/311; L/AG/14/13/1; L/AG/14/14/1; L/AG/14/14/2; L/AG/14/14/3; L/AG/14/14/5; L/AG/14/15/1; L/AG/14/17/1; L/AG/14/17/2; L/AG/24/36; L/AG/29/1/153; L/AG/37/4

India Office. Financial Department Records, c.1800–1948:
L/F/5/3; L/F/5/4; L/F/5/5; L/F/5/6; L/F/5/7; L/F/5/8; L/F/5/9; L/F/5/10; L/F/5/37; L/F/5/59; L/F/5/60; L/F/5/61; L/F/5/62; L/F/5/64; L/F/5/79; L/F/5/80; L/F/5/139; L/F/5/144; L/F/5/169; L/F/5/170; L/F/5/173; L/F/7/162; L/F/7/163; L/F/7/164; L/F/7/166; L/F/7/167; L/F/7/168; L/F/7/169; L/F/7/170; L/F/7/172; L/F/7/173; L/F/7/177; L/F/7/178; L/F/7/182; L/F/7/813; L/F/7/184; L/F/7/186; L/F/7/188; L/F/7/189; L/F/7/190; L/F/7/192; L/F/7/193; L/F/7/198; L/F/7/199; L/F/7/214; L/F/7/224; L/F/7/421–2; L/F/7/423; L/F/7/426; L/F/7/428; L/F/7/442; L/F/7/460; L/F/7/592; L/F/7/593; L/F/7/596; L/F/7/597; L/F/7/598; L/F/7/599; L/F/7/601; L/F/7/742; L/F/7/746; L/F/7/755; L/F/7/757; L/F/7/763; L/F/7/768; L/F/7/772; L/F/7/773; L/F/7/776; L/F/7/780; L/F/7/782; L/F/7/783; L/F/7/784; L/F/7/785; L/F/7/786; L/F/7/787; L/F/7/791; L/F/7/792; L/F/7/793; L/F/7/794; L/F/7/795; L/F/7/796; L/F/7/797; L/F/7/799; L/F/7/801; L/F/7/803; L/F/7/805; L/F/7/806; L/F/7/807; L/F/7/809; L/F/7/810; L/F/7/813; L/F/7/815; L/F/7/816; L/F/7/817; L/F/7/820; L/F/7/823; L/F/7/825

Crown Agents' Archive, Liverpool (CAAL)

L 266; WN 13

Crown Agents' Archive, Sutton (CAS)

1913 report, file 53; CA M 5, Memorandum on the procedures followed in connection with the issue of Crown colony loans, 1919; Notes on the issue of loans by the Crown Agents, 1926; Prospectuses

Guildhall Library, London

Prospectuses

Marshall Library, Cambridge

Keynes Papers, box 53a7

National Archives, Kew, London (NA)

Crown Agents Files:
CAOG 9/29; CAOG 9/33; CAOG 9/34; CAOG 9/35; CAOG 9/40; CAOG 9/76; CAOG 9/94; CAOG 9/101; CAOG 9/102; CAOG 9/103; CAOG 9/104; CAOG 9/107; CAOG 9/118; CAOG 9/147; CAOG 9/300; CAOG 9/324; CAOG 12/97

Colonial Office Files:
CO 48/439/9353; CO 54/667/35749; CO 129/370/11508; CO 137/552/2931; CO 167/773/28358; CO 247/111/4604; CO 273/332/16226; CO 323/364/5665; CO 323/393/11909; CO 323/453/32835; CO 323/591/9213; CO 323/870; CO 323/945; CO 323/1202/11; CO 323/1623/19

Treasury Files:
T 1/11261; T 1/11898; T 1/16802; T 20/6; T 120/1; T 120/2; T 160/472; T 160/474; T 160/649; T 172/238; T 175/70; T 233/1425

National Westminster Bank Archive, London

12915/212; 12917/220

Parliamentary Papers (PP)

PP 1831–32 [734–5] *Select Committee on the Affairs of the East India Company*
PP 1842 [409] *Exchequer Bills Forgery. Report of the Commissioners*
PP 1859 [201] *East India (Loans)*
PP 1868–69 [258] *East India (Registered Debt)*
PP 1871 [363] *Select Committee on Finance and Financial Administration of India*
PP 1872 [327] *Select Committee on Finance and Financial Administration of India*
PP 1873 [311] *Select Committee on Principles and Practice on which Public Departments Regulate the Purchase and Sale of Materials and Stores*

PP 1873 [354] *Select Committee on Finance and Financial Administration of India, Third Report*

PP 1874 [263] *Report from the Select Committee on Public Departments*

PP 1875 [351] *Report from the Select Committee on Banks of Issue*

PP 1875 [367] *Report from the Select Committee on Loans to Foreign States*

PP 1878 [333] *Report from the Select Committee on East India (Public Works)*

PP 1878 [C.2147] *Statistical Abstract relating to British India from 1867/8 to1876/7*

PP 1878 [C.2157] *London Stock Exchange Commission: Report*

PP 1878–79 [165] *Financial Statement of the Government of India, 1879–80*

PP 1878–79 [312] *Select Committee on Expediency of Constructing in India Public Works*

PP 1881 [205] *Financial Statement of Government of India, 1881–82*

PP 1882 [181] *Financial Statement of Government of India, 1882–83*

PP 1883 [135] *Financial Statement of Government of India, 1883–84*

PP 1884–85 [151] *Financial Statement of Government of India, 1885–86*

PP 1884–85 [352] *East India (Reduction of Expenditure)*

PP 1886 [C.4730] *Statistical Abstract relating to British India from 1875/6 to 1884/5*

PP 1887 [C.5099] *Gold and Silver Commission*

PP 1887 [C.5210] *Statistical Abstract relating to British India from 1876/7 to 1885/6*

PP 1888 [C.5512] *Gold and Silver Commission*

PP 1889 [123] *Financial Statement of Government of India, 1889–90*

PP 1890 [140] *Financial Statement of Government of India, 1890–91*

PP 1890–91 [225] *Financial Statement of Government of India, 1891–92*

PP 1890–91 [C.6502] *Statistical Abstract relating to British India from 1880–81 to 1889–90*

PP 1893–94 [207] *Financial Statement of Government of India, 1893–94*

PP 1893–94 [C.7060, 7060.I, 7060.II] *Indian Currency Committee*

PP 1894 [92] *Financial Statement of Government of India, 1894–95*

PP 1896 [166] *Financial Statement of Government of India, 1896–97*

PP 1896 [C.8238] *Statistical Abstract relating to British India from 1885/6 to 1894/5*

PP 1896 [C.8258] *Indian Expenditure Commission, Volume 1*

PP 1897 [193] *Financial Statement of Government of India, 1897–98*

PP 1898 [168] *Financial Statement of Government of India, 1898–99*

PP 1898 [C.9037] *Committee to Inquire into Indian Currency: Evidence*

PP 1899 [254] *Financial Statement of Government of India, 1899–1900*

PP 1899 [C.9222, 9390] *Committee to Inquire into Indian Currency*

PP 1899 [C.9376] *Committee to Inquire into Indian Currency*

PP 1900 [225] *Financial Statement of Government of India, 1900–01*

PP 1900 [Cd.130] *Indian Expenditure Commission, Volume 3*

PP 1900 [Cd.131] *Indian Expenditure Commission, Volume 4*

PP 1901 [171] *Indian Financial Statement for 1901–02*

PP 1902 [187] *Indian Financial Statement for 1902–03*

PP 1903 [151] *Indian Financial Statement for 1903–04*

PP 1904 [193] *Indian Financial Statement for 1904–05*

PP 1904 [Cd.1915] *Review of the Trade of India, 1898/9 to 1902/3*

PP 1905 [167] *Indian Financial Statement for 1905–06*

PP 1906 [162] *Indian Financial Statement for 1906–07*

PP 1906 [Cd.2754] *East India (Statistical Abstract), 1894–95 to 1903–04*

PP 1907 [140] *Indian Financial Statement for 1907–08*

PP 1908 [170] *Indian Financial Statement for 1908–09*

PP 1908 [Cd.3969] *Review of the Trade of India, 1902/3 to 1906/7*

PP 1909 [122] *Indian Financial Statement for 1909–10*

PP 1909 [Cd.4474] *Committee of Enquiry into the Organisation of the Crown Agents' Office*

PP 1909 [Cd.4670] *Report of the Royal Commission on Shipping Rings, Volume 3*

PP 1909 [Cd.4685] *Report of the Royal Commission on Shipping Rings, Volume 4*

PP 1910 [169] *Return of Indian Financial Statement and Budget for 1910–11*

PP 1911 [155] *Return of Indian Financial Statement and Budget for 1911–12*

PP 1913 [130] *Return of Indian Financial Statement and Budget for 1913–14*

PP 1913 [Cd.6783] *Review of the Trade of India, 1907/8 to 1911/12*

PP 1914 [232] *Return of Indian Financial Statement and Budget for 1914–15*

PP 1914 [Cd.7069] *Royal Commission on Indian Finance and Currency, Volume 1*

PP 1914 [Cd.7070] *Royal Commission on Indian Finance and Currency: Appendices, Volume 1*

PP 1914 [Cd.7071] *Royal Commission on Indian Finance and Currency: Appendices, Volume 2*

PP 1914 [Cd.7236] *Royal Commission on Indian Finance and Currency. Final Report*

PP 1914 [Cd.7238] *Royal Commission on Indian Finance and Currency: Appendices*

PP 1914–16 [233] *Return of Indian Financial Statement and Budget for 1915–16*

PP 1914–16 [Cd.7799] *East India (Statistical Abstract), 1903–04 to 1912–13*

PP 1916 [80] *Return of Indian Financial Statement and Budget for 1916–17*

PP 1916 [Cd.8343] *Review of the Trade of India, 1910/11 to 1914/15*

PP 1917–18 [94] *Return of Indian Financial Statement and Budget for 1917–18*

PP 1918 [61] *Return of Indian Financial Statement and Budget for 1918–19*

PP 1918 [Cd.9162] *East India (Progress and Condition), 1916–17*

PP 1919 [104] *Return of Indian Financial Statement and Budget for 1919–20*

PP 1919 [Cmd.234, 235, 236, 237, 238] *Report of the Indian Industrial Commission. Evidence, Volumes 1–5*

PP 1919 [Cmd.288, i–viii] *Royal Commission on Income Tax*

PP 1919 [Cmd.442] *Report on the Conditions and Prospects of British Trade in India at the Close of the War*

PP 1920 [103] *Return of Indian Financial Statement and Budget for 1920–21*

PP 1920 [Cmd.528] *Committee Appointed to Enquire into Indian Exchange and Currency, Volumes 1 and 2*

PP 1920 [Cmd.529] *Report of the Committee Appointed to Enquire into Indian Exchange and Currency, Volume 3*

PP 1921 [153] *Return of Indian Financial Statement and Budget*

PP 1921 [Cmd.1512] *Report of the Committee Appointed by the Secretary of State for India to Enquire into the Administration and Working of Indian Railways*

PP 1922 [Cmd.1778] *East India (Statistical Abstract), 1910–11 to 1919–20*

PP 1923 [128] *Return of Indian Financial Statement and Budget*

PP 1924 [115] *Return of Indian Financial Statement and Budget*

PP 1924 [Cmd.2033] *East India (Statistical Abstract), 1911/12 to 1920/1*

PP 1924–25 [201] *Report on the work of the India Store Department, 1924–25*

PP 1926 [108] *Return of Indian Financial Statement and Budget*

PP 1926 [Cmd.2687] *Royal Commission on Indian Currency and Finance*

PP 1928 [Cmd.3046] *East India (Statistical Abstract), 1916–17 to 1925–26*

PP 1929–30 [Cmd.3386] *Explanatory Memorandum, of the Accounts and Estimates for 1929–30*

PP 1930–31 [Cmd.3670] *Explanatory Memorandum, of the Accounts and Estimates for 1930–31*

PP 1930–31 [Cmd.3882] *East India (Statistical Abstract), 1919–20 to 1928–29*

PP 1931–32 [Cmd.3969] *Explanatory Memorandum, of the Accounts and Estimates for 1931–32*

PP 1931–32 [Cmd.4161] *East India. Accounts and Estimates, 1932–1933*

PP 1932–33 [112] *Report of the Joint Committee (Indian Constitutional Reform)*

PP 1932–33 [Cmd.4238] *Proceedings during the Third Session, 17th November to 24th December, 1932 (Round Table Conference (1930–31))*

PP 1932–33 [Cmd.4416] *East India. Accounts and Estimates, 1933–1934*

PP 1933–34 [Cmd.4695] *East India. Accounts and Estimates, 1934–1935*

PP 1934–35 [17] *Government of India: A Bill to make Further Provision for the Government of India*

PP 1934–35 [Cmd.5000] *East India. Accounts and Estimates, 1935–1936*

PP 1935–36 [Cmd.5158] *East India (Statistical Abstract), 1923–24 to 1932–33*

PP 1938–39 [Cmd.6079] *East India (Statistical Abstract), 1927–28 to 1936–37*

PP 1942–43 [Cmd.6441] *East India (Statistical Abstract), 1930–31 to 1939–40*

Periodicals

Banker's Magazine; *Board of Trade Labour Gazette*; *Canadian Jewish Chronicle*; *Daily List*; *Directory of Directors*; *The Economist*; *Financial News*; *India Finance*; *Investors Review*; *Journal of the Royal Society of Arts*; *Journal of the Statistical Society*; *Economist*; *Financial Times*; *New Witness*; *Pall Mall Gazette*; *Stock Exchange Official Intelligence*; *The Statist*; *Toronto World*; *Westminster Gazette*

Secondary sources

Ambedkar, B. R., *The Problem of the Rupee: Its Origin and its Solution*, London 1923

Anon, *The Investor's Handy Book of Active Stocks and Shares,* London 1910

Anon, *Indian Currency and Finance*, Bombay 1913

Anon, *Guidebook for Investors in Government of India Securities*, Calcutta 1921

Anstey, V., *The Economic Development of India*, London 1952

Atkin, J., 'Official Regulation of British Overseas Investment, 1914–31', *Economic History Review*, 23 (2) (1970), pp. 324–5

Attard, B., 'Marketing Colonial Debt in London: Financial Intermediaries and Australasia, 1855–1914', *Association of Business Historians Conference*, January 2004, pp. 1–2

Aubrey, W. H. S., *Stock Exchange Investments*, London 1896

Avigdor-Goldsmid, H. d', 'The Little Marconi Case', *History Today*, 14 (1964), pp. 283–6

Ayling, K., *My Father's Family*, London 1979

Bagchi, A., *Private Investment in India, 1900–1939*, Cambridge 1972

Bahl, V., 'The Emergence of Large-Scale Steel Industry in India under British Colonial Rule, 1880–1907', *Indian Economic and Social History Review*, 31 (4) (1994), pp. 413–60

Balachandran, G., 'The Sterling Crisis and the Managed Float Regime in India, 1921–1924', *Indian Economic Social History Review*, 27 (1990), pp. 1–31

Balachandran, G., 'Britain's Liquidity Crisis and India, 1919–1920', *Economic History Review*, 46 (3) (1993), pp. 575–91

Balachandran, G., *John Bullion's Empire: Britain's Gold Problem and India between the Wars*, Richmond 1996

Balachandran, G., 'Introduction', in G. Balachandran (ed.), *India and the World Economy, 1850–1950*, Oxford 2003, pp. 1–45

Balachandran, J. G., 'Power and Markets in Global Finance: The Gold Standard, 1890–1926', *Journal of Global History*, 3 (2008), pp. 313–35

Ball, M. and D. Sunderland, *An Economic History of London, 1800–1914*, London 2001

Banerjee, D., 'Is there Overestimation of 'British Capital' Outflow? Keynes' Indo-British Trade and Transfer Accounts Re-examined with Alternate Evidence', *Indian Economic and Social History*, 41 (2) (2004), pp. 43–64

Banerji, A., *Finances in the Early Raj: Investments and the External Sector*, London 1995

Banerji, A., 'Revisiting the Exchange Standard, 1898–1913: 1. Steps to the Exchange Standard', *Economic and Political Weekly*, 1 December 2001, pp. 4490–500

Banerji, A., 'Revisiting the Exchange Standard, 1898–1913: 2. Operations', *Economic and Political Weekly*, 6 April 2002, pp. 1353–62

Banerji, C. A. K., *Aspects of Indo-British Economic Relations, 1858–1898*, Oxford 1982

Baster, A. S. J., *The Imperial Banks*, London 1929

Bhattacharayya, S., *Financial Foundations of the British Raj*, Simla 1971

Black, E., *The Social Politics of Anglo-Jewry 1880–1920*, Oxford 1988

Bloomfield, A. I., *Monetary Policy under the International Gold Standard*, New York 1959

Bloomfield, A. I., *Short-term Capital Movements under the Pre-1914 Gold Standard*, Princeton 1963

Bordo, M. D., 'The Gold Standard: The Traditional Approach', in M. D. Bordo and A. J. Schwartz (eds), *A Retrospective on the Classical Gold Standard, 1821-1931*, London 1984, pp. 23–120

Bordo, M. D., and H. Rockoff, 'The Gold Standard as a "Good Housekeeping Seal of Approval"', *Journal of Economic History*, 56 (1996), pp. 389–428

Bose, A., 'Foreign Capital', in V. B. Singh (ed.), *Economic History of India, 1857–1956*, London 1965, pp. 490–520

British-Indian, *Finance and Commerce in Federal India*, Oxford 1932

Budheswar, P., *India and the First World War*, Delhi 1996

Cain, P. J. and A. G. Hopkins, *British Imperialism, Volume 1: Innovation and Expansion, 1688–1914*, London 1993

Cain, P. J. and A. G. Hopkins, *British Imperialism, 1688–2000*, Harlow 2002

Carabelli, A. M. and M. A. Cedrini, 'Indian Currency and Beyond: The Legacy of the Early Economics of Keynes in the Times of Bretton Woods II', *Journal of Post Keynesian Economics*, 33 (2) (2010/11), pp. 255–79

Cassis, Y., *City Bankers, 1890–1914*, Cambridge 1994

Chablani, H. L., *Indian Currency and Exchange*, Oxford 1925

Chablani, H. L., *Indian Currency, Banking and Exchange*, Oxford 1929

Chand, G., *The Financial System of India*, London 1926

Chapman, R., *Ethics in Public Service for a New Millennium*, Aldershot 2000

Chapman, S., *The Rise of Merchant Banking*, London 1984

Charlesworth, N., 'The Problem of Government Finance in British India: Taxation, Borrowing and the Allocation of Resources in the Inter-War Period', *Modern Asian Studies*, 19 (3) (1985) pp. 521–48

Chirol, Sir V., *India: Old and New*, London 1921

Cleaver, G. and P. Cleaver, *The Union Discount. A Centenary Album*, London 1985

Colebatch, H., 'Australian Credit as Viewed from London', *Economic Record* (November 1927), pp. 217–227

Cristiano, C., 'Keynes and India, 1909–1913: A Study of Foreign Investment Policy', *European Journal of the History of Economic Thought*, 16 (2) (2009), pp. 301–24

Crump, A., *The English Manual of Banking*, London 1879

Davies, A. E., *The Money and the Stock and Share Markets*, London 1909

Davis, L. E. and R. A. Huttenback, *Mammon and the Pursuit of Empire: The Economics of British Imperialism*, Cambridge 1988

de Cecco, M., *Money and Empire*, London 1974

de Cecco, M., *The International Gold Standard: Money and Empire*, London 1984

Desai, M., 'Drains, Hoards and Foreigners: Does the Nineteenth Century Indian Economy have any Lessons for the Twenty First Century India?', in K. Uma (ed.), *Indian Economy*, New Delhi 2004, pp.17–32

Dhar, B., *The Sterling Balances of India*, Calcutta 1956

Doraiswami, S. V., *Indian Finance, Currency and Banking*, Madras 1915

Dubey, D. L., *The Indian Public Debt*, London 1930

Dutton, J., 'The Bank of England and the Rules of the Game', in M. D. Bordo and A. J. Schwartz (eds), *A Retrospective on the Classical Gold Standard, 1821–1931*, London 1984, pp. 173–202

Edelstein, M., 'Realised Rates of Return of UK Home and Overseas Portfolio Investment in the Age of High Imperialism', *Explorations in Economic History*, 13 (3) (1976), pp. 302–6

Edelstein, M., *Overseas Investment in the Age of High Imperialism*, New York 1982

Edelstein, M., 'Imperialism: Cost and Benefit', in R. Floud and D. McCloskey, *The Economic History of Britain, Volume 2*, Cambridge 1984, pp. 197–216

Eichengreen, B., *Golden Fetters: The Gold Standard and the Great Depression, 1919–39*, Oxford 1992

Eichengreen, B., *Globalizing Capital: A History of the International Monetary System*, Princeton 1996

Elliot, R. H., *Our Indian Difficulties*, London 1874

Fawcett, H., *Indian Finance*, London 1880

Feldman, D., 'Jews and the British Empire, c.1900', *History Workshop Journal*, 63 (1) (2007), pp. 70–89

Ferguson, N., *The House of Rothschild*, New York 1998

Ferguson, N. and M. Schularick, 'The Empire Effect: The Determinants of Country Risk in the First Era of Globalisation, 1880–1913', *Journal of Economic History*, 66 (2) (2006), pp. 283–312

Ferguson, N. and M. Schularick, 'The "thin film of gold": Monetary Rules and Policy Credibility in Developing Countries', *NBER Working Paper*, no. 13918 (2008)

Fishlow, A., 'Lessons from the Past: Capital Markets during the Nineteenth Century and the Interwar Period', *International Organization*, 39 (3) (1985), pp. 383–439

Flandreau, M. and F. Zumer, *The Making of Global Finance*, Paris 2004

Foster, R. F., *Lord Randolph Churchill*, Oxford 1982

Gallarotti, G. M., *The Anatomy of an International Monetary Regime: The Classical Gold Standard 1880–1914*, Oxford 1999

Ghose, S. C., *Lectures on Indian Railway Economics, Part One*, Calcutta 1922

Ghose, S. C., *Lectures on Indian Railway Economics, Part Three*, Calcutta 1923

Gilbert, R. S., 'London Financial Intermediaries and Australian Overseas Borrowing, 1900–29', *Australian Economic History Review*, 10 (1) (1971), pp. 39–47

Goldsmith, R. W., *The Financial Development of India, 1860–1977*, London 1983

Goodhart, C. A. E., *The Business of Banking, 1891–1914*, London 1972

Goodman, M., 'Vice Versa: Samuel Montagu, the First Lord Swaythling', *Jewish Historical Studies*, 40 (2005), pp. 75–103

Green, E., 'The Influence of the City over British Economic Policy, c.1880-1960' in Y. Cassis (ed.), *Finance and Financiers in European History, 1880–1960*, Cambridge 1992, pp. 193–218

Gutwein, D., *The Divided Elite*, Leiden 1992

Gutwein, D., 'Jewish Financiers and Industry 1890–1914: Germany and England', *Jewish History*, 8 (1–2) (1994), pp. 177–89

Hall, A. R., *The London Capital Market and Australia, 1870–1914*, Canberra 1963

Hargrave, J. F., 'Competition and Collusion in the British Railway Track Fittings Industry: The Case of the Anderton Foundry, 1800–1960', University of Durham, PhD thesis, 1992

Harris, S. E., *Monetary Problems of the British Empire*, New York 1931

Hill, C. W. L., *International Business: Competing in the Global Marketplace*, London 2010

Hopkinson, D., 'Vintage Liberals', *History Today*, 28 (6) (1978), pp. 363–70

Howard, H. F., *India and the Gold Standard*, London 1911

Howson, S., 'Sterling's Managed Float: The Operations of the Exchange Equalisation Account, 1932–39', *Princeton Studies in International Finance*, 46 (1980), pp. 1–7

Husain, S. A., 'The Organisation and Administration of the India Office, 1910–1924', University of London, PhD thesis, 1978

Hyndman, H. M., *The Bankruptcy of India*, London 1886

Jain, L. C., *The Monetary Problems of India*, London 1933

James, H., *International Monetary Cooperation since Bretton Woods*, Oxford 1996

Jones, G., *British Multinational Banking, 1830–1990*, Oxford 1993

Jopling, W. F., *Foreign Exchange and Foreign Bills in Theory and Practice*, London 1925

Kale, V. G., *India's National Finance since 1921*, Delhi 1932

Keim, G. D., 'Corporate Social Responsibility: An Assessment of the Enlightened Self-Interest Model', *Academy of Management Review*, 3 (1) (1978), pp. 32–9

Keynes, J. M., *Indian Currency and Finance*, London 1913

King, F. H., *The History of the Hong Kong and Shanghai Banking Corporation, Volume 1*, Cambridge 1986

King, F. H., *The History of the Hong Kong and Shanghai Banking Corporation, Volume 2*, Cambridge 1988

Krishnaswami, A., 'Capital Development of India, 1860–1913', University of London, PhD thesis, 1941

Kumar, D., 'The Fiscal System', in D. Kumar (ed.), *The Cambridge Economic History of India, Volume 2, 1757–1970*, Cambridge 1983, pp. 905–46

Kynaston, D., *The City of London, Volume 1: A World of its Own, 1815–90*, London 1994

Kynaston, D., *The City of London, Volume 2: Golden Years, 1890–1914*, London 1995

Leavens, D. H., *Silver Money*, Bloomington 1939

Lindert, P. H., *Key Currencies and Gold, 1900–13*, Princeton 1969

Lowenfeld, H., *The Investment of Trust Funds in the Safest and Most Productive Manner*, London 1908

Lowenfeld, H., *All About Investment*, London 1909

Maddison, A., *Class Structure and Economic Growth: India and Pakistan since the Moghuls*, London 1971

Madon, B. F., *Exchange Fallacies Exposed: Being India's Exchange Problem, Part 2*, Bombay 1925

Mathews, R., 'Prejudice: Anti-Semitism in the Distributist Weeklies', at http://racemathews.com/Assets/Distributism/1999%20Distributism&AntiSemitism.pdf (accessed May 2010)

Mauro, P., N. Sussman and Y. Yafeh, *Emerging Markets and Financial Globalization: Sovereign Bond Spreads in 1870–1913 and Today*, Oxford 2007

McGuire, J., 'Exchange Banks, India and the World Economy: 1850–1914', *Asian Studies Review*, 29 (2005), pp. 143–63

Michie, R. C., *The City of London*, London 1992

Milgrom, P. and J. Roberts, *Economics, Organisation and Management*, Princeton 1992

Mitchell, B. R., *International Historical Statistics: Africa, Asia and Oceania, 1750–2000*, London 2003

Mitchener, K. J. and M. D. Weidenmei, 'Country Risk, Currency Risk, and the Gold Standard', at http://www.frbatlanta.org/news/CONFEREN/06workshop/mitchener.pdf (accessed August 2010)

Mooney, H. F., 'British Opinion on Indian policy, 1911–1917', *Historian*, 23 (2) (1961), pp. 191–210

Morgan, K. O., *Consensus and Disunity: The Lloyd George Coalition Government, 1918–1922*, Oxford 1979

Morrison, T., *The Economic Transition in India*, London 1911

Muirhead, S., *Crisis Banking in the East*, Aldershot 1996

Mukherjee, A., *Imperialism, Nationalism and the Making of the Capitalist Class, 1920–47*, London 2002

Mukherjee, A., 'The Depression Years: Indian Capitalists' Critique of British and Monetary Financial Policy in India 1929–39', in A. K. Bagchi (ed.), *Money and Credit in Indian History from Early Medieval Times*, New Delhi 2002

Nash, R. L., *A Short Inquiry into the Profitable Nature of Our Investments*, London 1880

Nishimura, S., *The Decline of Inland Bills of Exchange in the London Money Market, 1855–1913*, London 1971

Obstfeld, M. and A. M. Taylor, 'Sovereign Risk, Credibility and the Gold Standard 1870–1913 versus 1925–31', *Economic Journal*, 113 (487) (2003), pp. 1–35

Offer, A., 'Between the Gift and the Market: The Economy of Regard', *Economic History Review*, 50 (3) (1997), pp. 450–76

Officer, L. H., 'Gold Standard', at http://eh.net/encyclopedia/article/officer.gold.standard (accessed January 2011)

Oxford Dictionary of National Biography, Oxford 2004

Pandit, Y. S., *India's Balance of Indebtness, 1893–1913*, London 1937

Poduval, R. N., *Finance of the Government of India since 1935*, Delhi 1951

Poovey, M., *The Financial System in Nineteenth-Century Britain*, London 2003

Pope, A., 'Australian Gold and the Finance of India's Exports during World War I: A Case Study of Imperial Control and Coordination', *Indian Economic & Social History Review, 33 (2) (1996), pp. 115 –31*

Prasad, A., *Indian Railways: A Study in Public Utility Administration*, London 1960

Purkayastha, K. M., *The ABC of Indian Finance*, Calcutta 1924

Rag, P., 'Indian Nationalism, 1885–1905: An Overview', *Social Scientist*, 23 (263–5) (April/June 1995), pp. 69–97

Rai, L., *England's Debt to India*, London 1917

Report of the Controller of Currency, Delhi 1926–1934/5

Rothermund, D., 'The Great Depression and British Financial Policy in India, 1929–1934', *Indian Economic and Social History Review*, 18 (1) (1981), pp. 1–17

Rothermund, D., *An Economic History of India from Pre-Colonial times to 1991*, London 1993

Saul, S. B., *Studies in British Overseas Trade, 1870–1914*, Liverpool 1960

Sayers, R. S., *Gilletts in the London Money Market*, Oxford 1968

Sayers, R. S., *Bank of England Operations 1890–1914*, Connecticut 1970

Sayers, R. S., *The Bank of England 1891–1944, Volume 1*, Cambridge 1975

Searle, G. R., *Corruption in British Politics*, Oxford 1987

Sen, S., *Colonies and the Empire: India, 1890–1914*, London 1992

Sen, S. K., *Studies in Economic Policy and Development of India 1848–1926*, Calcutta 1966

Senate of the United States, Speech by Hon. William Stewart, 1 May 1888, at http://www.yamaguchy.com/library/uregina/stewart.html (accessed July 2012)

Shah, K. T., *Sixty Years of Indian Finance*, London 1927

Shirras, G. F., *Indian Finance and Banking*, London 1920

Silver, F., *Modern Banking: Commercial and Credit Paper*, New York 1920

Simha, S. L. N. and G. Balachandran, *History of the Reserve Bank of India*, Bombay 1970

Simon, M., 'The Pattern of New British Portfolio Foreign Investment, 1865–1914', in A. R. Hall (ed.), *The Export of Capital from Britain, 1870–1919*, London 1968, pp. 18–36

Sinha, J. C., *Indian Currency Problems of the Last Decade*, Delhi 1938

Spalding, W. F., *Eastern Exchange, Currency and Finance*, London 1920

Sunderland, D., *Managing the British Empire: The Crown Agents for the Colonies 1833–1914*, London 2004

Sunderland, D., *Social Capital, Trust and the Industrial Revolution, 1780–1880*, London 2007

Sunderland, D., *Managing British Colonial and Post-Colonial Development: The Crown Agents 1920–1980*, London 2007

Supple, B., *The Royal Exchange Assurance*, London 1970

Sweeney, S., 'Indian Railroading: Floating Railway Companies in the Late Nineteenth Century', *Economic History Review*, 62 (S1) (2009), pp. 57–79

Sweeney, S., *Financing India's Imperial Railways, 1875–1914*, London 2011

Tallman, E. W. and J. R. Moen, 'Lessons from the Panic of 1907', *Economic Review*, May/June 1990, pp. 2–13

Tomlinson, B. R., 'Monetary Policy and Economic Development', in K. N. Chaudhuri and C. J. Dewey (eds), *Economy and Society*, Oxford 1979, pp. 197–214

Tomlinson, B. R., *The Political Economy of the Raj 1914–47*, London 1979

Tomz, M., *Reputation and International Cooperation*, Oxford 2007

Triffin, R., 'The Evolution of the International Monetary System: Historical Reappraisal and Future Perspectives', *Princeton Studies in International Finance*, 12 (1964), pp. 1–8

Trivers, R. L., 'The Evolution of Reciprocal Altruism', *Quarterly Review of Biology*, 46 (1971), pp. 35–57

Tsokhas, K., 'Coldly Received: Australia and the London Capital Market in the 1930s', *Australian Journal of International Affairs*, 46 (1) (1992), pp. 61–80

Vakil, C. N., *Financial Developments in Modern India, 1860–1924*, London 1924

Vasudevan, R., 'The Borrower of Last Resort: International Adjustment and Liquidity in Historical Perspective', *Journal of Economic Issues*, 42 (4) (2008), pp. 1055–82

Vasudevan, R., 'International Trade, Finance and Uneven Development', *Export-Import Bank of India Occasional Paper*, 133 (2009), pp. 1–113

Wadia, P. A. and G. N. Joshi, *Money and the Money Market in India*, London 1926

Wainwright, D., *Government Broker: The Story of an Office and of Mullens & Co.*, London 1990

Waley, S. D., *Edwin Montagu: A Memoir and an Account of his Visits to India*, London 1964

Wattal, P. K., *The ABC of Indian Government Finance*, Delhi 1945

Webb, M. de P., *Britain's Dilemma*, London 1912

Williams, D., 'The Evolution of the Sterling System', in C. R. Whittlesey and J. S. G. Wilson (eds), *Essays in Money and Banking in Honour of R. S. Sayers*, Oxford 1968, pp. 266–97

Zakheim, D. S., 'The British Reaction to Zionism, 1895 to the 1990s', *Round Table*, 88 (350) (1999), pp. 321–32

Index